Chopin: pianist and teacher

DATE DUE

OC 7 '97		
AP 27 '98		
MY 15 '98		
MR 17 '99		
MR 2 8 '00		
MY 4 '00		
MY 18 '00		
JE 1 0 '00		
OC 13 '00		
OC 2 3 '00		
AP 2 '0		
JE 4 '04		

Chopin at the piano. Pencil drawing by J. Götzenberger, Paris,
October 1838.

Chopin: pianist and teacher
as seen by his pupils

JEAN-JACQUES EIGELDINGER
University of Geneva

Translated by
Naomi Shohet
with Krysia Osostowicz and Roy Howat

Edited by
Roy Howat

CAMBRIDGE
UNIVERSITY PRESS

Riverside Community College
Library
4800 Magnolia Avenue
Riverside, California 92506

ate of the University of Cambridge
gton Street, Cambridge CB2 1RP
York, NY 10011–4211, USA
igh, Melbourne 3166, Australia

© Cambridge University Press 1986

Originally published in French as *Chopin vu par ses élèves* by Editions
de la Baconnière, Neuchâtel (Switzerland), 1970 and © 1970 and 1979
Editions de la Baconnière

First published in English by Cambridge University Press 1986 as
Chopin: pianist and teacher – as seen by his pupils
Third, English edition © Cambridge University Press 1986
First paperback edition 1988
Reprinted 1990, 1991, 1993, 1995, 1996

Printed in Great Britain at
the University Press, Cambridge

British Library cataloguing in publication data
Eigeldinger, Jean-Jacques
Chopin: pianist and teacher as seen by his pupils.
1. Chopin, Frédéric 2. Composers – Poland –
Biography
I. Title II. Howat, Roy III. Chopin vu par
ses élèves. *English*
786.1'092'4 ML410.C54

Library of Congress cataloguing in publication data
Chopin vu par ses élèves. English.
Chopin: pianist and teacher as seen by his pupils.
Translation of: Chopin, vu par ses élèves.
Bibliography.
Includes indexes.
1. Chopin Frédéric, 1810–1849. 2. Chopin,
Frédéric, 1810–1849. Piano music. 3. Piano music –
Interpretation (Phrasing, dynamics, etc.)
I. Eigeldinger, Jean-Jacques. II. Title.
ML410.C54.C4913 1986 786.1'092'4 85-15141

ISBN 0 521 36709 3 paperback

SE

Contents

List of illustrations   *page* vii

Acknowledgements   ix

Explanation of references   xi

Editor's note   xiii

Abbreviations   xv

Introduction   1

Part 1: Technique and style   23

  BASIC TECHNIQUE: Definition of pianistic technique.   23
Mistakes in customary approaches to 'pure' technique.
Categories of technical study. Qualities required of a piano;
makes of piano. Daily practice: how to work and for how long.
Position at the piano and hand position. General suppleness.
Flexibility of the wrist and hand; freedom of the fingers.
Passivity of the arm and elbow. Cultivation of the touch;
control of hearing; variety of attack; predominance of *legato*.
Individuality and independence of the fingers. Five-finger
exercises for acquiring independence. Scales and arpeggios;
passing the thumb; evenness. Evenness of sound and tranquillity
of the hand as principles of fingering. Practice of trills. Octaves,
double notes and chords.

  MUSICAL STYLE: Musical prosody and declamation;   42
phrasing. *Bel canto* – a model for pianistic declamation and
fullness of tone. *Legato* and *cantabile*. Fingerings for *legato* and
cantabile playing. Agogics: rhythmic strictness and rubato.
Rubato and ornamentation (improvised or notated).
Ornamentation. Simplicity and poise as an ideal in playing.
Spontaneity and range of interpretation. Dynamic scale;
continuous gradation in nuances. Use of the pedal. Execution of

ornaments. Study of musical theory. Analysis of the form and
character of works studied. Curriculum. Composers studied by
Emilie von Gretsch. Works studied by Marie Roubaud.
Repertoire studied by Camille O'Meara (Mme Dubois). Works
of Chopin studied by Jane Stirling. Chamber music; four hands;
two pianos.

Part 2: Interpretation of Chopin's works   65

Andante spianato op. 22. *Ballade* op. 38. *Barcarolle* op. 60.   65
Concerto op. 11 (movements 1 & 2). Concerto op. 21 (2nd
movement). *Etudes* op. 10/1 & 3. *Etudes* op. 25 in general.
Etudes op. 25/1–3. *Fantaisie* op. 49. Impromptus opp. 29 & 51.
Mazurkas: general character; general character of Chopin's
playing; principles of accentuation; rhythmic and agogic
characteristics of Chopin's performance; improvised ornaments;
Chopin's pedalling. Mazurkas opp. 7/1 & 2; 17/4; 24/4; 30/3;
33/2 & 4; 41/3; 50/1. Nocturnes: from a pedagogical viewpoint.
Nocturnes opp. 9/2; 15/2 & 3; 27/1 & 2; 37/1; 48/1 & 2.
Polonaises opp. 26/1 & 2; 40/1; 53. Preludes op. 28/17 & 20.
Scherzos opp. 20; 31; 39. Sonata op. 35, trio of the 'Funeral
March'. Waltzes opp. 34/2; 42; 64/1 & 2; 70/2 & 3.

Notes   90
List of Chopin's pupils whose recollections are quoted in this
    book   161
Appendix I: Translated transcript of Chopin's 'Sketch for a
    method' (*Projet de méthode*)   190
Appendix II: Annotated scores belonging to pupils and associates
    of Chopin   198
Appendix III: Fingerings and annotations in the scores of pupils
    and associates   244
Appendix IV: Chopin's playing described by his contemporaries   267
Bibliography   297
Index of persons   310
Index of musical works

Illustrations

Chopin at the piano. Pencil drawing by J. Götzenberger, Paris,
October 1838. Coll. of the late André Meyer (photograph:
Roger Viollet, Paris) *frontispiece*

Fig. 1   Chopin's salon, Square d'Orléans. Unsigned watercolour,
now destroyed. Former coll. of Ludwika Ciechomska
(photograph: *F-Ppo*) *page* 7

Fig. 2   *Elèves et leurs Parens*, list of Chopin's pupils drawn up by
Jane Stirling. Coll., and photograph, *PL-Wtifc* 8

Fig. 3   Cover page of Chopin's appointments diary for 1848 with
autograph timetable of his lessons during his stay in
London. Coll., and photograph, *PL-Wtifc* 10

Fig. 4   Autograph page of Chopin's *Projet de méthode*. US-
NY*pm* (Lehman); photograph: De Jongh, Lausanne 24

Fig. 5   Basic exercises written by Chopin for his niece Ludwika
(Ludka) Jędrzejewicz. Autograph now destroyed; from
former coll. of Laura Ciechomska (photograph: *PL-Wtifc*) 35

Fig. 6   Carl Filtsch. Lithograph by Menut-Alophe, 1843. *F-Pn*,
Département des Estampes (photograph: *F-Pn*) 141

Fig. 7   Camille O'Meara (later Mme Dubois). Oil painting by
Ary Scheffer, 1851. Former coll. of Jean Dubois, Paris;
present location unknown. Photograph: former coll. of
Edouard Ganche 165

Fig. 8   Georges Mathias. Lithograph by Cossmann, *c.* 1850. Coll.,
and photograph, *F-Pn* 171

Fig. 9   Karol Mikuli. Photograph by Mazur and Roszkiewicz,
Lwów. Coll., and photograph, *PL-Wtifc* 173

Fig. 10 Friederike Müller (later Mme Streicher). Lithograph by
Anton Hähnisch, 1847 (photograph: *PL-Wtifc*) 183

Fig. 11 Chopin teaching Pauline Viardot: 'That's the "Listz" [*sic*]
way of playing! You mustn't play like that when
accompanying the voice.' Ink drawing by Maurice Sand,

from his first album, Nohant, June 1844. Paris, coll. of
Michèle Maurois   187

Fig. 12 First page of the *Etude* op. 10/2, proof for the original
French edition containing inked corrections, all by
Chopin. *F-Po* (photograph: *F-Pn*)   199

Fig. 13 Autograph note in pencil, by Chopin, on the back of the
cover of the Nocturnes op. 9 in Jane Stirling's printed
score, listing works to be studied (8 Preludes from op. 28
and the Polonaise op. 26/2). Coll., and photograph, *F-Pn*   203

Fig. 14 Beginning of the Mazurka op. 7/1 in Jane Stirling's score,
with inked fingering – sometimes inked over pencil – in
Jane Stirling's hand. Coll., and photograph, *F-Pn*   204

Fig. 15 Nocturne op. 15/1, bars 25ff, in Jane Stirling's score, with
musical modifications and pencilled fingering in Chopin's
hand. Coll., and photograph, *F-Pn*   206

Fig. 16 Beginning of the Nocturne op. 48/1 in Camille Dubois-
O'Meara's score, with pencilled fingering and annotations
by Chopin. Coll., and photograph, *F-Pn*   216

Fig. 17 Nocturne op. 15/1, bars 25ff, in the Jędrzejewicz score,
with musical modifications and pencilled fingering copied
by Jane Stirling from those of Chopin in her own score
(*cf.* Fig. 15). Coll., and photograph, *PL-Wtifc*   222

Fig. 18 Nocturne, op. 27/2, bars 44ff, in the Jędrzejewicz score,
with pencilled modifications of dynamics in Chopin's
hand. Coll., and photograph, *PL-Wtifc*   223

Acknowledgements

It would be impossible here to thank individually every person whose kind co-operation has enabled the present study to come to fruition. My gratitude goes particularly to Dr Dalila T. Turło and Mrs Hanna Wróblewska-Straus of the Fryderyk Chopin Society, Warsaw, who generously made their collections available and provided information with untiring good will; to M. André Clavier (Grivegnée/Liège), whose dedication and whose linguistic competence in matters Polish have helped me enormously, and M. Jean-Michel Nectoux, of the Bibliothèque Nationale, Paris, who amicably eased various tasks in the Department of Music. I dedicate a particularly affectionate thought to the late Ludwik Bronarski, the initial supporter of this enterprise, and extend especial thanks to Mme Marie-José Rieckel-Leroy, whose generosity has helped towards the costs of translating the book into English.

I should also like to thank Mmes Wanda Borkowska and Irena Gałęzowska (Bibliothèque Polonaise, Paris), Antoinette Couturier-André (Paris) and the late Yvonne Faure-André (La Croix-en-Touraine); the late regretted Dr Zofia Lissa (University of Warsaw), Dr Hedwig Mitringer (Gesellschaft der Musikfreunde, Vienna); Dr Michał Bristiger (Universities of Warsaw and Kraków), Dr Hellmut Federhofer (University of Mainz), Dr Franz Grasberger (Music Department of the National Library, Vienna), M. Jacques Horneffer (Library of the Geneva Conservatoire), Dr Jeffrey Kallberg (University of Pennsylvania, Philadelphia), M. François Lesure (Music Department of the Bibliothèque Nationale, Paris), M. Georges Lubin (Boulogne-sur-Seine), M. Laurent Pénicaud (Tonneins, Lot-et-Garonne), Mr Jerzy Stankiewicz (Kraków) and Mr J. Rigbie Turner (the Pierpont Morgan Library, New York).

To Roy Howat, the initiator of this English edition, I express special gratitude for having given unstintingly of his time and energy to see through all the necessary revision with a constant competence and dedication. My recognition extends equally to Naomi Shohet and Krysia Ososowicz for their translation of the major part of the book.

Finally I thank François Ditesheim for the warm sympathy with which he surrounded my work.

JEAN-JACQUES EIGELDINGER

Quebec, March 1978
Geneva, July 1983

Explanation of references

In referring to bibliographic sources, whenever an author is represented in the present book by more than one work, the source in question is identified by an added abbreviation (e.g., Lenz, *B*; Lenz, *GPV*; etc.), which prefaces the source's full entry in the Bibliography. When source references consist of two or more names separated by oblique strokes, the first name is that of the originator of the information, the last name that of the author whose publication is our source. For example, 'Dubois/Niecks' means that Mme Dubois, Chopin's pupil, passed her reminiscence (orally or verbally) to Niecks, who reproduced it in his publication; 'Mikuli/Bischoff/Federhofer' means that Mikuli passed his information (orally) to Bischoff, who put it in writing in a text published by Federhofer; 'Czartoryska/Działyńska/ Czartkowski–Jeżewska' means that the Princess Marcelina Czartoryska reported her information to a pupil, Cecylia Działyńska, who published it in an article reproduced in the book by Czartkowski and Jeżewska; and so on.

Note markers in the Introduction and Appendices refer to footnotes on the same page; those in the main part of the book (pages 23–89) refer to the body of notes on pages 90–159. Some notes are referred to more than once; note markers therefore do not always follow an exact numerical sequence.

Music examples have all been supplied by the author, except for those on pages 34, 37, 38, 39, 43, 79, which figure in the Kleczyński sources, those on pages 88 and 104 (note 45), present in Pugno's and Neuhaus's commentaries, those in note 127 on page 133, taken from Chopin's correspondence (various editions), and those in Appendix I.

Music examples quoting Chopin's works, including Appendix III, are given in *Urtext* form, based on autographs and the original French editions. Unless otherwise specified, all identifying references to Chopin's music follow the National Polish Edition of the Fryderyk Chopin Complete Works (*CW*; see Abbreviations below) as regards bar numbering and order of pieces within an opus – even though this latter order may differ from that in the original French editions, notably in the Mazurkas opp. 6, 7, 33 and 41. Some reprints of individual *CW* volumes have changed page numbering, so the page references to *CW* in the present book, which follow the currently available editions of *CW*, may not apply to all editions. The contexts always make clear, however, where the reader can find the reference.

Pitch notation

Editor's note

The first English edition is based on the second edition of *Chopin vu par ses élèves* (Neuchâtel, La Baconnière, 1979), supplemented by various author's revisions. In particular, Appendix I appears for the first time, and Appendix II has been largely reworked in the light of newly accessible sources.

All translations have been made directly from the original source languages. Some existing published English translations have been used (as indicated by the references); in these cases all passages quoted have been checked for accuracy of translation. The main examples are Hedley's translation of selected Chopin correspondence (*SC*) and the English editions of Kleczyński (*CGW*, *FCI*), issued during his life with his authorization. The English in the Kleczyński books has occasionally been tacitly modernized, and references to the old English fingering (+, *1*, *2*, *3*, *4*) have been changed to the modern system (1–5).

Abbreviations

General abbreviations

l.h., r.h.	left hand, right hand
m.g., m.d.	*main gauche, main droite*
ms, mss	manuscript, manuscripts
n.d.	no date
OEE	original English edition
OFE	original French edition
OGE	original German edition
op. no., opp.	opus number, opuses
op. posth.	opus posthumous

Bibliographical abbreviations

BWV	Schmieder, Wolfgang, *Bach-Werke-Verzeichnis*, Leipzig, Breitkopf & Härtel, 1950
CFC	Chopin's correspondence, French edn (see Bibl., Chopin)
CGS	George Sand's correspondence (see Bibl., Sand)
CW	Chopin, Fryderyk, *Complete Works*, ed. Ignacy J. Paderewski, Ludwik Bronarski and Józef Turczyński, Warsaw and Kraków, PWM, 1949–, 21 vols
KFC	Chopin's correspondence, Polish edn (see Bibl., Chopin)
OXF	*The Oxford Original Edition of Frédéric Chopin*, ed. Edouard Ganche, London, Oxford University Press, [1932], 3 vols
PIW	Państwowy Instytut Wydawniczy [(Polish) National Publishing Institute]
PM	Chopin's *Projet de méthode* (see p. 90, note 1)
PWM	Polskie Wydawnictwo Muzyczne [Polish Musical Editions]
PWN	Państwowe Wydawnictwo Naukowe [Polish National Scientific Editions]
RGMP	*Revue et gazette musicale de Paris*

SC   Chopin's correspondence, English edn (see Bibl., Chopin)
TiFC   Towarzystwo im. Fryderyka Chopina [Fryderyk Chopin
            Society (Warsaw)]

Library and museum sigla

F: France
   Pn   Paris, Bibliothèque Nationale (Music Department unless
                  otherwise specified)
   Po   Paris, Bibliothèque de l'Opéra
   Ppo   Paris, Bibliothèque Polonaise

PL: Poland
   Kj   Kraków, Biblioteka Jagiellońska
   Kjm   Kraków, Muzeum Uniwersytetu Jagiellońskiego
   Wn   Warsaw, Biblioteka Narodowa
   Wtifc   Warsaw, Towarzystwo im. Fryderyka Chopina
                  [Fryderyk Chopin Society]

US: United States of America
   NYpm   New York, the Pierpont Morgan Library, Robert O.
   (Lehman)   Lehman deposit

Introduction

True science does not constitute a separate branch of knowledge from art. On the contrary, science, when envisaged like this and demonstrated by a man like Chopin, is art itself.
Delacroix

The authentically minded interpreter who wishes to do justice to masterpieces of the past faces a multitude of complex problems. Musicology, established now for a century as a positive science, has seen its objectives broaden and diversify. Performance practice, without being altogether a new sphere, is now a field in which musicology is proving itself to the greatest effect. In recent times musicological studies have contributed towards revitalizing or reconsidering the interpretation of gregorian chant, Renaissance polyphony and concertante style, also shedding a clearer light on the realization of *continuo*, ornamentation and improvisatory elements of Baroque music. The combined efforts of organologists, instrument makers and performers enable us to-day to enjoy all the sumptuousness of Monteverdi's instrumental colouring; in Mozart the woodwind take on a new savour, emerging with unaccustomed clarity.

But with the music of the last century, and with Romantic piano music in particular, only recently have we begun to realise that they too present the performer with problems analogous to those encountered in the music of more remote periods. This new preoccupation arises from an awareness that our epoch, no longer comfortably attached to the end of the preceding century, has broken away from it altogether. The last bastion of post-Romanticism, the inter-war period, rediscovered the Baroque; a similar impulse is now urging us to rethink our relationship with the nineteenth century. As soon as a period becomes history, a resurgence of interest arises for its artists and their works, not necessarily restricted to its foremost figures. Those talents not blessed with genius nevertheless become a rich source of information, sometimes delight. In the field of Romantic piano, our knowledge of Weber, Schubert, Mendelssohn, Schumann, Chopin or Liszt is enhanced and placed in better perspective through familiarity with Alkan, Field, Heller, Henselt, Hummel and Moscheles, even Kalkbrenner or Thalberg. We are now better acquainted with these pianist-composers thanks to recent editions, studies and recordings. It is for this context of modern research into musical Romanticism that the present collection of annotated texts is offered.

I

The idea for this book arose from a desire to approach Chopin's pianistic and stylistic practices as closely as possible – a desire that entailed thorough study of his views on piano playing and teaching, as well as of their musical and aesthetic surroundings. The aim was not to write a historical essay, although historical perspective is rarely absent from the commentary. The interpretative, fragmentary and highly diversified nature of our sources does not lend itself to a straightforward historical treatment, which would in any case have stifled the subject in its cradle. It seemed preferable to adopt a somewhat didactic approach, letting the texts speak for themselves rather than using them as pretexts. The documents thus retain their own life, independent of their accompanying editorial notes.

The present volume may be seen as a critical synthesis of Kleczyński's two books with those written by Karasowski, Niecks and Hoesick: a synthesis elaborated in the light of various other texts, many of them not previously available in translation. The whole project has been based exclusively on documents whose weight and authenticity are undisputed.[1]

We have the following main sources of information on Chopin's teaching activity and methods:

- Chopin's memoranda books for the years 1834, 1848 and 1849.
- His correspondence (*CFC*; *KFC*; *SC*) and, in addition, that of George Sand (*CGS*).
- A 'sketch for a method' (*Projet de méthode* – *PM*) in its two fragmentary versions, one an autograph draft (transcribed in full as Appendix 1 on pp. 190–7 below)[2] and the other a partial fair copy made by the composer's older sister.
- The annotated scores of pupils and associates.[3]
- The statements of Chopin's own students in diaries, letters and reminiscences, written, dictated or conveyed by word of mouth.[4]

[1] Among various examples of apocryphal testimonies there are the alleged reminiscences of Laura Rappoldi-Kahrer (pupil of von Bülow and Liszt) concerning a commentary, on the Preludes op. 28, supposedly emanating from Liszt, Lenz and Mme Kalergis (pupil of Chopin); Kapp (see Bibliography) quoted these reminiscences in an article, judging them as 'almost authentic'. Incidentally, the facsimile reproduced in Edvige Calza's monograph *Interpretazione letteraria dei Preludi di Chopin attribuita a Liszt* (Bologna, Editrice Compositori, 1968) is none other than an Italian translation of Kapp's text. Similar caution should be applied to Victor Gille's *Souvenirs romantiques*, in which imagination sometimes supplants reality (see Bibliography, and note 21 on p. 98 below). On the other hand some credit, albeit subject to caution, has been accorded here to some souvenirs of F.-H. Peru (see Bibliography); this is explained in the passage under his name in the *List of pupils*, pp.174–6 below.
[2] See p. 90 below, note 1, for a full description of the sources of the *Projet* and their history.
[3] See Appendices II and III, pp. 198–266.
[4] Documents contemporary with their subject are traditionally regarded as the most trustworthy ones. In the case of Chopin's pupils, however, their correspondence and private diaries are not merely as rich or as vivid as their reminiscences set down at later dates; mundane details naturally dominate the former, and the pupil is often too overwhelmed by the revelation to be able or even wish to write it down. Even if the time lapse gives rise to inaccuracies of detail, it cannot detract from the authenticity of impressions which are profoundly anchored in the memory.

This last category, providing our main source, comprises over twenty names, including the best authorities on the subject (Princess Czartoryska, Mme Dubois-O'Meara, Emilie von Gretsch, Gutmann, Lenz, Mathias, Mikuli, Mme Peruzzi, Mme Rubio, Jane Stirling, Friederike Streicher-Müller, Tellefsen, Pauline Viardot). Supplementing these are documents supplied by the pupils of Chopin's pupils or by friends, pianists and composers, music critics and journalists who heard Chopin play;[5] for Chopin the teacher is logically a reflection of Chopin the pianist. These people's reminiscences have been edited to omit anecdotes and opinion, retaining only the musical indications given by Chopin or originating from him, as well as passages describing his teaching and occasionally his playing. These fragments are reassembled in two main sections here, one concerned with the technical and stylistic principles of piano playing in general, and the other with Chopin's indications for performing and interpreting his own works.

The first section, *Technique and Style* – two notions inseparable in Chopin's mind – arranges these fragments in an order intended to reconstruct Chopin's own order of approach. Passages on the same topic by different authors have been juxtaposed; some fragments appear unashamedly in more than one place when they apply to more than one topic. As for the documents whose views are not corroborated by other sources, they figure in this book only where their authenticity appears beyond doubt; otherwise they are relegated to the notes or rejected entirely. In the second section, *Interpretation of Chopin's Works*, works are arranged by alphabetical order of their titles, rather than by chronological order (or opus number), for easier reference and so that each genre (Mazurka, Nocturne, etc.) can be dealt with as a whole.

The book thus takes on the aspect of a sort of handbook to Chopin's teaching methods, and consequently to his aesthetic beliefs. Its interest and novelty reside undoubtedly in the juxtaposition of original and partly unpublished documents which, illuminating one another with some remarkable correspondences, offer a coherent, if inevitably still incomplete, picture of Chopin's piano teaching. The chronological diversity of these testimonies does not detract from their agreement, since Chopin's teaching principles did not so much change with time as increase in refinement – as did his playing and his compositions.

How can we account for the scarcity of comprehensive documents? Why is

---

[5] These documents are gathered mainly in Appendix IV, but some fragments appear in the main text. To avoid confusion, here is the list – in order of appearance – of the *non-pupils* of Chopin whose reminiscences are quoted in the main text: Liszt, Hipkins, Schelling, Franchomme, Kleczyński, Karasowski, Moscheles, Marmontel, Mendelssohn, Hallé, Berlioz, Schumann, Schindler, Seligmann, Fontana. Chopin's pupils may be identified by references to the *List of pupils* (pp. 161–89 below), devoted exclusively to the 23 pupils whose reminiscences have been quoted in the main text.

the available coverage so fragmentary in character? The reasons may be summarised in two general points:

1. Chopin, by nature a pure musician, was always shy of committing ideas to paper: 'The pen burns my fingers,' he would say by way of excuse. We know what a chore it was for him to write even a simple letter, be it in Polish or in French. It is therefore hardly surprising that his correspondence, so reserved with regard to his work as a composer,[6] carries scarcely any mention of his activities as a teacher, and is completely silent as to the tenor of his teaching. Nor is it surprising that he never completed his long-term project of writing a piano method, for which only a few initial sketches survive; even had he lived longer, he would probably have recoiled from the constraint of such a task. Besides, Chopin did not like to express himself on matters close to his heart except through music. He hardly ever spoke of his own aesthetic, pianistic or pedagogical views outside the narrow circle of his pupils and a few close friends (notably Franchomme and Delacroix). Gifted with the lightning lucidity of momentary insight, he had no patience with reasoned explanations, still less with manifestos. George Sand noted:

Chopin speaks little and seldom about his art; but when he does, it is with a wonderful clarity, a soundness of judgement and of intent that could annihilate quite a few heresies were he to speak his mind openly.

But even in private he is reserved, and only at the piano does he really open his heart. Still, he has promised to write a *method* in which he will deal not only with technique, but also with theory [*non seulement du métier, mais de la doctrine*]. Will he keep his word?

(Sand, *Impressions et souvenirs*, p. 88)

2. Unlike Clementi, Hummel, Kalkbrenner or Czerny, Chopin did not create a school or institute a set tradition. It was not in his nature to impose his personality on pupils, in the way that the Liszt of Weimar did. Too much of an aristocrat and poet to become a leader, Chopin was content to suggest and imply, winning devotion without any attempt to convince. Such an attitude could hardly be conducive to an analytic approach on the part of his disciples. And then it has its corollary: with the exception of a very few professionals,[7] the core of Chopin's clientèle consisted of ladies of the Faubourg-St-Germain or of the Slavonic aristocracy exiled in Paris. Talented

[6] One could hardly be more laconic than Chopin in his references (in letters) to two of his most daring inspirations: the finale of the Sonata op. 35 is described as follows: 'The left hand and the right hand gossip in unison after the March' (SC, p. 181), and the Prelude op. 45 – a constantly shifting vision tinted successively with all the colours of the harmonic spectrum – merely as 'well modulated'. As for the *Berceuse* op. 57, it is designated by the term 'variants'.

[7] 'Professionals' here refers to those who took up careers as concert artists or teachers in official musical establishments. Nevertheless it is well to remember that in the nineteenth century there was much less of a gap between the categories of professional and amateur. The latter included some highly accomplished musicians who contributed actively to the dissemination of new music.

as they may have been (many of them were), their social status effectively forbade them to perform in public except for charity functions. Princess Marcelina Czartoryska, generally recognized as Chopin's most faithful disciple, fits the description exactly. And people of this category rarely communicated anything more than anecdotal reminiscences – by no means without value! – and fragmentary indications of the training received.[8]

Questioned once on the subject of Chopin's pedagogical posterity, Liszt replied, 'Chopin was unfortunate in his pupils' (Niecks, II, 174). This remark is confirmed in many cases. Three of Chopin's most promising young talents died young (Filtsch, Caroline Hartmann, Paul Gunsberg). Among the most brilliant of his students, two renounced their careers at a very early stage (Emilie von Gretsch, Friederike Streicher), another two confined themselves to private teaching (Mme Dubois, Mme Rubio); while Pauline Viardot, a pianist of repute, had already taken to a singing career by the time she received any musical ideas from Chopin. We are left with about ten students, all men, who eventually embraced a serious professional career. Apart from Tellefsen (who balked at the task of completing Chopin's 'Sketch for a Method', and produced instead an inaccurate edition of his works), two important names emerge in the teaching profession: Mathias in the West, and Mikuli in the East. Koczalski, Mikuli's heir, represents the last link in the chain of direct descendants.

In fact, all the evidence indicates that Chopin's teaching was not oriented towards the concert platform. Did he not declare to a female student that 'concerts are never real music; you have to give up the idea of hearing in them the most beautiful things of art' (Grewingk, p. 19.)? Such words reveal the aesthetic of a chamber musician – an aesthetic that must inevitably have influenced his conception of teaching. Add to this a certain confidential atmosphere in Chopin's lessons, and one understands better why their contents are recorded so incompletely.

The diversity of context and provenance of the documents assembled here may give the text an impression of bittiness. Here Chopin speaks or plays, there the pupil relates personal impressions; now a lightning sketch carries us into the intimacy of the salon where the lesson is taking place; or again, a

---

[8] The accounts in the Countess Elizavieta Cheriemietieff's *Journal* are typical in this respect, never entering into detail. More lamentable is the complete silence of Mme Kalergis – of whom Chopin notes that she 'plays very well' (*CFC*, III, p. 312) – in her letters to her daughter (see La Mara, *Marie von Mouchanoff-Kalergis . . . in Briefen an ihre Tochter*, Leipzig, Breitkopf & Härtel, 1911, 2nd edition); Liszt and von Bülow both considered her one of the best interpreters of Chopin's works. On the other hand, the silence of Princess Czartoryska on the subject may well have been due to a scrupulous sensitivity to the memory of the master whose music she recreated perhaps best of all. She nevertheless did communicate some indications through her teaching and agreed to pass on some fragments of information to Kleczyński and Michałowski.

discursive passage will take us out of the immediacy of the moment. In one place Chopin proclaims a general truth; in others his comments are tailored to the precise needs of a pupil with a particular problem to overcome. In their gradual unfolding, our texts suggest the aspect of a mosaic, tempered by the ravages of time and reconstructed by the archaeologist, in unavoidably abbreviated form, but always using the original pieces and respecting the main outlines of the composition. It is left to the present-day interpreter, whether pianist or musicologist, to complete the blanks with the aid of his restorative intuition and his musical culture. My own contribution to this task is to be found in the notes accompanying the texts (pp. 90–159 below).

If Chopin was persuaded to give some lessons in the years before leaving Warsaw, it was against his will and only as a special favour to friends.[9] His real teaching career began only after his establishment in Paris, and occupied the latter part of his life, from 1832 to 1849. During this period he divided his time equally between composing and teaching, dedicating himself to each in turn in summer and winter respectively; this at any rate was the norm after his return from Majorca until the time of his separation from George Sand.[10] For six months of the year, from October or November to May, Chopin received an average of five pupils daily.[11] Rising early, he would spend the morning and at least the first half of the afternoon teaching. Each lesson lasted theoretically between 45 minutes and an hour, but would sometimes stretch out over several hours in succession, particularly on Sundays, for the benefit of gifted pupils whom he particularly liked (see the memoirs of Mme Streicher, Emilie von Gretsch, Mikuli). Pupils would receive one lesson weekly or more often two or three,[12] depending on their teacher's availability, their own individual needs and their talents – and, secondarily, on the state of their finances. Some pupils maintain that Chopin unofficially

---

[9] See CFC, I, pp. 92–3, 104, 161, 184.

[10] Knowing how much his teaching and his Parisian obligations would fill his time, Chopin wrote from Nohant in 1845: 'I simply must finish certain manuscripts [opp. 60, 61, 62] before I leave here, for I cannot compose in winter' (SC, p. 254).

[11] The number may have been greater before Majorca: in 1847, Chopin deplores having to give seven lessons (CFC, III, p. 272); the pace eases up in 1848–9. For information on the outer facts of Chopin's teaching activity (periods of teaching, lists of daily lessons, times, duration, fees, etc.) the principal sources are: Chopin's pocket diaries for 1834, 1848, and 1849 (PL-Wtifc); CFC, II, pp. 84–5, 121, 131, 206–7, 254; III, pp. 183, 225, 265, 268–9, 270, 272, 273, 311–12, 313, 316, 328, 329, 342, 344, 346, 347, 348, 356, 401, 408; CGS, V, pp. 160, 522–3, 783; VI, p. 253; VIII, p. 470; Balzac, C, IV, p. 499; LH, II, p. 8; Hallé, pp. 209–10; Hiller, BU, pp. 149, 150; Karasowski, II, pp. 98–9; Karłowicz, pp. 136–42 and passim; Niecks, passim. See also the memoirs of the following students: Harder/Adelung; Roubaud/Ganche, DSFC; Gretsch/Grewingk; J. de Caraman/Hedley, NUC; Zaleska/Hordyński; Lenz, GPV 1872; Mikuli; Cheriemietieff/Niesmieyanova-Siemienowski; Streicher/Niecks; Tellefsen.

[12] Maria von Harder's assertion that she was given daily lessons (Adelung, p. 122) is isolated. Even Filtsch did not, in principle, receive more than three lessons per week.

1   Chopin's salon, Square d'Orléans. Unsigned watercolour, now destroyed.

taught them practically free of charge, or that they were offered numerous additional lessons.

Chopin's lessons were even more in demand than those of Liszt or Kalkbrenner; they were also expensive, since the fee was invariably fixed at 20 gold francs, the equivalent of a 'Louis d'or' (£1 sterling of that time), or 30 francs if Chopin was to teach at the pupil's home.[13] It is only fair to add that teaching was Chopin's main source of income – hence his talk of a 'treadmill' to describe the succession of lucrative hours. Publishers grasped exclusive rights-in-perpetuity of his compositions in exchange for a lump sum; as for his public concerts in Paris and Scotland, only six or seven of them brought him anything approaching a reasonable profit.[14]

How many pupils did Chopin have? This is difficult to assess with any degree of precision. If anyone who received his advice at some time is to qualify as a pupil, then the number of identified pupils to date is about 150.[15]

---

[13] See *CGS*, V, pp. 522, 523.

[14] Information on the material circumstances of Chopin's life may be found in the documents compiled by Suzanne and Denise Chainaye.

[15] In an article on the subject, Bronarski (*EC*) quotes about 100 names; these are reproduced and added to in Holland's thesis, which contains a total of 126 names. There is reason to discard about ten of these (either dubious or the result of errors) but then to add about another 30 new ones, listed

2 *Elèves et leurs Parens*, list of Chopin's pupils drawn up by Jane
Stirling.

But this figure is certainly higher than the number of proper pupils; one also has to be sceptical of various biographers' claims regarding alleged 'pupils' of Chopin. In Chopin's life-time it was already fashionable and even advantageous to claim to be his pupil, and Chopin, aware of this, would respond, 'I never gave him lessons; but if it's of any use to him to pass as my pupil, then let him be. Let him remain one!' (Karasowski, II, p. 98). In addition, various categories of students may be distinguished: with the large majority made up of 'dilettantes' (in the positive eighteenth-century sense of the term), the number of professionals bordered on twenty. If a small number studied with Chopin for four or five years, others cannot have had more than four or five lessons in all – such as the 'Lady de Liverpool', who hastened down to London to be taught for just one week! (Chopin, CFC, III, p. 356; SC, p. 325).

In any case, Chopin saw straight through the motives of many of these. Some artists also came to him for advice on furthering their studies: we find even Moscheles and Kalkbrenner not above requesting an interview or some advice, one for his daughter, the other for his son. Finally one can add that Chopin devoted himself with particular care to his compatriot pupils, though this did not prevent him from taking under his wing various other pianists who travelled from all over Europe to study with him. His reputation as pianist and pedagogue reached far and wide: one finds his pupils coming not only from France and Poland but also from Lithuania, Russia, Bohemia, Austria, Germany, Switzerland, Great Britain, Sweden and Norway.

Chopin did not accept children or beginners. Nor was he easy to approach:

Chopin was surrounded, adulated and protected by a small entourage of enthusiastic friends who defended him from unwelcome visitors or second-rate admirers. Access to him was difficult; as he himself told Stephen Heller, one had to make several attempts before one could succeed in meeting him

related Marmontel (PC, p. 9). This characteristic tale recurs in the memoirs of a good dozen pupils, and by no means the least significant, who at first regularly found themselves confronted with a polite refusal.[16] Talent or

by Jaeger, who also looks critically at the existing list and eliminates a few names erroneously taken for pupils.

Apart from other names still to be found, here are those figuring in Chopin's pocket diaries: Planat, Gaymüller (1834); Wedgwood, Cooper, Carter, and [the daughter of the Duchess of] Sutherland (1848); Champlatreux (1849). Two new names appear in the list drawn up by Jane Stirling (see also Fig. 2, page 8 opposite): [Mr] Gailloux [E. Gaillard?], and the Viscountess of Ludre (not Sudre, as printed by Karłowicz and Hoesick).

[16] See Harder/Adelung, p. 122; Roubaud de Cournand/Ganche, DSFC, p. 85; Gretsch/Grewingk, p. 14; Anonymous Scottish lady/Hadden, p. 157; Zaleska/Hordyński, p. 157; Lenz, GPV 1872, pp. 333–5; Dubois/Niecks, II, p. 178; Peruzzi/Niecks, II, p. 339; Streicher/Niecks, II, p. 340; Gutmann/Stavenow, pp. 96–8; Tellefsen, pp. 142–3.

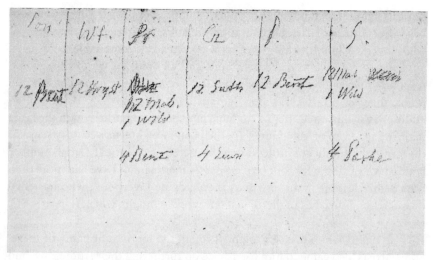

3   Cover page of Chopin's appointments diary for 1848 with autograph timetable of his lessons during his stay in London.

artistic personality would always serve to overcome these initial obstacles. Once the ice was broken, Chopin revealed personal qualities felt as exceptional by all his pupils. We should not underestimate the affectionate atmosphere suffusing many of the lessons given to the refined, talented and chastely enthusiastic young ladies of the aristocracy; doubtless these conditions stimulated progress by creating an intense state of receptiveness in the pupil. The special quality of these pupil–teacher relationships – demonstrated by numerous album pages and dedications of works – helps to explain why Chopin's teaching was not suited to mass popularization or to the establishment of a definite 'tradition'. Its character was more personal, to some extent initiatory. As a rule Chopin's lessons were private (some dubious testimonies present them as an occasion for social gatherings!). Sometimes certain pupils would be allowed to attend the lessons of a colleague: Mikuli and Lenz were both to benefit from these stimulating circumstances.

Exceptionally, Chopin once organized at his home a special dress rehearsal on two pianos for Filtsch, who was to perform the E minor Concerto op. 11 in society events and concerts. At certain times Chopin would employ an assistant – notably Mme Rubio, and occasionally Gutmann and Marie de Rozières.

It would be wrong to imagine that Chopin saw his teaching as a 'pensum' or a poor substitute for the concerts he no longer gave. On the contrary, he was highly aware of the importance of his task and presented himself for lessons with meticulous punctuality – which only ill health eventually impeded – and with the zeal of an apostle. Mikuli relates:

Chopin daily devoted his entire energies to teaching for several hours and with genuine delight [. . .] Was not the severity, not so easy to satisfy, the feverish vehemence with which he sought to raise his pupils to his own standpoint, the ceaseless repetition of a passage till it was understood, a guarantee that he had the progress of the pupil at heart? A holy artistic zeal burnt in him then, every word from his lips was stimulating and inspiring.

(Mikuli, p. 3).

Exactingness, fire, patience and firmness were united in Chopin; he wished for certain immediate results that would herald the future achievements towards which he tirelessly schooled the pupil's inner vision. The intensity of his concentration equalled that of his lucidity:

Chopin was a born teacher; expression and conception, position of the hand, touch, pedalling, nothing escaped the sharpness of his hearing and his vision; he gave every detail the keenest attention. Entirely absorbed in his task, during the lesson he would be solely a teacher, and nothing but a teacher

related Maria von Harder (Adelung, p. 122). Chopin preferred pupils to follow the text carefully rather than always play from memory, and he would mark the score as it lay on the music stand. Generally seated at his small upright *pianino* while the student played on the large Pleyel, he would tirelessly point out each error, each carelessness, each weakness – more profuse with examples than with words. 'Often the entire lesson passed without the pupil's having played more than a few bars,' related Mikuli (p. 4). Chopin's usual courtesy, even playfulness, could give way on days of illness or irritability to fits of anger, as violent as they were brief; the male pupils seem to have been more prone to these '*leçons orageuses*' than were the women. Then again, repeated negligence or careless playing would sometimes exasperate him, with positively glacial results.[17] But more often, without in any way relaxing his demands, Chopin showed a humane understanding of his students' personal, musical and technical problems. He knew how to inspire self-confidence and to find the right words of encouragement to free the pupil's inner resources at the right moment.[18] Then he was a subtle guide blessed with an absolute sureness of intuition and psychological penetration. This aspect of Chopin's teaching has not yet been given the attention it deserves. By way of compensation here is a passage from one of Emilie von Gretsch's letters, dated 30 April 1844:

[17] See quotation from Zaleska/Hordyński, p. 28 below.
[18] For instance, to Paul Gunsberg, a very talented pupil who died young: 'If you lose the present time, you'll never regain it!' (related in a letter from Jane Stirling to Ludwika Jędrzejewicz, Chopin's sister [5 March 1852]; quoted in Wróblewska-Straus, *LSJ*, p. 136). To Elizavieta Cheriemietieff: 'Perfect! Couldn't be played better' (Cheriemietieff, *Journal*, 30 December 1842). To Mme Peruzzi: 'What a good idea of yours that is!' (Niecks, II, p. 339). To Emilie von Gretsch: 'You'll soon be playing this [some Nocturnes] as I do; it's no trouble [*une bluette*] to you' (Grewingk, p. 13; see also *ibid.*, p. 10).

Yesterday at Chopin's I tried to play his Nocturnes. I knew, I still felt clearly within myself the way in which he had played them. But partly because of uncertainty with the notes, and partly through a certain inhibition which comes out in our bearing and our performance when we are anxious or unhappy, I found myself unable to express the music as I heard it in my head; I did not have the strength to realize it in sound. It is wonderful then to see how tactfully Chopin puts one at one's ease; how intuitively he identifies, I might say, with the thoughts of the person to whom he is speaking or listening; with what delicate nuances of behaviour he adapts his own being to that of another. To encourage me, he tells me among other things, 'It seems to me that you don't dare to express yourself as you feel. Be bolder, let yourself go more. Imagine you're at the Conservatoire, listening to the most beautiful performance in the world. Make yourself want to hear it, and then you'll hear yourself playing it right here. Have full confidence in yourself; make yourself want to sing like Rubini, and you'll succeed in doing so. Forget you're being listened to, and always listen to yourself. I see that timidity and lack of self-confidence form a kind of armour around you, but through this armour I perceive something else that you don't always dare to express, and so you deprive us all. When you're at the piano, I give you full authority to do whatever you want; follow freely the ideal you've set for yourself and which you must feel within you; be bold and confident in your own powers and strength, and whatever you say will always be good. It would give me so much pleasure to hear you play with complete abandon that I'd find the shameless confidence of the *"vulgaires"* unbearable by comparison.'   (Grewingk, pp. 10–11)

Such testimony is by no means unique in Chopin's pupils' memoirs.[19]

In his lessons, Chopin worked simultaneously with music and words. Not content with demonstrating a few passages over the pupil's shoulders, he would often play the piece from beginning to end, even repeating it several times, constantly striving for greater perfection. And many a lesson was prolonged while he sat at the piano playing one piece after another, not only his own works but also those of other composers. Several of his pupils agree in saying that Chopin the pianist was never greater, never more complete and more ideal than in these transcending moments of grace. He did not, however, neglect to make the pupil analyse the formal structure of the works studied, and readily resorted to images or analogies to evoke the mood of a piece and to arouse the right musical impulse in the pupil. In order to obtain a particular expressiveness and sonority, for instance, he once suggested to Georges Mathias during a section of Weber's Sonata in A flat (op. 39) that 'an angel is passing over the sky' (first movement, bars 81ff). Where the young

---

[19] See Friederike Streicher-Müller's memoirs: 'At a *soirée* (20 December 1840) he made me play the Sonata with the "Funeral March" before a large assemblage. On the morning of the same day I had once more to play over to him the Sonata, but was very nervous. "Why do you play less well today?" he asked. I replied that I was afraid. "Why? *I* consider you play it well", he rejoined very gravely, indeed, severely. "But if you wish to play this evening as nobody has played before you, and nobody will play after you, well then!"' . . . These words restored my composure. The thought that I played to his satisfaction possessed me also in the evening; I had the happiness of gaining Chopin's approval and the applause of the audience' (Niecks, II, p. 342).

Liszt in 1832, making use of his freshly acquired education, sought to stimulate the pupil's imagination by reading him a page of Chateaubriand or a poem by Hugo, Chopin achieved the same result with a single, concise image – so intensively was he imbued with the reality of his vision even as he translated it into words. These spontaneous creations of the mind, evoking here a legion of capricious spirits, there a house of the dead, elsewhere a dialogue between a tyrant and his victim, are the result not so much of a literary temperament as a visionary imagination and a feeling for poetry rooted in popular Slavonic legend.

Sometimes a pupil's sensitivity would meet with Chopin's recognition on a higher, privileged level, as is shown by this astonishing declaration to Juliette de Caraman: 'I give you *carte blanche* to play all my music. There is in you this vague poetry, this *Schwärmerei* that is needed to understand it' (Hedley, NUC, p. 8). We know Chopin was generally quite strict about the exact comprehension and performance of his works, and it required no less than the genial personality of the young Filtsch to make him admit: 'We each understand this differently, but go your own way, do as you feel, it can also be played like that.'[20] Professional or not, many pupils experienced a feeling of revelation and liberation through Chopin's teaching; his absolute novelty opened wide to them the doors of all music, not just of piano playing. Then it would not be long before they noticed radical changes in their playing, their listening and their mental attitude. Chopin for his part did point out these improvements to them. Emilie von Gretsch relates:

During the last lesson [. . .] Chopin showed me how best to practise the *Etudes*. Some of them required no comment from him, 'since you understand them perfectly' – that was his opinion. It was a special joy to me to be able to play easily what had previously seemed to involve perilous difficulties, particularly when I was working on these *Etudes* with Henselt. Chopin (I think he can read hearts), at the precise moment when this agreeable discovery about my progress crossed my mind, told me: 'This seems perfectly easy to you now, doesn't it? – not like it was before. Well! In this short time you've made miraculous progress!' He told me that within a few months I'd be more aware of it, or, at any rate, he presumed that I would, since he had found this happened with his best students.[21]

The student could then forge ahead powered by creative energy, since his work was now based on a natural method, revealed by a poet who could turn his hand equally to dialectic.

What are the fundamental principles governing Chopin's technical instruction; how was he an innovator? It is hard to answer that without giving an outline of his musical aesthetic. His piano teaching is as closely bound up with stylistic views as it is with his contribution to the technique of the instrument.

[20] Denis (under the date 20 April 1843), p. 125.   [21] Dated 20 May 1844; Grewingk, p. 13.

For Chopin, as for most of the Romantics – but even more so the Baroque and Classical composers – music is a language. Through the specific medium of organized sounds it seeks to express a world of thoughts, feelings and sensations.[22] Even if Chopin seems to share Goethe's view of music as the language of the inexpressible, for him this does not make it any less subject to the principal laws of verbal language. There are revealing parallels on this subject which Chopin frequently established between the arts of oratory and musical interpretation, between the means and ends common to spoken declamation and musical discourse.[23] In both cases the purpose is to move and convince the listener by means of intonation and accentuation appropriate to the meaning of the text. Just like a piece of prose or verse, a score consists of an arrangement of sections, paragraphs, phrases, periods and clauses; a system of punctuation aims to ensure correct articulation, the general sense of direction and the main breathing points; prosodic laws determine the long and short syllables, accented or soft, and so forth.

It is hardly surprising, then, that Chopin was very early on attracted towards the art of singing, and particularly by its embodiment in *bel canto*. The great vocal school of the 1830s, in which the art of declamation and its dramatic expression in music were harmoniously united, represented for him the ideal and definitive model for interpretation. It was on the singing styles of Rubini, of Pasta,[24] that Chopin based his own style of *pianistic declamation*, the key to his playing and the touchstone of his teaching. We find him repeatedly exhorting his pupils to listen to the great dramatic artists, even to the extent of declaring: 'you must sing if you wish to play' (Niecks, II, p. 187). For Chopin, singing constituted the alpha and omega of music; it

---

[22] Among the tentative definitions of the art of music put forward by Chopin in his *Projet de méthode*, we find:
  - The expression of thought through sounds.
  - The manifestation of our feelings through sounds.
  - The art of expressing one's thoughts through sounds.
  - The expression of our perceptions through sounds.
  - The undefinite (indeterminate) language [*parole*] of men is sound.
  - We use sounds to make music just as we use words to make a language.
  - The indefinite language [*langue*] music.
  - One abstract sound doesn't make music, just as one word doesn't make language.
  Many of these definitions appear already from Rameau: 'In a word [*sic*], the expression of thought, of feeling, of passion, must be the real object of Music' (*Code de musique pratique*, Paris, 1760, p. 170). Schumann-Florestan, the spokesman of German Romanticism, exclaims in his turn: 'It would be an insignificant art that consisted only of sounds, without language or signs to express states of the soul!' (Schumann, *GS*, I, p. 30) – this despite Chopin's musical aesthetic being in other ways diametrically opposed to Schumann's.

[23] The expression '*dire* un morceau de musique' (to 'tell' a piece of music) was current in French musical circles of the last century and even at the beginning of this one. Chopin uses it with eloquent insistence.

[24] See pp. 110–11, note 75.

formed the basis of all instrumental training, and the more piano playing drew its inspiration from vocal models, the more convincing it became.[25] Hence Chopin's art of transforming the piano into a leading tenor or a prima donna and creating the impression of human breathing; hence that pre-eminence given to broad *cantabile* style, that intense *legato*, that inimitable sense of line and phrasing, that fullness of sound, that 'cello-like quality which the piano can suddenly reveal. Even his particular conception of rubato is vocal and Baroque in essence, in that it seeks, wherever apt, to release the melodic part from all metrical fetters and let it expand with the perfect freedom of inflection found in singing.[26] Moscheles writes of Chopin's playing: 'So one does not miss the orchestral effects which the German school requires from a pianist, but allows oneself to be carried away as by a singer who, unpreoccupied by the accompaniment, gives full rein to his feelings' (Moscheles, II, p. 39). This predilection for vocal art may be put beside Chopin's abhorrence of all massive effects, and his insistence on naturalness and simplicity in piano playing. Nothing was more foreign to Chopin's nature than overemphasis, affectation or sentimentality: '"Je vous prie de vous asseoir", he said on such an occasion with gentle mockery' (Niecks, II, p. 341). But dry and inexpressive playing was equally unbearable to him, and in such cases he would implore the student: 'Put all your soul into it! [*Mettez-y donc toute votre âme!*]' (Karasowski, II, p. 91) – and what happiness he felt when innate musicality expressed itself spontaneously: 'She [Wanda Radziwiłł] has plenty of genuine musical feeling and you don't have to tell her *crescendo* here, *piano* there, quicker, slower and so on' (Chopin, *SC*, p. 37).

Piano technique should be no more than a means; and so it should come directly out of an imperative need for musical self-expression. There Chopin opens the way to a modern conception of music teaching, resolutely turning

[25] This is one of the fundamental traits linking Chopin to the Baroque aesthetic (for other points such as the *Affektenlehre*, *cantabile*, rubato, improvisation and execution of ornaments, the Bach cult, etc., see notes 70, 77, 82, 95, 103, 126, 128, 137 and 184 below). Seventeenth and eighteenth century treatises make constant reference to vocal models for instrumental playing. This '*cantabile* Art', recommended by Bach in his introduction to the Inventions and Sinfonias, was particularly prominent in Germany in the first half of the eighteenth century. Forkel reports that Bach 'knew how to introduce such variety to his performance that each piece, under his fingers, sounded just like a speech' (*Über Johann Sebastian Bachs Leben, Kunst und Kunstwerk*, Kassel and Basel, Bärenreiter, 1950, p. 33). The same aesthetic ideal is extended to a different style and instrument in Wolfgang Amadeus Mozart's comment about a pianist: 'She plays wonderfully; only in the *cantabile* she lacks the real feeling of singing' (Mozart, III, p. 135 – 27 June 1781). We are almost at Chopin's *bel canto*.

[26] See pp. 118–19, note 95. We can understand this as *one* of the components of Chopin's rubato, as the expression of his musical personality: a natural flair for improvising together with a Slavonic flexibility that rounds off sharp corners.

his back on many piano professors of his time[27] – and after! – whose teaching is based on a mechanistic conception of instrumental playing. With the exception of pianists such as Cramer, Field, Hummel and Moscheles, the pedagogues descended from the Classical generation regarded the acquisition of virtuosity as a collection of recipes (catalogued in innumerable *Methods*) to obtain a well-determined position of the fingers, hand, forearm, etc. One concentrated on the physical act of producing the sound, forgetting that the desire to create a certain sonority engenders the appropriate movement and in this way contributes to the education of the fingers. So the presumed way to virtuosity lay in a daily regime consisting of long hours of digital gymnastics and stubborn repetition of *Etudes de mécanisme* like those of Czerny, Kalkbrenner, Herz and others prolific in the genre.[28] Galvanised into action by Paganini's enchanted violin, Schumann and above all Liszt helped to pull piano teaching out of this rut, drawing new resources out of the instrument with their adaptations and transcriptions of Paganini's *Caprices*.[29]

Chopin, on the contrary, self-taught (his only piano teacher, Żywny, was a violinist) and an outsider to all Schools, with no taste for transcribing, offered in place of the narrowly mechanistic views a new, artistic conception of technical work. In place of the mental numbness caused by mechanical repetition of exercises, he advocated an intense listening concentration, an element reflected in the work, and playing, of Leimer and Gieseking.[30] In this concentration reside the two complementary factors indispensable to a good sonority: refinement of the ear, and muscular control and relaxation. One can hardly overstress that in Chopin's definition of technique, sound production, or the art of touch, comes *before* the acquisition of virtuosity: 'One needs only to study a certain positioning of the hand in relation to the keys to obtain with ease the most beautiful quality of sound, to know how to play long notes and short notes and [to attain] unlimited dexterity' (PM). And further: 'A well-formed technique, it seems to me, [is one] that can

---

[27] Some years later, Stephen Heller reacted similarly with his *Etudes* opp. 16, 45, 46 and 47, studies in style and expression, concerned with musical problems rather than exclusively mechanical formulae. Though falling short of the transcendental character of Chopin's opp. 10 and 25, they are by no means musically negligible.

[28] Liszt himself in those days (1832) did not escape the mechanistic conception of technique inherited from Czerny, his former teacher. Mme Boissier's notes (see Bibliography) testify to this. On this subject see pp. 94 and 96–7 below, notes 14 and 18.

[29] Schumann, *Studien nach Capricen von Paganini*, op. 3 (1832); *Sechs Concert-Etüden nach Capricen von Paganini*, op. 10 (1833). Liszt, *Etudes d'exécution transcendante d'après Paganini* (1838), revised and published in 1851 under the title *Grandes Etudes de Paganini*. Contemporary with these (and of no less importance pianistically) are Liszt's transcription of Berlioz's *Symphonie fantastique* (1833) and his first forays into the Beethoven symphonies (1837).

[30] See p. 95, note 16.

control and vary [*bien nuancer*] a beautiful sound quality' (*ibid.*). This is really the fundamental article of Chopin's pianistic *credo*, illustrated equally well by an axiom attributed to Liszt: 'All technique originates in the art of touch and returns to it.'[31]

A maximum of suppleness ('*facilement, facilement*' he would repeat tirelessly), and a cultivation of sensitivity of hearing and touch – these were the purposes of the exercises he prescribed in the first lessons. Chopin's famous predilection for the black keys springs from his understanding of the keyboard's proper relationship to the physiognomy of the hand, as the black keys favour a natural, comfortable position of the longer second, third and fourth fingers. This is why he made his pupils begin with the scales of B, F♯, and D♭ (following the basic fingertips *1-2-3-1*, *2-3-4-1* and *2-3-1* respectively). Contrary to the pedagogues of the time, who sought to equalize the fingers by means of laborious and cramping exercises, Chopin cultivated the fingers' individual characteristics, prizing their natural inequality as a source of variety in sound: 'As many different sounds as there are fingers' (*PM*). In this way he would quickly develop a great variety of colours in his pupils' sound meanwhile sparing them much tedious labour in fighting their own physiognomy. As for evenness of fingers and the *jeu perlé*, that touchstone of Romantic pianists, Chopin achieved it by two original means: innovatory fingering conducive to producing a flowing succession of sounds, and, in scales and arpeggios, a light movement of the hand in the direction of the run.[32]

By making his students study his own compositions, Chopin communicated to them something of the secret of the innovations with which he had enriched the pianistic art. In the first quarter of the nineteenth century, Beethoven, Weber and Schubert, each in his own way, founded the Romantic piano style by bursting through the fetters of the eighteenth-century fortepiano. But it was left to the following generation, and principally to Chopin and Liszt, to explore the resources of the newly developed instrument (Erard, Pleyel) in the service of a new aesthetic. To draw up a detailed list of Chopin's pianistic innovations would exceed the purpose of this introduction; in any case, the process cannot be dissociated from Chopin's contribution to the techniques of composition and the development of musical language.[33] But one can aptly outline the general tendency of these innovations and define their main points.

[31] Quoted in Paul Locard and Rémy Stricker, *Le Piano*, Paris, P.U.F. 'Que sais-je', No. 263, 1974, 5th edition, p. 44.

[32] See Mikuli's text, p. 37 below, and p. 106, note 59.

[33] This idea emerges from comments by Liszt on the innovations brought about by Chopin: 'It is to him that we owe the extension of chords, whether struck together, arpeggiated or in whole successions; the chromatic and enharmonic meanderings of which his music offers such striking

'Everything is a matter of knowing good fingering [. . .] Just as we need to use the conformation of the fingers, we need no less to use the rest of the hand, the wrist, the forearm and the upper arm. One cannot try to play everything from the wrist, as Kalkbrenner claims' (PM).[34] With these innocuous-sounding phrases, Chopin indeed sums up his own contribution to piano technique, aimed essentially at increasing the suppleness in all senses of playing. He is no longer content, like most of his contemporaries, solely with finger articulation aided at best by the wrist. In Chopin's playing, the fingers activate the whole arm: all his technical innovations rest upon the feeling of perfect continuity from the shoulder to the tips of the fingers. Naturally, these innovations are reflected in his piano writing being substantially richer than that of his immediate predecessors, such as Hummel, Field and Weber, and of his contemporaries. The first of all his *Etudes*, op. 10/1, composed in 1829, illustrates this perfectly by extending over the entire length of Chopin's keyboard in its opening phrase. This reflects Chopin's particular physiological discovery: in covering distances on the keyboard, the central pivoting finger is not the third, but the index finger, leading finger *par excellence*. From that are largely derived the following innovations:

- Flexible extension of the right hand (*Etudes* opp. 10/1 and 10/8).[35]
- Extended left-hand writing (*Etude* op. 10/9; Nocturnes op. 27/1 and 2; Prelude op. 28/24).
- Simultaneous extensions in both hands (*Etudes* op. 25/1, Prelude op. 28/19).
- Elaboration of scale passages to patterns alternating stepwise motion with larger intervals (*Etudes* opp. 10/4 and 25/2).[36]
- Extension of broken chords to the whole length of the keyboard (*Etudes* opp. 10/1 and 25/12).
- Extended chords either struck together or rapidly arpeggiated (*Etude* op. 10/11, Nocturne op. 48/1).

examples; the small groups of added grace notes, falling like tiny drops of speckled dew over the melodic figure. To this kind of ornamentation, previously modelled solely upon the *fioritura* of the great old Italian school of singing, he gave an unexpectedness and a variety beyond the reach of the human voice, which had hitherto been slavishly copied by the piano in embellishments that eventually became stereotyped and monotonous. He invented those wonderful harmonic progressions which would enhance with a serious aspect even those pages which, considering the lightness of their subject, did not seem to aspire to such importance' (Liszt, pp. 14–15).

[34] See pp. 95–6 and 108, notes 17 and 65.

[35] The comparison with Cramer's *Etude* no. 18 (84 *Etüden*, Peters edition, I, pp. 40–1) is most telling with regard to Chopin's novelty. The same goes for the *Etude* no. 77 (IV, pp. 28–9), concerning the extension of the left hand.

[36] From all the evidence Chopin avoids writing in scales. Among the rare works featuring scales are the end of the Impromptu op. 36 and the closing bars of the *Barcarolle* op. 60, both in F sharp and thus including a maximum of black keys. The same applies to the second theme of the finale of the Sonata op. 58, and to some extent to the end of the fourth Scherzo, op. 54.

- Writing in double octaves (*Etude* op. 25/10; Nocturne op. 48/1; Polonaise op. 44; Scherzo op. 39).
- Writing in double notes using all the intervals from the 2nd to the 7th (*Etude* op. 10/7).

Chopin's pianistic writing reveals two other innovations that involve the inspirational element – even improvisation – as much as technique. First, playing twos against threes, each in a separate hand, which requires perfect independence of the hands for the parts to fall harmoniously into place (Etude op. 25/2, *Nouvelles Etudes* nos. 1 and 3, [*Fantaisie-*]*Impromptu* op. 66, Waltz op. 42; see the fives against threes at the end of the Nocturnes opp. 32/2 and 55/2). Secondly, those 'small groups of added grace notes, falling like tiny drops of speckled dew over the melodic figure,'[37] something Chopin definitively transplanted into piano writing from *bel canto* (*Andante Spianato* op. 22, Concertos opp. 11 and 21, Impromptus opp. 29 and 36, Nocturnes, and elsewhere).

Those of Chopin's fingerings that have come down to us[38] are an indispensable guide to understanding his technical advances and originality. 'Everything is a matter of knowing good fingering', he wrote, as we have already seen (*PM*); he always adopted 'the easiest fingering, although it might be against the rules, that came to him', related Hipkins (p. 5) after having seen and heard Chopin play. From these two quotations, we see that Chopin was no slave to the traditions of fingering laid down by theoreticians and publishers. On the contrary, good fingering was a matter of finding the most comfortable succession of fingers, best suited both to the form of the hand and to conveying the musical discourse. So it was precisely by breaking many a Classical rule that Chopin opened new horizons with his revolutionary way of fingering.[39] His contribution in this field may be summed up in the following points:

- Emancipation of the thumb, which is allowed the freedom of the black keys (*Etude* op. 10/5) and entrusted with melodic fragments (*Etude* op. 25/7, *Nouvelles Etudes* no. 1).
- Letting the 3rd, 4th and 5th right hand fingers cross over one another in chromatic passages (*Etude* op. 10/2) and in singing legato lines (*Berceuse* op. 57, Nocturne op. 9/2, Prelude op. 28/15, and elsewhere).

---

[37] See note 33 above.
[38] These come through first editions, the manuscript or autograph copies used for making these editions, rough-draft autographs, proofs of the *Etude* op. 10/2 corrected by Chopin, and the principal printed scores with his annotations, formerly used by pupils and associates (Jane Stirling, Mme Dubois-O'Meara, Ludwika Jędrzejewicz and Franchomme). For these last sources, see Appendix II and III below.
[39] See in particular the texts of Kleczyński and Mikuli (pp. 38–40 below plus the relevant notes – 85, pp. 116–17; 91, p. 117–18), and also Appendix III.

- Crossing over these same fingers in passages of chromatic thirds (*Etude* op. 25/6, *Berceuse* op. 57, Prelude op. 28/24).
- Passing the 5th finger over the thumb (*Etude* op. 25/11, Impromptu op. 29, and elsewhere).
- Using the same finger on successive notes in a melodic line, diatonic as well as chromatic (Nocturne op. 37/1 and elsewhere).
- Notes repeated with the same finger, as far as the writing and the tempo permit it.[40]

Chopin also expanded piano technique by developing a new dependence on pedal, a factor that decisively influenced his piano writing, of which it acts as an integrating element (unlike with Hummel). The progress made by French and English piano manufacturers enabled particularly the bass strings' vibrations to be substantially prolonged by using the damper pedal. The fingers could then elaborate over a bass note which could be held on the pedal without dwindling too rapidly. Chopin also took advantage of this to develop his writing for the left hand. It is this extension of suppleness that underlies the accompanying voice in compositions such as the *Andante spianato* op. 22, the *Berceuse* op. 57, most Nocturnes (particularly opp. 27/1 and 2), and the trio in the 'Funeral March' from the Sonata op. 35.

If Chopin's technique perhaps appears to us as the most beautiful flower of Romantic pianism, it obviously does not represent *all* the technique that has since been applied to the instrument. It is naturally suited to the music of its creator, to that of several of Chopin's contemporaries and also, to a large extent, of many of his successors, particularly Grieg, Fauré, Debussy, Scriabin, Albéniz and Granados. After Chopin came Liszt, who exhausted the technical possibilities of the Romantic piano by fully exploring the paths opened up by his predecessor, and joining to them his own discoveries. Chopin, the aristocrat, was a pianist *da camera*; Liszt, the eloquent tribune, was a man of the stage. Chopin brought to the piano the refined art of *bel canto*; from the same piano Liszt wrenched sonorities evoking Berlioz or Wagner. While the Pole's aesthetic is based on the voice, the Hungarian's is inspired by the orchestra.[41] Liszt's choice here is what underlies the great innovations he brought to piano technique: the use of not only the whole arm

[40] Naturally this cannot apply to examples like the opening of the Waltz op. 18; see fingerings on Appendix III, pp. 252–3 – and, by way of contrast, p. 263 for the end of the Nocturne op. 32/1.

[41] Liszt writes: 'In its span of seven octaves [the piano] embraces the range of an orchestra; the ten fingers of a single man suffice to render the harmonies produced by the combined forces of more than 100 concerted instruments [. . .] We make arpeggios like the harp, prolonged notes like wind instruments, staccatos and a thousand other effects which once seemed the special prerogative of such and such an instrument' (*Pages romantiques*, Paris, Alcan; Leipzig, Breitkopf & Härtel, 1912, p. 136). Addressed to Adolphe Pictet in the form of a letter, this text was first published in the *Revue et gazette musicale de Paris*, V/6, 11 February 1838, pp. 57–62.

in playing but also the active participation of shoulders and back; and from this the notion of weight, hitherto unimagined to such an extent, and those massive movements of the arm, transporting immense blocks of sound from one end of the keyboard to the other.

Pianistically speaking, Liszt's place comes between Beethoven and Ravel, in a line of composers seeking essentially to give the piano a symphonic character. Chopin, rather, is Mozart's heir and Debussy's precursor.[42] The only musical genius of the nineteenth century whose pianism does not emulate the orchestra of his era, he lies at the heart of a tradition of vocal inspiration, with its prime emphasis on refinement of touch. Liszt's art evolved considerably in the course of a long, rich and eventful career, while Chopin, by 1830, had decisively mastered all the constituent elements of his genius. While Liszt was still following the avenues of pianistic virtuosity, Chopin's transcendent perspicacity and maturity had already placed him foremost among modern pianist-pedagogues.

[42] See pp. 127–30, notes 120, 121 and 122.

Part 1: Technique and style

BASIC TECHNIQUE

Time is still the best critic, and patience the best teacher.

Chopin

Definition of pianistic technique

Intonation being the tuner's task, the piano is free of one of the greatest difficulties encountered in the study of an instrument. One needs only to study a certain positioning of the hand in relation to the keys to obtain with ease the most beautiful quality of sound, to know how to play long notes and short notes, and [to attain] unlimited dexterity. Chopin, *PM*[1]

Mistakes in customary approaches to 'pure' technique

To those who are studying the art of playing the piano I suggest some practical and *simple* ideas which I know from experience to be really useful. As art is infinite within the limits of its means, so its teaching should be governed by the same limits in order to give it boundless potential [. . .] So we are not dealing with more or less ingenious theories, but with whatever goes straight to the point and smoothes the technical side of the art [. . .] People have tried out all kinds of methods of learning to play the piano, methods that are tedious and useless and have nothing to do with the study of this instrument. It's like learning, for example, to walk on one's hands in order to go for a stroll. Eventually one is no longer able to walk properly on one's feet, and not very well on one's hands either. It doesn't teach us how to play the *music* itself – and the type of difficulty we are practising is not the difficulty encountered in good music, the music of the great masters. It's an abstract difficulty, a new genre of *acrobatics*. Chopin, *PM*

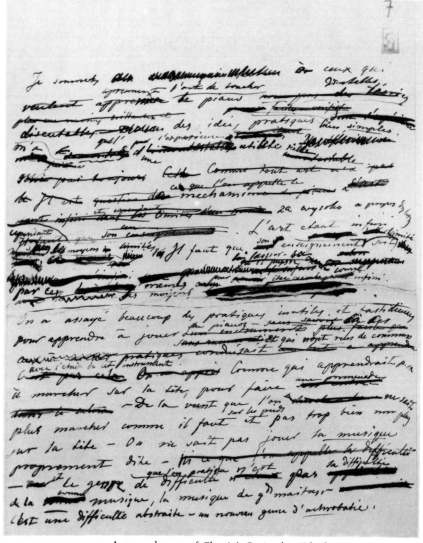

4 Autograph page of Chopin's *Projet de méthode*.

Categories of technical study

I am not, let it be understood, dealing here with musical feeling or style, but *purely* with the *technical* aspect of playing, what I call the *mechanism*. I divide the study of piano *mechanism* into three parts.

1st Teaching both hands to play adjacent notes (notes a tone apart and a semitone apart), that is, scales – *chromatic* and *diatonic* – and *trills*. Since there cannot be devised any *fourth* theoretical combination of adjacent notes,[2] whatever we invent to be played using *tone and semitone intervals* has to be a combination or selection of scales or trills.

2nd Notes farther than a tone or semitone apart, that is, intervals of a tone and a half upwards: *the octave divided* in minor thirds,[3] with each finger thus occupying a key, and the *common chord* with its inversions (disjunct notes).[4]

3rd *Double notes* (in two parts): *thirds, sixths, octaves*. (When you can play your thirds, sixths and octaves, you are then able to play in three parts – as a result [you have] chords, which you will know how to divide from your knowledge of disjunct intervals [category 2 above].) The two hands together will give four, five, six parts – and there is nothing more to be invented for study as far as mechanism *of piano playing* is concerned.[5]   Chopin, PM

Qualities required of a piano; makes of piano

[At Chopin's house] the pupil played always on a magnificent concert grand, and it was part of his duty to practise only on best quality instruments.

                         Mikuli, p. 4

Pleyel's pianos are the last word in perfection.[6]

            Chopin, *SC*, p. 101 (12 December 1831)

Chopin played a Pleyel, an instrument with a light touch on which one can nuance with more ease than on a fleshy-sounding instrument.

                Lenz, *GPV* 1872, p. 62

[. . .] these Pleyel pianos which he particularly cherished for their silvery and slightly veiled sonority and their lightness of touch. Liszt, p. 146

'When I feel out of sorts,' Chopin would say, 'I play on an Erard piano
where I easily find a ready-made tone. But when I feel in good form and
strong enough to find my own individual sound, then I need a Pleyel piano.'[7]

                                        Chopin/Karasowski,[8] II, p. 96

Until now I have worked more on heavy keyboards than on light ones: this
has greatly strengthened my fingers. However, on this type of piano it is
impossible to obtain the subtlest nuances with movements of the wrist and
forearm, as well as of each individual finger. These nuances – I've
experienced them as Chopin's on his beautiful piano, with its touch so close
to that of the Viennese instruments. He himself calls it 'a perfidious traitor'
[un traitre perfide]. Things that came out perfectly on my solid and robust
Erard became abrupt and ugly on Chopin's piano.[9] He found it dangerous to
work much on an instrument with a beautiful ready-made sound like the
Erard. He said these instruments spoil one's touch: 'You can thump it and
bash it, it makes no difference: the sound is always beautiful and the ear
doesn't ask for anything more since it hears a full, resonant tone.'

                                        Gretsch/Grewingk, p. 15

Broadwood, [who is the] real [London] Pleyel . . .

                                        Chopin, KFC, II, p. 268 [August 1848]

[Chopin] especially liked Broadwood's Boudoir cottage pianos of that
date [1848], two-stringed, but very sweet instruments, and he found pleasure
in playing on them.[10]   Hipkins,[11] p. 7

Our modern pianos, with their vast sonority, are equally different in their
touch from the pianos of Chopin's time. The large, heavy hammers, the depth
of touch, almost double that of the pianos of 1845, demand to-day a totally
different strength, suppleness and training.   Schelling,[12] p. 69

[Chopin] could not bear too loud a sound on the piano, and called it 'a dog
barking'. But according to Mikuli it does not follow that we have to avoid
stronger gradations and accents when interpreting Chopin nowadays. We
should take into account that piano manufacture has undergone an
extraordinarily important evolution. Formerly on those small, delicate
instruments, forte could indeed sound positively disagreeable. To-day's forte,
however, has a round sonority and a remarkable 'substance'.

                                        Mikuli/A. Michałowski,[13] p. 75

Daily practice: how to work and for how long

He feared above all . . . the *abrutissement* [stupefaction by overwork] of the pupils. One day he heard me say that I practised six hours a day. He became quite angry, and forbade me to practise more than three hours.[14]

Dubois/Niecks,[15] II, pp. 183–4

He always advised the pupil not to work for too long at a stretch and to intermit between hours of work by reading a good book, by looking at masterpieces of art, or by taking an invigorating walk.[16]

Gretsch/Grewingk, p. 20

He never tired of inculcating that the appropriate exercises are not merely mechanical but claim the intelligence and entire will of the pupil, so that a twentyfold or fortyfold repetition (even nowadays the worshipped arcanum of so many schools) does no good at all; while one hardly dare mention the kind of practice advocated by Kalkbrenner,[17] during which one may occupy oneself reading (!).[18]   Mikuli, p. 3

In complete opposition to Chopin, Liszt maintains that the fingers should be strengthened by working on an instrument with a heavy, resistant touch, continually repeating the required exercises until one is completely exhausted and incapable of going on. Chopin wanted absolutely nothing to do with such a gymnastic treatment of the piano.

Mikuli/Bischoff[19]/Federhofer, p. 85

Chopin invented a completely new method of piano playing that permitted him to reduce technical exercises to a minimum.   Mikuli/Koczalski,[20] p. 56

Georges Mathias told me that Chopin required his pupils to practise from the first slowly and *legato*,[21] with a full tone.   Mathias/Philipp,[22] p. 15

If I was at a loss to understand a passage, he played it slowly to me [. . .] Sometimes he went to the other piano and murmured an exquisite impromptu accompaniment.[23]   Anonymous Scottish lady/Hadden, p. 158

He makes you practise so thoroughly in his presence that you cannot fail to make progress.   Cheriemietieff/Siemienowski, p. 128

To satisfy her feared but venerated teacher the next time, she sould sometimes have to prepare a whole sonata in the time from one lesson to another – on a practical as well as a theoretical level – and learn it by heart, or at other times solve a difficult harmony exercise, or overcome some technical difficulties.   Harder/Adelung, p. 122

I sat down at the piano.
– 'What about the score?'
– 'I didn't bring it, I play this Nocturne [op. 9/2] by heart.'
– I don't want any of this: are you reciting a lesson? I want to teach either precisely or not at all. I've already told you you don't know how to work. I gave you the Clementi [*Préludes et Exercices*] and by the next lesson it had mysteriously vanished, just like the Moscheles *Etudes* [probably op. 70]. You played my Impromptu [op. 29? 36?] twice, and that was it already despatched; now it's a Nocturne, and you forget to bring the score!'
                    Zaleska/Hordyński, p. 150

Mr Wotpol,[24] a virtuoso contemporary with Chopin living in our circle – whom Chopin even called his 'colleague' – while not contesting what I have said above about practising from the score, advises us none the less not just to stop using the score in the final stages of preparation, but even to refrain from looking down at the keyboard – as he claims Chopin himself recommended him to do.[25] Wotpol, surprised to see Chopin looking always in the same direction while playing, his eyes fixed on a point to the left above him,[26] questioned him about the habit and received by way of reply the following advice: 'As soon as you know a piece from memory, practise it at night in the dark! When the eyes can see neither notes nor keys, when all disappears, only then does the hearing function with all its sensitivity; then you can really hear yourself, noticing every fault, while the hand acquires an assurance and boldness that it cannot find when the player is constantly looking at the keys.'[27]   Wotpol/Działyńska[28]/Czartkowski–Jeżewska, p. 376

Position at the piano and hand position

Sit slightly high at the piano and make as few movements as possible.
                    Courty/Aguettant, p. 196

Position yourself so as to be able to reach both ends of the keyboard without leaning to either side. The right foot on the sustaining pedal without operating the dampers. The elbow level with the white keys, the hand turned neither to the left nor the right.[29]

Find the right position for the hand by placing your fingers on the keys, E, F♯, G♯, A♯, B:[30] the long fingers will occupy the high [= black] keys, and the short fingers the low [= white] keys. Place the fingers occupying the high [= black] keys all on one level and do the same for those occupying the white keys, to make the leverage relatively equal; this will curve the hand, giving it the necessary suppleness that it could not have with the *fingers straight*. A supple hand; the wrist, the forearm, the arm, everything will follow the hand *in the right order*.   Chopin, *PM*

The pivot is the index finger, which divides the hand in half when it spreads open.   Chopin, *PM*/Jędrzejewicz copy[1]

General suppleness

'Have the body supple right to the tips of the toes,' [Chopin used to say].[31]
                                    Franchomme/Picquet/Anonymous,[32] p. 39

Suppleness was his great object. He repeated, without ceasing, during the lessons: 'easily, easily' [*facilement, facilement*]. Stiffness exasperated him.
                                                    Dubois/Niecks, II, p. 182

On beginning a lesson, Chopin's main concern was to do away with every stiffness and convulsive or cramped movement of the hand, in order to obtain the primary requisite of good playing: *souplesse* [suppleness] and with it independence of the fingers.   Mikuli, p. 3

One day, Chopin forbade Mikuli ever to work on Hummel's Septet [op. 74] again, since Mikuli had remarked that his hand was hurting in an octave passage.   Mikuli/Bischoff/Federhofer, p. 85

[After a long break] I am astonished that my fingers don't stiffen. What a way of teaching he has – it's marvellous.   Stirling/Ganche,[33] *DSFC*, p. 123

Flexibility of the wrist and hand; freedom of the fingers

He could play *legato* in the most difficult arpeggios made up of very wide intervals, since it was his wrist and not his arm that was in constant motion.
                                                    Mikuli/Koczalski, p. 56

[He] gently found fault with my stiff wrist.   Streicher/Niecks, II, p. 340

I had not played many bars before he said: 'Laissez tomber les mains' [Let your hands fall]. Hitherto I had been accustomed to hear 'Put down your hands', or 'Strike' such a note. This *letting fall* was not mechanical only: it was to me a new idea, and in a moment I felt the difference.

Anonymous Scottish lady/Hadden, p. 157

The hand should be supple and trained to flex as far as possible, without ever having to resort to the force of the elbow, except in *fortissimo* passages, and not always even then. Furthermore the hand should fall softly on the keys just with its own weight – as though to play *pianissimo*, often seeming to caress the keys; sometimes lying as though dead at the wrist, but keeping always a living, active link from each finger to the hand, concentrating the sensorial power in the extreme tips of the fingers. When the wrist is not passive, the sensorial power runs through the whole hand right through to the fingers, paralysing them; this robs them of their freedom and tires the player, and the stiff hand prevents him from playing what he would be able to manage perfectly well by being relaxed.

Czartoryska/Działyńska/Czartkowski–Jeżewska, p. 373

He recommended [. . .] that the fingers should fall freely and lightly.

Kleczyński,[34] FCI, pp. 38–9

The fingers should be free [*déliés*], running over the keys without the slightest effort – but not superficially 'tickling' the keyboard, except in the most delicate passages.

Czartoryska/Działyńska/Czartkowski–Jeżewska, p. 374

As gymnastic aids he recommended bending the wrist inward and outward, repeated wrist strokes, and stretching the fingers, but all this with an earnest warning against over-fatigue.   Mikuli, p. 3

Passivity of the arm and elbow

Chopin kept his elbows close to his sides and played only with finger touch, no weight from the arms.[35]   Hipkins, p. 5

The arms should be the *slaves* of the fingers, yet the opposite always tends to occur; one should keep one's mind off the arms[36] and just use them as naturally as possible: fingers elongated for singing passages and closely bent for that special cloudy fluency of ornaments or appoggiaturas.

Courty/Aguettant, p. 195

Young Leszkiewicz[37] plays very well, but most of the time still from the elbow.   Chopin, KFC, I, p. 119

[For] all rapid passages in general [. . .] the hands must be slightly turned, the right hand to the right, and the left hand to the left; and the elbows should remain close to the body, except in the highest and lowest octaves.

Kleczyński, FCI, p. 34

Cultivation of touch; control of hearing; variety of attack; predominance of 'legato'

The goal is not to learn to play everything with an equal sound, [but rather,] it seems to me, a well-formed technique that can control and vary [bien nuancer] a beautiful sound quality.[38]   Chopin, PM

The basis therefore of this method of teaching consisted in refinement of touch; and this alone would suffice to distinguish it from all others. Everyone, it is true, recognized the utility of a good touch, but often spoilt it by an abuse of exercises badly comprehended [. . .] Thus the first few lessons [with Chopin] were a perfect martyrdom; the touch of the pupil always appeared too hard and rough.   Kleczyński, FCI, p. 26

The fingers should sink, immerse themselves somehow in the depths of the piano[39] – in piano as well as in forte playing – drawing from it that sustained, melancholy sound which – the fingers reluctant to leave the keys – is able to bring out from even the least melodious instrument a singing quality close to that of the Italian singers whom Chopin recommended as models.

Czartoryska/Działyńska/Czartkowski–Jeżewska, p. 374

'Caress the key, never bash it!' Chopin would say. And his pupil Georges Mathias would add, repeating Chopin's advice, that 'You should, so to speak, mould the keyboard with a velvet hand and feel the key rather than striking it!'   Mathias/Piron, p. 115

'Play this note properly, don't let it bark.'[40]

Chopin/Zaleska/Hordyński, p. 152

As to Chopin's method of teaching, it was absolutely of the old *legato* school, of the school of Clementi and Cramer. Of course, he had enriched it by a great variety of touch (*d'une grande variété dans l'attaque de la touche*); he obtained a wonderful variety of tone and nuances of tone.[41]

Mathias/Niecks, II, pp. 181–2

He made me practise first of all constantly varying the attack of one single note, and showed me how he could obtain diverse sonorities from the same key, by sriking it in twenty different ways.   Peru, p. 29

He treated the different types of touch very thoroughly, especially the full-toned [*tonvolle*] *legato*.   Mikuli, p. 3

Chopin called playing that was not *legato* 'a pigeon hunt' [*chasse aux pigeons*].[42]
                           Lenz, B, p. 304

In *legato* playing, you should not merely join the notes, but bind them together, clinging to the keys – practising (as Moscheles also recommends) obtaining every colour of sound just by modifying the weight of the fingers falling on the keys. As for *staccato*, it should be just like the dot over an *i* – like the buzz of a string plucked on the harp or the guitar – like a violin *pizzicato*.[43] You can make this marvellous vibration of the string not so much by snatching your hand away from the key, as by using a short, dry touch – almost grazing it like a fly brushing against it with its wing.

Czartoryska/Działyńska/Czartkowski–Jeżewska, p. 374

He insisted that, unless specially indicated, the hand should not be lifted too quickly: 'Did it burn you?' he would ask.

Franchomme/Picquet/Anon., p. 39

Individuality and independence of the fingers

For a long time we have been acting against nature by training our fingers to be all equally powerful. As each finger is differently formed, it's better not to attempt to destroy the particular charm of each one's touch but on the contrary to develop it. Each finger's power is determined by its shape: the thumb having the most power, being the broadest, shortest and freest; the fifth [finger] as the other extremity of the hand; the third as the middle and the pivot; then the second [illegible], and then the fourth, the weakest one, the

Siamese twin of the third, bound to it by a common ligament, and which people insist on trying to separate from the third – which is impossible, and, fortunately, unnecessary.[44] As many different sounds as there are fingers.

Chopin, *PM*

[. . .] Chopin, from the first lesson, unceasingly directed the attention of the pupil to the freedom and independence of the fingers. He differs in this, I believe, from other professors who do not come to the independence of the fingers until after a long course of study. Chopin recommended, with this object, that the fingers should fall freely and lightly, and that the hand should be held as though suspended in the air (without weight); he objected to rapid movements at too early a stage of the pupil's progress, and wished that they should learn to execute all passages *fortissimo* and *pianissimo*. From this method the various qualities of tone came of themselves, and the hand was never fatigued. This frequent employment of *piano*, for the purpose of avoiding heaviness and clumsiness of [the] hand, is a characteristic feature in the method of Chopin. Kleczyński, *FCI*, pp. 38–9

Five-finger exercises for acquiring independence

In order to give the hand a position at once advantageous and graceful (and in his estimation these two qualities always went together), he caused it to be thrown lightly on the keyboard in such a manner that the five fingers rested upon the notes E, F♯, G♯, A♯, B; this he considered the normal position. Then without change of position the hand was required to play exercises calculated to ensure the independence and equality of the fingers. He almost always instructed the pupil to commence these exercises playing the notes *staccato* (A). The *staccato* effected by a free movement of the wrist is a wonderful means of counteracting heaviness [. . .] A second set of exercises consisted of a *legato staccato*, or heavy *staccato*, in which the finger rests somewhat longer on the key (B).[45] Then we come to the true slurred manner by modifying the *legato staccato*, making it an accented *legato* (C). Then we use a *legato* executed with the fingers raised considerably above the keyboard;[46] and, finally, we have the *legato* performed *ad lib.*, with a movement of the fingers more or less marked, modifying at pleasure the volume from *ff* to *pp*, and the movement from *andante* to *prestissimo* (D):

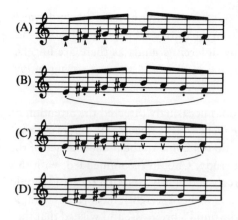

Kleczyński, *FCI*, pp. 27–8, 29

Scales and arpeggios; passing the thumb; evenness

It is useless to start learning scales on the piano with C major, the easiest to read, and the most difficult for the hand, as it has no pivot. Begin with one that places the hand at ease, with the longer fingers on the black keys, like B major for instance.

Chopin, *PM*

Chopin made his pupils begin with the B major scale, very slowly, without stiffness.

Dubois/Niecks, II, p. 182

The scales with many black keys (B, F♯ and D♭) were studied first, whereas C major, as the most difficult, came last.[47]

Mikuli, p. 3

Start with the B major scale and work through them one by one to C major, moving back [*reculant*] one finger each time.[48]

Chopin, *PM*/Jędrzejewicz copy

He made his pupils practise scales with a full tone, as *legato* as possible,[49] very slowly at first and only gradually advancing to a quicker tempo, and with metronomic evenness. To facilitate passing the thumb under the other fingers and passing the fingers over, the hand was to be given a corresponding turn inward.[50]

Mikuli, p. 3

He recommended *daily* work on scales and arpeggios played *with regularity* [presumably of rhythm], and set great store by scales lightly accented in groups of three or four, or even played three against four and vice versa.[51]

Gretsch/Grewingk, p. 20

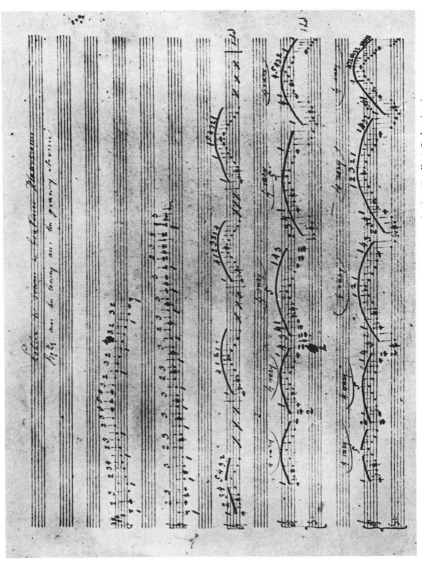

5 Basic exercises written by Chopin for his niece Ludwika (Ludka) Jędrzejewicz.

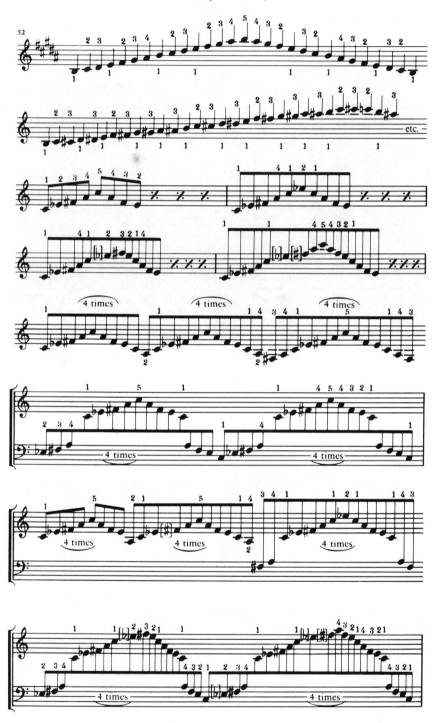

The chromatic scale:
1. With the thumb, index finger and middle finger.[53]
2. With the little finger, fourth and middle finger.[54]
3. In thirds with the same fingerings at once.[55]
4. In sixths.[56]
5. In octaves.

Divide the hand alternately in two parts:
1. The thumb, index and middle finger
2. The middle finger, fourth and little finger.

Chopin, PM/Jędrzejewicz copy

No one will notice the inequality of sound in a very fast scale, as long as the notes are played in equal time.[57] Chopin, PM

According to Chopin, evenness in scales (and in arpeggios) depended not merely on equal strengthening of all fingers by means of five-finger exercises, and on entire freedom of the thumb when passing under and over, but above all on a constant sideways movement of the hands (with the elbow hanging freely and always loose);[58] continuous and even-flowing rather than in steps, a movement he illustrated by a *glissando* over the keys.[59] Mikuli, p. 3

[After the first five-finger exercises] the second series is for the purpose of preserving the even and tranquil position of the hand during the passage of the thumb in scales and arpeggios. [. . .] Now Chopin, from the very first lesson, insisted upon the hand's retention of its position; he preferred that the notes should at first be disconnected, rather than that the hand should alter its normal position. He also at the commencement caused all exercises and scales to be played *staccato*, without troubling about the passage of the thumb. Taking it that each scale has two fundamental positions, viz., that of thumb, 2, 3, 4, and of thumb, 2, 3; his pupils commenced with the scale of B major for the right, and D flat major for the left hand (these being the easiest scales for the respective hands), forming the hand in the manner already described at each fundamental position:

By this *staccato* exercise the hand was rendered familiar with the successive positions; then by the various steps of *legato staccato*, accentuated *staccato*, etc., the pupil got to the point when, raising the fingers high, the thumb was passed by the action of the muscles alone, the hand still retaining its horizontal position; the hand was thus prepared for the more difficult scales, and for arpeggio passages, in which the wide intervals were eventually reached without effort and without greatly raising the fingers. I know from experience that by this method an equal and steady style of performance is attainable even when it is necessary to pass the thumb after the fourth or fifth finger, as in the Scherzo in B flat minor [op. 31] (A), in the *Etude* in A minor [op. 25/11] (B), in the *Impromptu* in A flat [op. 29] (C), etc.:[60]

These exercises also explain to us how Chopin executed his very difficult accompaniments, accompaniments unknown before, and consisting of notes at great distances apart, for instance, in the Nocturnes in D flat [op. 27/2], and in C sharp minor [op. 27/1], in the 'Marche funèbre' (Trio) [op. 35], in the Nocturne in G [op. 37/2], etc.   Kleczyński, *FCI*, pp. 29–32

Evenness of sound and tranquillity of the hand as principles of fingering

[The exercises immediately above] also explain to us those fingerings – so original that they shocked the old pianists[61] – the object of which is to keep the hand in its proper position, even by passing the 3rd or 4th finger over the 5th:[62] for instance, the chromatic scales with the 3rd, 4th and 5th fingers, *Etude* op. 10/2; the passage to the second motif of the Nocturne in B flat minor [op. 9/1] (A), the *Berceuse* (B), the Nocturne in C sharp minor [op. 27/ 1] (C), etc.:[63]

[... This fingering] arises from a perfectly true and rational idea, from a natural position of the hand, to which position it ought to conform in most passages; and this is one of Chopin's greatest merits so far as piano technique is concerned. If we take as the normal position for the right hand, E, F♯, G♯, A♯, B, and for the left hand C, B♭, A♭, G♭, F♮ [*sic*], we perceive that the two hands must be slightly turned in contrary directions.

Kleczyński, *FCI*, pp. 32–4

Chopin marked fingering on his scores liberally, especially the type peculiar to himself. Here pianoforte playing owes to him great innovations which, through their expediency, were soon widely adopted, notwithstanding the horror with which some authorities, like Kalkbrenner, at first regarded them. Thus Chopin unashamedly used the thumb on black keys, or passed it under the fifth finger (with a decided inward turn at the wrist, to be sure), if it helped to facilitate performance and lend it more evenness and quietness. He often used the same finger to play two adjoining notes consecutively (and this not only when sliding from a black key to a white key), without the slightest noticeable break in the continuity of line. He frequently crossed the longer fingers over one another without the help of the thumb (see the *Etude* op. 10/2),

and this not only in places where, for example, the holding of another note with the thumb made it necessary to do so. The fingering for chromatic thirds based on this device (as he marked it himself in the *Etude* op. 25/6 [bars 5–6])

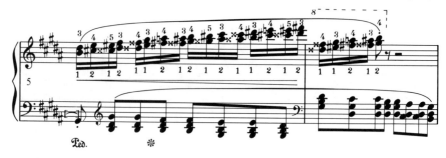

makes it much easier than ever before to obtain the smoothest *legato* in the quickest tempo, and with a perfectly unstrained hand.   Mikuli, p. 4

As many different sounds as there are fingers – everything is a matter of knowing good fingering. Hummel[64] was the most knowledgeable on this subject. Just as we need to use the conformation of the fingers, we need no less to use the rest *of the hand*, the wrist, the forearm and the upper arm. One cannot try to play everything from the wrist, as Kalkbrenner claims.[65]

Chopin, *PM*

Gutmann told me that his master's playing was particularly smooth, and his fingering calculated to attain this result.   Gutmann/Niecks, II, p. 95

In every kind of touch the evenness of his scales and passage work was unsurpassed, indeed phenomenal [. . .]   Mikuli, p. 2

He used a simple, natural position of the hands as conditioned by scale and chord-playing, adopting the easiest fingering, although it might be against the rules, that came to him.   Hipkins, p. 5

. . . in addition [he showed] me the special fingering, on which so much depended, and about which he was very strict.

Anonymous Scottish lady/Hadden, p. 158

Mathias said that Chopin was very particular about fingerings, demanding that the student should learn a fingering once and for all, and then never alter it.   Mathias/Schelling, p. 70

Practice of trills

Trill with three fingers at least, and four when practising.[66]

Chopin, *PM*/Jędrzejewicz copy

Octaves, double notes and chords

Octaves were to be played from the wrist, it is true,[67] but without thereby losing any of their fullness of tone.   Mikuli, p. 4

In simple repeated notes and octaves don't leave the key, but simply let the finger be softly pushed back up by the key itself.

Franchomme/Picquet/Anon., p. 38

For playing double notes and cords, Chopin demanded that the notes be struck strictly simultaneously; breaking was allowed only where the composer himself had specified it.[68]   Mikuli, p. 4

MUSICAL STYLE

We use sounds to make music just as we use words to make a language.

Chopin, PM

Musical prosody and declamation; phrasing

Here are the chief practical directions as to expression which Chopin often repeated to his pupils:

A long note is stronger, as is also a high note. A dissonant is likewise stronger, and equally so a syncopated note. The ending of a phrase, before a comma, or a stop, is always *weak*. If the melody ascends, one plays *crescendo*, if it descends, *decrescendo*. Moreover, notice must be taken of *natural* accents. For instance, in a bar of two, the first note is strong, the second weak, in a bar of three the first strong and the two others weak. To the smaller parts of the bar the same direction will apply. Such then are the rules: the exceptions are always indicated by the authors themselves.[69]

Kleczyński, CGW, pp. 41–2

Under his fingers each musical phrase sounded like song, and with such clarity that each note took the meaning of a syllable, each bar that of a word, each phrase that of a thought. It was a declamation without pathos; but both simple and noble.   Mikuli/Koczalski, p. 53

Chopin insisted above all on the importance of correct phrasing. Wrong phrasing would provoke the apt analogy that it seemed to him as if someone were reciting a laboriously memorized speech in an unfamiliar language, not merely failing to observe the right quantity of syllables, but perhaps even making full stops in the middle of words. Similarly, by his illiterate phrasing the pseudo-musician reveals that music is not his mother tongue but something foreign and unintelligible to him; and so, like that orator, he must relinquish all hope of his speech having any effect on the listener.[70] Mikuli, p. 4

All the theory of the style which Chopin taught to his pupils rested on this analogy between music and language, on the necessity for separating the various phrases, on the necessity for pointing and for modifying the power of the voice and its rapidity of articulation [. . .] Here follow some principal rules for musical punctuation and elocution.[71]

In a musical phrase composed of something like eight measures,[72] the end of the eighth will generally mark the termination of the thought, that which, in language written or spoken, we should indicate by a full-point; here we should make a slight pause and lower the voice. The secondary divisions of this phrase of eight measures, occurring after each two or each four measures, require shorter pauses – that is to say, they require commas or semi-colons. These pauses are of great importance; without them music becomes a succession of sounds without connection, an incomprehensible chaos, as spoken language would be if no regard were paid to punctuation and the inflection of the voice. A short example will make the matter clear. Let us take the well-known Waltz in A flat (op. 69/1); the musical thought is divided into periods of two measures, and thus the concluding note of each second measure should be shorter and weaker than the preceding notes. Written thus:

The above should be executed as follows:

[. . .] From these general rules, Chopin arrived at the following conclusion, to which he attached much importance: *do not play by too short phrases*; that is to say, do not keep continually suspending the movement and lowering the

tone on too short members of the thought; that is again to say, do not spread
the thought out too much, by slackenings of the movement – this fatigues the
attention of the listener who is following its development. If the thought is
short, as in an Adagio, the movement may be slackened, but never when it
consists of more than four measures.   Kleczyński, *FCI*, pp. 49, 50–3

He advised his pupils not to fragment the musical idea, but rather to carry
it to the listener in one long breath.   Karasowski, II, p. 94

At phrasing a melody, at bringing out a thematic fragment, at making a
'line', he was inimitable.   Mathias/Schelling, p. 70

On declamation and performance in general, he gave his pupils invaluable
and sensible instructions and hints, but conveyed his meaning by repeatedly
playing not just single passages but whole pieces, and this with a
conscientiousness and enthusiasm that listeners in a concert hall could not
have had the opportunity of hearing.[73]   Mikuli, p. 4

'Bel canto' – a model for pianistic declamation and fullness of tone

Chopin's advice was, that this theory [of musical declamation] should be
grounded upon the rules which guide vocalists, and that it should be
perfected by hearing good singers.[74]   Kleczyński, *FCI*, p. 55

The best way to attain naturalness in performance, in Chopin's view, was
to listen frequently to Italian singers, among whom there were some very
remarkable artists in Paris at the time.[75] He always held up as an example to
pianists their broad and simple style, the ease with which they used their
voices and the remarkable sustaining powers which this ease gave them.
                                                   Karasowski, II, p. 93

As regards style, one should follow that of Pasta,[75] of the great Italian
school of singing.[76]   Lenz, *UB*, p. 297

Chopin questioned me as to [my previous training], and I told him I had
learned more from listening to singing than anything else. He remarked:
'That is right; music ought to be song.' And truly in his hands the piano *did*
sing, and in many tones.   Anonymous Scottish lady/Hadden, p. 159

To Madame Rubio he said: 'You must sing if you wish to play'; and he made her take lessons in singing.   Rubio/Niecks, II, p. 187

During lessons Chopin would repeat indefatigably: '*Il faut chanter avec les doigts!*'[77]   Gretsch/Grewingk, p. 20

Chopin played me four Nocturnes I had not heard before – what enchantment! – it was unbelievably beautiful. His playing is entirely based on the vocal style of Rubini, Malibran and Grisi, etc.; he says so himself. But it's a purely pianistic 'voice' that he uses to recreate the particular style of each of these artists, while they have other means at their disposal. This is not to suggest that Chopin achieved this to the detriment of having a personal style:[78] his sense of harmony ensures a synthesis of all these elements. I listen to his playing – noble and sonorous, yet at the same time soft and delicate – with a deeper attention that Grisi can command from me with her jubilant, passionate singing, often astonishing, but also often not beautiful at all.

Today Chopin showed me another new, simple way of obtaining a marvellous result. I had felt in what respect my playing was lacking, but without knowing the solution. True to his principle of imitating great singers in one's playing, Chopin drew from the instrument the secret of how to express breathing. At every point where a singer would take a breath,[79] the accomplished pianist [. . .] should take care to raise the wrist so as to let it fall again on the singing note with the greatest suppleness imaginable. To attain this *souplesse* is the most difficult task I know. But once you succeed in doing it, then you laugh with joy at the beautiful sound, and Chopin exclaims, '*C'est cela, parfait! merci!*'   Gretsch/Grewingk, pp. 9–10

The wrist: respiration in the voice.[80]   Chopin, *PM*

Chopin attached great importance to these [phrasing slurs], which by the way are not always correctly drawn in the greater part of his works;[81] whenever this mark terminated he detached the hand after having diminished the tone.   Kleczyński, *FCI*, p. 55

He loved to find in piano playing what we understand by *portamento* in singing.[82]   Karasowski, II, p. 94

[In interpreting Chopin] carry one sound to the next, but only at the last moment; don't ever, ever, exaggerate.   Courty/Aguettant, pp. 195–6

'Legato' and 'cantabile'

Under Chopin's hands the piano needed to envy neither the violin for its bow nor wind instruments for their living breath. The tones melted into one another as wonderfully as in the most beautiful singing [. . .] The tone he could *draw* from the instrument, especially in *cantabile*, was immense [*riesengross*]; in this regard John Field[83] alone could be compared with him.

Mikuli, p. 2

Field's[84] and his own Nocturnes also figured to some extent as *Etudes*, for through them the pupil would learn – partly from Chopin's explanations, partly from observing and imitating Chopin, who played them indefatigably to the pupil – to recognize, love and produce the beautiful 'bound' [*gebunden*] vocal tone and the *legato*.

Mikuli, p. 4

His playing was always noble and beautiful, his tones always sang, whether in full *forte* or in the softest *piano*. He took infinite pains to teach the pupil this *legato*, *cantabile* way of playing. 'Il (ou elle) ne sait pas lier deux notes' [He (or she) doesn't know how to join two notes together] was his severest censure.

Streicher/Niecks, II, p. 341

Fingerings for 'legato' and 'cantabile' playing

He often used the same finger to play two adjoining notes consecutively (and this not only when sliding from a black key to a white key), without the slightest noticeable break in the continuity of line.[85]

Mikuli, p. 4

(Nocturne op. 9/2, bars 4–6)[86]

Frequent use of the same finger in melodies between one note and the next.

Courty/Aguettant, p. 196

(Nocturne op. 9/2, bars 26–8)[87]

The third finger is a *grand chanteur*.

Courty/Aguettant, p. 196

(Nocturne op. 48/1, opening)[88]

(Nocturne op. 37/1, bars 5–6)[89]

He changed fingers upon a key as often as an organ-player.[90]

Hipkins, p. 5

Substitute fingers as much as possible.[91]

Franchomme/Picquet/Anon., p. 38

[For repeated notes in a moderate tempo] Chopin could not tolerate the alternation of fingers [. . .] He preferred the repeated note to be played with the fingertip, very carefully and without changing fingers.

Franchomme/Picquet/Anon., pp. 12–13

His hand always remained tranquil and flexible, even in the repeated
attack of a single key.   Mikuli/Koczalski, p. 56

Agogics: Rhythmic strictness and rubato

[Chopin] required adherence to the strictest rhythm, hated all lingering and
dragging, misplaced rubatos, as well as exaggerated *ritardando*s. 'Je vous
prie de vous asseoir' [Pray do take a seat] he said on such an occasion with
gentle mockery.   Streicher/Niecks, II, p. 341

In keeping time Chopin was inexorable, and some readers will be surprised
to learn that the metronome never left his piano. Even in his much maligned
tempo rubato,[92] the hand responsible for the accompaniment would keep
strict time, while the other hand, singing the melody, would free the essence
of the musical thought from all rhythmic fetters, either by lingering hesitantly
or by eagerly anticipating the movement with a certain impatient vehemence
akin to passionate speech.   Mikuli, p. 3

Through Mme Viardot [. . .] I learned the true secret of tempo rubato [. . .
where] the accompaniment holds its rhythm undisturbed while the melody
wavers capriciously, rushes or lingers, sooner or later to fall back upon its
axis. This way of playing is very difficult since it requires complete
independence of the two hands;[93] and those lacking this give both themselves
and others the illusion of it by playing the melody in time and dislocating the
accompaniment so that it falls beside the beat; or else – worst of all – content
themselves with simply playing one hand after the other.[94] It would be a
hundred times better just to play in time, with both hands together.
                                        Viardot/Saint-Saëns, QM, pp. 386–7

Everyone knows that rubato is an indication often encountered in old
music;[95] its essence is fluctuation of movement, one of the two principal
means of expression in music, namely the modification of tone and of tempo,
as in the art or oration, whereby the speaker, moved by this or that emotion,
raises or lowers his voice, and accelerates or draws out his diction. Thus
rubato is a nuance of movement, involving anticipation and delay, anxiety
and indolence, agitation and calm; but what moderation is needed in its use,
and how all too often it is abused! [. . .] There was another aspect: Chopin, as
Mme Camille Dubois explains so well, often required simultaneously that
the left hand, playing the accompaniment,[96] should maintain strict time,
while the melodic line should enjoy freedom of expression with fluctuations
of speed. This is quite feasible: you can be early, you can be late, the two

hands are not in phase; then you make a compensation which re-establishes the ensemble. In Weber's music, for example, Chopin recommended this way of playing. He often told me to use it, it's as though I still hear him: in the Sonata in A flat [op. 39], in the A flat passage of the *agitato* in the *Concertstück* [op. 79, first movement bars 57ff] . . .   Mathias, p. 5

What characterized Chopin's playing was his rubato, in which the totality of the rhythm was constantly respected. 'The left hand,' I often heard him say, 'is the choir master [*Kapellmeister*]: it mustn't relent or bend. It's a clock. Do with the right hand what you want and can.'[97] He would say, 'A piece lasts for, say, five minutes, only in that it occupies this time for its overall performance; internal details [of pace within the piece] are another matter. And there you have rubato.'[98]   Lenz, GPV, p. 302

How did Chopin understand rubato? Was it synonymous with complete freedom and arbitrariness of rhythm, or was it just the expression of a living undulation of tempo which avoided exact coincidence with the strict metric framework [. . .] Mikuli, on the basis of his personal reminiscences, answered as follows:

Chopin was far from being a partisan to metric rigour and frequently used rubato in his playing, accelerating or slowing down this or that theme. But Chopin's rubato possessed an unshakeable emotional logic. It always justified itself by a strengthening or weakening of the melodic line, by harmonic details, by the figurative structure. It was fluid, natural; it never degenerated into exaggeration or affectation.

Mikuli/A. Michałowski, pp. 74–5

[. . .] rubato is never a defect in the time; the idea of rhythm, and consequently of the relative value of the notes, must never be lost, apparent changes and momentary incongruities notwithstanding. I shall now give the result of my own reflections on the rubato of Chopin:

1. Precise rules for it cannot be given, because a good execution of the rubato requires a certain musical intuition, that is to say, a certain particular talent.

2. Every rubato has for its foundation the following idea: each musical thought contains moments in which the voice should be raised or lowered, moments in which the tendency is to retardation or acceleration. The rubato is only the exaggeration or bringing into prominence [of] these different parts of the thought: the shadings of the voice make themselves more marked, the differences in the value of notes more apparent. Hence there arises in the mind an image of the musical thought more full of vitality and of poetry, but always in accordance with law and order [. . .]

We in all cases *borrow* the time from notes of smaller importance for the
purpose of giving it to the principal notes.   Kleczyński, *FCI*, pp. 58–9

In his playing the great artist [Chopin] rendered most exquisitely that kind
of agitated trepidation, timid or breathless [. . .] He always made the melody
undulate like a skiff borne on the breast of a powerful wave; or sometimes he
made it hover like an airy apparition suddenly sprung up in this tangible and
palpable world. In his writings, he at first indicated this way of playing –
which gave such an individual stamp to his virtuosity – by the term 'tempo
rubato': stolen, broken time – a rhythm simultaneously supple, abrupt and
languid, vacillating like the flame under the breath that agitates it, like the
corn in the field waving under the soft pressures of the warm air, like the tops
of trees bent hither and thither by a strong breeze.

But as the term taught nothing to whoever already knew, and said nothing
to those who did not know, understand, and feel, Chopin later ceased to add
this explanation to his music,[99] persuaded that if one had the sense of the
music, it would be impossible not also to divine this rule of irregularity. Also,
all his compositions must be played with that kind of speech-like, accented
lilt, that softness [*morbidezza*], the secret of which it was difficult to grasp if
one had not often heard him play in person. He seemed to wish to teach this
style of playing to his numerous pupils, especially his compatriots to whom,
more than to any others, he wanted to communicate the breath of his
inspiration.[100]   Liszt, pp. 115–16

'Look at these trees!' [Liszt] said, 'the wind plays in the leaves, stirs up life
among them, the tree remains the same, that is *Chopinesque rubato*.'
                                                          Liszt/Niecks, II, p. 101

Some of Chopin's students have assured me that in the rubato the left hand
ought to keep perfect time, whilst the right indulges its fancy; and that in such
a case Chopin would say, 'The left hand is the conductor of the orchestra.'
Many passages of the *Berceuse* can be executed in this manner [. . .] It is,
nevertheless, my belief that this means can only be employed in certain
particular cases; and I, therefore, can only regard it as a demi-rubato. There
are passages in the works of Chopin, in which not only do the leaves tremble
(to continue the comparison of Liszt), but the trunk totters. For instance: the
Polonaise in C sharp minor (op. 26/1), 3rd part, measures 9–14 [= 59–63];
Nocturne in A flat (op. 32/2), the middle part [bars 27–50]. We may quote
also the Impromptu in A flat [op. 29]; here everything totters from
foundation to summit, and everything is nevertheless so beautiful and
clear![101]   Kleczyński, *FCI*, p. 57

Rubato and ornamentation (improvised or notated)

In the fluctuations of speed, the holding back and pushing on [*Hangen und Bangen*],[102] in rubato as *he* understood it, Chopin was charm itself; each note was rendered in the most perfect taste, in the noblest sense of the word. If *he* happened to improvise a *fioritura* – a rare occurrence – it was always somehow a miracle of good taste.[103]   Lenz, *GPV* 1872, p. 47

Chopin took particular pleasure in playing [. . .] Field's Nocturnes, to which he would improvise the most beautiful *fioritura*s.   Mikuli, p. 3

He marked a few small but very important modifications into my score [of the Nocturne, op. 9/2].[104]   Lenz, *GPV* 1872, p. 42

When playing his own compositions, Chopin liked here and there to add ornamental variants. Mikuli told me he had a particular predilection for doing this in the Mazurkas.[105]   Mikuli/Koczalski, p. 203

Ornamentation

[In the] *Fantasia on Polish National Airs*, op. 13 [. . .] the small-note embellishment written into the upper part of the 10th bar of the first *polonais* theme (Andante 6/8, bar 65) is characteristic of Chopin's ornamentation and should be studied by all those wishing to master this aspect of his music:

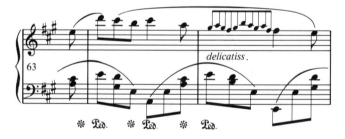

[. . .] It looks so simple! Chopin used to say of these ornaments that 'they should sound as though improvised,[106] the result not of studying exercises but of your sheer mastery of the instrument'. He himself provided the perfect example of this: like Field playing in Paradise!   Lenz, *UB*, p. 283

These ornamental passages, these *gruppetti* of a certain number of notes, most frequently appear when the same motif returns several times; first the motif is heard in its simplicity; afterwards, surrounded with ornaments, richer and richer at each return. It is, therefore, necessary to render this motif with very nearly the same shadings, whatever may be the form in which it reappears. For example, compare, in the Nocturne in F sharp (op. 15/2), the third and eleventh measures, and then [bar 51,] the return of the principal motif; or compare the thirteenth and fifty-fourth measures of the Romance of the Concerto in E minor [op. 11]; in the second motif of the Impromptu in A flat [op. 29], consider the different forms in which the phrase in F minor [bars 35–82] appears, etc. Again, these ornamental passages should not be slackened, but rather accelerated towards the end; a *rallentando* would invest them with too much importance, would make them appear to be special and independent ideas, whereas they are only fragments of the phrase, and, as such, should form part of the thought, and disappear in it like a little brook which loses itself in a great river; or they may be regarded as parentheses which, quickly pronounced, produce a greater effect than they would if they were retarded. Here are examples of these ornamental passages which should be played more slowly at the commencement and accelerated towards the end:

(a) Nocturne in E flat (op. 9/2), measures 16 and 24:

(b) *Larghetto* of the Concerto in F minor [op. 21], measures 26, 28, 30, 40, 75, and 77.

The following parentheses should be delivered rapidly and *pianissimo*:

Nocturne in A flat op. 32/2, measures 14 and 22.
Nocturne in F op. 15/1, measure 20; also upon the return of the motif [bar 68].
Nocturne in G minor op. 37/1, measure 36:

Chopin differed, in his manner of using arabesques and parenthetical ornamentations, from the usual manner of his time, which was to dwell upon such passages and to endue them with importance, as in the cadenzas attached to the airs of the Italian School.   Kleczyński, *FCI*, pp. 48–9

Simplicity and poise as an ideal in playing

'Simplicity is everything. After having exhausted all the difficulties, after having played immense quantities of notes, and more notes, then simplicity emerges with all its charm, like art's final seal. Whoever wants to obtain this immediately will never achieve it: you can't begin with the end. One has to have studied a lot, tremendously, to reach this goal; it's no easy matter.'[107]

Chopin/Streicher/Niecks, II, p. 342

For all the warmth of Chopin's temperament, his playing was always measured, chaste, distinguished and at times even severely reserved.

Mikuli, pp. 2–3

Naturalness, naturalness, no forcing, and a taut and balanced [*cadencé*] rhythm, characteristic of the beloved teacher's country; all this, in conjunction with an extreme poetic sense – *without any exaggeration*, above all in the tempo – goes to make up that unparalleled beauty characteristic of the true pupils of this exquisite school, one so often misunderstood [. . .] No noises, no 'effects', just simplicity, as in all that is beautiful.

Courty/Aguettant, p. 196

This style is based upon simplicity, it admits of no affectation, and therefore does not allow too great changes of movement. This is an absolute condition for the execution of all Chopin's works and more especially of his Concertos; the richness and variety of the embellishments would tend to sickliness and affectation if the execution were not as simple as the conception.   Kleczyński, *FCI*, p. 47

[In Chopin's works] when huge slurs extend over entire musical periods, they indicate this *spianato*[108] playing, without nuances or discontinuities in the rhythm – impossible for those whose hands are not graced with perfect suppleness.   Viardot/Saint-Saëns, *QM*, p. 386

Chopin had a horror of all exaggerated accentuation, which, in his opinion, took away the poetry from playing and gave it a sort of dry pedantry.[109]   Karasowski, II, p. 94

I sat down at the Pleyel. Feeling that I really owed it to Liszt,[110] I played Beethoven's theme [*Andante con Variazioni*, first movement of the Sonata op. 26 in A flat] just *so*, in the mood of an autumnal landscape illuminated by a ray of the summer sun! – with the three well graduated *crescendos* (to be well felt) on the five consecutive A flats [semiquaver group, bars 9 and 27]. There were many other things, including a certain pause before the demisemiquaver *gruppetto* [bars 4, 12, 15, 20 . . .] I was playing well and glowing like a live coal; it could have been a kind of challenge – except that I was communing with myself alone. At the end of the theme I stopped playing and calmly looked into Chopin's eyes. He put his hand amicably on my shoulder and said, 'I'll tell Liszt about this; I have never come across this before; yes, it's beautiful, only does one really always have to speak in such a declamatory way?'[111]   Lenz, *GPV* 1872, pp. 39–40

Spontaneity and range of interpretation

The difference between [Kalkbrenner] and Chopin was remarkable: the latter never played his works twice with the same expression, and yet the result was always ideally beautiful, thanks to the ever-fresh inspiration, powerful, tender or sorrowful. He could have played the same piece twenty times in succession, and you would still listen with equal fascination.

Peru, p. 25

Chopin *never* played his own compositions twice alike, but varied each according to the mood of the moment, a mood that charmed by its very waywardness;[112] his playing resembled nothing so much as the tender delicate tints seen in mother-o'-pearl, and rendered apparently without the least effort.   Hipkins, p. 7

I am entirely indebted to him for the ever-different expression he taught me to obtain in my playing of his works. That is why I so often wept after having worked on one of his pieces which he would then play for me; to show me the style, he would make me hear it in an entirely different way from the previous time. And yet it was wonderful each time! [. . .] How often have I seen him rise from the couch where he was lying and take my place at the piano in order to play, as he felt it, the piece that I had played – badly – that is to say, in an entirely different manner, though I had worked long and hard on it! That finished the lesson, for I did not want to forget this experience to which I had so religiously listened. At the following lesson, almost satisfied with the imitative fashion in which I had worked on the piece, I would play it again. Unfortunately, when I had finished, Chopin, once again stretched on his couch, would rise and, with a brusque reprimand, seat himself at the piano, saying, 'Listen, this is how it should go', and he would proceed to play it yet again in an entirely different way.[113] I could respond only with tears to this demonstration which in no way resembled the first one. Discouragement filled my whole being. Then he felt sorry for me, saying, 'It was almost good, only not the way I feel it.'

                                                                      Peru, pp. 28–30

Dynamic scale; continuous gradation in nuances

He gave a noble, manly energy to appropriate passages with overpowering effect – energy without roughness – just as, on the other hand, he could captivate the listener through the delicacy of his soulful rendering – delicacy without affectation.

                                                                      Mikuli, p. 2

In performance you should develop an ample, full and rounded tone; shade the scale of nuances with infinite gradations between *pianissimo* and *fortissimo*,[114] though in *pianissimo* avoid any indistinct muttering, just as in *fortissimo* avoid the sort of pounding that would hurt a sensitive ear.

                                                                      Mikuli/Koczalski, p. 12

His speciality was extreme delicacy, and his *pianissimo* extraordinary. Every little note was like a bell, so clear.   Peruzzi/Niecks, II, p. 339

Chopin played generally very quietly, and rarely, indeed hardly ever, *fortissimo*.[115]   Gutmann/Niecks, II, pp. 96–7

I may tell you that he had an extraordinary vigour, but only by flashes [*ce ne pouvait être que par éclairs*].   Mathias/Niecks, II, p. 182

According to Mikuli, Chopin played with a delicate touch, avoiding strong and shrill accents. He never dazzled by pure technique, nor overpowered by sheer sonorous power. He could not bear too loud a sound from the piano, and called it 'a dog barking' [. . .][116] Chopin's touch was by nature deep and resonant [. . .] and yet Mikuli himself played with a rather small and weak sound. When I asked him why he avoided playing *forte*, he answered that Chopin used to forbid him to play with a stronger touch: 'Chopin objected to my *forte*, and I suffered on more than one occasion as a result. The *Maître*'s criticisms distressed me all the more because he seemed far more accommodating and understanding towards other pupils.'[117]

                                                                      Mikuli/A. Michałowski, pp. 75–6

To play with great strength was German; as he told Mrs Goddard in Paris, when she took her daughter Arabella Goddard,[118] child of seven or eight, to play to him. 'Why,' said he, 'she plays like a German', and when they left the house, as Mrs Goddard told me lately, Chopin's last words were, 'Never let the child play loud.'   Hipkins, p. 7

Chopin's *piano* is so like a soft breath that he needs no vigorous *forte* to bring about the desired contrasts; and one does not miss the orchestral effects that the German school demands of a pianist.   Moscheles, II, p. 39

He abhorred banging a piano;[119] his *forte* was relative, not absolute; it was based upon his exquisite *pianos* and *pianissimos* – always a waving line, *crescendo* and *diminuendo*.[120]   Hipkins, pp. 6–7

In dynamic shading he insisted on a real and exactly graduated increase and decrease of loudness.   Mikuli, p. 4

Only with Chopin can one appreciate the quality of sound to infinitesimal levels [*le charme du son jusqu'à l'infini*]; as an entirety as well as in its smallest detail, his *decrescendo* is as enchantingly beautiful as it is difficult to attain.   Gretsch/Grewingk, pp. 15–16

However, Chopin himself warned against becoming prisoners of excessive shading [in nuances], as he wrote [?]: 'We are concerned with the end result' – repeated Chopin – 'the goal, the response evoked in the listener, not the means used to evoke it. You can be struck dumb with astonishment at unexpected news, equally whether it is shouted out loud, or barely whispered in your ear.'   Czartoryska?/Działyńska/Czartkowski–Jeżewska, p. 377

Use of the pedal

In the use of the pedal he had likewise attained the greatest mastery, was uncommonly strict regarding the misuse of it, and said repeatedly to the pupil: 'The correct employment of it remains a study for life.'
                                    Streicher/Niecks, II, p. 341

Use the pedal with the greatest economy.[121]   Mikuli/Koczalski, p. 13

'Learn to make a *diminuendo* without the help of the [*una corda*] pedal;[122] you can add it later', [said Chopin].   Franchomme/Picquet/Anon., p. 39

Chopin did not want [me to use the] pedal, yet he himself used it, particularly the soft pedal – without however indicating this to his pupils, in order not to exaggerate or overstep its resources. Courty/Aguettant, p. 196

Chopin used the pedals with marvellous discretion. He often coupled them to obtain a soft and veiled sonority, but more often still he would use them separately for brilliant passages, for sustained harmonies, for deep bass notes, and for loud ringing chords. Or he would use the soft pedal alone for those light murmurings which seem to create a transparent vapour round the arabesques that embellish the melody and envelop it like fine lace. The timbre produced by the pedals on Pleyel pianos has a perfect sonority,[123] and the dampers work with a precision very useful for chromatic and modulating passages; this quality is precious and absolutely indispensable.

Marmontel,[124] *HP*, pp. 256–7

Chopin brought [the combined use of the pedals] to perfection. We know those graces which are so beautiful when played with the help of the soft pedal (the Nocturne in F sharp, part 2 [op. 15/2, bar 51]; the Nocturne in G Minor [op. 37/1]; the *Larghetto* of the Concerto in F minor [op. 21]; the trio of the Impromptu in A flat [op. 29 bars 35–82]; the Nocturne in D [flat, op. 27/2], etc. Chopin frequently passed, and without transition, from the open to the soft pedal, especially in enharmonic modulation. These passages had an altogether particular charm, especially when played on Pleyel's pianofortes. For instance, the first measure of the solo in the *Larghetto* of the Concerto in F minor [op. 21], on the note E flat [bar 6]; Polonaise in C minor (op. 40/2), upon the return of the motif of the trio [bars 81–2]; the Mazurka in A minor (op. 17/4), eighth [*sic* – eighteenth?] measure; the Polonaise in C sharp minor (op. 26/1), second part, ninth measure [= bar 33], etc. [. . .] Notwithstanding the charming effects of the soft pedal, it should be employed with due caution; many passages are best when played simply and without the use of either pedal. This may be said of [the first section of] the Nocturne in F (op. 15/1), and the middle part, in 3/4 time, of the *Andante spianato* (op. 22).[125]

[. . .] Frequently the *una corda* pedal attaches to melodies truly divine; melodies which remove us from earth. For example: the trio of the Prelude in F sharp [op. 28/13 bars 21–8]; the Waltz in C sharp minor [op. 64/2 bars 65–96]; the Scherzo in B minor [op. 20 bars 305–88]; the Nocturne in C minor [op. 48/1 bars 25–38], etc. Kleczyński, *FCI*, pp. 44–5, 59

Execution of ornaments

Chopin considered that trills should begin *on the upper note*. When they are preceded by a small note (at the same pitch as the principal note), that does not mean that this note should be repeated, but merely that the trill should begin on the principal note and not, as normally, on the upper note.[126]

Viardot/Saint-Saëns, *QM*, p. 387

Trills, which he mostly began with the auxiliary note, were to be played not so much rapidly as with great evenness, and with the ending [turn] tranquil and not at all precipitate.

For the turn [*gruppetto*][127] and the appoggiatura,[128] he recommended the great Italian singers as models.

Mikuli, p. 4

Study of musical theory

Chopin insistently advised his students to take up basic theoretical studies as early as possible; through his recommendation many pupils received instructions in this field from Chopin's friend Mr Henri Reber, whom Chopin esteemed highly both as theoretician and as composer.[129]

Mikuli, p. 4

Analysis of the form and character of works studied

Any work selected for study should be carefully analysed for its formal structure, as well as for the feelings and psychological processes which it evokes.[130]

Mikuli/Koczalski, p. 13

My next lesson began with the Sonata [Beethoven, op. 26]. He called my attention to its structure, to the intentions of the composer throughout; showing me the great variety of touch and treatment demanded [. . .] From the Sonata he passed to his own compositions. These I found fascinating in the highest degree, but very difficult. He would sit patiently while I tried to thread my way through mazes of intricate and unaccustomed modulations, which I could never have understood had he not invariably played to me each composition – Nocturne, Prelude, Impromptu, whatever it was – letting me hear the framework (if I may so express it) around which these beautiful and strange harmonies were grouped.   Anonymous Scottish lady/Hadden, p. 158

Curriculum

In conjunction with scales and in the same tonal sequence,[131] Chopin made his pupils study Clementi's *Préludes et Exercices*, a work whose usefulness he valued very highly.

Mikuli, p. 3

The pupils of Chopin, however advanced, were required, besides the scales, to play with care the second book of Clementi's *Préludes et Exercices*, and above all to study the first *Exercice* in A flat.[132] Every hard, rough or uneven note had to be played again and carefully corrected. To complete his misery the pupil encountered at the commencement an arpeggio:

which has caused many tears to flow. It was necessary that it should be executed rapidly, crescendo, but without abruptness. It was this arpeggio which brought upon one unfortunate student this somewhat too sharp rebuke from the master, who springing up on [*sic*] his chair, exclaimed: 'What was that? Was that a dog barking?'[133] I had this story from the late Mme B[ohdana] Zaleska [Zofia Rosengardt], who herself has said some sharp things to me whilst showing me some peculiarities in Chopin's manner of performance.

This unfortunate study had to be worked in every possible way; it was played quickly and slowly, *forte* and *piano*, *staccato* and *legato*, until the touch became equal, delicate and light without feebleness.

Zaleska/Kleczyński, *FCI*, pp. 34–5

He then prescribed a selection from Cramer's *Etudes*,[134] Clementi's *Gradus ad Parnassum*, Moscheles's *Stylstudien zur höheren Vollendung* [*sic*, probably op. 95, possibly op. 70] which he especially liked;[135] and J.S. Bach's Suites[136] and individual Fugues from *Das Wohltemperirte Clavier* [...] His own Etudes op. 10 and 25 he entrusted only to the most advanced students.   Mikuli, pp. 3–4

Madame Dubois says that Chopin made her begin with the second book of Clementi's *Préludes et Exercices*, and that she also studied under him the same composer's *Gradus ad Parnassum* and Bach's forty-eight Preludes and Fugues. Of his high opinion of the teaching qualities of Bach's compositions we may form an idea from the recommendation to her at their last meeting

[1848] to *'toujours travailler Bach – ce sera votre meilleur moyen de progresser'* (practise Bach constantly – this will be your best means to make progress).[137]   Dubois/Niecks, II, pp. 190, 107

Clementi, Bach and Field [were] always the composers most [set for work to] *débutants*.[138]   Mathias/Niecks, II, p. 189

Chopin held that Clementi's *Gradus ad Parnassum*, Bach's pianoforte Fugues, and Hummel's compositions[139] were the key to pianoforte-playing, and he considered a training in these composers a fit preparation for his own works.   Gutmann/Niecks, II, p. 189

Field's and his own Nocturnes also figured to some extent as *Etudes*, for through them the pupil would learn – partly from his explanations, partly from observing and imitating Chopin, who played them indefatigably to the pupil – to recognize, love and produce the beautiful 'bound' [*gebunden*] vocal tone and the *legato*.   Mikuli, p. 4

Composers studied by Emilie von Gretsch[140]

For Chopin, Emilie von Gretsch played mostly Bach, Beethoven, and the Master's own works; he gave absolute priority to Bach.
                                Gretsch/Grewingk, p. 19

Works studied by Marie Roubaud[141]

Among the works she studied with him, Mme Roubaud cited: the Sonata in A flat [op. 39] by Weber and that by Beethoven [op. 26], of which he was very fond. Among his own compositions, he prescribed the Polonaise in E flat [op. 22?] the Nocturne in C minor [op. 48/1] and the Sonata in B minor [op. 58], whose *Largo*, when he once played it to her, had his pupil in tears.
                                Roubaud/Ganche, DSFC, p. 85

Repertoire studied by Camille O'Meara (Mme Dubois)[142]

Hummel:
Rondo brilliant mêlé d'un Thème russe [op. 98],
La Bella Capricciosa [polonaise op. 55],
Sonata in F sharp minor [op. 81],
Concertos in A minor [op. 85] and B minor [op. 89],
Septet [op. 74];

Field:

several Concertos – including the one in E flat [no. 1, 3, 4?] – and several Nocturnes: 'He always liked Field' [*Field lui était très sympathique*];

Beethoven:

the Concertos and several Sonatas [op. 26, 27/2, 57);[143]

Weber:

the Sonatas in C [op. 24] and A flat [op. 39] – Chopin made his pupils play these two works with extreme care;[144]

Schubert:

the *Ländler* and all the Waltzes,[145] and some of the piano duets [listed on p. 63 opposite];

Mendelssohn:

only the G minor Concerto [op. 25] and the *Songs without Words*;[146]

Liszt:

only [his transcriptions of] Rossini's *Tarentelle* [*La Danza*, no. 9 of Rossini's *Soirées musicales*] and of the Sextet[147] in *Lucia* – 'but this kind of music did not appeal to him';

Schumann: *nothing*.[148]   Dubois/Niecks, II, p. 190

Works of Chopin studied by Jane Stirling[149]

- *Ballades* op. 38 and 47,
- Concerto op. 21,
- *Etudes* op. 10 and 25,
- *Fantaisie* op. 49,
- Impromptus op. 29, 36 (and 51),
- Mazurkas op. 7, 24, 33 (and 56),
- Nocturnes op. 9, 15, 32, 37, 48 and 55,
- Polonaises op. 26,
- Preludes op. 28,
- Sonatas op. 35, 58 and 65,
- Waltzes op. (34 and) 64.

Chamber music; four hands; two pianos

Chopin earnestly recommended ensemble-playing and cultivation of the best chamber music – but only together with highly accomplished musicians.

Those with no such opportunity were to make up for it by playing four-hand piano duets.   Mikuli, p. 4

I sight-read piano duets with Chopin.
                                        Thun-Hohenstein/Simonides, p. 77

[Chopin made me study] some of [Schubert's piano] duets – the Marches, Polonaises, and the *Divertissement Hongrois* [op. 54] which last piece he admired *sans réserve*.[150]   Dubois/Niecks, II, p. 190

We very often passed mornings at his house, where he asked me to play with him all Weber's duets.[151] This was delightful to me, the more so, as he complimented me on my reading and entering at first sight into the spirit of the music. He made me acquainted with the beautiful duet of Moscheles, [*Grande sonate* in E flat major op. 47], and was the first with whom I played Hummel's splendid duet [probably the *Grand Duo* in A flat, op. 92] [. . .] I studied so many things with him, among others his two Concertos. The one in E minor [op. 11] I once played accompanied by himself on a second piano.
                                        Peruzzi/Niecks, II, p. 339

Chopin had always a cottage piano [*pianino*] by the side of the grand piano on which he gave his lessons. It was marvellous to hear him accompany, no matter what compositions, from the concertos of Hummel to those of Beethoven.[152] He performed the *rôle* of the orchestra most wonderfully (*d'une façon prodigieuse*). When I played his own concertos, he accompanied me in this way.[153]   Dubois/Niecks, II, p. 188

Then he played with me the *Andante* [*sic*] of his F minor Concerto [op. 21], which he accompanied magnificently on the second piano.
                                        Streicher/Niecks, II, p. 342

Part 2: Interpretation of Chopin's works
(listed in alphabetical order of genre)

Chopin's compositions have opened a new era in the piano's history. But they run the risk of being misunderstood if one has not known the master's way of playing, his intentions and his conception of the instrument – since their result on paper is quite different from that of the sound world in which they really live.   Lenz, 1872

Any deliberate misreading of his compositions [Chopin] resented sharply.   Hallé

Andante spianato op. 22, G major

[. . .] But of all he played when I heard him, I best remember the *Andante Spianato* [. . .] Physical weakness was not, however, the cause of his tenderly-subdued style of playing.[120] This was his own, and inseparable from his conception of pianoforte touch; it was incapable of modification from any influence whatever. His *fortissimo* was the full pure tone without noise, a harsh inelastic note being to him painful. His nuances were modifications of that tone, decreasing to the faintest yet always distinct *pianissimo*. His singing *legatissimo* touch was marvellous. The wide extended arpeggios in the bass were transfused by touch and pedal into their corresponding sustained chords, and swelled or diminished like waves in an ocean of sound. He kept his elbows close to his sides, and played only with finger-touch, no weight from the arms. He used a simple, natural position of the hands as conditioned by scale- and chord-playing, adopting the easiest fingering, although it might be against the rules, that came to him. He changed fingers upon a key as often as an organ-player.   Hipkins, p. 5

Chopin played the G major Nocturne[154] [before the *Grande Polonaise brillante*] for Mendelssohn, who then gave a very poetic description of it: it was like a vision opening up of a garden peopled by beings walking in silence amidst fountains and strange birds; by this Mendelssohn wanted to convey the music's sense of complete envelopment.

Mendelssohn/Schumann, *EFM*, p. 68

Ballade op. 38, F major

Mme Viardot told me that Chopin had often played her the opening Andantino, but never the rest.[155] He played this Andantino without any

65

nuances at all, except for the two indicated [bars 18–21, 22ff.?] which he strongly brought out.   Viardot/Saint-Saëns, *EV*, p. 22

Barcarolle op. 60, F sharp major

At the last public concert he gave in Paris, at the [. . .] beginning of 1848, he played the latter part of his 'Barcarolle', from the point where it demands the

utmost energy, in the most opposite style, *pianissimo*, but with such wonderful nuances, that one remained in doubt if this new reading were not preferable to the accustomed one. Nobody but Chopin could have accomplished such a feat.   Hallé,[156] p. 36

Concerto op. 11, E minor

ALLEGRO MAESTOSO

In this piece the pianist must be first tenor, first soprano – always a singer and a bravura singer in the runs, which Chopin wanted the pianist to take pains to render in the *cantabile* style. This was the way he taught Filtsch,[157] his specially favoured young pupil, to understand this first movement. At that time (1842), Chopin himself no longer played the piece, as he had already given up performing in public.[158] Still, he played us the themes indescribably beautifully and gave us hints for playing the runs and passage-work. He wanted the runs *cantabile*, with a certain measure of strength and bravura within, trying to bring out as much as possible the slightest thematic fragments, using the most delicate touch, even where the runs are no more than runs – which in this piece is the exception. The second and third movements were never mentioned [. . .] Filtsch studied the work with Chopin solo section by solo section; he was never allowed to play the movement right through, since it would affect Chopin too powerfully; Chopin maintained besides that the entire work's power was contained within each solo section.

[. . .] When at last Filtsch was allowed to play the whole movement – an occasion for which he had prepared himself by Roman Catholic fasting and prayer as well as by reading the score under Chopin's direction (practising had been forbidden) – Chopin said, 'Now this movement is sufficiently "in place" for us to play it: I'll be your orchestra' [. . .] With his incomparable way of accompanying, Chopin evoked all the ingenious and elusive qualities of the orchestration. He played from memory. I have never heard anything comparable to that first *tutti* as he played it himself at the piano. As for the lad [Filtsch], he worked marvels. It was the experience of a lifetime.

Lenz, UB, pp. 282–3

ROMANCE

The *Adagio* [*sic*] of my new *Concerto* is in E major. It is not meant to create a powerful effect; it is rather a Romance, calm and melancholy, giving the impression of someone looking gently towards a spot which calls to mind a thousand happy memories. It is a kind of reverie in the moonlight on a beautiful spring evening. Hence the accompaniment is muted: that is, the violins are stifled by a sort of comb which fits over the strings and gives them a nasal and silvery tone.[159]

Chopin, SC, p. 45

This andante [*sic*] transports the auditorium into an ecstatic calm; [. . .] the last note drops like a pearl in a golden vase, and the audience, absorbed in its contemplation, hold back the applause for a few moments: they are listening still. It is like having watched the half-tints of an evening twilight dissolve harmoniously, and then staying motionless in the darkness, the eyes still fixed on the point in the horizon whence the light has just vanished.[160]

Berlioz/Boschot, p. 282

Concerto op. 21, F minor

This concerto, dedicated to the countess Delphina Potocka,[161] was particularly dear to Chopin's heart.

Mikuli, p. 2

LARGHETTO

[. . .] the *Adagio* [*sic*] of the second *Concerto*, for which he had a marked predilection and which he liked to play frequently.

Liszt, p. 18

Etude op. 10/1, C major

[Chopin] bade me practise it in the mornings very slowly. 'Cette étude vous fera du bien' (this *étude* will do you good), he said. 'If you study it as I intended it,[162] it widens the hand and enables you to play runs of wide broken chords, like bow strokes. But often, unfortunately, instead of making people learn all that, it makes people unlearn it.' I am quite aware that it is a generally-prevalent error, even in our day, that one can only play this study well when one possesses a very large hand. But this is not the case, only a supple hand is required.

Streicher/Niecks, II, p. 341

Etude op. 10/3, E major

Chopin said to Gutmann that he had never in his life written another such beautiful melody (*chant*); and on one occasion when Gutmann was studying

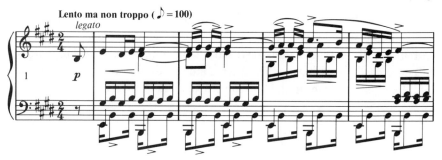

it the master lifted up his arms with his hands clasped and exclaimed: 'O, my fatherland!' [O, *ma patrie!*][163]   Gutmann/Niecks, II, p. 253

Etudes op. 25 in general

I have heard Chopin play most of them – and very much *à la Chopin* [. . .] Imagine an Aeolian harp capable of all sonorous levels, and an artist's hand animating it, adding here and there all kinds of fantastic embellishments, always, however, with a strong bass audible and, in the treble, a softly flowing cantilena, and you have some idea of his playing.[164]

Schumann, GS, II, p. 73

Etude op. 25/1, A flat major

It is said that Chopin explained to one of his pupils the manner in which this study should be executed. 'Imagine,' he said, 'a little shepherd who takes refuge in a peaceful grotto from an approaching storm. In the distance rushes the wind and the rain, while the shepherd gently plays a melody on his flute.'

Kleczyński, CGW, p. 19

It would be a mistake to suppose that he made all the small notes individually audible: it was more an undulation of the A flat major chord, lifted here and there high up on the keyboard, with the help of the pedal. But, exquisitely entangled in the harmony, one perceived the wonderful, deep-toned melody, and just in the middle section [bars 17–20] did a tenor voice emerge clearly from the chords to join the principal melody:

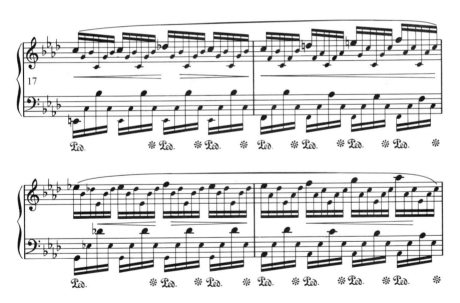

And when the *étude* was ended, we felt as though we had seen a radiant picture in a dream which, half awake, we ached to recover [. . .] Then he played the second *étude* in the book, in F minor.[165]

Schumann, GS, II, p. 73

Etude op. 25/2, F minor

Again one in which his individuality impresses itself unforgettably: so charming, dreamy, and soft that it could be the song of a sleeping child.

Schumann, GS, II, p. 73

Etude op. 25/3, F major

Here the concern was more with bravura, but of the most pleasant kind, and in this respect too Chopin deserved the highest praise.

Schumann, GS, II, p. 73

Fantaisie op. 49, F minor

In the march-like introduction, Chopin played the enharmonic modulation in bar 17 strictly in time, which only enhanced its effect.[166]

Lenz, UB, p. 298–9

Impromptus op. 29 and 51, A flat major and G flat major

Chopin had a predilection for these, especially for the third Impromptu in G flat.

Lenz, UB, p. 298

Mazurkas: general character

[. . .] these productions which he loved to hear us call 'paintings on the easel' [*tableaux de chevalet*].

Liszt, p. 68

'Liszt said of the Mazurkas that each one of them should harness itself to a different, first-class pianist.' 'Liszt's always right,' replied Chopin, 'Do you think I'm satisfied with myself when I play them? Never! It has happened once or twice at an annual concert, where I felt inspired by the atmosphere in the hall;[167] that's as often as I should be heard, once a year; the rest is work!'

Lenz, GPV 1872, p. 37

'These are Heine's *Lieder* in terms of the piano!' When I made this remark to Chopin, he replied: 'Yes, you understand me; that's why I take pleasure in listening when you play something for the *first time*, because then *you give me ideas.*'

Lenz, GPV, p. 301

Mazurkas: general character of Chopin's playing

[. . .] His melodies, all impregnated with Polish elements, have something naïvely untamed about them that charms and captivates by its very strangeness [. . .] Unfortunately, virtually nobody but Chopin himself can play his music and give it this unusual turn, this sense of the unexpected which is one of its principal beauties; his interpretation is shot through with a thousand nuances of movement of which he alone holds the secret, and which are impossible to convey by instructions.

There are unbelievable details in his Mazurkas; and he has found how to render them doubly interesting by playing them with the utmost degree of softness, *piano* in the extreme, the hammers merely brushing the strings, so much so that one is tempted to go close to the instrument and put one's ear to it as if to a concert of sylphs or elves.[168]

Berlioz, Le Rénovateur II/345, 15 December 1833

In the details of the performances, in the natural elegance – born of his feelings without being intentional or studied – in the taste and inwardness evidenced by all his interpretations, Chopin the pianist was a phenomenon of incomparable originality, a *Polish* (Sarmatian) phenomenon, French in education and habits, with the advantages and drawbacks of both factors. Lacking in physical strength, Chopin concentrated all his energies in a singing style [*Gesangsstyl*], in transitions and joining together, in the details. In that respect he was a pastel painter 'such as there had never been before him'. Chopin's Mazurkas are the diary of his soul's journey through the socio-political territories of his Sarmatian dream-world! There his playing was truly at home; *in them resided* Chopin's originality as a pianist. He represented Poland, *the land of his dreams*, in the Parisian salons under Louis-Philippe – salons which *his* viewpoint allowed him to use as a political platform. Chopin was the *only political* pianist. He *incarnated* Poland, he *set* Poland *to music*!

Lenz, GPV 1872, p. 86

Chopin's inner ideal reveals itself, as is well known, in the very original and absolutely inimitable way in which he interprets his nationalistic Polish pieces, with a genuinely characteristic stamp. For that reason he himself, in his own music, could not be a model to imitate. Even the playing of his students gives the impression just of a lithograph of an original oil canvas radiating colours.

                                                    Schindler, *BLB*, p. 489

Mazurkas: principles of accentuation

In the national dances such as the Polonaise, Mazurka, Krakowiak, Kujawiak, the main rhythmic notes should be strongly accentuated, followed by a gentle release of the rhythmic impulse wherever the accent (or long-held accented note) is omitted or displaced.[169] But this must never degenerate into mere lack of rhythm.

                                                    Mikuli/Koczalski, pp. 12–13

Mazurkas: rhythmic and agogic characteristics of Chopin's performance

Manifesting a certain preference for strength as opposed to lightness, Henselt's[170] priority when playing the Mazurkas is the beat and the barline; passages of delicately wrought workmanship he paints over with big brush strokes and a big sonority. His rubato is not Chopin's: it is a shifting of accents within a maintained tempo, rather than a radical readjustment of the whole field of vision to view the piece in its entirety as if seen through reversed opera glasses.

                                                    Lenz, *GPV* 1872, p. 102

A remarkable feature of his playing was the entire freedom with which he treated the rhythm, but which appeared so natural that for years it has never struck me. It must have been in 1845 or 1846 that I once ventured to observe to him that most of his Mazurkas (those dainty jewels), when played by himself, appeared to be written, not in 3/4, but in 4/4 time, the result of his dwelling so much longer on the first note in the bar. He denied it strenuously, until I made him play one of them and counted audibly four in the bar, which fitted perfectly. Then he laughed and explained that it was the national character of the dance which created the oddity. The more remarkable fact was that you received the impression of 3/4 rhythm whilst listening to common time. Of course this was not the case with every Mazurka, but with many. I understood later how ill advised I had been to make that observation to him and how well disposed towards me he must have been to have taken it with such good humour, for a similar remark made by Meyerbeer, perhaps in a somewhat supercilious manner, on another occasion, led to a serious quarrel, and I believe Chopin never forgave him.   Hallé, p. 34

Once Meyerbeer arrived in Chopin's room during my lesson. He did not announce his arrival, of course: he was a king. We were playing the Mazurka in C op. 33[/3] – one page of music which seems nevertheless to contain hundreds. I called it the *epitaph* of the Mazurka, so full does it seem of grief and sorrow – the weary flight of an eagle:

Meyerbeer took a seat and I continued. 'That's in 2/4', said Meyerbeer. I had to repeat it while Chopin, pencil in hand, beat time on the piano; his eyes were blazing. '2/4', Meyerbeer calmly repeated. Only once have I have ever seen Chopin lose his temper, and it was at that moment – and what a wonderful sight he was! A faint red suffused his pale cheeks. 'It's in 3/4', he said in a loud voice. 'Give me that piece as a ballet in my opera', retorted Meyerbeer (he was then working in secret on *L'Africaine*), 'I'll prove it to you.' 'It's in 3/4', Chopin almost yelled, he who never normally raised his voice above a murmur. He pushed me aside and sat at the piano himself. *Three times* he played the piece, counting aloud and stamping out the beat with his foot; he was beside himself! Meyerbeer still held his own and they parted on bad terms. It pained me to have witnessed this scene. Without taking leave of me, Chopin had disappeared into his study. He was right, all the same: for though the third beat loses some of its value, submerged as it is in the flow of the melody, still it does not cease to exist.

                                                                Lenz, *GPV*, p. 302

Moscheles[171] told me that his married daughter [Emily Roche], who took lessons from Chopin, had played [for Moscheles], among other things, a new Chopin Mazurka, with such a rubato that the entire piece gave the impression of being in 2/4 instead of 3/4.[172]   Moscheles/Bülow, I, p. 133

Mazurkas: improvised ornaments

While playing his own compositions, Chopin liked to introduce ornamental variations in some places. Mikuli told me that he was particularly fond of doing so in the Mazurkas.[173]

Mikuli/Koczalski, p. 203

Mazurkas: Chopin's pedalling

[. . .] So Czerny abused this [damper] pedal from the beginning, employing it too often in *fortes*, while it is more advantageous in *piano* passages, particularly when it is tempered by the soft pedal, which, quietening the sound, allows one to prolong it by raising the dampers at the beginning of each bar. This was Chopin's own procedure in his poetic compositions [Mazurkas].[174]

Schindler, *HVOB*, p. 335

Mazurkas op. 7/1 and 2, B flat major and A minor

Studying Chopin's B flat major and A minor Mazurkas op. 7, I learnt much about piano-playing in general from Liszt. In both pieces he made me aware of important little variants and was very strict with me, particularly concerning the deceptively simple-looking bass in the major section of the A minor Mazurka. What pains he took with me there! 'Only an ass could believe that this is easy,' he said, 'it's these *legato slurs* [*Verbindungen*] that identify a virtuoso! Play it like *this* to Chopin and he'll notice it; it will please him. These stupid French editions bungle everything of his;[175] this is how you should read these slurs in the bass! If you play to him like *this*, then he'll give you lessons.'

Lenz, *GPV* 1872, p. 26

[At Chopin's concert in Glasgow] he was encored for his well-known Mazurka in B flat (op. 7, no 1) which he repeated with quite different nuances from those of the first [time].

Seligmann[176]/Hadden, p. 123

Mazurka op. 17/4, A minor

Even in Chopin's presence we called it 'the mourner's face' [*das Trauergesicht*] – he was quite happy about this name.

Lenz, *UB*, p. 291

Mazurka op. 24/4, B flat minor

Chopin taught us that the third section [bars 54–62] is a mixed choir; the opening unison is answered by the chords:

Nobody ever managed to satisfy him with these unisons, which have to be played very lightly; the chords were an easier matter. But these unisons! 'They're the women's voices in the choir', he would say, and they were never played delicately enough, never simply enough. One was barely allowed to breathe over the keyboard, let alone touch it![177]   Lenz, *UB*, pp. 291–2

Mazurka op. 30/3, D flat major

'It seems like a Polonaise for a coronation festivity,' said someone to Chopin. 'Something like that,' was his reply.   Lenz, *UB*, p. 291

Mazurka op. 33/2, D major

Despite her advanced years, Princess Czartoryska gave in to my pleas and played a few Mazurkas, among others the well-known Mazurka in D major. I was struck by the way she interpreted its main theme. At first she played it in a brash, forthright way, with no subtlety of nuance. It was only towards the end of the piece, at the theme's second appearance [bar 74 to the end], that she played it with a soft, caressing touch, utterly subtle and refined.[178] When I asked her about this contrasting treatment, she replied that Chopin had taught it to her that way: in this piece he wanted to present the contrast between the 'tavern' and the 'salon'. That was why he wanted the same melody played so differently: at the beginning it was to evoke the popular atmosphere of the tavern, and, towards the end, the refinement of the salons . . .   Czartoryska/A. Michałowski, p. 73

Mazurka op. 33/4, B minor

This piece is a *Ballade* in all but name. Chopin himself taught it as such, stressing the narrative character of this highly developed piece, with its ravishing trio [B major: bars 129ff].[179] At the end a bell tolls a heavy bass carillon G–C–G–C[180] – and the sudden arrival of the final chords sweeps away the cohort of ghosts, Chopin would say.   Lenz, *UB*, p. 291

Mazurka op. 41/3, B major

Chopin used to say that this piece opens with a chorus of guitars and that it is
particularly difficult to render because of the tangle of groups of dancers
changing direction at every moment. Here the modulations are bold. The
first four bars and their repetitions [bars 9–12, 21–4, 29–32, 76–8] are to be
played in the style of a guitar prelude, progressively quickening the tempo:

The Mazurka proper starts only at the fifth bar. These were Chopin's
instructions.   Lenz, *UB*, p. 291

Mazurka op. 50/1, G major

Chopin considered it difficult to play. He set great store by the modulation to
E flat [bars 41ff][181] being well rendered: Lenz, *UB*, p. 291

Nocturnes: from a pedagogical viewpoint

Field's[84] and his own Nocturnes also figured to some extent as *Etudes*,[182] for through them the pupil would learn – partly from Chopin's explanations, partly from observing and imitating Chopin, who played them indefatigably to the pupil – to recognize, love and produce the beautiful 'bound' [*gebunden*] vocal tone and the *legato*.   Mikuli, p. 4

During the lesson, Chopin played as I never heard him play before. He seemed to want to attain the ideal of his poetic soul; the first time he played me his Nocturnes, he apologized for not having 'said it' in the way he wanted me to hear it, and he repeated them with even more perfection.

Gretsch/Grewingk, p. 12

Nocturne op. 9/2, E flat major

This work, apparently so innocent and innocuous, poses particular problems of performance – as the composer himself frequently repeated [. . .] Chopin's teaching of it is worth reproducing here. The piece is 34 bars long. The first four bars introduce the theme which leads to the first variation (bars 5–8), followed by a ritornello (bars 9–12) and a transition leading to the second variation (bars 13–16), then a ritornello (bars 17–20), and the third variation (bars 21–4), and finally (bars 25 to 34), by a ritornello and cadenza.

Chopin wanted 'the bass to be practised first by itself, divided between the two hands; and each of the chords following the main bass beats in the 12/8 should sound like a chorus of guitars. Once the bass part is mastered – with two hands – with a full but *piano* sonority and in strict time, maintaining an absolutely steady *allegretto* movement without the 12/8 lapsing into triplets [? – presumably he means avoiding an oom-pah-pah effect], then the left hand can be trusted with the accompaniment played that way and the tenor invited to sing his part in the upper voice.' The second variation was to be an Andante, the third a moving Adagio, and the theme and second variation were to be sung full-voiced, expressive but without any sentimentality. The style should be modelled upon Pasta[75] and the great Italian school of singing, and the pathos should increase throughout the variations.

On the upbeat introducing the first variation (end of bar 4), Chopin replaced the single B♭ with the following run of notes like a string of pearls, wonderfully swift but *delicatissimamente*:

He took the *F♯* and the *G* both with the third finger, gliding from a black to a white key, for the best possible *legato* [. . .] Between the *F* (bar 5, last note) and the *G* (bar 6, first note) he would slip a passing *F♯* to ensure a better transition:

This addition is by no means unimportant: Chopin insisted on this *F♯* and its repetition in parallel passages (bars 13 and 21). The [printed] cadenza presents the simple *gruppetto* C♭, B♭, C♮, A♮, repeated twelve times in a row. Chopin replaced it with a ravishing figuration which he copied into the scores of his favourite pupils.[184]

                                                    Lenz, *UB*, p. 297

Gutmann played the return of the principal subject in a way very different from that in which it is printed, with a great deal of ornamentation, and said that Chopin played it always in that way. Also, the cadence at the end of the Nocturne had a different form.

                                        Gutmann/Niecks, II, p. 263, n. 32

[Here is] a variant [bar 24] often added by Chopin and indicated to me by Mr Makomaski, a pupil of Tellefsen:

185

Tellefsen/Kleczyński, CGW, pp. 36–7

Nocturne op. 15/2, F sharp major

In spite of the metronome marking [♩=40], I think this Nocturne is generally played too fast. The tradition was passed on to me by my teacher Georges Mathias who himself studied it with Chopin, and it seemed to me that the metronome marking would correspond better to a bar at 4/8 than to the 2/4 time indicated. I played it at 52 to the quaver, respecting the change in the second section [*Doppio movimento*, bars 25ff]. Otherwise, at a different tempo, this Nocturne loses all its character of enveloping intimacy.[186]

Mathias/Pugno, C, p. 66

Nocturne op. 15/3, G minor

[. . .] It was originally intended to be called 'After a representation of the tragedy of *Hamlet*'. Afterwards Chopin abandoned this notion, saying: 'Let them guess for themselves.'[187] Kleczyński, CGW, p. 46

Nocturne op. 27/1, C sharp minor

In most of the pieces where, as in this one, the left hand accompaniment consists of an undulating figure, Chopin wished it to be played very soft and subdued. Gutmann/Niecks, II, p. 264, n. 33

Nocturne op. 27/2, D flat major

[. . .] the principal theme, which [. . .] occurs [. . .] three times [bars 2, 26, 46], should appear each time with a different strength and a different shade of expression. The first time, for instance, it should be given *piano*, with softness and simplicity; the second time, *pianissimo* – assisted by the second [*una corda*] pedal, which is perfectly justified by the character and the modulation which prepares it; and the third time *forte* and *entirely* contrary to the printing of the text, which directs that it is to be taken *delicately and diminuendo*. This was once demonstrated to me by the late Julian Fontana;[188] and it is very logical, for after the entire middle part, which develops itself *crescendo*, the theme resumed for the third time in a feebler manner produces no effect. Why the faulty marking was never rectified in Chopin's lifetime, and why the long [ornamental] passage [bars 51–2] after the return of the theme, has been directed to be played *con forza* instead of *con delicatezza*,[189] I am at a loss to understand.

Fontana/Kleczyński, CGW, pp. 38–40

Nocturne op. 37/1, G minor

Gutmann played [the middle section, bars 41–65] quicker than the rest, and said that Chopin forgot to mark the change of movement.[190]

Gutmann/Niecks, II, p. 264, n. 34

Nocturne op. 48/1, C minor

How exacting and finicky Chopin was over the four opening bars – which appear so simple!

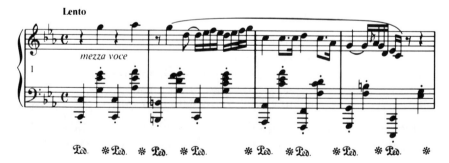

. . . He was not easy to satisfy with the first bar of the Nocturne: the crochets G, A♭, should emerge as thematic elements, but were always too loud or too soft for his liking [. . .] In the second bar the final semiquaver G was to glide smoothly into the following C (first beat of the third bar), and Chopin was never satisfied. He told me: 'Since it lies within your *capabilities*, you *must* be able to do it.' I finally succeeded, after long efforts: either the G would be too short and the C arrive too soon, or else the reverse. 'It must have an intention', said Chopin. He was no less exacting when it came to the descending C before the quaver rest at the end of the semiquaver group (fourth bar, third beat); the C was either too short or too long. I found a way out by 'combing' this with the thumb, that is by sliding the finger along the key and releasing it only upon reaching the outer edge. This way the end of the phrase at last satisfied him; but that was nothing beside Chopin's own playing in these two passages! [. . .] He wanted a *question* on the G–C [bars 2–3],a *response* in the C [bar 4].[191]   Lenz, GPV 1872, pp. 61–2

Nocturne op. 48/2, F sharp minor

When Gutmann studied [this] Nocturne with Chopin, the master told him that the middle section (the *piùlento*[192] in D flat major) [bars 57–100] should be played as a recitative:

'A tyrant commands' (the first two chords), he said, 'and the other asks for mercy.'   Gutmann/Niecks, II, p. 265

Polonaises op. 26/1 and 2, C sharp minor and E flat minor

As for the E♭ minor Polonaise – with its gripping trio in C♭, written enharmonically in B major – the same thing happened as with the B♭ minor Scherzo [op. 31]: Chopin refused to let me play it. 'You cannot play this piece,' he retorted laconically.[193] I did, however, manage to play the C♯ minor Polonaise to his satisfaction.   Lenz, UB, pp. 290–1

Polonaise op. 40/1, A major

As for interpretation, I remember Chopin's advice to feel the Polonaise in quavers. A 6/8 counted aloud in *allegro con brio* can determine the exact tempo with absolute certainty, for the simple reason that nobody will be able to count six quavers in a clear and loud voice in too fast a tempo.[194]

Mikuli?/Pozniak, p. 65

After the D major trio section, I play the return of the first theme [bars 65ff] softly, and then loud again in the following section [bars 73ff]. Chopin did not particularly observe this nuance himself, but he liked it when I did so: in fact he was thoroughly satisfied.   Liszt/Lachmund, pp. 230–1

Polonaise op. 53, A flat major

I remember how, on one occasion, in his gentle way he laid his hand upon my shoulder, saying how unhappy he felt, because he had heard his 'Grande Polonaise' in A flat *jouée vite!* [played fast], thereby destroying all the grandeur, the majesty, of this noble inspiration.[195]   Hallé, p. 34

The A flat major Polonaise (op. 53), for instance, he could not thunder forth in the way we are accustomed to hear it. As for the famous octave passages which occur in it,[196]

he began them *pianissimo* and continued thus without much increase in
loudness.   Gutmann/Niecks, II, p. 97

[With regard to the F minor episode – bars 138–51 – after the return of the
four flats:] 'In this register of the piano, don't just play the basses *sforzando*,
that is, reinforced,' said Liszt, 'but give them a slightly lingering accentuation, like the muffled rumbling of a distant cannon. The pedal will help to
obtain this effect. The idea isn't my own,' he added, 'I've often heard Chopin
play it like that.' Liszt then sat down at the piano and played the passage.
These bass notes, accented intermittently at first and then in each bar,
produced a unique effect which was like a revelation to us.
                                                            Liszt/Lachmund, p. 81

Prelude op. 28/17, A flat major

I remember once when I was playing the 17th Prelude of Chopin, Madame
Dubois said that Chopin himself used to play that bass note in the final
section [bars 65 ff.] (in spite of playing everything else *diminuendo*) with
great strength. He always *struck* that note in the same way and with the *same*
strength, because of the meaning he attached to it. He accentuated that bass
note – he proclaimed it, because the idea of that Prelude is based on the sound
of an old clock in the castle which strikes the *eleventh* hour. Madame Dubois
told me that I should *not* make that note *diminuendo* as I intended, in
accordance with the right hand which plays *diminuendo* continually, but
said that Chopin always insisted the bass note should be struck with the *same*
strength – no *diminuendo*, because the clock knows no *diminuendo*. That
bass note was the clock speaking.[197]   Dubois/Paderewski, p. 154

Prelude op. 28/20, C minor

I played what I had always called 'La Prière' (the prayer), the Prelude in C
minor, the 20th, in the second volume [in the original edition] [. . .] Those
chords [played by Chopin] sounded more celestial than of this earth, and
contained an aspiration that extended into eternity.
                                        Stirling/Wróblewska-Straus, *LSJ*, p. 110

Scherzo op. 20, B minor

In the trio [bars 305–88],

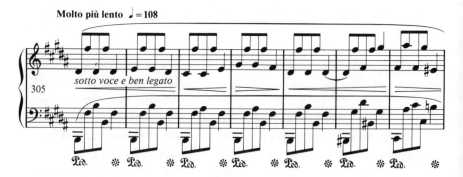

Chopin's playing produced an indescribable impression.[198]

Lenz, UB, p. 290

The tradition for playing the *ritardando* [*ritenuto*] transition, which precedes in particular the *agitato* [bars 160–84] and the middle section [bars 276–304] has been transmitted only by word of mouth. Chopin marks this passage the same way each time: *piano* at first, then *forte*, *diminuendo*, and then again *piano*. But Johanna Laurecka, for many years Mikuli's assistant, has assured me that before the middle section and also before the coda [bars 540–69] Chopin would feverishly intensify the passage, making a *crescendo* and *stringendo*. This would be relaxed only on the very last chord preceding the middle section [bar 304]; but the intensification would continue before the coda, so that the piece finished with tremendous impetus.

Mikuli/Pozniak, p. 55

Scherzo op. 31, B flat minor

Right from the first bar there was a problem: the repeated triplet group A♮–B♭–D♭ (bars 1–2),

so innocent-seeming, could never be played to Chopin's satisfaction. 'It must be a question,' taught Chopin; and it was never played questioningly enough, never soft enough, never round enough (*tombé*), as he said, never sufficiently weighted (*important*). 'It must be a house of the dead', he once said. [. . . In his lessons] I saw Chopin dwell at length on this bar and again at each of its reappearances. 'That's the key to the whole piece,' he would say. Yet the triplet group is generally snatched or swallowed. Chopin was just as exacting over the simple quaver accompaniment of the cantilena [second theme, bars 65ff], as well as the cantilena itself:

'You should think of [the singer] Pasta,[75] of Italian song! – not of French Vaudeville,' he said one day with more than a touch of irony.

Lenz, UB, p. 290

Scherzo op. 39, C sharp minor

It is dedicated to Gutmann,[199] and it was probably with his prize-fighter's fist in mind that the bass chord in bar 6 was thought out,

a chord that no left hand can take – least of all that of Chopin, who arpeggiated it on his light-touch, *narrow-keyed*, Pleyel.   Lenz, *GPV* 1872, p. 48

Sonata op. 35, B flat minor: trio of the 'Funeral March'

The expression which Chopin gave this trio is indescribable. Only Rubini[75] could sing like that, and even then only in certain arias ('il mio sasso' in [Bellini's] *Il Pirata*; 'fra poco' in Donizetti's *Lucia*). Nothing is easier than to reduce this trio to the tritest platitude, nothing more difficult than to raise its melodic spell to the level of the sorrow that hangs over the whole poem which this 'Funeral March' is. And this is what it is about: never in Chopin's interpretation did his subdued expression in the trio section strike me as contradicting the character of the March – despite many critics' remarks to that effect. This trio is a touchstone for recognizing whether the performer is a poet or merely a pianist; whether he can tell a story or merely play the piano.

Lenz, *UB*, p. 289

Waltz op. 34/2, A minor

'Here's the *Valse mélancolique*. Never in your life will you [be able to] play this piece, but since you understand it well, I want to write something in it for you.' In bar 8, in the upper part, there is a *D* (crotchet, 2nd beat) then a *D–G♯* (crotchet, 3rd beat). Above the *D* play *G♯–C*, then *G♯–B*, and the added voice will enrich the polyphony:[201]

Lento

It produces a lovely effect to repeat this whenever the phrase recurs.

Lenz, GPV 1872, p. 37

Waltz op. 42, A flat major

This waltz, springing from the eight-bar trill, should evoke a musical clock, according to Chopin himself. In his own performance it embodied his rubato style to the fullest; he would play it as a continued *stretto prestissimo* with the bass maintaining a steady beat. A garland of flowers winding amidst the dancing couples!

Lenz, UB, p. 298

Waltz op. 64/1, D flat major

A great lady who was present at Chopin's last concert in Paris (1848), when he played among other works his *Valse* in D flat (op. 64/1), wished to know *'le secret de Chopin pour que les gammes fussent si coulées sur le piano'* [Chopin's secret for making his scales so fluid]. Mme Dubois, who related this incident to me, added that the expression was felicitous, for this *'limpidité délicate'* had never been equalled.

Dubois/Niecks, II, p. 95

Chopin would compress the first four bars[202] almost into two bars: 'It should unroll like a ball of yarn', he said; the real tempo came in with the bass in the fifth bar.[203]

Lenz, UB, p. 298

Waltz op. 64/2, C sharp minor

Chopin could hardly be satisfied in the second Waltz: only he knew how to tie the one (!) semiquaver[204] convincingly to the following crotchet, in bars 3–4.

Lenz, UB, p. 298

An up-bow effect [*retiré*][205] contributes a great deal to the flexibility of the contours. To demonstrate this, returning to the Waltz op. 64/2 [. . .] we shall apply this gesture to the third beat left hand chords of each bar. 'Chopin did this', Schiffmacher told me; in the same way, he would anticipate the F double-sharp [of bar 2], as is indicated for the G [sharp] of the first bar.

Played this way, this waltz takes on a great elasticity and a truly artistic allure. It becomes impossible, with such a touch, to strike the notes unvaryingly.

Schiffmacher/Tasset, p. 50

[bars 9–16:] Don't forget that all this forms one single phrase; here is the extract complete with nuances:

This tradition comes directly from Chopin.   Mathias/Pugno, V, p. 53

Waltz op. 70/2 (posth.), F minor

Although he never had the Waltzes [of op. 70] published, Chopin valued them highly, at least the one in F minor. I often heard him play it, and how incomparably! This nostalgic piece could be entitled *Malinconia*.[206]

Lenz, UB, p. 298

Waltz op. 70/3 (posth.), D flat major

In the trio, the bass melody must dominate until the violin's E♮ in the fifth bar [bars 33–7];

but I don't need to tell you, because you'll feel it anyway.

Chopin, KFC, I, p. 108 [3 October 1829]

Notes

1   *PM: Projet de Méthode* (Sketch for a Method)

This is a collection of autograph notes, consisting of texts in various stages of completion, for the beginning of a piano method. The manuscript comprises twelve separate folios, single or double (ordinary or music paper of varying formats), giving a total of sixteen covered sides and twenty blank sides. Written in ink, with one musical example and two corrections or additions in pencil, the *PM* is particularly difficult to read owing to numerous revisions and superimpositions, as well as to uncertain pagination. After Chopin's death this autograph was taken by Ludwika Jędrzejewicz, the composer's elder sister, who made a fair copy of parts of it (now at *PL-Wtifc*: M/429), but who also included some fragments absent from the original as we know it. In the present book these fragments are indicated by *PM*/Jędrezejewicz copy. Chopin's sister gave the original manuscript in 1850 to Princess Marcelina Czartoryska (see also pp. 112–13 below) who subsequently bequeathed it to the pianist Natalia Janotha. The latter published for the first time some extracts from it, in a rather free English translation, as an introductory chapter to Kleczyński (*CGW*). Among these excerpts, arbitrarily chosen and revised, are some passages neither in the manuscript known at present nor in the Jędrzejewicz copy: this would suggest that certain pages of the manuscript have since gone astray (see p. 113, note 80). In 1936 Chopin's manuscript was acquired in London by Alfred Cortot, who kept it until his death in 1962; it is now in *US-NYpm* (Lehman).

Cortot, in his book *Aspects de Chopin* (pp. 56–66), presented the first almost complete transcription of the autograph. This, however, is marred by omissions and numerous misreadings; Cortot's introductory comments are equally subject to caution, the illustrious pianist having underestimated and misunderstood the exceptional value of this document. Some of these misreadings have been corrected in a Polish translation made from photocopies and signed A. in *Ruch Muzyczny*, XII/12 (1968), pp. 5–7; but the music examples reproduced in facsimile are incomplete. Appendix I below (pp. 190–7) supplies a complete transcription of the autograph. This, plus some previously unpublished pages and the variants in the Jędrzejewicz copy, and supplemented with a commentary and history of the problems involved, is the subject of the present writer's forthcoming publication 'Le "Projet de Méthode" de Chopin'.

On the basis of the autograph studied in *US-NYpm*, the pages above quote excerpts of the *PM* when relevant, grouping them according to subject regardless of the uncertain order of the manuscript. Spelling and punctuation have been tacitly corrected (but not in Appendix I).

2   That is to say, all intervals foreign to the equal temperament system. Chopin's reasoning here is exclusively pianistic; indeed, the entire reasoning of the *PM* – including some theoretical notions – is founded on the structure of the (equal tempered) keyboard.

3   Namely the diminished seventh arpeggio (identical, pianistically speaking, in its

root position and inversions) with which Chopin would introduce the study of arpeggios (see music example on p. 36 and Fig. 5). In the basic position C–Eb–F♯–A–C, the longer fingers naturally take the black keys and supple extension is facilitated by the equal distance of the intervals. This is doubtless why Chopin does not mention other types of seventh. At a more advanced level, he doubtless required all types of arpeggios to be studied, as being indispensable to the performance of his *Etudes* opp. 10/1 and 25/12.

4　By this Chopin designates all disjunct intervals from the augmented second (or minor third, basic component of the diminished seventh chord) upwards: namely, broken chords, arpeggios, other arpeggiated figures and all types of leap.

5　Such a radical simplification of technical categories cannot be found in any of the principal piano methods of the nineteenth and twentieth centuries. Concerning himself solely with the keyboard – since that is the instrument to master – Chopin allies healthy pragmatism with an accomplished dialectic in order to reduce his classification to three categories:

　　1. monodic conjunct playing,
　　2. monodic disjunct playing,
　　3. polyphonic playing and chords.

6　As Chopin really commenced his teaching career only after settling in Paris, the present book omits statements relating to pianos previously used by him. For brief references on this topic (particularly to Viennese instruments, with a preference for Graf) see *SC*, pp. 22, 23, 25, 30, 33, 39, 59, 60, 67, 69, 72, 76. For general information on instruments played by Chopin, see Steglich, *CK*.

7　Karasowski's source could be Blaze de Bury (p. 118) who quotes Chopin's statement in identical form. Marmontel quotes it thus: 'If I am not feeling on top form, if my fingers are less than completely supple or agile, if I am not feeling strong enough to mould the keyboard to my will, to control the action of keys and hammers as I wish it, then I prefer an Erard with its limpidly bright, ready-made tone. But if I feel alert, ready to make my fingers work without fatigue, then I prefer a Pleyel. The enunciation of my inmost thought and feeling is more direct, more personal. My fingers feel in more immediate contact with the hammers, which then translate precisely and faithfully the feeling I want to produce, the effect I want to obtain' (*HP*, p. 256).

Lenz in turn recalls: '[The piano] was a Pleyel; I had been told that Chopin played on no other instrument. Of the French makes these were the ones with the easiest touch. The instrument responded more easily then my Erard' (*GPV* 1872, pp. 34–5). Further on Lenz describes Chopin's piano as 'a docile Pleyel with narrow keys' (*ibid.*, p. 48).

Although both derived from the English mechanism, Pleyels and Erards of 1830–50 differ substantially in several respects. The double escapement, perfected by Erard in 1823, and from then on used in all his instruments, was not systematically adopted by Pleyel; piano No. 7267 (of 1839) which belonged to Chopin has a single escapement. Other aspects of the Erard design result in a more resistant action and consequently a heavier touch. In a little known book, Montal (a contemporary technician) describes some of the Pleyel's characteristics: 'M. Pleyel, by modifying the English mechanism with a well-combined leverage system, has succeeded in overcoming the stiffness of the keyboard and giving it a facility, an evenness and a rapidity in repeated notes, which both artists and makers had thought impossible [. . .] the striking of the hammers has been calculated so as to produce a sound that is pure, clear, even and intense; the carefully made up hammers – very hard in the middle, then covered with a soft and elastic skin – bring out in *piano* playing a soft and velvety tone, gaining in brightness and volume with stronger pressure on the keyboard [. . .] In 1830, M. Pleyel introduced veneered sound boards to his pianos

[. . .] veneering the pine boards with mahogany across the grain of the pine. The result was the same, that is to say, the sound did not augment in volume, but acquired instead a particularly satisfying quality, the upper register becoming bright and silvery, the middle one accentuated and penetrating, and the lower clear and vigorous' (pp. 223, 230–1).

In their sonorous qualities, if not in details of workmanship, the Pleyels of those days were closer to some Viennese instruments (Graf) than to the Erard. These characteristics, in perfect harmony with Chopin's playing and taste, explain his well known predilection for the Pleyel.

The last Pleyel (No. 14810) in Chopin's possession, from 1847 until his death, is at present in PL-Wtifc. A recording by Zbigniew Drzewiecki (issued by Polskie Nagrania: Muza X 0117) gives an approximate idea of its sound despite his excessively heavy handling of the instrument, most inappropriate to the bringing out of its character. On the matters raised here about problems of manufacture, see Marmontel (HP), Montal, Harding, and Hirt.

8 **Karasowski**, Maurycy (1823–92): 'cellist, musical writer and, together with Kleczyński, one of the foremost Polish music critics of his time. He was author of the first two monographs on Chopin to be based on first-hand documentation: *Młodość Fryderyka Szopena* [The Youth of FC] (Warsaw, 1869); and the biography originally written in German, listed in the present book's Bibliography. If by present-day standards Karasowski often lacks scientific rigour, his principal merit rests in having copied (though not without numerous omissions and corrections) some of Chopin's letters then in the possession of his second sister, Izabela Barińska. The originals of these letters, together with many other souvenirs, were destroyed by Russian soldiers during the plunder of the Zamoyski palace in Warsaw in September 1863. Izabela also gave Karasowski information and family recollections, to which the author has sometimes given a 'literary' turn at the expense of accuracy.

9 An identical experience is related to by Lenz (see note 7 above) who adds, 'Erard-Pleyel! Liszt-Chopin!' (*GPV*, p. 300), summarizing thus all that separated his two teachers in their aesthetic and consequently in their choice of favourite instrument. The same formula occurs in this passage from an article in the musical periodical *Le Pianiste* (1834/9, p. 130; signed L.D.): 'Give Liszt, Herz, Bertini and Schunke an *Erard*; but to Kalkbrenner, Chopin and Hiller give a *Pleyel*; a *Pleyel* is needed to sing a Field romance, to caress a Chopin *mazourk* [sic], to sigh a Kessler Nocturne; for the big concert an *Erard* is necessary. The bright tone of the latter carries no further, but in a clearer, more incisive and distinct fashion than the mellow tone of the Pleyel, which rounds itself and loses a little of its intensity in the corners of a large hall.'

It is also known that Liszt was a firm supporter of the Maison Erard and its 'salons', just as Chopin was of Camille Pleyel – dedicatee of the Preludes op. 28 in the OFE and OEE, works whose rights Pleyel had bought.

10 This Broadwood model is a small upright piano (117 cm high) with vertical strings, English double escapement, a compass of six octaves (*F′* to *f″″*), and two pedals, first launched by the maker Wornum in 1811. This instrument quickly became popular in England where it was soon christened the 'cottage piano'. The first mention of the 'Boudoir' model in question appears in Broadwood's price list of January 1840 (see Harding, pp. 228–32, 382).

Chopin undoubtedly valued Broadwoods in general, but we should qualify Hipkins's assertions in view of the fact that he was employed by Broadwood as a technical adviser, and that Chopin was under contract with Broadwood for the duration of his tour of Britain. Chopin's ultimate preference in grand pianos emerges from a letter dated 13 May

1848: 'I have three pianos. In addition to my Pleyel I have a Broadwood and an Erard, but I have so far only been able to play on my own' (*SC*, p. 317).

Introduced in France from 1815 by Henri Pape, Wornum's 'cottage piano' was improved upon by Pleyel and christened 'pianino'; it gradually usurped the square piano – which Chopin, unlike Liszt, still liked to use. The Pleyel pianino is described thus by Montal (pp. 240–1): 'These small instruments, no wider than their keyboard, with a proportionate height and depth, consequently occupy little space and so are very convenient in small rooms. The bass is single strung and the rest of the keyboard double strung, all vertically. The keyboard is able to slide from left to right by means of a pedal so that the hammers strike only one string, producing an effect analogous to that of the celesta pedal. These small pianos are distinguished by a pure, mellow and singing sound; their keyboard speaks easily, repeats well, and their tone has considerable volume in relation to their dimensions and number of strings; they have also been a commercial success.'

In his salon at the Square d'Orléans, Chopin had, in addition to his large concert Pleyel, a pianino of the type described above (but with six and a half octaves). He used it for demonstrating during his lessons, or for playing the part of the orchestra when the pupils were studying concertante works. It was on a similar instrument in Valldemosa that he put the final touches to the Preludes op. 28.

11   **Hipkins**, Alfred James (1826–1903): English pianist, harpsichordist, organist, theoretician and musicologist. An associate of Broadwood, whom he joined in 1840 as technical adviser, he made Chopin's acquaintance in London in 1848. He was then Chopin's piano tuner (we know how exacting Chopin was in that respect) and heard him play several times, notably (on one occasion in private) two of the op. 64 Waltzes and the *Andante spianato* op. 22. Strongly influenced by Chopin's style, particularly by his *legato cantabile*, Hipkins is believed to be the first English pianist to have dedicated entire recitals to the Polish composer, whose works were still relatively little known in Britain in the middle of the century. From the 1880s he made himself known as a specialist in old keyboard instruments and played a major role in England in the restoration of the clavichord (performance of Bach's *Chromatic Fantasy*) and the harpsichord (first performance of the *Goldberg Variations*). He was also the first to point out certain stylistic links between Chopin and the Baroque aesthetic. Besides important contributions to the original Grove's *Dictionary of Music and Musicians* (some of which survive still in *The New Grove*) and studies of various acoustic problems, Hipkins published *A Description and History of the Pianoforte* (London and New York, 1896; 3rd edition, revised, 1929).

His reminiscences of Chopin's playing were published by his daughter Edith J. Hipkins. There are no grounds to doubt their authenticity even though they were published later, despite Hedley's assertions (*C*, p. 119, note 1) and Karasowski's (p. 212). The only question is that of how closely Hipkins's own 'diaries and note-books' correspond to his daughter's published text. In this regard the first half of the latter's notes on Chopin (Hipkins, pp. 4–5) match, word for word – except for paragraph grouping – the version given by Diehl and Mangold (pp. 42–4) which specifies the text as that of a letter addressed to Alice Mangold by Alfred J. Hipkins. Edith J. Hipkins's publication, forty years later, therefore introduces no variant; all she does is add another text by her father, dated 1899 (pp. 6–8).

12   **Schelling**, Ernest (1876–1939): American pianist, composer and conductor, of Swiss extraction. A child prodigy, he was accompanied by his father to Paris at the age of seven in order to enrol at the Conservatoire. In view of his youth he was admitted as a

listener to Mathias's class, where Isidore Philipp was a fellow student. For almost three years Schelling was privately taught twice weekly by Mathias, who passed on to him many indications about Chopin's interpretations. In Paris he also profited from Moszkowski's tuition and then, briefly, from Leschetizky's in Vienna. Later on he met Paderewski who kept him for three years as his only student; Schelling stood in for him in 1910 at a recital in Lwów commemorating the centenary of Chopin's birth. He subsequently made a brilliant career in both America and Europe. Besides his output as a composer, Schelling devoted several articles to piano teaching, notably in *The Oxford Piano Course* (New York, 1929–32) of which he was a participating editor. In a short article (see Bibliography) he recorded some of his childhood memories from the lessons with Mathias.

13 **Michałowski**, Aleksander (1851–1938): Polish pianist-composer and teacher. After working in turn with Moscheles, Reinecke and Tausig, he studied with Mikuli in Lwów, and also knew Princess Marcelina Czartoryska during her last years. From these two Chopin disciples Michałowski learned the Chopin tradition, which comes through in an important article containing indications which felicitously complement those of Mikuli's Preface. Better known as a teacher than as concert artist, he taught among others Wanda Landowska and Heinrich Neuhaus at the Warsaw Institute of Music. Some idea of his playing may be gleaned from a recording of the Waltzes op. 64/1 and 2 (Pearl Records, *Great Virtuosi of the Golden Age*, vol. 8: GEM 108).

14 Chopin, whose first priority was mental concentration, did not build his technique through hours of purely mechanical exercises: '. . . you know the mechanics of piano-playing occupied little of your time and that your mind was busier than your fingers', wrote Nicolas Chopin to his son (*SC*, p. 94), when the latter was still considering submitting himself for three years to Kalkbrenner's discipline.

In this respect (as in many others) Chopin turns his back on most pianistic schools of his time and even on Liszt, who, at that time, had not yet discovered that 'technique is a product of the mind' and who set great store by purely mechanical exercises: '. . . I spend 4 to 5 hours on exercises (thirds, sixths, octaves, tremolos, repeated notes, cadences, etc., etc.). Ah! provided it does not drive me mad – you'll discover an artist in me!' wrote Liszt to Pierre Wolff (Paris, 2 May [1832]) after hearing Paganini (La Mara, I, p. 7). And at this time he demanded hardly less of the pupil: 'Again he recommended simple and broken octaves in all keys; notes struck with all the fingers, holding down those not in use on the keys; fast and loud scales, in short the entire gymnastics of the hand for at least two hours daily' (Boissier, p. 35).

Thus the maximum three hours of daily study (including exercises, *études* and specific pieces) which Chopin did not want exceeded would barely have sufficed even for the finger exercises practised and taught by Liszt at that time. Chopin shared the opinion of Hummel, who observes: 'Many already advanced pianists believe that they must practise up to six or seven hours daily in order to reach the required standard; they are mistaken; I can assure them that three hours of regular and attentive study are quite sufficient; for any further prolonged exercise stupefies the mind, produces soulless mechanical playing, and nearly always results in the inconvenience of quickly becoming unfit if forced to interrupt this sustained routine: if suddenly asked to play at such a time one finds oneself embarrassed unless one has a few days in which to recover agility' (p. iv, 'Advice to parents and teachers'). These apt remarks, as valid now as then, find confirmation in one of Chopin's letters describing preparations for his first concert in Vienna, on 11 August 1829: 'Three *Instrumentenmacher* wanted each to put a huge piano [*pantaléon*] at my disposal. I thanked them and refused, for my room was too small; anyway, these few hours of practice wouldn't have been much use, since I was to play forty-eight hours later' (*KFC*, I, p. 104) – and this in spite of his legendary stage-fright!

15   Niecks, Frederick (1845–1924): Scottish musician, critic and musicologist, of German extraction; professor at Edinburgh University. He was the author of one of the most remarkable and detailed monographs devoted to Chopin's life and personality; this work remains an indispensable source to all researchers (see Bibliography). As Hoesick was later to do in Poland, Niecks contacted numerous old pupils and associates of Chopin living outside Poland at the time (up to 1888) when he was preparing material for his book. Those mentioned by him are Mme Dubois, Mme Rubio, Mlle Gavard, Mme Streicher, Gutmann, Mathias, Brinley Richards, Lindsay Sloper; Liszt, Hiller, Franchomme, Alkan, Heller, Edward Wolff, Hallé, Osborne, Kwiatkowski, Chodzko, L. Niedźwiecki, Jenny Lind, Hipkins, Dr Łyszczuński and his wife; the publishers Breitkopf & Härtel, Kistner, Schuberth, Hofmeister, Ashdown, Richault, etc. (Preface, p. viii). Many later biographies are indebted to Niecks for a huge amount of information, and more than once they borrow the structure of his work (Hadden, 1903; Leichtentritt, 1905; Valetta, 1910; Hoesick, 1910–11; Ganche, FC, 1913; Murdoch, 1934; Hedley, C, 1947; Wierzyński, 1949; Czartkowski and Jeżewska, 1958; Belotti, FCU, 1947 – the dates listed are those of the first editions). The inaccuracies in Niecks's monograph are minor in the face of its documentary value, exceptional for the period in which it was compiled. In addition to a biography of Schumann, published posthumously (London and Toronto, 1925), we are indebted to Niecks for an important stylistic study, Programme Music in the Last Four Centuries (London and New York, [1907]).

16   This programme of study (three hours daily) punctuated by rest periods anticipates a fundamental principle of the Karl Leimer method: 'The uninterrupted concentration of from twenty to thirty minutes will probably tire the pupil. It is then useless to continue practising, as results thus gained are not worth mentioning. In the beginning, therefore, I forbid my pupils to practise longer than the given time [. . .] After having practised a short time, the pupil should pause for a while, and then commence work again in about an hour's time, beginning with the phrases he had last practised. It is sufficient even for concert players to practise one half-hour five or six times a day' (Gieseking–Leimer, p. 48). And further, regarding intense concentration: 'At any rate, the number of hours devoted to study is of far less significance than the intensity and attention one puts into them' (Gieseking, p. 95).

17   It is hard to imagine anything further removed from Chopin's personality and conceptions than the teachings of Kalkbrenner (1785–1849). And yet, on his arrival in Paris, the young Chopin was captivated – as were many others – by the tranquil mastery of this man who, at the time, reigned over the world of Parisian pianists and pedagogues. 'Just imagine how curious I was to hear Herz, Liszt, Hiller and the rest – they are all nobodies compared with Kalkbrenner. I confess I have played as well as Herz, but I long to play like Kalkbrenner. If Paganini is perfection itself, Kalkbrenner is his equal but in quite a different field. It is impossible to describe his calm, his enchanting touch, his incomparable evenness and the mastery which he reveals in every note – he is a giant who tramples underfoot the Herzes, Czernys and of course me!' writes Chopin to his confidant Tytus Woyciechowski (SC, p. 98; 12 December 1831). If this fascination is partly explicable by the classicism underlying Chopin's pianistic aesthetic (Kalkbrenner had been a pupil of Clementi), it lasted only a few weeks before the spell was broken and Chopin perceived the scholastic coldness, the unnaturalness and lack of inspiration in Kalkbrenner's style. He then discreetly kept his distance when the latter suggested 'giving him a schooling' entailing three years of tuition – a proposal that horrified Mendelssohn, then in Paris (see Hiller, FMB, pp. 21–2). We may note in passing that a similar proposal was made in 1838 to Stephen Heller, who declined it quite sharply! Having finally resolved his hesitation Chopin wrote to Elsner: 'I would even agree to three years' work if I could thereby make a

great step forward in my plan for the future. I am firmly convinced that I shall not be an imitation of Kalkbrenner: *he* has not the power to extinguish my perhaps too audacious but noble wish and intention to create for myself a new world' (*SC*, pp. 103–4). This statement to his former composition teacher shows that Chopin had grasped once and for all that his piano playing was the expression of his entire personality, as much as were his musical creations; indeed, he was at this time working on his op. 10 *Etudes*.

Kalkbrenner's method could not satisfy Chopin because of the importance given to purely mechanical study, the almost exclusive emphasis on finger action and the use of the *guide-mains* [hand-guide]. Invented by Logier and called *chiroplaste*, this apparatus was perfected by Kalkbrenner who imposed its use on his assistants and students – at considerable financial advantage to himself; he was moreover affiliated to the Maison Pleyel. The *guide-mains* consists of a rod fixed to the front of the keyboard at a slightly raised level, permitting the forearm to rest on it and supposedly alleviating all possible tension (?) in the wrist, freeing the fingers of all weight and facilitating their independent action. Chopin was probably alluding to this device when he wrote in the *PM*: 'People have tried out all kinds of methods of learning to play the piano, methods that are tedious and useless [. . .] It's like learning, for example, to walk on one's hands in order to go for a stroll.' Another essential part of Kalkbrenner's doctrine is the articulated use of the fingers and wrist only, without recourse to the forearm and upper arm. The pianist Hallé (see note 156, p. 140 below) encountered this in his first visit to Kalkbrenner: '. . . he stopped me and asked why I played the octaves with my arms and not from my wrists. "You are quite out of breath," he said, (which was the case); *he* could play scales in octaves for an hour without the least fatigue; and why had God given us wrists? He was sure, if the Almighty had ever played the piano, He would play from the wrist!' (Hallé, p. 213). On this particular point Chopin, who did use – and how – the wrist joint, specifically opposed the pedagogue: 'One cannot try to play everything from the wrist, as Kalkbrenner claims' (*PM*); Chopin's own music, moreover, makes the point, whether played on an old or modern piano.

In the year following Chopin's arrival in Paris his relationship with Kalkbrenner evolved into a somewhat distant politeness. Even if the dedication of the Concerto op. 11 (1833) 'A Monsieur F. Kalkbrenner' illustrates a polite deference, Chopin explained it to Lenz: 'It was when I had just arrived in Paris. Kalkbrenner then reigned supreme; it was necessary to pay court to him a little' (Lenz, *UB*, p. 282). The dedication of his op. 10 *Etudes* to Liszt in the same year shows that Chopin had modified his initial hasty judgement of *l'illustre égal*, and that he was aware of moving at his side to the discovery of a new world. In 1845 Kalkbrenner in his turn humbly approached Chopin for 'quelques conseils' intended for his pianist son (*SC*, pp. 260–1). Mickiewicz, for his part, clearly discerned the utter incompatibility of Chopin's and Kalkbrenner's methods. 'In each science or art, whoever appears as professor gathers around himself students and not masters. Of what use would it be to Chopin, for instance, to visit Kalkbrenner during his teaching hours and there and then to maintain that his lessons were based on a bad method? Both teachers would equally be wasting their time', he writes to the Abbé Jełowicki (p. 258).

18 In the Preface to his *Méthode* (p. 4) Kalkbrenner relates: 'After a few days I understood all the advantage that this new working method [the *guide-mains*] gave me; my hand-position could no longer be incorrect, I had nothing more to occupy me, playing only five-finger exercises. Soon I decided to try reading while feeding my fingers their daily nourishment. For the first few hours it seemed difficult, by the next day I was already accustomed to it. Since then I have always read while practising.'

In 1832 even Liszt succumbed to this barbarity: 'He therefore prescribes that each finger in turn should be exercised for quarter of an hour every day. This exercise should be carried out while reading, to avoid boredom' (Boissier, pp. 56–7). At that time Liszt temporarily adopted the use of Kalkbrenner's *guide-mains* (see note 17 above).

19 **Bischoff**, Ferdinand (1826–1915): Moravian lawyer, musical writer and music collector. An enlightened amateur, he lived for ten years (1855–65) in Lwów where he became friendly with Mikuli who was at the centre of musical activities in the town. At the end of August 1869 Mikuli, who had just spent several weeks in Rome (where he had been in daily contact with Liszt), visited Bischoff's home in Graz and gave him a detailed account of his impressions of Liszt's playing and teaching. Bischoff hastened to commit this narrative to paper. The autograph, currently in the possession of Professor Hellmut Federhofer (Mainz) was published with the latter's commentary in an article (see Bibliography), which also includes a list of the *Chopiniana* offered by Mikuli to Bischoff (now in the possession of the Library of the Graz Cantonal Conservatoire, and in the private collection of Prof. Federhofer, who kindly informed me of it). This documentation partly completes the information given in Zofia Lissa's article on the unpublished *Chopiniana* in Lwów. We have Bischoff to thank also for the publication of Delfina Potocka's decisive evidence on the controversial question of which works were sung by her at Chopin's death-bed (see note 161, pp. 143–4 below).

20 **Koczalski**, Raoul (1885–1948): Polish pianist-composer and teacher. A child prodigy, he performed quite regularly in public from the age of four and was composing at five; at seven he performed his op. 46! Extraordinarily acclaimed all over Europe, his talent was comparable to that of Filtsch (see note 157 below). The prodigy's childhood years are retraced in a pamphlet by Bernhard Vogel. From 1892, for four consecutive summers, Koczalski was subjected to Mikuli's rigorous discipline in Lwów: 'It was no trifle; each lesson lasted two full hours, and these were daily lessons; I was never permitted to work alone,' he remembered (Vogel, p. 10). The elderly master took special care over the child's education, seeing him to some extent as heir to the Chopin tradition. 'Strictly based on Chopin's method, his teaching was so revolutionary that even today it commands all my admiration. His analyses opened my eyes and trained me not to dissociate technique from mental work. Nothing was neglected: posture at the piano, fingertips, use of the pedal, *legato* playing, *staccato*, *portato*, octave passages, *fiorituras*, phrase structure, the singing tone of a musical line, dynamic contrasts, rhythm, and above all the care for authenticity with which Chopin's works must be approached. Here there is no camouflage, no cheap rubato and no languishing or useless contortions' (*ibid.*, p. 11). These reminiscences are from a valuable volume in which Koczalski assembles Mikuli's remarks together with his own experience of interpreting Chopin, to whom he dedicated most of his career. Among Chopin's numerous disciples-by-proxy, Koczalski undoubtedly appears to be the one to have preserved this living tradition most purely. In this respect his recordings constitute a document of prime importance. These are listed in the discography by Panigel–Beaufils:

Ballades opp. 23; 38; 47; 52	Nocturnes opp. 9/2; 15/2; 27/2; 32/1; 48/1;
Berceuse op. 57	62/1
Ecossaises op. 72/3–5	Polonaises op. 40/1; 53
Etudes op. 10/1–12; op. 25/1–12	Preludes op. 28/7, 9–14, 17, 20
3 Nouvelles Etudes [without op. no.]	Prelude op. 45
Impromptus opp. 29; 36	Scherzo op. 31
[*Fantaisie-*] *Impromptu* op. 66	Sonata op. 35, 'Funeral March' only
Mazurkas opp. 33/4; 68/2–3	*Tarentelle* op. 43
	Waltzes opp. 18; 34/1–3; 42; 64/1–3; 69/1;
	70/1; E minor [without op. no.]

To this can be added the Concerto op. 21, recently reissued – with opp. 34/2–3, 64/1 and 3, 66 – by the Italian company Replica (RPL 2462).

21 '"Never hurry into a difficulty", [Chopin] advised, "but play through it slowly, in a supple way, for you'll probably discover a hidden treasure. *Powoli bardzo* [very slowly]"' relates Victor Gille (p. 163).

Gille (1884–1964), grandson of Victor Massé and son of the writer and librettist Philippe Gille, was a pianist, pupil of Diémer at the Paris Conservatoire – and renowned for his extravagances and certain semi-spiritualist séances in the course of which he most liked to play Chopin and Liszt. His *Souvenirs romantiques*, dictated late in life, contain, besides some pages of probable fantasy, some interesting comments relative to Chopin's teaching. Gille grew up at the turn of the century amongst several former pupils of Chopin whom he names; in addition to some well-established names (Mme Dubois, Laure Duperré, Baronne d'Ivry, Mathias, Mme Roubaud, Mme Veyret) he lists Peru and about ten others who are otherwise unknown – for example, Charles Delioux (1825–1915) who taught Gille's mother and Gille himself, and to whom he refers both as Chopin's 'pupil' (p. 20) and as Chopin's 'friend' (p. 39). In his chapter on Delioux, Marmontel (*VC*, pp. 227–33) mentions Delioux as a student of Zimmermann – who was in fact Chopin's immediate neighbour at no. 7, Square d'Orléans. Whatever the answer, Gille's *Souvenirs* certainly seem to contain some authentic information, perplexingly mixed with other undoubtedly fictitious material; for that reason I have kept them out of the main texts above.

22 **Philipp**, Isidore (1863–1958): pianist and teacher of Hungarian origin, he established himself in Paris, then in the U.S.A. (1941) before ending his days in France. On arrival in Paris he worked with Mathias, Théodore Ritter, and Saint-Saëns who introduced him to the then aged Stephen Heller. Author of numerous didactic works, he trained generations of pianists at the Paris Conservatoire where he taught for forty years. To a certain extent Philipp inherited the Chopin tradition from Mathias, who wrote the preface to his collection of *Exercices quotidiens tirés des oeuvres de Chopin*. This influence is very noticeable in Philipp's ideas on teaching: 'You must appeal to the pupil's intelligence and reason, lead him to work more with the mind than with the fingers, to think and concentrate more. He must clearly understand that the important thing is not the quantity but the quality of his work, and that purely mechanical work, with no thought, is useless. Above all you must show him how to work so as to achieve the best results in the shortest time and so that his virtuosity may equally become a means of expression' (Philipp, p. 6).

23 This is corroborated by Victor Gille (pp. 48–9): 'During the lesson he had the habit of sketching some capricious arabesques with his right hand, in the upper reaches of the piano, and his improvisations would render enjoyable even the hardest and most thankless of technical studies.'

Although in this particular case there is no arabesque, this previously unpublished descant copied into Mme Dubois's score of the Waltz op. 34/2, bars 122–36, shows one example of this reported habit of Chopin:

24 Very little is known about the personality of this Michał **Wotpol** or **Wodpol** (d. after 1882), who passed on Chopin's words to Cecylia Działyńska; that Chopin may have called him his 'colleague' is no proof that he had given him lessons. In his biographical dictionary Sowiński gives Wotpol a concise entry (p. 574): 'Talented pianist, resident for some time in Le Mans, where he married. For several years this artist has been living in the south of France where he devotes himself to teaching the piano.'

25 This indication finds implicit corroboration in Chopin's facetious description of Scottish ladies at the piano: 'They all look at their hands and play wrong notes most soulfully' (SC, p. 348).

26 This attitude at the piano is very noticeable in the pencil sketch made by Delacroix (summer 1838) in preparation for the (unfinished) portrait of Chopin and George Sand.

27 These remarks may be compared with the reminiscences of a female pupil who took lessons at the Square d'Orléans: 'Behind the piano hung a painting by Frère representing a caravan in the desert. Marie Roubaud would look at it too much while playing, and Chopin told her: "You must stop this habit of staring at the painting, otherwise you'll find yourself unable to play without having it in sight"' (Ganche, DSFC, p. 86). Kwiatkowski mentions a pastel drawing by Jules Coignet representing Les Pyramides d'Égypte (Niecks, II, p. 135, note 17).

28 Cecylia **Działyńska** (1836–99): Polish pianist. A pupil of Planté in Paris, she frequented the salon of Marcelina Czartoryska who gave her much information on Chopin's teaching. During a stay in Britain in 1858, Działyńska was also in contact with a less talented pupil of Chopin, the Scottish Lady Murray – by then considerably aged, since Chopin had referred to her ten years previously as one of his 'sixty-year-old pupils' in London (SC, p. 327). Działyńska compiled the information given to her by Marcelina Czartoryska in a booklet published in Poznań in 1882. The present book quotes the essential points of this text as reproduced by Czartkowski and Jeżewska.

29 This last sentence comes from the head of the sheet intended by Chopin for his niece Ludwika (see Fig. 5, p. 35 and note 52). The main *PM* manuscript gives the variant above the fingered B major scale: '. . . the hand [pointing] neither in [*dedans*] nor out [*dehors*]' (p. 190 below).

Chopin's advice on posture at the piano and the position of the hand can be compared with Hummel's: 'You should sit facing the centre of the keyboard, at a distance of six to ten thumb's lengths, depending on the size and length of the arm; the right hand can then easily reach the highest notes, and the left hand the lowest notes, without disturbing the position of the body. You should sit neither too high nor too low, so that both hands may rest quite naturally, so to speak, upon the keys. [. . .] The body must be straight, leaning neither forward nor to the side; the elbows should be close in but without touching it [. . .] One must keep the hands free, rounded, and [turned] a little outwards: this facilitates the use of the thumb on the black keys. The hands should be neither higher nor lower than is necessary to reach the key with the pad of the finger, bending only the last two phalanges, so that the extremities of the little finger and thumb form a line parallel to the keyboard' (Hummel, p. 1, points 1–2). But while Chopin places the hand on *E, F♯, G♯, A♯ B*, Hummel remains a slave to *solfège*, commencing his five-finger exercises exclusively in C major.

30   Heinrich Neuhaus elaborates (pp. 84–5): 'These five notes *E, F♯, G♯, A♯, B♯* [*sic*], are the contents of Chopin's first lesson in piano playing. Perhaps not the first he actually gave, but the first from the point of view of systematic teaching.

In time, by no means immediately, I came to the conclusion that it is with these five notes that one must begin the whole methodology and heuristic of piano playing, of learning the piano, that they are its cornerstone, its Columbus's egg, the seed of wheat which yields a thousandfold harvest. This little formula is truly weightier than many heavy tomes. What is it in this formula that so attracts me?

Chopin, as we know, used to place the pupil's hand on these five notes which represented the most convenient, the most natural, the most relaxed position of the hand and fingers on the keyboard, since the shorter fingers – the thumb and little finger – are on the white keys which are lower, and the longer fingers (second, third and fourth) are on the black keys which are higher. You cannot find anything more natural on the keyboard than this position. Anyone can see how much less convenient is the position of the five fingers on only the white keys: *C, D, E, F, G*.'

The distinguished Russian teacher pays tribute there to Chopin as a pioneer of a revolutionary teaching concept, one radically dissociating piano apprenticeship from the basic principle of the theoretical *solfège* system. Giving precedence to physiological considerations (the hand) and physical ones (the keyboard), Chopin is in effect the first to emancipate himself from 'tyrant C', ruler of non-pianistic tonality.

Chopin's renowned preference for keys loaded with sharps or flats can be largely explained by this concern for pianistic comfort. To illustrate this statistically, the following compositions are written in key signatures comprising four or more sharps or flats: the four Impromptus; three out of four Scherzos; eleven out of seventeen Waltzes (Henle edition); fifteen out of 27 *Etudes*; eleven out of 21 Nocturnes (including the *Lento con gran expressione* without op. no., Henle edition) and nine out of sixteen Polonaises. Naturally this is not to deny the choice of these tonalities for the expressivity of their moods; it is no coincidence that Chopin's beloved A♭ is the key of the *Ballade* op. 47, the *Etudes* opp. 10/10 and 25/1 and the third of the *3 Nouvelles Etudes* [without op. no.], the Impromptu op. 29, the Prelude op. 28/17 and the Waltzes opp. 34/1, 42, 64/3 and 69/1. The B♭ minor of the Sonata op. 35 is also that of the Prelude op. 28/16 and the Scherzo op. 31, the ecstatic F♯ tonality of the *Barcarolle* op. 60 that of the Impromptu op. 36, the Nocturne op. 15/2 and the Prelude op. 28/13, and so on.

31   Chopin's physical suppleness was legendary, particularly in the context of his famous improvised mimes: 'According to Gutmann, he could, like a clown, throw his legs over his shoulders [. . .] Stephen Heller told me that it was a wonderful sight to see one of those small hands expand and cover a third of the keyboard. It was like the opening of the mouth of a serpent which is going to swallow a rabbit whole. In fact, Chopin appeared to be made of caoutchouc' [rubber] (Niecks, II, p. 96). Mme Peruzzi remarked, 'His fingers seemed to be without any bones; but he would bring out certain effects by great elasticity' (Niecks, II, p. 339).

32   This and other following passages are taken from a booklet published with no author's name, entitled *Conseils aux jeunes pianistes* (see Bibliography: [Anonymous]), which compiles various indications given during lessons by Mme Charles Picquet (née Jeanne Pillot, 1840–1904) and approved by her. The niece of Franchomme and a pupil of Mme Dubois, Mme Picquet gathered some elements of the Chopin tradition, particularly from Franchomme.

Auguste **Franchomme** (1808–84): eminent 'cellist and professor at the Paris Conservatoire. He was one of the first, and eventually the closest, of Chopin's French friends. An unfailing friendship based on mutual esteem linked the two musicians until Chopin's death: Chopin's last surviving letter is addressed to Franchomme. Not only did Franchomme participate in two of Chopin's important Paris concerts (21 February 1842 and 16 February 1848), but also, and above all, he collaborated with him in writing two works for piano and 'cello: the *Grand Duo Concertant sur des Thèmes de Robert le Diable* published in 1833 (without opus number), and the Sonata op. 65, of which he is the dedicatee and which was the last piece published in the composer's lifetime. Chopin, who had spent the summer of 1833 and part of April 1846 (see *CGS*, VII, p. 315 and note 2) in Touraine with Franchomme's family and friends, become very fond of his children: Cécile (1838–1903), a budding pianist and pupil of Mme Dubois, and René (1841–60), a gifted 'cellist who died prematurely. Chopin had given the latter a music album (which was never used) on the cover of which is embossed: *Souvenir de Chopin/ a Réné [sic] Franchomme*; a partial autograph (bars 1–42) of the Mazurka op. 63/2 is inset inside the front cover (collection of the late Mme Yvonne Faure, La Croix-en-Touraine).

Franchomme transcribed many of Chopin's compositions for 'cello and piano, either with a view to publication or for his own personal use; the autographs of these transcriptions are mostly in *F-Pn*. The *Deux Nocturnes de Chopin dédiés à Mad.elle Sterling [sic] arrangés pour le violoncelle avec acc*[ompagnemen]*t de piano par Aug. Franchomme . . . op. 55*, issued by Brandus at the beginning of 1846, cannot have been published without the composer's consent. Besides, Chopin wrote to his family: 'Franchomme [. . .] has arranged my sonata with the March [op. 35] for orchestra. Yesterday he brought me a Nocturne which he has adapted to the words *O Salutaris* – it goes well as a song' (8 June [1847]; *SC*, p. 290). Might this be the transcription sung by Delfina Potocka in 1849, according to Delacroix's *Journal*: '. . . this evening I saw Mme Potocka again, at Chopin's. Her voice was wonderful as ever. She sang parts of Nocturnes and other Chopin piano music, among them the *Moulin de Nohant*, which she had arranged for an *O Salutaris*. It worked admirably' (I, p. 286; 11 April 1849)?

Franchomme applied himself in various ways to perpetuating the memory of Chopin, whose best pupils became his musical partners in public and in the salons. To him we owe the manuscript fair copies of various of the posthumous works, including the realization of the last Mazurka as published by Fontana in the volume of *Oeuvres posthumes* and reproduced as op. 68/4 in CW (X, no. 51). Franchomme having omitted a section of sixteen bars in F major, a more satisfactory reconstruction has been suggested by Jan Ekier in a separate edition of the piece (Kraków, PWM, 1965, no. 5817). Two other reconstructions have been produced, by Wojciech Nowik ('Próba rekonstrukcji *Mazurka f-moll* op. 68 nr 4 Fryderyka Chopina' [Attempted reconstruction of FC's F minor Mazurka op. 68/4], *Annales Chopin* VIII, 1969, pp. 44–85) and by Ronald Smith (*Chopin. The final composition. Mazurka in F minor op. posthumous (Fontana op. 68 no. 4)*, *a completely new realization*, New York, Hansen House, 1975). Franchomme also participated in helping the collected Chopin editions by Tellefsen (see pp. 184–5 below) and by Mikuli (see pp. 172–4 below), and also the edition by Breitkopf & Härtel (Leipzig, 1878–80, 14 vols.) edited in collaboration with W. Bargiel, Brahms, Liszt, C. Reinecke and E. Rudorff.

With Jane Stirling, Mme Dubois, Marcelina Czartoryska and Delacroix, Franchomme belongs to a group of people loyal to the memory of the composer: 'Perform Chopin's works with the same accuracy as you do the works of the old masters. Bear in mind that a note repeated from the arm, a third beat unduly accented, a note lifted too hastily all suffice to distort the poetry of the composer's work and place you in the category of his *massacreurs*', he warned! ([Anonymous], pp. 39–40.) Franchomme's present-day descendants have carefully kept letters, musical autographs, first editions of Chopin, and family portraits and other memorabilia connected with Franchomme, Chopin, and their artistic milieu.

33 Despite the reference to *DSFC*, the text here is taken directly from Ganche's handwritten copy of Jane Stirling's letters to Ludwika Jędrzejewicz, now in *F-Pn* (see p. 181 below). Ganche in fact modified the original text and made numerous cuts in *DSFC*.

Edouard **Ganche** (1880–1945) was a French musical writer. After a medical training he devoted most of his life to study of Chopin's personality, life and works. From 1911 he carried on intense activity as founder-president of the Société Frédéric Chopin in Paris. Besides the three works listed in the present Bibliography (*DSFC*, *FC*, *VAFC*), he published a psycho-physiological study *Souffrances de Frédéric Chopin* (Paris, 1935), and numerous articles, prefaces, lectures and conference papers, some of them included in the above-listed volumes. His name remains mostly remembered through his editorship of *The Oxford Original Edition of Frédéric Chopin*['s *Works*] (*OXF*), based on annotated scores formerly belonging to Jane Stirling (see Appendix II, pp. 200–11) and on a few separate autograph or other manuscript copies. Between the two World Wars Ganche gathered a collection, which counted among the most important private collections made up this century, of documents and other objects to do with Chopin. During the last war most of this collection was taken to Poland and it is now deposited at *PL-Kj* and *Kjm* – with the exception of Jane Stirling's annotated scores. Ganche's researches brought him into contact with several of Chopin's last surviving contemporaries (notably Chopin's pupil Marie Roubaud) and with some descendants of Chopin's entourage, among them Jane Stirling's great-niece who enriched his collection with some invaluable items. Despite specific musical and philological limitations, Ganche's work shows a careful use of proper sources and places its author in the top rank of pre-war Chopin scholarship.

34 **Kleczyński**, Jan (1837–95): Polish pianist, composer, teacher and musical author. Kleczyński never worked with Chopin; but during a long stay in Paris (1859–66) he studied the tradition with three of Chopin's most distinguished students, Marcelina Czartoryska, Mme Dubois and Georges Mathias (who wrote introductions for the French edition (1880) of *FCI*), as well as with Fontana and Zofia Zaleska-Rosengardt. On returning to Poland (where he became one of the foremost music critics of his time), he endeavoured to re-express the technical and stylistic basis of Chopin's teaching in order to attain a synthesis of what he had learnt – one imbued at times with personal or foreign elements. Kleczyński passed on the results of his research in his remarkable teaching – both private and public – at the Warsaw Music Institute, and then the Conservatory, between 1887 and 1889 (he was one of Wanda Landowska's teachers), in his edition of Chopin's works (Warsaw, Gebethner & Wolff, 1882, 10 vols), and in two basic books: *FCI* and *CGW*, whose original Polish editions appeared respectively in 1879 and 1886 (the French version of *FCI*, 1880, is probably by Kleczyński himself). In the first of these books it is difficult at times to distinguish between what came from Chopin's own pupils and other ideas attributable to other sources (notably Mathis Lussy and Hans Schmitt). The above pages reproduce only those excerpts which appear the most authentic, taking care to indicate in the notes any possibly dubious details. For Kleczyński's works, personality and musical activities, the reader is referred to M. Woźna's remarkable study.

35 This phrase is taken from the description of Chopin's playing in the *Andante spianato* op. 22 (see complete text, p. 65 above); I have allowed it out of context to cover a broader meaning, since the make-up of this piece (broad cantilena over a rolling bass) applies equally to many other compositions in similar or derived forms, particularly among the Nocturnes.

36 This probably signifies that Chopin did not use the passive weight of the arm and forearm on the hand, but rather wanted them to follow the movements of the wrist freely, the fingers remaining always free and in control of the contact with the keyboard. The reader who has tried playing a pre-1850 piano (particularly a Pleyel or a Viennese instrument) will need little persuasion about how the weight of the arm on such instruments can be a hindrance.

37 Leszkiewicz, Antoni (1818–after 1886): pianist and composer. A child prodigy, he started performing in public at the age of seven, but appears to have ceased giving concerts after 1830. Chopin refers here to Leszkiewicz's concert with the violinist Antoni Orłowski at the Warsaw National Theatre on 2 April 1830; in March 1838 Chopin was to play in Rouen at a benefit concert for this same violinist, who had by then emigrated to France.

38 Realistic dialectician that he was, Chopin subordinated the means to the ends. Thus his definition of technique (see *PM* text, p. 23 above) places tone production, and consequently the art of touch, *before* the acquisition of velocity – which in itself is just the product of ever-increasing comfort at the keyboard. The chief aim being vested in the quality of sound and control of nuance, the point is not to pursue an exact equality of fingers, but rather to develop their individual qualities, using their natural conformation to produce above all the maximum variety of sound in terms of quality as well as intensity and duration. As for evenness of touch – in which no one could rival him – Chopin achieved it through strict control by the ear, carefully calculated fingering and, in scales and arpeggios, with the help of lateral movement of the hand in the direction of the run (see Mikuli's text, p. 37 above).

39 One may note the evocative strength of this image, illustrating the notion of free fall into the keyboard, of letting the strings speak with their full sonority. It recalls Debussy's phrase: 'Above all make me forget, as I listen to you, that the piano has hammers' (Durand, [I], p. 74).

40 Chopin used the expression 'a dog barking' frequently to describe an aggressive and uncontrolled attack: see Mikuli/A. Michałowski, p. 56 above, and Zaleska-Rosengardt/Kleczyński, p. 60 above.

41 Mathias's observations correspond perfectly with those of Marmontel, who heard Chopin at different times in his life; *cf.* the first paragraph of Marmontel's text, p. 274 below.

Chopin's general aesthetic, and pianistic aesthetic in particular, were greatly influenced by his constant admiration for the composers he studied in his adolescence; hence his distaste for most contemporary productions, his short-lived infatuation with Kalkbrenner, low esteem for Thalberg, Herz and the like, his reservations about Liszt and his musical aloofness from Berlioz. Chopin remained attached to the tradition of Classical pianists: Hummel, Clementi, Field, Cramer, and – more distantly – Moscheles, who represents the transition between the post-Classical and Romantic generations. The programmes of study which he gave his students speak for themselves here, as does his first Parisian letter to Tytus Woyciechowski: 'I surprised M. Kalkbrenner, who at once questioned me as to whether I was a pupil of Field, for he found that I have the style of Cramer and the touch of Field. I was terribly pleased to hear that [. . .]' (SC, p. 98; 12 December 1831). Moreover, Chopin's contemporaries frequently compared his touch to that of Field, while acknowledging that the Pole had a transcendent virtuosity far beyond that of the Irishman. For reference to the way in which Chopin's variety of sonority and nuance seems to anticipate Debussy, see notes 120–2, pp. 127–30 below.

42　The same expression is used by Wodziński (p. 254) in his account of Chopin's caricatures and pantomimes [*polichinades*]: 'We would then imitate this or that famous artist, the playing of some of his pupils or some of his compatriots, hitting the keyboard with sweeping gestures of the hands and arms, in a wild, dishevelled manner which he called "going on a pigeon hunt" [*aller à la chasse aux pigeons*].'

43　These comparisons are revealing about Chopin's ideas of sonority. While the art of *bel canto* is constantly proposed as a model for pianistic *legato* – the basis of Chopin's playing and the cornerstone of his teaching – he tends rather to make comparisons with instrumental sounds (harp and guitar, for instance) for the characteristics of *staccato*. In the case of violin *pizzicato*, a particular articulation is meant. This suggests that Chopin considered *staccato* (rare, at least in its pure state, in his compositions) secondary to *legato*, the real basic type of articulation. Tartini, in his *Regole per le Arcate*, drew a similar distinction between *cantabile* and *sonabile*, in similarly evocative terms (*Traité des Agréments de la Musique*, appended facsimile, p. [2]).

44　None the less, in August 1848 (at a time when he barely had either the strength or the desire to work) Chopin complained to Fontana in his characteristic half-joking, half-disillusioned tone: 'All that is left to me is a long nose and a fourth finger out of practice' (SC, p. 330). One notices also that Chopin avoids arriving on the fourth finger in his exercises of diminished sevenths, except for the final arpeggio (see p. 36 above).

45　Neuhaus (p. 85) comments on the relevance of this exercise: 'Chopin made his pupil play these five notes in turn, not *legato* (which could have caused a certain tenseness or stiffness with the inexperienced beginner) but as a light *portamento*, using the wrist, so as to feel in every point complete freedom and flexibility. Thanks to this simple exercise the beginner immediately makes friends with the instrument, and feels that the piano and keyboard are not an alien, dangerous and even hostile machine but a familiar, friendly being [. . .] But instead of this, how many hundreds and thousands of pitiful beginners – and during how many years – when brought by their teachers into contact with the keyboard for the first time, tried to turn their living hand with its nerves, muscles, flexible joints and pulsating blood, into a piece of wood with curved hooks, to extract with these hooks such offensive combinations of sound as, for instance,

[This exercise, recommended by the *Méthodes* of Kalkbrenner and Herz, still appears in most of the 'methods' of this century, including the Malwine Brée–Leschetizky and Cortot methods.]

46 This last suggestion is debatable: no pupil of Chopin ever affirmed having worked with the fingers raised very high. This gymnastic exercise was probably part of Kleczyński's own method – as also of other teachers. Similarly, Kleczyński claims that this exercise helps the fingers to acquire equality – which flagrantly contradicts many principles Chopin set forth in his *PM*; it is for this reason that two passages have been cut here from Kleczyński's text. In Chopin's view this type of exercise is primarily intended to develop awareness of each finger's individuality and independence.

47 Neuhaus comments (p. 86): 'As we know from Mikuli, Chopin used to suggest to his pupils that they should first play scales with many black keys (the most convenient to start with is the B major for the right hand and the D flat major for the left) and only then, gradually decreasing the number of black keys, come to the most difficult scale of all, that of C major. This is the reasoning of a realist, a practician, one who knows his stuff not from hearsay, but from inside, from its very substance. And in spite of the fact that this composer, pianist and teacher of genius, Chopin, lived so long ago, after his time (to say nothing of what went on before him!) hundreds and thousands of exercises, *études* and educational pieces have been written in that beloved C major with an obvious disregard for the other tonalities with many sharps and flats. [. . .] Please do not think that I am so naive as to ignore the logic of the circle around which our scales are built and the centre of which is C. I merely stress that the theory of piano playing which deals with the hand and its physiology is distinct from the theory of music. Chopin, as a teacher of the piano, was a dialectician, whereas the authors of educational compositions were schematists, not to say scholasters.'

These pertinent considerations also point out implicitly why Cortot misinterpreted the *PM*; great pianist though he was, the exercises in his *Principes Rationnels de la Technique Pianistique* (Paris, Salabert) almost all begin in C major – then to be transposed into all the other keys!

Finally one may note that Chopin had his students practise Clementi's *Préludes et Exercices* in the same tonal sequence as the scales; they would commence with the second volume, comprising studies with four and more sharps or flats (see under Mikuli, also Zaleska/Kleczyński, on pp. 59–60 above).

48 Chopin may mean by this a continuous sequence of scales passing through all the keys, descending chromatically from B to terminate on C. It could mean, alternatively, descending by fifths, removing one black note each time (and thus pulling back one more finger to a white note), corresponding with Neuhaus's belief (note 47 above).

49 On the basis of evidence from Mme Dubois, Niecks (II, p. 184, note 10) rightly questions Karasowski's assertion according to which Chopin made his students practise 'the major and minor scales, from *piano* to *fortissimo*, and *staccato* as well as *legato*' (Karasowski, II, p. 91). Concerning *staccato*, Karasowski probably misinterpreted the information he had gathered. On this occasion Kleczyński's explanation (see texts, pp. 33–4, 37–8 above) is the most plausible: Chopin resorted to non-*legato* in order to loosen the hand by allowing use of the wrist in five-finger exercises, and in order to facilitate passing the thumb when beginning to study scales. According to Mathias, Mikuli, Marmontel and others, constant use of *staccato* in scales is quite contrary to Chopin's predominant *legato* aesthetic.

50 This statement does not contradict Chopin's indication quoted in note 29: 'the hand [pointing] neither in nor out'. The latter advice concerned the neutral position of the fingers while stationary on the keys. When there is a rapid and continuous movement a slight inclination of the wrist in the direction of the run gives assurance and facilitates coherent, even playing of scales and arpeggios.

51 This indication is confirmed by Karasowski (II, p. 19): 'To this were added scales with accents on every second, third or fourth note', and by Kleczyński (*FCI*, p. 39): 'He had the scales played with an accent on every third or fourth note.'

52   The chart of basic scales and arpeggios was intended for Chopin's niece Ludwika Jędrzejewicz (familiarly called Ludka, later Mme Ciechomska). Preceded by the instructions 'the elbow level with the white keys, the hand [turned] neither to the left nor the right', the chart occupied the first recto of a ruled double sheet of Italian format; the document (see Fig. 5, p. 35), part of the collection of Maria and Laura Ciechomskie (Warsaw), Chopin's great-nieces, was destroyed during the last war. We have seen (p. 100, note 29) a variant of the above phrase in the *PM* autograph, which gives only the fingered B major scale and, on the verso in pencil, a scale on E without any accidentals indicated (see p. 190 below).

53   Played with this fingering, starting respectively on each of the twelve semitones, the chromatic scale gives the hand a ductility which refines the sense of contact with the keyboard.

54   See Chopin's fingering all through the *Etude* op. 10/2 (music example, p. 40 above). Koczalski (p. 56) reports after Mikuli that 'Chopin most often played chromatic scales with the three last fingers.' However, the fragment reproduced on p. 36 above specifies the so-called French fingering for the chromatic scale, ascending thus from *B*: *1-2-3-1-3-1-2-3-1-3-1-3*, etc. This need imply no contradiction: in a didactic passage, Chopin specifies the latter fingering (generally employed today), which was then taking over (in the *Méthodes* of Hummel, Cramer and Kalkbrenner) from the old fingering advocated by Marpurg and Türk (*1-2-3-1-2-1-2-3-1-2-1-2-1* etc. always starting on *B*): see Fétis–Moscheles, pp. 40–1 and note 1.

55   That is, the fingerings specified by Chopin in the *Etude* op. 25/6 (see music example on p. 40 above).

56   See the fingerings indicated by Chopin in the *Etude* op. 25/8 bars 3, 7, 32–3.

57   According to Chopin's synthetic conception of musical flow (embracing the rubato principle), rhythmic correctness within a given beat takes precedence over the purely qualitative exactness of each single note, taken in sequence. Since the aim here is towards *dynamic* order (the attainment of rapidity and ease), it cannot be approached by *static* means – that is, through exercises intended to impose artificial equality of force on unequally constructed fingers – but, on the contrary, by profiting from this very inequality; which is the art of fingering. Again Chopin's healthy pragmatism is evident: it is useless to block the development of velocity by fixing on the notion of equality at the expense of a varied, animated trajectory of sound propelled by the rhythmic impulse.

58   Mikuli's observation is illustrated by Hipkins's description (p. 5) of Chopin's playing of the *Andante spianato* op. 22, in which the left hand follows a rotary arpeggiated pattern: 'He kept his elbow close to his sides, and played only with finger-touch, no weight from the arms. He used a simple, natural position of the hands as conditioned by scale and chord-playing.'

59   Victor Gille in turn recalls: 'He so loved *legato* playing that at times in a scale he would tilt the hand towards the little finger when ascending and towards the thumb when descending; he liked to make a *glissando* with the nail of his third finger, in order to give the wrist and hand the desired inclination' (p. 161). This participation of the hand by an imperceptible lateral movement in the direction of the run was one of the conditions of the evenness of Chopin's playing, so much admired by his contemporaries. There lay, perhaps, 'Chopin's secret for making his scales so fluid [*si coulées*] over the piano', in the words of one listener after a performance of the Waltz op. 64/1 (Niecks, II, p. 95).

60   (A)   bars 476–9 and 488–9; Kleczyński's fingerings are neither specified by Chopin

in the OFE nor indicated in any of his traced pupils' scores. They figure
partly in Mikuli's edition (contemporary with Kleczyński's text).

(B)   bars 17–18; fingerings from the OFE.

(C)   bars 81–2; fingerings corroborated in the scores of Dubois, Franchomme and
Stirling.

61   That is, the pianists of the Classical school: Clementi and his pupils Cramer, Field,
Berger, Bertini, Kalkbrenner; Boieldieu, Adam and Zimmermann in Paris; in Vienna,
principally Czerny (Hummel being a notable exception). Moscheles himself, although
something of a transition to the Romantic generation, had been shocked by Chopin's
innovations prior to hearing him perform (I, pp. 271, 294; II, pp. 38–9; for the latter text see
pp. 272–3 below). Questioned about Chopin, Cramer told Lenz, 'I don't understand him,
but he plays beautifully and correctly, oh! very correctly; he doesn't let fly [*er lässt sich
nicht gehen*] like other young people; but I don't understand him' (Lenz, *GPV* 1872, p. 30).
Field, on hearing some of Chopin's *Etudes* played by Edward Wolff, exclaimed 'Such
youth really is diabolical' (*KFC*, I, p. 259).

62   Kleczyński is referring to the old fingerings in use up to the days of François
Couperin and J. S. Bach; harpsichordists and organists did not pass the thumb under in
scales and runs but resorted (according to country) to crossing over the second, third and
fourth fingers (even in the sixteenth century Tomás de Santa María was making
exceptions by passing the thumb in certain runs).

I dispute the repeated assertion (Leichtentritt, *ACK*; Abraham; Hedley, C) that Chopin
'rediscovered' the old fingerings in his *Etude* op. 10/2. Not only is the chromaticism (and
the appropriate fingering) thought out here in terms of the equal temperament system
unknown to the *clavecinistes*, but also, and above all, it is the fruit of an entirely new and
personal pianism, stemming from Chopin's autodidactic concept of the keyboard and his
purely pianistic sense. In any case, Chopin's lack of interest in musical archaeology is well
known.

63   (A)   bars 18–19; these fingerings appear also in Mikuli's edition. This 4-5-4
crossing, certainly used by Chopin and frequently encountered in right hand
cantilenas and arpeggios, is virtually unknown in undulating bass figurations in any of his pupils' annotated scores. It appears in the OFE of the
Concerto op. 11, first movement, bars 291–3, and among the fingerings in the
Fontana edition of the Nocturne op. 72/1, bars 34 and 45.

(B)   bars 49–50; OFE fingering.

(C)   bars 6–7; Kleczyński's fingering corresponds to one of the two suggested by
Mikuli;
bars 27–8; this fingering is either of Kleczyński's invention or from an
unknown source. It is contradicted by the annotations in the Stirling and
Jędrzejewicz scores, which divide the arpeggio between the two hands, the
right hand taking the top notes.

64   This is a reference to Hummel's *Méthode*, which Chopin valued very highly as
being the first rational method of fingering. Far ahead of all the didactic theories of his
time, Hummel prepared the way for Chopin by flouting some pianistic taboos and so
opening a range of future techniques. In the second part of this *Méthode*, the following
sections are of particular interest: 6 (*Use of the thumb and 5th finger on black keys*), 7
(*Crossing one finger over a shorter one or under a long one*), and 8 (. . . *to use the same
finger on two or more different keys*). This source reveals some principles of fingering
underlying many innovations traditionally attributed to Chopin; and indeed the layout of
the *PM* – as far as one can tell with its uncertain pagination – seems to be based on the
opening of Hummel's *Méthode*.

In my opinion, Hummel's influence on Chopin's aesthetic, pianism and compositions was more considerable than Field's – not just in Chopin's adolescence but equally in later life. The chapter on this subject by Branson (pp. 145–67) is well worth reading, particularly the comparison of the Concerto op. 11 with Hummel's Concerto op. 85 in A minor, even if one may not share all the conclusions drawn. The importance given in Chopin's teaching to the works of his predecessor (who for two years was Mozart's pupil) confirms his unremitting admiration for him (see texts on pp. 61 and 63 above).

65   Kalkbrenner resorts exclusively to finger and wrist articulation, considering his *guide-mains* as a universal panacea: 'It prevents the student from grimacing [*sic*!] and playing from the arm or shoulder', his Preface asserts (p. 5). And later in the main body of the book: 'Sixths and octaves must be played from the wrist without stiffening the arm [. . .] Octaves are to be practised like sixths, without stiffness; only the hands should be raised and lowered, by articulating the wrist' (pp. 48–9). Such repeated protestations against tension might suggest that it was a problem to which Kalkbrenner's system was particularly prone!

66   Some fingerings for trills in various contexts, taken from the annotated scores of pupils and associates:

Berceuse op. 57, bar 44, second a♭', $\overgroup{1\ 3}$ (Dubois);

Concerto op. 21, first movement, bar 72, r.h., $\overgroup{3\ 5}$; bar 87, $\overgroup{1\ 3}$; second movement, bar 7,

   $\overgroup{2\ 4}$ (Dubois);

Etude op. 25/7, bar 25, $\overgroup{1\ 3}$ (Dubois);

Grand Duo Concertant [without op. no.], Introduction, bar 10, $\overgroup{2\ 3}$; bar 22, $\overgroup{3\ 2\ 3\ 1}$

   (Franchomme);

Nocturne op. 62/1, bar 69, d♯'', $\overgroup{3\ 5}$ (Dubois);

Nocturne op. 62/2, bar 23, $\overgroup{1\ 3}$ (Dubois);

Nocturne op. 72/1, bar 37, $\overgroup{3\ 5}$ (Fontana edn);

Prelude op. 28/18, bar 18, r.h., $\overgroup{1\ 3\ 2}$ (Dubois);

Waltz op. 34/2, bar 5, $\overgroup{1\ 2}$ (Stirling);

Waltz op. 42, bars 1–8, $\overgroup{2\ 4}$ (Dubois).

In the *Barcarolle* op. 60, the OFE indicates $\overgroup{5\ 4}$ – $\overgroup{5\ 3}$ in bars 23–4 for the double trill.
                                              $1\ 2$ – $1\ 2$

67   This assertion seems too restrictive, reflecting Kalkbrenner's views more than Chopin's (see pp. 95–6, note 17; above, note 65). Even if the double octaves, nearly all conjunct, of the *Etude* op. 25/10 and Nocturne op. 48/1 can at a pinch be managed exclusively from the wrist, those in the Polonaise op. 44, and even more in the Scherzo op. 39, need the participation of at least the forearm if not more.

68   This is in reaction to the sentimentalizing fashion of spreading this or that chord or beat, an abuse that reached its peak at the turn of this century. That said, there are places in Chopin's compositions where the spreading of chords, though necessary, is not always clearly specified, probably bearing in mind the different hand spans of pianists. The Nocturne op. 48/1 provides a very clear example, at the beginning of the second section (bars 25–38).

In the Prelude op. 28/6 (bar 7), the Dubois score indicates the following arpeggiation, very common with Chopin, but which does not appear in the OFE:

The same applies in the Nocturne op. 32/1 bars 9, 32, etc.

69   Analogous remarks, though less developed, are found in Kleczyński's other book – *FCI*, p. 53.

The general rules given here about metric accents have no rapport with the type of rhythmic accentuation – deriving from Graeco-Latin prosody – practised by Beethoven, who studied and applied it systematically; see his marginal notes and comments to Cramer's *Etudes*, prosodically analysed by him according to a system of long–short contrasts, in J. B. Cramer, *21 Etüden für Klavier nach dem Handexemplar Beethovens* (edited by Hans Kann; Vienna, Universal Edition, 1974). Schindler (*BLB*, p. 471) also described his master's playing: 'It was the *rhythmic* accent which he preferred to bring out most strongly (and wanted to be heard as brought out), while the *melodic* (or grammatic, as they were known) accents were handled more according to necessity; he took special care only over appoggiaturas, especially semitone ones in cantabile, giving them more emphasis than one hears from others.' Chopin, on the contrary, gives precedence to continuity in the cantilena, whose line he does not want broken by pronounced accentuation (see Karasowski's texts, pp. 44 and 54 above). Hence Lenz's astonishment at the way Chopin phrased the variations in Beethoven's Sonata op. 26 (see pp. 277–8 below).

70   This revealing comparison links Chopin directly to the Baroque and Classical aesthetic, particularly to the theory of *affect* (*Affektenlehre*) out of which arose the principles of musical declamation expounded in the important vocal and instrumental treatises of the eighteenth century. Chopin's views coincide with Bérard (pp. 50–1), Lacassagne (pp. 156–7), Quantz (pp. 100–1), Leopold Mozart (pp. 107–8, note *c*), and particularly Türk (pp. 340ff), the principal German theoretician of the Classical keyboard whose *Klavierschule* was perhaps known to Chopin. All these writers emphasize the means and ends common to musical discourse and the art of oratory, on which musical performance is to model itself. These principles were also practised and taught by Clementi (after his purely virtuosic phase) and subsequently reinterpreted through him by Beethoven, who adopted Clementi's views and planned, late in life, to write a method whose substance is summarized by Schindler (*BLB*, p. 452): 'While the poet can fashion his monologue or dialogue within a continuous rhythm, the orator has to punctuate his speech with added periods and rests in order to convey the sense which he intends; such devices can be adapted to musical performance, where the freedom of their use is limited only by the number of performers.'

This explains Chopin's remark to a female pupil trained in the Classical style: 'You understand Beethoven marvellously, just as he should be understood and as nobody at present seems able to do, except for a small number of people, to which you belong' (Grewingk, p. 10). Chopin, who avoided the corruptions in musical style stigmatized by Schindler (*BLB*, pp. 469–72 particularly), evidently deplored the loss of the tradition in Beethovenian declamation.

For matters of style and interpretation (polyphony, *cantabile*, ornamentation, rubato, etc.) linking Chopin to the Baroque and Classical aesthetic, see Abraham; Basso; Belotti

(*OIRC*); Dunn; Eigeldinger (*CHB*); Hipkins; Kamieński; Kreutz; Meister; Ottich; Wiora; Zagiba.

71   On Kleczyński's own admission (*FCI*, p. 49) these ideas were strongly influenced by the views of Mathis Lussy. It is difficult there to distinguish between what Kleczyński took from Lussy and what is attributable to Chopin. This paragraph is quoted, however, since it accords with Chopin's indications in an area otherwise sparsely documented.

72   This pronouncement takes into consideration only the general rule of regular phrase-lengths. Yet Chopin, while frequently conforming to it, often broke it or widened its context. Among many notable instances, see the *Etude* op. 10/3; Mazurkas opp. 7/1, 24/3, 33/4; Nocturnes opp. 15/3, (see p. 153, note 187), 32/1; Preludes op. 28/2, 4, 14, 18; finale of the Sonata op. 35.

73   Mikuli adds later: 'One can say without exaggeration that only Chopin's pupils knew the pianist in his entire unrivalled greatness' (p. 4). This quite plausible assertion is vulnerable to the charge of generalization: anyone who has participated in a master class knows how a teacher's art can flourish in close communion with the pupils, when dealing with a masterpiece. Other sources relate how in the course of a lesson Chopin would repeat the same piece several times in succession, always with increasing perfection. Those who did not attend his lessons generally share Berlioz's opinion: 'In order to appreciate him fully I believe he has to be heard from close by in the salon rather than the concert hall' (see p. 272 below). Chopin's aesthetic sense is still that of a man of the eighteenth century, an aristocratic pianist *da camera* for whom the atmosphere of the concert in the Romantic sense disturbs the listening conditions and the quintessence of the musical message: 'Concerts are never real music; you have to give up the idea of hearing in them the most beautiful things of art,' he once declared (Grewingk, p. 19).

74   Another feature linking Chopin to the instrumental treatises of the late Baroque: see C. P. E. Bach (I, pp. 121–2); Leopold Mozart (pp. 50, 107–8); Quantz (p. 96), and also Hummel (p. 438).

75   The singers of the Théâtre-Italien who most impressed Chopin on his arrival in Paris were:

Prima donnas

Mme Cinti-Damoreau (1801–63)	soprano for whom Rossini composed several roles. She was the author of a *Méthode de chant* (Paris, Meissonnier, 1849).
Giulia Grisi (1811–69)	soprano who premiered the principal female roles in Bellini's *I Puritani* and Donizetti's *Don Pasquale*.
la Malibran (1808–36)	renowned for the range of her voice (soprano-contralto like her younger sister, Pauline Viardot); excelled particularly in Rossini and Bellini's *Norma*.
la Pasta (1797–1865)	soprano who, with Rubini, premiered Bellini's *La Sonnambula*, then *Norma*. Donizetti composed several roles for her.
Men	
Lablache (1794–1858)	initially a comic bass, he later performed serious roles; he was the author of a *Méthode de chant* (Paris, Canaux, n.d.), and sang in Mozart's *Requiem* at Chopin's funeral.
Nourrit (1802–39)	a tenor, he was the first to sing Schubert Lieder in France and premiered roles in operas by Rossini, Bellini and Donizetti. Chopin played the organ at his funeral in Marseilles.
Rubini (1794–1854)	'the king of tenors', he was renowned for the range of his voice in the high register and for his musical intelligence. He premièred

roles in operas by Rossini, Donizetti and Bellini (*La Sonnambula, I Puritani*).

Tamburini   baritone who premiered the principal roles in Bellini's *Il Pirata,*
(1800–76)   *La Straniera, I Puritani* and Donizetti's *Don Pasquale.*

Rubini, la Pasta, la Malibran and Mme Cinti-Damoreau were complete revelations for the young Polish pianist, who was forever to remember these artistic experiences. Of Rubini, whom he first heard singing Rossini (*The Barber of Seville, Otello, The Italian Girl in Algiers*), he wrote: 'Rubini is an excellent tenor. He sings true notes, never falsetto [or 'in a full voice, never from the head'] and sometimes his ornamental runs go on for hours (but sometimes his decorative passages are too long and he deliberately uses a *tremolo* effect, besides trilling endlessly – which, however, brings him the greatest applause). His *mezza voce* is incomparable' (*SC*, p. 100). As for Pasta and Malibran, he cannot decide at first which he prefers: 'They say that Pasta has gone off, but I never saw anything more sublime. Malibran impresses you merely by her marvellous voice, but no one *sings* like her. Miraculous! Marvellous!' (*ibid.*). And two days later: 'Today, unquestionably, it is not Pasta but Malibran (Garcia) who is the leading European *prima donna* – she is fabulous!' (*SC*, p. 104). Mme Cinti-Damoreau's singing 'could not be bettered – I prefer her to Malibran. Malibran amazes you – the other ravishes you, and she does her chromatic scales better than Tulou, the famous flautist. Impossible to have a more perfectly trained voice, and it seems to cost her so little effort that she coquettes with the public. Nourrit, the French tenor, sings with extraordinary feeling' (*SC*, p. 101). We shall see that Chopin integrated these singers' qualities into his playing; he constantly presented Rubini as a model for pianistic declamation.

This is not the place to enlarge on Chopin's knowledge of operatic matters and his fascination with *bel canto*, which he had learnt to appreciate in Warsaw whose National Theatre had been completely Italianized under the direction of Kurpiński; on this subject, see Pukińska-Szepietowska; Sandelewski (*PERP*); Lisowska. On Chopin and *bel canto* in general, see Abraham; Bronarski (*CI*); Meister; Sandelewski (*BCOC; IROC*).

As living evidence of Chopin's love for *bel canto*, there exists an autograph sketch of an accompaniment to the cavatina *Casta diva* from *Norma* (former collection of Gregor Piatigorsky, now collection of Mrs Daniel Drachman, Stevenson, Maryland; microfilm copy in the Library of Congress, Washington). This sketch was probably intended for Pauline Viardot who sang the role for the first time at St Petersburg in November 1844. A transcription and realization of this has been undertaken by W. Nowik (*ZCB*).

76   In Lenz's souvenirs this remark applies to the particular case of the Nocturne op. 9/2. It is quoted here in detached form in view of its wider applicability not only to the Nocturnes in general but also to all cantilena passages in Chopin. Lenz, indeed, repeats the observation with regard to the Concerto op. 11 (first movement), the Scherzo op. 31, second theme (bars 65ff) and the Sonata op. 35 (trio of the 'Funeral March').

77   Telemann observed: 'Whoever plays an instrument must have some knowledge of singing' (cited in R. Rolland, *Voyage musical au pays du passé* (Paris, 1922), p. 82). This was the type of playing advocated by the German treatises of the eighteenth century and called *Cantable Art* by Bach in his preface to the Inventions and Sinfonias. This tradition was continued through the Classical and pre-Romantic periods, codified by Türk (p. 331) and Hummel (p. 438) and eminently practised by Mozart and by Clementi (after his reform). Even Beethoven was aware of it, having 'himself heard from Clementi how the latter, after much experiment and research towards positive rules of musical performance, had finally found the solutions in the art of singing. As a singer himself, he [?] sought to

carry the rules of prosody over right down to the smallest phrases in instrumental music'
(Schindler, *BLB*, p. 468). As the Romantic piano became increasingly exploited for the
orchestral effects made possible by the development of its manufacture, the *cantabile*
tradition of keyboard playing declined. Thalberg, among others, attempted to revive it
with his collection *L'Art du chant appliqué au piano*, consisting of transcriptions of vocal
works in various styles. Despite the principles laid down in its introduction, this enterprise
proved almost as sterile in its efforts as some of Kalkbrenner's ideas; we know Chopin's
facetious opinion of Thalberg's playing (*SC*, p. 76). The Polish master was certainly the
one best equipped to continue this tradition, reviving it through his genius as a composer
rather than through transcriptions. In this regard Liszt paid a notable homage to him by
declaring, after leaving Venice in 1838: 'One should sing more at the piano, an advantage
for the most mediocre voice. If we were to hear one evening, on a deserted beach, the
singing of a Chopin Nocturne, what an emotion!' (d'Agoult, p. 154).

78   The implication of this is that Chopin, while adopting the *bel canto* style and the
manner of the best singers of the time, was not in any way compromising his pianistic
technique. He integrated these adaptations within the framework of his own pianistic
aesthetic, influenced as he was by Field and particularly by Hummel in his concern for
legato, *cantabile* and, to a certain extent, ornamentation and dynamics.

79   In contrast to the annotated scores of other students or associates, those of Mme
Dubois often feature oblique strokes (single or double) across the staff, which appear to
have been marked with the score on the music stand. These strokes indicate breaks, of
various kinds depending on the musical context. Sometimes it means lifting the hand
before a change of pattern or a new motive (Impromptu op. 36, bar 101 on the quaver rest;
Sonata op. 58, slow movement, bars 20, 22, 90, 106, 109, 110, before the chords; Prelude
op. 28/24, bars 54–5 before the run in chromatic thirds). At other times it is placed over a
rest, lengthening it to stress the following note (Nocturnes op. 15/1 bar 38, op. 48/1 bar 23,
Polonaise op. 40/2 bar 3). More often it intervenes before a key note in the musical line,
indicating a breath as in a *bel canto* line, implying the wrist movement described by Emilie
von Gretsch:

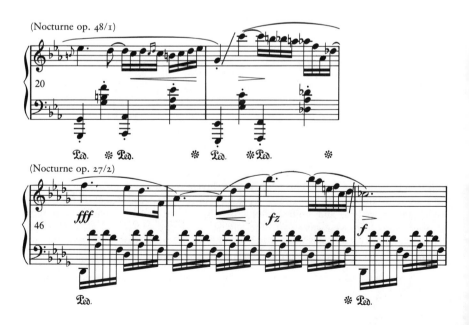

(Nocturne op. 48/1)

(Nocturne op. 27/2)

In the Nocturnes alone this type of breathing is indicated in the following places: op. 9/2 bars 12 and 20 after the $b\flat'$ in the middle of the bar (the same in the Jędrzejewicz score), bar 27 after the top g'''; op. 15/2 bar 6 before the $f\sharp''$, bar 15 before the b', bar 57 after the top $g\sharp''$; op. 27/2 bar 8 after the c'' in the middle of the bar, bars 48–9 before the $c\flat''$; op. 32/2 bar 9 after the $a\flat''$, bars 27, 31, 39 and 43 after the fourth quaver, bar 52 after the first c''; op. 48/1 bar 7 after the $e\flat''$, bar 21 before the c'''. There are similar cases in the Etude op. 10/3 between bars 69 and 70; in the Preludes op. 28/1 bar 21 on the semiquaver rest; op. 28/11 bar 23 before the $c\sharp\sharp$; op. 28/17 bar 49 after the first $c\sharp''$, etc.

80   This key statement appears in isolation at the head of a ruled sheet of paper now in PL-*Wtifc* (M/613). This page, containing a reference to keys in German, in pencil and in Chopin's writing, was originally to be part of the *PM*. The fragments of the latter published by Natalia Janotha in English translation include the following version of the phrase: 'The action of the wrist is analogous to taking breath in singing' (Kleczyński, *CGW*, p. 15). Since this phrase does not appear in the *PM* as it was acquired by Robert Owen Lehman after Cortot's death, we must conclude that this particular sheet became detached before Cortot bought the manuscript in 1936 (see p. 90 above, note 1).

Chopin's statement underlines once more how closely his technical thinking is allied to the musical reality, conditioned as it is by the stylistic element. Victor Gille (p. 172) for his part quotes Anna de Lichocherstoff as being taught by Chopin, that 'the *Luft-Pause* which gives the hand the elegance of a wing . . . The suppleness of the wrist, independent of the forearm, was the virtuoso's prime consideration'.

81   These are long slurs encompassing and defining phrases and periods, thus indicating the main agogic punctuation. Kleczyński's remark on the lack of precision of these phrasing marks is correct; some autographs do not always show clearly where they begin and end (see the first section of the *Ballade* op. 38, the *Etude* in A$\flat$ of the *3 Nouvelles Etudes* [without op. no.], etc.). The original French and German editions often exacerbate the problem by offering conflicting readings.

82   Originally, the *portamento di voce* (from *portar la voce*: to carry the voice) was an improvised ornament in the *bel canto* of the eighteenth and beginning of the nineteenth centuries. It is mentioned by Tosi (pp. 99–100) and defined by his German translator and commentator Agricola (pp. 56–7). The ornament consists of filling an ascending interval – in appropriate places – with a supple chromatic *glissando*. It was immediately adopted by the violin, a most suitable instrument for that purpose. Chopin, in his pianistic stylization of *bel canto*, took the opportunity to use this ornament in places: Concerto op. 21, first movement, bar 127; Nocturnes op. 9/2 bar 24, op. 72/1 bar 37; Nocturne in C minor [without op. no.] bars 25, 41; Waltz op. 69/1, bars 11, 35 (*ossia* versions in the autograph given to Maria Wodzińska: see Bory, p. 105); Variations op. 2, *tema*, bar 31. A diatonic version of it occurs in the Concerto op. 11, slow movement, bar 17; the *Grand Duo Concertant* [without op. no.], introduction, bars 10 and 12; and the Nocturne op. 72/1, bar 35. But it was also known for Chopin, faithful to the vocal tradition, to improvise this *portamento* in his own compositions, in the manner of singers (see Caswell, pp. 486, 488–9). Mikuli records two such instances in the Nocturne op. 9/2, bars 4–5 and 31 (see *CW*, VII, p. 118). The first one, for which Lenz gives a diatonic version (see music example on p. 78 above), is also specified by a sign added to the Dubois and Jędrzejewicz scores (see p. 150, note 183). Fontana recorded the same ornament for the Nocturne op. 27/2, bar 21 (see *CW*, VII, p. 123). For further information on *portamento*, *strascino* (its inversion) and their combinations and derivatives in Chopin's music, see Belotti (*OIRC*, pp. 17–18, 36–7), Eigeldinger (*CHB*, pp. 62–5) and Ottich (pp. 26ff).

From the beginning of the nineteenth century the term *portamento*, frequently confused with *portando* or *portato*, was often used incorrectly to indicate the articulation of repeated notes in a slow or moderate tempo. This is how it was understood by Liszt (see Lachmund, p. 245) and even Thalberg – despite his researches on the subject – who notes in his *L'art du chant appliqué au piano*: 'The notes bearing the indication [. . .] ⌢⌢⌢⌢, should be neither slurred nor detached, but carried as by a human voice, the first ones slightly heavier than the second ones' (p. 3). This definition really belongs to the vocal ornament properly known as *parlando* in *bel canto*, and generally referred to as *portando* in instrumental scores. The latter does of course appear in Chopin's works, notated as in Thalberg's description: see the slow movement of the Concerto op. 21 bars 32, 68, 76; *Etude* op. 10/9 bars 29–30, 33–4 and parallel passages; Nocturnes, op. 9/1 bars 1, 4 and similar; op. 9/2 bar 10; op. 15/2 bars 1 and similar, 19, 24; op. 27/1 bars 3 and similar; Variations op. 2, Introduction, bar 16. Many other places in Chopin's works contain expressive repeated notes which, even in the absence of the above-mentioned marking, nevertheless ask to be played the same way: *Ballades*, op. 38 bar 46; op. 52 bars 11 and similar; Concertos, op. 11, slow movement, bar 29; op. 21, first movement, bar 224; Mazurka op. 17/4 bars 28–9, 52–3; Nocturnes, op. 27/2 bar 28 – where, in the Dubois score, the dotted crotchet is articulated into three quavers to obtain this effect; op. 37/1 bars 16 and similar, 66–7 (with a *crescendo* sign in the Dubois score); op. 55/1 bars 24 and similar; op. 72/1 bars 35, 40–1; Polonaises, op. 26/1 bars 9 and similar, 33–4; op. 40/2 bars 81–2.

How then are we to understand Karasowski's statement ('He loved to find in piano playing what we understand by *portamento* in singing')? Is he referring to the improvised ornament of the Baroque tradition, or to the pianistic *portando* as defined by Thalberg? I suggest the latter for two reasons: first, that the original tradition of improvised *portamento* seems to have fallen into disuse by the second half of the nineteenth century, when Karasowski's book was published (1877). Second, Chopin (who used both types of ornament) does not appear to make any terminological distinction, if we refer to his judgement on the singer Sontag: 'Her *diminuendi* are *non plus ultra*, her *portamenti* wonderful and her scales, particularly *ascending chromatic*, excellent' (*KFC*, I, p. 127; my emphasis). Apparently he means to define two different things by distinguishing between ascending chromatic scales and *portamenti* – which in their other, original meaning are precisely fragments of ascending scales joining the extremes of an interval.

Chopin's works also show the stylized use of another vocal ornament related to the *portamento* and *strascino*, namely the *cercar della nota*. As defined by Johann Walther (p. 152), it consists of an auxiliary note which emphasizes an interval by repeating the first note just before the second note sounds. Prohibited in singing *méthodes*, this ornament was widely practised in *bel canto*. Chopin also made use of it, notating it as a crossed appoggiatura before the following note; in a slow to moderate tempo the appoggiatura is to be played simultaneously with the bass note that accompanies the ornamented note. A particularly eloquent example of this stylization occurs in the Nocturne op. 48/1 bars 18–19, with this timing specified in the Dubois score:

This device appears frequently in the Nocturnes: op. 9/2 bars 8 and 22; op. 9/3 bars 14, 17 and similar; op. 15/1 bars 9 and 56; op. 15/2 bars 12 and 52 (to be played as shown above, marked in the Dubois score); op. 27/2 bars 8 and 21; op. 32/2 bars 9 and similar; op. 37/1 bars 10, 12 and similar; op. 62/1 bar 15; also in other works like the *Andante spianato* op. 22, bars 19 and 44; Concerto op. 11, first movement, bars 397, 607 and 609, slow movement, bars 49 and 98; Mazurkas, op. 7/2 bars 11–12; op. 7/3 bars 14–15 and similar, 28–9 and similar, 94–5; op. 17/4 bars 6 and similar; op. 24/1 bars 7–8 and similar; op. 68/2 bar 36; Polonaise op. 26/1, bars 11 and similar.

83   John **Field** (1782–1837): Irish pianist, composer and teacher, known as the inventor of the piano Nocturne, a genre ideally suited to the taste of adolescent Romanticism, combining the melancholy charm of the romance with the elegance of the salon. Field, together with Hummel, was universally regarded as the master of *cantabile* (see Schindler, *BLB*, p. 469); his playing was further distinguished by its delicacy, precision, and Classical correctness. Chopin – who must have heard Maria Szymanowska in 1827 – then held his pianism in great esteem, and in 1830–2 Chopin's contemporaries readily compared his playing to Field's: 'I surprised M. Kalkbrenner, who at once questioned me as to whether I was a pupil of Field, for he found that I have the style of Cramer and the touch of Field. I was terribly pleased to hear that [...]' (*SC*, p. 98; see also *CFC*, i, pp. 218–19; II, pp. 76 and 84). It seems that on hearing Field later he was disenchanted; but this is not certain (see *SC*, p. 115; *CFC* II, pp. 144–5). Whatever the case, Chopin gave a large place in his teaching to studying the Irishman's *oeuvre*.

It would be wrong to assume that Chopin obtained his *cantabile* solely through his fingers linking each successive note, as in the Classical pianoforte school. He produced this impression of a perfect *legato cantabile* as much through original fingerings (see pp. 116–17, note 85) as through refinements of touch and a discreet, subtle use of the pedal. Lenz's remark on this subject (*B*, pp. 203–4) is revealing: 'After my lessons, Chopin would play for me whatever I had brought of the music of the great masters. The Allegretto of Beethoven's C♯ minor sonata [op. 27/2] had its turn. When it came to the chord sequence of which we have spoken,

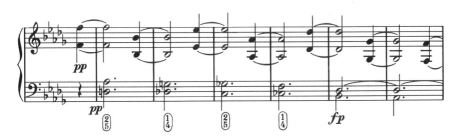

Chopin played it *legato*, it is true, on his beautiful Pleyel; but solely through nuances of touch. I suggested Liszt's fingering. 'This isn't your fingering, is it?' he asked in his quiet, pleasant voice. 'It's Liszt's,' I said. 'Ah! You see, he has these ideas that nobody else would ever think of.' And Chopin began to try out the fingering. 'But this way you can travel down the keyboard like a crab going back to the water; this fingering is perfect – I shall use it!'

84   It is interesting to see von Bülow (*V*, p. 246) recommending Field's Nocturnes as preparation for Chopin's: 'I have studied four of Field's Nocturnes with great pleasure and unexpected profit. Please do the same, for it is an exercise like no other as regards taste

and delicacy in *nuances* of touch. In any methodical teaching [. . .] Field's Nocturnes should *definitely* precede those of Chopin.'

Chopin believed himself indebted to Field, if we are to believe Lenz: 'Field's first Nocturne [in E♭; 1812], despite a few harmonic and rhythmic naïveties – delightful besides – is the father of the modern Nocturne. Chopin himself often told us that' (*B*, p. 149). On the subject of this influence, see Branson (some of whose conclusions are debatable in that they underrate the *bel canto* influence on Chopin in favour of that of Field) and Chmara.

While playing Field's Nocturnes, Chopin liked to introduce ornamental variants just as in his own works (see Mikuli's text, p. 52 above), doubtless in order to give them a more personal touch. An idea of these variants may be formed through those gathered by the Mikuli and *OXF* editions for the Nocturne op. 9/2 (see *CW*, VII, p. 118).

85 Here are some examples of successions of the same finger printed in the OFE or noted in the scores of the most reliable pupils or associates:

– *Repeated 5th finger in a melody:*
Nocturne op. 9/3 bars 16 and similar, *a♯″–b″* (OFE);
Nocturne op. 15/2 bar 13, *d♮″–c♯″*, bar 57, *g♯″–g♮″*, *f♮″–e♮″* (Dubois).
– *Repeated 5th finger in an arpeggiated bass:*
Nocturne op. 27/1 bars 13–14, *C♯–G♯′–G♯* . . . *G♯–G♯′–C♯–G♯* (Stirling; Jędrzejewicz).
Nocturne op. 32/1 bar 7, *G♮–e*; bar 26, *A♯′–A♯* (Stirling); bar 37, *B♯–b♯*, *C♯–c♯* (Stirling; Jędrzejewicz).
– *Repeated 4th finger:*
Nocturne op. 32/1 bar 58, *f♯″–e♯″* (Dubois);
Prelude op. 28/15 bars 3 and similar, *g♭″–f″* (Dubois); bar 14, *g♭″–f″* (Dubois); bars 16–17, *g♭″–f″* (Dubois), bars 78–9, *g♭″–f″–f″* (Stirling);
Sonata op. 35, trio of the 'Funeral March', bars 31 and similar, *g♭″–f″* (Stirling);
Beethoven, Sonata op. 14/2, first movement, bars 194–5 (Lenz, *B*, pp. 306–7):

– *Repeated 3rd finger:*
Etude op. 25/7 bar [1], *c♯′–c♯′–b♯* (Stirling);
Mazurka op. 24/3 bars 5–6, *a♭′–g′–f′–e♭′* (Stirling);
Mazurka op. 63/2 bars 7–8, *g♭′–f′–e♮′–c′* (OFE);
Nocturne op. 32/1 bar 29, *a♯′–b′* (Stirling);
Nocturne op. 37/1 bars 6 and similar, *b♭′–a′–g′–f♯′* (OFE); bars 9 and similar, *b♭′–b♮′* (Stirling; Dubois);
Prelude op. 28/4 bars 4–5, *b♭′–a′* (Stirling);
Prelude op. 28/6 bars 17–18, *F♯–G* (Jędrzejewicz).
– *Repeated 2nd finger:*
Prelude op. 28/6 bar 6, *f♯′–e♯′* (Stirling; Jędrzejewicz); bars 17–18, *F♯–G* (Stirling);
Beethoven, Sonata op. 14/2, first movement, bars 187–8, *a♯′–b′* (Lenz, *B*, p. 306).

– *Repeated thumb in a melody:*
Berceuse op. 57 bars 47–8, *b'♭–a♭'* (Stirling); bars 48–9, *g♭'–f'* (Stirling: Dubois);
Etude op. 25/7 bars 4–5 (OFE), 48–9, *c♯–d♯–e* (Stirling).
3 Nouvelles Etudes/1 (F minor) bars 40–1 and similar, *d♭'–c♭'–b♭* (OFE);
Impromptu op. 29 bar 65, *d♭''–c''* (Stirling; Dubois; Jędrzejewicz; Franchomme);
Prelude op 28/21 bar 49, *B♭–A* (Stirling);
Waltz op. 34/2 bar 169, *a–g* (Dubois).

– *Repeated thumb in a counter-melody or arabesque:*
Berceuse op. 57 bar 13, *f'–e♭'–d♭'* (Stirling; Dubois), *b♭'–a♭'* (Dubois; Franchomme);
Concerto op. 21 slow movement, bar 31, *e♭'–f'–g'* (OFE);
Impromptu op. 51 bars 37–8 and similar, *d♮'–d♭'–c♮'–c♭'–b♭* (OFE);
Nocturne op. 55/2 bars 36–7, *e♮'–e♭'–d'–c'*, bar 48, *f'–f♭'–e♭'*, bar 50, *g'–g♭–f*
(Dubois).

– *Repeated thumb in an arpeggiated bass:*
Nocturne op. 9/1 bars 26 and similar, *b♭♭–a♭* (Stirling; Franchomme);
Nocturne op. 32/1 bar 12, *a♯–b* (Stirling; Jędrzejewicz);
Nocturne op. 37/2 bar 81, *g–f♯*, bar 82, *f♮–e* (Dubois).

One more typical example of a repeated finger is worth listing, in this instance designed
not for obtaining suppleness in a *cantabile* but rather for obtaining a firm tone: r.h. third
finger repeated on the *c♯'–c♯'–c♯'–c♯'–c♯'–c♯'–d♭'* in the antepenultimate bar of the
Nocturne op. 32/1, and then at the instruction *adagio*, on *a♯–a♯–b* (Stirling;
Jędrzejewicz).

86   The repetitions 5–5 and 4–4 appear in the Dubois, Jędrzejewicz and Franchomme
scores. Stirling and Zaleska–Rosengardt give only 5–5.

87   The circled fingerings are those of the OFE.

88   The third fingers appear in the Dubois score; the OFE, however, indicates 2 on the
a♭'' in bar 5.

89   The circled fingerings are those of the OFE.

90   This statement is extracted from Hipkins's description of Chopin's playing in the
Andante spianato op. 22. It is allowed out of its context here since the *Andante* concerned
embodies *par excellence* the essence of the Chopinian cantilena.
    Among the rare fingerings in the Dubois score of the *Andante spianato* there appears
one single 5̂ 1̂ substitution on the last *d♮''* in bar 36.
    As for the reference to the organ, it is known that Chopin had considerable knowledge
in the field. He took a few lessons from Würfel (1790–1832) who taught an organ class at
the Warsaw Conservatory. In his adolescence Chopin frequently played the organ for
school services in the Church of the Visitandines.

91   The substitutions marked in the scores of students (occasionally in the OFE) are of
two main kinds. Some – the traditional type – aim at a *legato* solely through finger action:
Berceuse op. 57 bar 5, *d♭''*, 4̂2; *e♭''*, 3̂2 (Stirling); Mazurka op. 7/3 last bar, *f''*, 5̂1
(Stirling); Nocturne op. 15/2 bar 17, *g♯'*, 3̂1 (Dubois); Nocturne op. 72/1 bar 8, second *f♯*,
1̂5; bar 16, *d*, 1̂5; bar 17, *d♯*, 1̂5; bar 31, first *E*, 3̂5; bar 45, top *b*, 2̂1; bar 46, first *E*, 3̂5
(posthumous OFE by Fontana: to be taken with caution). Some others allow the holding
of a note: Mazurka op. 33/4 bars 124–5, *f♭''*, 1̂3 (Stirling; Jędrzejewicz); Nocturne op. 15/
1 bar 8, l.h., *g♯*, 1̂3 (Stirling; Jędrzejewicz); Nocturne op. 37/1 bar 66, *d'*, 5̂1 (Stirling); bar
90, r.h., *g'*, 2̂5 (Stirling). The second kind, the really innovatory substitutions, are to bring
out the tonal possibilities characteristic of a particular finger, or to maintain evenness in a
melody: Prelude op. 28/6 bar 15, *e*, 3̂1; bar 23, *d'*, 2̂1; bar 24, *b*, 2̂1 (Stirling); Prelude op.
28/15 bars 1 and similar, *a♭'*, 1̂2; bar 2, *c''*, 3̂1 (Stirling); Waltz op. 34/2 bars 2 and 4 [and
similar], *f*, 1̂2 (Stirling).

Chopin's fingerings in these three compositions are among the most revealing examples of his art of utilizing the natural conformation of the fingers and hand to obtain the desired effect most logically. These fingerings are reproduced in Appendix III below, pp. 248–9 and 255–6, and also on pp. 86–7 above.

92 Of those who heard Chopin play, rarely did any criticize his rubato. Those who did were non-Poles: Berlioz (see p. 272) who was little of a pianist and whose symphonic aesthetic was quite contrary to Chopin's, and Mendelssohn (see p. 267) who expressly declared allegiance to a more metrical conception. Moscheles's sudden change of mind (I, pp. 271, 294; II, p. 39) is significant; he recognized, though, that Chopin's music in the hands of other players could well degenerate into mere lack of rhythm [*Taktlosigkeit*]. We know how much any such accusation irritated Chopin if directed against himself (see Peruzzi/Niecks, II, p. 339). The quotations reproduced here concerning Chopin's rubato all reject this accusation and come from the most reliable pupils.

In fact, Mikuli is referring here to generations of pianists subsequent to Chopin's; victims of a pseudo-tradition, they submitted his music to agogic distortions in the name of the vague and convenient term 'rubato'. This practice was in vogue from before the second half of the nineteenth century up to the 1930s. The statements where Chopin's pupils denounce such abuses – which Chopin was accused at the time of having fathered – all date from that period: Streicher (around 1879), Mikuli (1879), Mathias (1897), Viardot/Saint-Saëns (1910). Kleczyński – a pupil of some of Chopin's pupils – reacted similarly in 1880 (*FCI*). It was only with the gradual return to respecting the letter of scores (which carries its own dangers), from the years 1930–40 or so, that this type of pseudo-rubato disappeared from most playing.

93 This independence of the two hands, aiming at a complex complementarity, is one of Chopin's characteristic traits. It cannot be fortuitous that he chose to be represented in the Fétis–Moscheles *Méthode des méthodes* [1840] by three *Etudes* of which two are based on polymetric principles: the first (F minor) with threes against fours and the third (A♭) with threes against twos. The [*Fantaisie-*]*Impromptu* op. 66 offers a juxtaposition of these two systems through its constituent sections; similarly the *Etude* op. 25/2 is based entirely on 'rhythmic exchanges'. Similar ideas occur at bars 249–72 and 849–75 of the Scherzo op. 54, as also in the Waltz op. 42, which Lenz called 'the most typical embodiment of Chopin's rubato style' (*UB*, p. 298).

94 This practice, criticized by Saint-Saëns, is clearly recognizable in the recordings of 'renowned' Chopin players of the time, notably Leschetizky, Pugno, Pachmann, Friedman and, to a lesser extent, Paderewski and Maurycy [Moritz] Rosenthal.

95 *Tempo rubato*: stolen time. Although this expression first appears in 1723 in the treatise by Tosi (Bolognese theoretician of *bel canto*), the musical reality which it reflects can be traced back at least to the beginnings of accompanied monody in Italian humanist circles. The following postulates emerge from Tosi's seminal writings (pp. 81–2, 99, 105): for the intelligent use of the singer in particularly expressive passages [mostly in slow tempi] in various pieces [recitatives, arias, *ariosi*], rubato is a system of compensation whereby the value of a note may be prolonged or shortened to the detriment or gain of the succeeding note. This metric 'larceny' is best applied to improvised ornaments [taking the sense of the words into account as much as the music] *over the imperturbable movement of the bass* (underlined by Tosi). It results from counterpoint between the solo line and the bass line and is characterized, vertically speaking, by moments of metric displacement between the two parts; it is left to the singer's discretion to use it with moderation, according to the rules of good taste. Here we have the pure tradition of Italian Baroque *bel canto*, linked with the art of improvising suitable ornaments, and deriving from the theory of *affetti*.

Bel canto, dominant in Europe at the end of the seventeenth and above all the eighteenth century, was transposed together with the art of rubato into the domain of instrumental music in its chamber, concertante and solo genres. Thus it came to be codified fairly accurately in the important instrumental treatises of the period: C.P.E. Bach (I, pp. 6–8, note) for the keyboard, Leopold Mozart (pp. 262–3 and note e) for the violin, and Quantz (pp. 256–7) for the transverse flute. Wolfgang Mozart, who had been well schooled, proudly related to his father (Augsburg, 24 October 1777): 'They all are amazed that I play accurately in time. They can't grasp that in *tempo rubato* in an Adagio the left hand goes on unperturbed; with them the left hand follows suit' (II, p. 83). If this independence of the hands is applied to some places in the B minor Adagio (K540), the *adagio* sections of the Fantasies in D minor (K397) and C minor (K475), the various reprises in the A minor Rondo (K511) or even to some slow movements in the sonatas and concertos, one can feel how closely Mozart anticipated Chopin!

This tradition was maintained in the instrumental field well into the Classical era, and codified once again by Türk in 1789 (pp. 374–5). *Tempo rubato*, still very much alive in Romantic *bel canto* (and, exceptionally, in Paganini's Concertos – Chopin heard him in 1829 when the latter gave ten concerts in Warsaw) was, by the beginning of the nineteenth century, gradually supplanted in instrumental music by larger-scale tempo fluctuations. The Frenchman Louis Adam, educated in the old tradition, observed (p. 160): 'Some people have tried to start a trend of playing out of time, playing all genres of music like a fantasy, prelude or capriccio. It is thought to enhance the expression of a piece, while serving in effect to distort it beyond recognition. Naturally, expressivity requires certain notes of the melody to be slowed or quickened; however, these fluctuations must not be used continually throughout the piece, but only in places where the expression of a languorous melody or the passion of an agitated one demands a slower or a more animated pace. In this case it is the melody that should be altered, while the bass should strictly maintain the beat.' The notion of rubato is then confused with that of *tempo ad libitum* in pieces written in free style. According to Schindler (*BLB*, p. 462), Beethoven finally adopted the term rubato in this new and incorrect sense designating fluctuations of tempo. In 1828 Hummel denounced this latest practice: 'Lately several artists have been trying to replace natural feeling with manufactured feeling; as for instance [...] by slowing down the beat (*tempo rubato*) at every possible opportunity to the point of satiation' (p. 438). Hummel, who was a pupil of Mozart, continues to recommend the use of traditional rubato in Adagios, but no longer designates it by this name (p. 452, *Remarques 1° and 2°*).

Thus Chopin practised and taught rubato in its traditional and original meaning, at a time when that practice was on the decline, if not already abolished, in other piano music. His attachment to the Baroque aesthetic may be explained by two factors: first, his training from Żywyny and Elsner, both products of the pre-Classical era and raised within Italianized circles (Prague and Vienna respectively); second, Chopin's own taste for *bel canto*, evident from in his adolescence on – we have seen how assiduously he frequented the Warsaw National Theatre, where Italianism dominated as much through Rossini as through the operas of Kamieński and Kurpiński. One might add that the singing class at the Warsaw Conservatory was then directed by the Piedmontese teacher Carlo Soliva. Faithful to the aesthetic of his education, Chopin was to transmit it through his own teaching (whence the continual appearance of indications along these lines in the annotated scores of Mme Dubois).

For more information on Chopin's connections with Baroque and Classical rubato, see particularly Belotti (*OIRC*), Eigeldinger (*CHB*), Kamieński, Kreutz, and Sobiescy.

96 This assertion of course applies equally to the inverse case, when the melody is in the left hand and the accompaniment in the right. Amongst many examples can be mentioned the *Etude* op. 25/7, Prelude op. 28/6, Mazurka op. 7/3 (bars 56–73), Polonaise op. 26/1 (bars 66–82), Waltz op. 34/2 (principal motif and bars 169–88), etc.

97 Chopin was fond of this metaphor and used it often. It appears with small variants or commentaries in the following texts:
– Lenz, *GPV* 1872, p. 47; *B*, p. 226
– Peruzzi/Niecks, II, p. 339
– Kleczyński, *FCI*, p. 57
– Dubois/Kleczyński, *FCI* French edition (only), p. [x]
– Franchomme, Potocka, Czartoryska/Planté, p. 36
– Franchomme/Picquet/Anonymous, p. 10
– Mikuli/Koczalski, p. 57
– Alkan/Bertha, p. 146
– Karasowski, II, pp. 94–5

Mme Peruzzi recalls Chopin 'calling his left hand his *maître de chapelle* and allowing his right to wander about *ad libitum*.' This corresponds precisely to the impression received by Moscheles (who had a more fundamentally metric conception) on first hearing Chopin: 'His *ad libitum* playing, which with other interpreters of his music tends to degenerate into a mere lack of rhythm [*Taktlosigkeit*], in his hands is the most graceful and original feature of the discourse [. . .] one feels drawn as by a singer who, unpreoccupied with the accompaniment, completely follows his or her feelings' (II, p. 39).

98 . This text and the preceding one (Mathias) are of prime importance. Originating from Chopin's students, they are the only ones that let us assume that his rubato took two different forms, by no means mutually exclusive. Kleczyński was of this opinion (see p. 51 above), followed recently by Higgins (*CI*, p. 94–102). I share this view, with the added nuance that a third component of Chopinian rubato is derived from the mobile rhythm of the Mazur (see pp. 145–6, note 169, pp. 147–8, note 172). The first type of rubato, descended from the Italian Baroque tradition, has been discussed in note 95, (pp. 118–19); it occurs principally in works with broad cantilenas. The second, more common type consists of fleeting changes of pace relative to the basic tempo; these agogic modifications may affect a whole section, period or phrase, slowing down or accelerating the flow depending on the direction of the music. This rubato is to be applied not arbitrarily but as a function of the musical texture and the basic laws of declamation. These agogic fluctuations are called rubato by extension only, since they affect the musical structure from top to bottom, not merely the melodic line. It is not unusual for these nuances of tempo to be specified in Chopin's music. Thus the sections of the Waltz op. 64/2 are differentiated by the indications *tempo giusto – più mosso – più lento – più mosso – tempo I – più mosso*. Within a section the tempo is also to be progressively accelerated, then slowed down, by the indications *agitato – sempre più mosso – calando – smorz. – riten.* (*Ballade* op. 23, bars 40–67) – similarly within a musical period by the complementary coupled indications *stretto – riten.* (*Etude* op. 10/3 bars 7–8, 15–16) or *poco riten. – accel.* (Polonaise op. 26/2 bars 1–6 and similar). The coda of the Mazurka op. 24/4 is a remarkable example of progressive *rallentando* specified by *riten. – calando – mancando – sempre rallent. – smorzando* (bar 129 to end). (On the subject of his musical editing, we may note the growing scarcity of agogic and other expressive markings from op. 25 onwards, as discussed in note 99 immediately below.)

The above considerations merely distinguish the two basic types of rubato employed by Chopin; they cannot by any means convey all the subtle flexibility of movement in his playing, of which we know only that it was conditioned by an acute awareness of the length of the piece and by an internal logic commanding the tempo nuances in relation to the basic pulse.

Koczalski's explanation of rubato (Koczalski, pp. 57–9) – although he himself mastered it to perfection – is unconvincing, which is why it is not quoted here.

99   Chopin ceases in effect to mark the word 'rubato' from op. 24 onwards. (This goes with a parallel progressive decrease in indications of mood or character and metronome markings, very frequent and diversified in his early works, but thereafter tending towards an increasing sobriety visible at all levels of Chopin's musical editing.) Liszt's explanation is convincing: doubtless Chopin realized that the word was insufficient to convey his intentions and could be misleading to his contemporaries – who did indeed criticize his attempts to notate 'to a certain extent' some aspects of 'his rubato' (see *Le Pianiste*, 1834–1835), pp. 78–9, on the subject of his op. 15).

But what meaning (or meanings) does this word have in the thirteen compositions in which it occurs? Does it refer to the Italian vocal tradition, as Kamieński maintains? – or, as Kreutz believes, to both the types described in note 98 above, according to the context? Or rather, as Jadwiga and Marian Sobiescy believe, does it emphasize the mobile agogic rhythm derived from Polish folk melodies? To attempt an answer to this thorny question we have to examine the musical contexts and genres in which this notation is used.

With the exception of the G♯ minor Polonaise [without op. no., *c*. 1823], where the term is used improperly in the final cadences of bars 12 and 27 to indicate an approaching *senza rigore*, the term 'rubato' occurs in two broad types of context:

1*a*   At the beginning of a piece (opp. 15/3; 24/1; 67/3 – in the last case according to the Fontana edition, the manuscript being lost).

1*b*   At the beginning of a new motif which is to direct the piece towards the final cadence (op. 9/2 bar 26).

2*a*   At the repetition of a phrase or half-phrase (op. 6/1 bar 9; op. 6/2 bar 65; op. 7/1 bar 49; op. 7/3 bars 17 and 93; op. 21, finale, bar 173; op. 24/2 bar 29).

2*b*   In the second half – last four bars – of a phrase (op. 8, first movement, bars 22–4 and 159–61; op. 16 bar 132; op. 21, finale, bar 157).

As for the genre of compositions featuring this notation, a good three-quarters of these works are genres connected with Polish folk music. Concerning tempo, all the above-mentioned pieces are in a quick tempo with the exception of the Nocturnes op. 9/2 and 15/3 and Mazurkas op. 24/1 and 67/3. These last three pieces are marked *rubato* at the first bar; thus placed, the indication applies to the entire piece or at least to its first section. It therefore concerns agogic fluctuations, the second type of rubato described in note 98. As for op. 9/2, a perfect example of *bel canto* adapted to the piano, it arises out of the Italian tradition: even if the rubato here is applicable to various other points in the same piece, it belongs essentially to one particular phrase of a more *pathétique* character – to use Tosi's own words. This definition also applies logically to the above-mentioned passages of the Trio op. 8, the Rondo op. 16 and the Concerto op. 21, even though all of these are in a quick tempo: underneath the piano melody, the violin and 'cello parts, or the orchestral parts, bear no mention of rubato but keep the beat. At the same time, the passages marked *rubato* in op. 21 derive directly from the Mazur and so relate also to categories 2*a* and 2*b*, of pieces inspired by the mobile rhythm of Polish folk music (see pp. 145–6 below, note 169). In each case Chopin took the trouble to *notate* a 'rhythmic rubato' (Belotti, *OIRC*, pp. 30–4) in the melodic line; thus the term 'rubato' serves there merely to underline the precise flexibility required for these subtle nuances. This type of 'national' rubato, the third component of Chopinian rubato, is by no means incompatible with that derived from the Italian Baroque: the best Polish folk musicians, in monodic chants, employ the compensatory system (lengthening or shortening one note value to the detriment or gain of the next), while stamping a strict triple metre with the foot. This brings one final point: of the twelve compositions examined, nine are in triple time (op. 8 is in 4/4, op. 9/2 in 12/8 and op. 16 in 2/4); moreover, the Nocturne op. 15/3 features many folkloric characteristics (see p. 153, note 187). This supports an argument in favour of this 'national' rubato having been instinctively applied by Chopin, harmoniously combined in his music with the other two types, each in its context.

If, then, Chopin's rubato may be seen to take diverse meanings, when he marks it explicitly it seems to be the 'national' element that takes precedence. As for the Italian tradition, it evidently applies to works with a broad cantilena, as much in slow tempi as in more restless fiery passages. It is easy to conclude from this that Chopin, after op. 24, renounced the use of a term which he would have had to employ constantly without the slightest assurance of his intentions being correctly understood.

100   Altogether Liszt's poetic evocation alludes to the Italian vocal tradition adapted to the piano by Chopin. This is confirmed in an excerpt from Lachmund's diary (p. 62, on the subject of the sixth of Liszt's *Consolations*): 'On this occasion [Liszt gave us] an important insight into the Lisztian rubato, consisting of subtle variations of tempo and expression within a free declamation, entirely different from Chopin's give-and-take system [*Eilen und Zögern*]. Liszt's rubato is more a sudden, light suspension of the rhythm on this or that significant note, so that the phrasing will above all be clearly and convincingly brought out. While playing, Liszt seemed barely preoccupied with keeping in time, and yet neither the aesthetic symmetry nor the rhythm was affected.'

Towards the end of his description Liszt singles out the Polish students to whom Chopin devoted the greatest care; this might also suggest that Liszt was equally aware of the mobile rhythm of Polish folk music as a component of Chopin's rubato. In fact Chopin readily affirmed that the purely national aspects of his playing and his music tended to escape foreigners: 'When one of his French pupils played his works to the approval of the listeners, Chopin would often remark that the performance had indeed been good but that the *Polish element* and the *Polish inspiration* were lacking' (Karasowski, II, p. 92). This is corroborated by Marie Roubaud: 'He often said that the French did not understand his Mazurkas, and that one had to be Polish to feel the subtleties of the national rhythm, and to render the proper local colour' (Ganche, *DSFC*, p. 86). This is vividly illustrated, too, by Chopin's dispute with Meyerbeer, and by Hallé's and Moscheles's astonishment at the rhythm Chopin imparted to the Mazurkas (see pp. 72–3 above).

101   In the case of the Impromptu op. 29, Kleczyński is probably referring to the two outer sections since the middle section (bars 35–82) does not lend itself to this manner of performance.

102   This expression defies exact translation, so closely does it belong to the essence of German Romanticism: it portrays a kind of breathless and vaguely troubled rhythm. Lenz uses the same expression to characterize the Waltz op. 64/3, declaring it to be the apotheosis of this genre of inspiration in Chopin's music (*UB*, p. 298).

103   This passage again emphasizes Chopin's affinity with Baroque tradition in that it implies a connection between rubato and the improvisation of ornaments, the former being a consequence of the latter – as indeed Tosi specifies; the reference to good taste also tallies with the Italian theoretician. Chopin had already, in his youth, learned the art of ornamenting a cantilena, as is proved by the indication *Simplice, senza ornamenti* heading the theme of the *Variations sur un Air national allemand* [without op. no.]; the presumed autograph of this was copied out for the use of performers other than the composer – hence this heading. The same instruction appears at bar 103 of the Rondo for two pianos, op. posth. 73.

104   See Lenz's comments (pp. 77–8 above) and notes 183–4 (pp. 150–2).

105   This and the two preceding texts (Mikuli, Lenz) indicate that Chopin improvised

ornaments precisely in the two genres where his rubato was at its most characteristic: the Nocturnes (a pianistic stylization of *bel canto* calling for a rubato of the Baroque type, brought about by *fiorituras*) and the Mazurkas (inspired by folkloric elements in which 'national' rubato predominates). These assertions of Lenz, Mikuli and Mikuli/Koczalski are fully corroborated in the ornamental variants passed on by Chopin's pupils or associates, either through the annotated scores of Jane Stirling, Mme Dubois and Ludwika Jędrzejewicz, through Mikuli's edition, or through the reminiscences of Lenz, Tellefsen, Gutmann and Fontana. With the exception of the two small variants for the Concerto op. 11 indicated by Mikuli (first movement, bars 153 and 583), and a *fioritura* (not in any edition) in the same work's slow movement (Stirling score), the ornamental embellishments provided by these sources all affect Nocturnes and Mazurkas: about twenty for the Nocturnes (opp. 9/2, 15/2, 27/2, 32/1, 48/2, 55/2, 62/2 – fourteen of them in op. 9/2, and seven of these near-duplications between different sources), and five for the Mazurkas (three of which are in op. 24/1 and op. 7/2, with one such near-duplication). Four of the five ornamental variations in the Dubois score, almost illegible, remain unpublished (Nocturne op. 32/1 bar 49; Mazurka op. 7/2 bars 23 and 27; Mazurka op. 24/1 bar 60 – see pp. 148–9, note 173).

For the nature of the ornaments introduced in the Nocturnes, see the texts on pp. 77–8 above, and pp. 150–2 notes 183–4. Generally these various *fiorituras* may be considered as representative of Chopin's improvised ornamentation.

106   This art of improvising ornaments in a *cantabile*, still alive in Romantic *bel canto* and in Paganini's violin playing, gradually fell into decline after Hummel or else became stereotyped in the hands of some pianists. These 'small groups of added grace notes, falling like tiny drops of speckled dew over the melodic figure' (Liszt, p. 14) are frequently printed in Chopin's music in small notes which give the impression of improvised ornaments. Here are some examples of these embellishments, minute or luxuriant, whose performance requires both a mastery of the keyboard and the evanescence of spontaneous creativity:

– *Andante spianato* op. 22 bars 17, 41, 43, 49
– Concerto op. 11, first movement, bar 572; slow movement, bars 26 and 58
– Concerto op. 21, first movement, bars 148, 273, 275
– Impromptus: op. 29 bars 45 and 48; op. 36 bars 17, 29, 71
– *Lento con gran espressione* [without op. no.] bars 58–61
– Mazurka op. 17/4 bars 15, 31, 55
– Nocturnes: op. 15/1 bars 20 and 68; op. 15/2 bars 11, 18, 20, 51; op. 32/2 bars 14, 22, 62, 70; op. 37/1 bars 19, 36, 85–6; op. 62/1 bars 26, 71, 73, 75; op. 62/2 bars 25 and 31; op. 72/1 bar 35
– Waltz op. 69/1 – in the autograph written for Maria Wodzińska – the *ossia* versions, bars 11 and 35

One should beware, though, of automatically attributing an *improvisando* style to all ornaments marked in small characters; these are also often used to notate a *gruppetto* or other passages and embellishments containing irregular numbers of notes relative to the time signature. Chopin generally (but not always) notates in ordinary type when the arabesque forms an integral part of the melodic line, or when it enlivens a previously heard melody by repeating or anticipating notes within it (as in the *Berceuse* op. 57), or in the varied reprises (Nocturne op. 15/1 bars 54 and 56; Prelude op. 28/15 bars 4, 23, 79; first and second movements of the Concertos op. 11 and 21, etc.). He also occasionally mixes the two typographic sizes (Nocturne op. 62/2 bar 31); therefore we have to be wary of reading any dogmatic system into his melismatic script.

On the various aspects and components of Chopin's ornamentation (affinities with *bel canto*, influences of Hummel and Field, degree of personal stylization, and connection with improvisation and virtuosity) see Abraham, Belotti (*OIRC*), Branson, Dunn, Eigeldinger (*CHB*), Holcman, Meister, Ottich.

107   Chopin pronounced this piece of aesthetic *credo* on hearing his pupil Friederike Müller (later Mme Streicher) describe her impressions of Liszt's performance at Erard's, on 20 April 1840. This was an important event for two reasons: since his pianistic joust with Thalberg, Liszt had not performed publicly in Paris; also he was now inaugurating the new form of public recital. On this occasion he played his own transcriptions of Beethoven's *Pastoral Symphony* (scherzo, storm, finale), and Schubert's *Ständchen* and *Ave Maria*, as well as his own Fantasia on *Lucia di Lammermoor*, an *Etude transcendante* and his *Grand Galop chromatique*. If Chopin's words betray some irritation with Liszt's prowess, they show even more his aloofness from the Hungarian. Chopin had previously greatly admired Liszt's transcendental playing: 'I am writing without knowing what my pen is scribbling, because at this moment Liszt is playing my studies and putting honest thoughts out of my head: I should like to rob him of the way to play my own studies', he wrote to Ferdinand Hiller (*SC*, p. 117) in 1833, a time when Chopin and Liszt were still friends. By 1840, besides personal reasons distancing him from Liszt, Chopin disapproved of such a great talent being frittered away, as he saw it, on transcriptions and adaptations whose mounting difficulties only detracted from musical clarity: '*ce genre de musique ne lui allait pas*' wrote Mme Dubois (Niecks, II, p. 190). Mathias (p. 5) relates a revealing anecdote in this respect: 'I remember once seeing Chopin in a blue rage over a fermata in Liszt's transcription of *Adelaïde*, a dreadfully platitudinous fermata, a stain deposited by Liszt on Beethoven's marvellous cantilena. Chopin had just received the *Gazette musicale* issue containing this transcription [*RGMP* 1840/12, 9 February] and his anger would not subside, he just could not get over this wretched pause, he railed on and on about it. He seemed to feel a kind of indignant regret towards his former comrade-in-arms.'

A similar incident, though less pronounced, occurred during Chopin's first meeting with Lenz, who, having been asked to play something, decided on the Mazurka op. 7/1, embellishing it with a lengthy ornamental variant invented by Liszt. 'He does have to put his stamp on everything; well, he may, he plays for *thousands* of people and I rarely play for *one*!' (Lenz, *GPV* 1872, p. 35). The words carry some bitterness as well as revealing Chopin's conviction that Liszt was becoming intoxicated with success to the detriment of the '*bon goût*' so prized by the aristocratic Pole. 'Chopin could not bear anyone to interfere with the text of his works. The slightest modification was a gross error for which he would not pardon even his closest friends, not even his fervent admirer Liszt,' reports Marmontel (*PC*, pp. 11–12).

108   Term signifying *levelled*, and therefore equal, smooth, simple. This idea derives from *bel canto*, especially Bellini's, according to Blaze de Bury (p. 112): 'After the vivid and brilliant graces, the glittering colours and the sometimes overloaded ornamentation of Rossini's method, the composer of *Norma* and *I Puritani* introduced a new style of tender cantilena, moving and palpitating – in short, *spianato* singing, as it is called in Italy, in all the eloquence of its expression.' The description applies admirably to the only work by Chopin bearing this indication, the *Andante spianato* op. 22 (*tranquillo*, $\goodbreak \; = 69$, according to the OFE). This type of playing is equally appropriate to other works characterized by a similarly tranquil type of respiration, such as the outer sections of the Nocturnes op. 15/1 and 27/1, of the Prelude op. 28/15, and so on.

Before Chopin, Paganini had already brought these vocal concepts to instrumental music: in 1829 he performed in Leipzig (and probably in Warsaw) a *Cantabile spianato e Polacca brillante* – a combination which surely has some bearing on the curious juxtaposition of the two pieces comprising Chopin's op. 22.

109 Once again the allusion is to pedantically metrical playing where the natural prosodic elements (strong beats, syncopations, etc.) are reinforced at the expense of the musical line. The *Wiener Theaterzeitung* review of Chopin's first Viennese concert is revealing here: 'He accentuates only gently, like a person conversing in the company of cultured people, avoiding that rhetorical aplomb considered indispensable amongst virtuosos.' It then adds a significant reservation about Chopin's 'inobservance of the accent marking the beginning of new musical ideas' (see pp. 288–9 below). In the latter case we may suppose that the accentuation peculiar to Mazovian folk music has something to do with Chopin's individual agogic style.

110 During his first stay in Paris in 1828, Lenz had studied with Liszt, working in particular on Beethoven's Sonata op. 26 (see *B*, pp. 187–9; *GPV* 1872, pp. 22–3). In the autumn of 1842 he re-established contact with Liszt who then introduced him to Chopin.

111 On the subject of Chopin's interpretation of the variations in Beethoven's Sonata op. 26, see Lenz's account, pp. 277–8 below.

112 Kleczyński gives a similar account: 'He himself played his own compositions in different styles, according to the inspiration of the moment, and always charmed his audience' (*FCI*, p. 62). Nothing was more foreign to Chopin's improvisatory genius than a learnt, immutably fixed interpretation. His contemporaries are unanimous in emphasizing this stamp of miraculous spontaneity which characterized his playing and affected his listeners in an absolutely unique way.

These changes of the character, even of the meaning, of a given piece under Chopin's fingers probably came through most in the agogic rhythm, ornamentation and dynamics, but equally in the choice of basic tempo, pedalling and other elements. Undoubtedly the different types of rubato used contributed in various ways to produce these 'thousands of nuances of movement' which so struck Berlioz (see p. 272 below). For variants in ornamentation, see the passages above concerning the Nocturne op. 9/2 and their corresponding notes, also pp. 122–3, note 105. As for changes of dynamics, Hallé's account of the *Barcarolle* op. 60, and the story of Czartoryska/A. Michałowski about the Mazurka in D, op. 33/2, are eloquent. For divergences of tempo and mood indications between autograph sources and first editions, see Higgins, *TCC*. On this subject an ambiguous case is the pencilled *Largo* (Chopin's hand?) replacing the printed *Allegro* in Jane Stirling's score of the Prelude op. 28/14. Is this to be regarded as an alternative possibility, modifying the piece's character (as Ganche interpreted it, printing it in *OXF* as definitive – probably regarding it as an agreement with the existing *pesante*), or was this an instruction specifically for Jane Stirling? I would suggest the latter, seeing the *Largo* as applying to a phase of her piano practice, also since the introduction appears in no other scores of Chopin's pupils and since the autograph indeed specifies the ₵ time signature.

Besides those pedal effects which no written source can convey, Chopin was able to modify his interpretation in many other ways. For instance, the antepenultimate bar of the *Etude* op. 25/2 in the Dubois score is taken up an octave higher than the printed c''' – a variant not listed in Paul Badura-Skoda's *Wiener Urtext* edition of the *Etudes* opp. 10 and 25. The Nocturnes opp. 48/2 (bars 113–14) and 62/2 (bar 68) contain the annotation 8va in the Dubois scores, similarly implying an extension of the arpeggiated figures from the upper octave (see the proposed realization in Jan Ekier's *Wiener Urtext* edition of the Nocturnes, pp. 82 and 104). Jane Stirling's score of the Mazurka op. 7/1 contains, in bars

56–8, an example of the melodic variants which Chopin was wont to introduce at the reprise of a motif. According to Seligmann/Hadden (p. 123), it was this same Mazurka that Chopin encored in Glasgow 'with quite different nuances from those of the first [time]'.

113   Peru experienced this especially with op. 15/2, according to what he told Ludwika Ostrzyńska (p. 3): 'Over six months I played this Nocturne at Chopin's and every time I began to play it as Chopin had shown me at my previous lesson, he would sit down at the piano himself, saying "But it's not that at all!", and he would play it completely differently from the time before.'

114   Chopin's works nevertheless contain both lower and higher dynamic indications than those given by Mikuli:

ppp: *Andante spianato* op. 22 bar 109; Concerto op. 21, finale, bar 315; Nocturnes: op. 9/1 bars 24, 61, 84; op. 9/2 and 9/3, final bar; op. 37/2, penultimate bar; Polonaise op. 26/2, final bar (modified to *fff* in the Stirling score and to *ff* in Jędrzejewicz score); Variations op. 2, end of the Introduction and Var. V bar 10. But one more often finds:

fff: Ballade op. 23 bars 124, 258, 206 (*il più forte possibile*); Concerto op. 11, first movement, bars 473 and 478, finale, bar 411; Concerto op. 21, finale, bar 485; *Etudes*: op. 10/4 bars 70–1 (*con più fuoco possibile*); op. 10/12 bar 83 (autograph); op. 25/10 bar 115 (*il più forte possibile*); op. 25/11 bar 93; op. 25/12 bar 82; Nocturnes: op. 27/1 bars 49 and 81; op. 27/2 bar 46 (Stirling and Jędrzejewicz scores); Polonaises: op. 26/1, bars 3 and 15; op. 26/2 bars 11, 59, 115, 163, 175 (the last in Stirling); op. 40/1 bars 33, 49, 57; op. 40/2, penultimate bar; Scherzos: op. 20 bars 110, 226, 490, 594, 623; op. 39 bar 644; Preludes: op. 28/18 penultimate bar; op. 28/24 bars 61 (autograph) and 73; Sonata op. 35, first movement, bar 240. (Notably, these *ppp* and *fff* indications all affect works published up to 1840.)

Undoubtedly these indications are not meant to have absolute significance. They are relative, and conditioned as much by the instruments at Chopin's disposal (see pp. 91–3, notes 7, 9 and 10) as by his personal range of dynamics. On this last point Moscheles is particularly detailed: *cantabile* being the basis of Chopin's playing, his dynamic range is naturally oriented more towards *p–pp* than towards *f*. This consideration suggested to Badura-Skoda (p. 19) the following table:

(for Chopin)			(for us)
ff	corresponds approximately to		*mf*
f	,,	,,	,, *mp*
p	,,	,,	,, *pp–ppp*
pp	,,	,,	,, almost inaudible

According to his students, however, Chopin's *pp* was always distinct. Apart from that, this table would suggest that we have to banish from modern instruments even the sort of supple *fortissimi* that remain beautiful, elastic and unaggressive. I cannot agree, given Mikuli's and Mathias's categorical statements on the subject. Besides, we have to remember that Chopin himself one day, feeling too weak to play the Scherzo op. 39 the way he wanted for Moscheles, entrusted it to Gutmann (see Moscheles, II, p. 39; Stavenow, pp. 101–2). It seems to me that an authentic interpretation on modern pianos has to take into account Chopin's dynamics while *adapting* them to present pianos, keeping in mind the composer's aesthetic of sonority. In this regard Badura-Skoda's table does act as a judicious warning to many interpreters, including some renowned ones. Here again Koczalski's recordings can serve as a good model.

115   Coming from Gutmann, notorious for his muscular playing, this last assertion is

happily balanced by the following passages from Mathias/Niecks, which are doubtless closer to the truth.

116   Here there is a relevant digression by Michałowski (p. 75), which follows after the passage reproduced on p. 26 above: 'Are we to believe that Chopin, had he known the modern pianoforte, would not have explored all its sonorous effects? According to Mikuli, Chopin had a naturally deep and resonant touch. On today's Bechsteins and Steinways it would certainly suffice to produce the level of *forte* which in former times demanded a forcing of the sound and resulted in an artificial and unpleasant tone.' In their 'humanist' orientation these considerations seem well founded: in the case of Chopin the authenticity of an interpretation goes beyond the instruments he had at his disposal. This said, though, playing on an 1840 Pleyel is a highly educational experience for any interpreter.

117   This refers to Gutmann, whose athletic playing was diametrically opposed to his teacher's conceptions. Lenz (*GPV*, p. 302; *GPV* 1872, p. 47) puts Chopin's blindness down to Gutmann's flourishing health and herculean constitution, which supposedly overawed the composer.

118   Arabella **Goddard** (1836–1922), pianist of English origin; she studied in Paris with Kalkbrenner, then with Thalberg. She then married the music critic James William Davison, author of *An Essay on the Works of Frederic Chopin*, and subsequently an unjust detractor of the composer. In the second half of the nineteenth century, Arabella Goddard made herself famous in England for her interpretation of Beethoven's last sonatas; she gave up her career around 1880.

119   Chopin's dislike of noisy undisciplined playing is amusingly illustrated by the character-sketch in a letter of 25 December 1831: 'If I'm in the middle of a letter I can't bear it when the bell rings and in strides a huge, fully-grown, powerful, bewhiskered creature who sits down at the piano, improvises God knows what, storms, bangs like a madman, writhes about, crosses his hands and hammers on one note for fully five minutes with one enormous finger which Heaven intended for holding the whip and reins of some farm-steward away in the Ukraine – such is the portrait of Sowiński [1805–80] who has no other merits than a good appearance and a kind heart. Never could I have a better opportunity of conceiving what is meant by charlatanism or stupidity in art than just now, when I so often have to listen to him as I move about my room while getting washed. I blush to the ears' (*SC*, p. 107).

120   Hipkins himself heard Chopin only during the latter's stay in London in 1848, at a time when circumstances and failing health no longer let him display all the desired energy. He was able to introduce contrasts into his playing by means of infinite tiny nuances within a limited dynamic range – aptly illustrated by Hallé's description of the performance of the *Barcarolle* op. 60.

Even if Chopin's great physical weakness affected his treatment of the instrument, these extreme refinements of dynamics were nonetheless the result of conscious research dating back to his adolescence. From his very first concert in Vienna (11 August 1829) Chopin was criticized for the delicacy of his touch: 'The general opinion is that I play too quietly, or rather too delicately for those accustomed to the banging of the Viennese pianists [. . .] It doesn't matter. There must always be some kind of "but . . ." and I should prefer it to be that one rather than have it said that I play too loudly' (*SC*, p. 25; see also *CFC*, I, pp. 127 and 146–7). So his choice was deliberate from the start; subsequently this 'small sonority', much admired by musicians, was to become the critics' leitmotif, from the *Wiener Theaterzeitung* of 1829 to the British journals of 1848. Fétis noted in 1832: 'He draws little sound from the instrument' (see p. 290 below). Three years later a little-known review reported: 'in a duo for two pianos, played by the composer and M. Chopin, we once again had occasion to observe M. Hiller's qualities, though they came together with a few faults not worth mentioning here; we should add, however, that M. Chopin was not heard sufficiently and that many details of his part must have been lost to the listeners. M. Chopin's otherwise perfect talent is so delicate, so full of imperceptible nuances which only a sensitive and trained ear can discern, that in our opinion it is not to his advantage to be heard together with someone else' (*Le Pianiste* 1835/9, p. 69). Finally, there is the pianist Marmontel's brief comment (*HP*, p. 254): 'I heard Chopin during his first year in Paris, and his playing already had an exquisite beauty, a natural sensitivity, a suave, hazy sonority based essentially on the delicacy of his touch and his quite individual use of the pedals.'

In 1842, at the height of Chopin's career, Lenz (*GPV* 1872, p. 39) criticized his teacher for not defining the outlines more vigorously in the variations of Beethoven's Sonata op. 26 (in A♭, a key beloved of Chopin): '"I indicate", replied [Chopin] without a trace of touchiness, "it's up to the listener to complete [*parachever*] the picture"' – a revealing insight into an art of nuance based on an aesthetic of suggestion, and opening the way to musical impressionism, to whose advent Chopin contributed more than anyone else. Many gems in his Mazurkas already indicate this tendency, such as the ritornello (with the astonishing pedalling indicated in the OFE) at the beginning and the end of the mazurka in the *Andante spianato* op. 22, the coda of the Nocturne op. 27/2, the Prelude op. 28/21, the Nocturne op. 37/2, the 3 *Nouvelles Etudes* [without op. no.]; even more the Prelude op. 45 and the *Ballade* op. 47. From op. 52 onwards the musical texture, progressively tighter and more complex, becomes a more and more intimate reflection of Chopin's pianism. This evolution, anticipating Debussy – to mention only the standard model of musical 'impressionism' – is a vast subject, impossible to pursue here. But we may remember the veneration in which the composer of *Pelléas* held the Polish master, his careful editing of Chopin's works for the Durand edition in 1914–15, his own *Douze Etudes* of 1915 dedicated to Chopin's memory, and his declaration of having 'worn down his fingers' [*s'être usé les doigts*] (M. Long, p. 37) on the third (A♭ major) of the 3 *Nouvelles Etudes* (his own *Etude* no. IV, 'Pour les sixtes', bears this out firmly in bars 21ff). As for Debussy's playing, his publisher describes it thus: 'A full sonority, a remarkable delicacy, a perfect mastery of *nuance*, an impeccable finish, an imperceptible rubato always framed within the beat, an astounding use of pedal: all this was what defined Debussy's playing' (Durand, II, p. 21). Were this passage taken out of context with Debussy's name omitted, one would almost certainly attribute the description to Chopin's playing!

Back on the subject of the scale of nuances, Emma Debussy-Bardac left a valuable comment: 'Debussy like Chopin nearly always played in a perpetual *demi-teinte*, but nevertheless with a full, deep sonority without any hardness in the attack. The scale of *nuances* must go from triple *piano* to [triple?] *forte*, without ever producing confused sounds where the subtlety of the harmonies is lost' (Janine-Weill, p. 87). We know, too, how attached Debussy was to his upright Bechstein with its supple and obedient keys – precisely the qualities Chopin prized in Pleyel instruments.

121   But we know also that Chopin made frequent and very refined use of the pedal: 'Chopin, on the contrary, while making constant use of the pedal, obtained ravishing harmonies, melodic whispers that charmed and astonished,' relates Marmontel (*PC*, pp. 4–5). So how are we to interpret the above *caveat*? – is it directed at those who abuse the pedals to produce a sound too rich in overtones, or at those who resort to it to conceal a lack of finger *legato*? Or does it refer to certain stages of study, not necessarily to be

applied to the final result? The comments of Courty/Aguettant suggest this last sense, supported (though less concretely) by Debussy* (p. 150): 'I have very precise recollections of what Mme Mauté de Fleurville told me. [Chopin] wanted his pupils to practise without the pedal, and, except on very rare occasions, to avoid its use altogether. Besides, it's this art of using the pedal as a kind of *respiration* that I noticed in Liszt's playing, when I had the chance of hearing him in Rome.' It seems, then, that Chopin's warning stems from his Classical instincts and from an anxiety that the multiple iridescences of his own playing should not be exaggerated. 'The way he used the pedal was a revelation,' reported Mathias (Schelling, p. 70) – a report that reveals not only the pedal's possibilities in tone colouring, but also in agogics, since the pedal helps give life to a phrase and to define its outline (the *respiration* which Debussy mentions?). If today we have to imagine these sound effects from the past, there is still one source that gives a partial graphic indication of them: the most carefully detailed of Chopin's manuscripts (intended for engraving) where the pedalling is very precisely indicated – in relation, be it remembered, to the instrument he used. Unfortunately the first editions and today's critical editions do not always reproduce it exactly (the Henle and Wiener Urtext editions are the most accurate in this respect). Higgins (*CI*, pp. 66–76) has studied the pedal markings as they appear in the autograph facsimiles published by PWM (edited by Hordyński); his conclusions, drawn mostly from examination of opp. 28, 31, 38, 47 and 54, are thus not exhaustive nor exempt from some over-generalizations and debatable interpretations. Higgins summarizes Chopin's characteristic uses of the pedal in the following points:

1   Chords with or without pedal
2   Pedal in scales and diatonic passages
3   Pedal in sounds foreign to the harmony
4   Pedal blurring together harmonies of different function
5   Variations of pedalling between similar or identical passages within one work
6   Application and release of pedal independently of phrase marks
7   Juxtaposition of pedalled and unpedalled passages within a work
8   Absence of pedal when the writing indicates one predominant voice, and in 'solo' passages
9   Use of pedal during rests
10   Omission, at the end of a piece, of the sign indicating release of the pedal.

(Other cases may be imagined, such as the absence of *una corda*, the almost total absence of pedal markings in polyphonic passages, etc.) The urgent question arises of how to adapt these indications to modern instruments, whose louder and more sustained sonority can overload Chopin's calculated effects. A single example of this illustrates point 3 above: the autograph of the Prelude op. 28/15 indicates the pedal for the whole of bar 1 and its repetitions in bars 5, 20, 24 and 80, but not for the return of the same motif

---

* Mme Mauté, Debussy's first teacher, claimed to have studied with Chopin, although there is no known documentation sufficient to prove or disprove this. Her daughter Mathilde (ex-Mme Paul Verlaine) later wrote: 'My grandmother made [my mother] take lessons with Chopin who perfected her talent; it was with the composer himself that she learnt to play his Polonaises and Impromptus so beautifully' (*Mémoires de ma vie* (Paris, Flammarion, 1935), p. 56). However, these memoirs are too full of name-dropping and dubieties for this passage to be accepted as indisputable. In his monograph on Debussy, Dietschy (pp. 22–3) denies the Chopin–Mauté link without offering any real supporting argument. Lockspeiser (I, pp. 19–22) suspends judgment, while Belotti (*FCU*, II, pp. 1069–70 and note 40) is more certain. Whatever the answer, Debussy's fleeting reminiscences on his lessons from Mme Mauté are in no way contradictory with Chopin's teaching. One fact remains certain, that Marmontel was Debussy's teacher at the Paris Conservatoire.

after the second section, bar 76, where the pedal is to be raised on the fourth beat. It is evident there that Chopin intends two different treatments. On an 1840 Pleyel the sound clears more rapidly and the melodic move to B♭ colours it without however affecting its clarity, whereas on a modern piano it blurs the harmony. Renewing the pedal just before the fourth beat would effectively negate Chopin's intention of reserving this effect for bar 76; so we are left with the possibility of a half-pedal, more practicable on modern pianos than on old ones. Exact knowledge of Chopin's pedal markings (the *Barcarolle* op. 60 and the *Polonaise-Fantaisie* op. 61 are particularly complete examples) is therefore indispensable for its adaptation to modern pianos, as it also is for the performer's own conception.

One last remark: the CW editors (I, p. 69) observe judiciously that 'The passages in which Chopin has not marked the pedalling are most often explained by the fact that the required pedalling is very simple, and is therefore self-evident; or, on the contrary, that it is so subtle as to be too complicated, if not impossible, to indicate.' The latter case seems to be illustrated in the *Etudes* op. 10/2, 6 and 7; op. 25/10 (outer sections); *Etude* in A♭ from 3 *Nouvelles Etudes*; Preludes op. 28/2 and 14; finale of the Sonata op. 35. I also suggest that the absence of pedal markings can equally signify in some cases that the passage is to be played practically without pedal: the *Andante spianato* op. 22, bars 67–95, and the outer sections of the Nocturne op. 15/1.

122   This injunction is implicitly corroborated in Chopin's rather cutting criticism that Thalberg 'produces *piano* with the pedal instead of with the hand' (*SC*, p. 76).

To my knowledge, no autograph or original edition of Chopin contains the instruction *una corda* or *u.c.* (with the exception of some annotations in the Nocturne op. 15/2; see p. 152, note 186). At first sight this seems the more surprising since the last Beethoven sonatas abound in indications of the type *una corda – poco a poco tutte le corde* (op. 101); *poco a poco due e poi tre corde – una corda – tutte le corde* (op. 106), etc. But, aside from the fact that Chopin probably did not play these works, they were written for instruments equipped with a more complex assembly of pedals than post-1830 Pleyel grands, limited to the two pedals familiar today (regarding pedal mechanisms of eighteenth and nineteenth century pianos, see Harding, pp. 69–72 and *passim*; Hirt, pp. 119–24 and *passim*). From the accounts of Courty/Aguettant, Marmontel and Kleczyński it appears that Chopin made frequent, highly diversified and refined use of the soft pedal and that he resorted to it not merely to soften the sound but more for its quality of *timbre*, in the manner of a registration. This probably explains his advice: 'You can add it later.' Chopin probably considered the coloration provided by *una corda* a matter of personal interpretation, and judged it better not to specify it in his music – again revealing a Classical type of thinking in the editing of his own music. But as far as we can tell from contemporary accounts, Chopin's use of pedal opened the way for Debussy, who took particular pleasure in what he called *l'alchimie sonore*: 'Like Chopin, too, Debussy had a preoccupation with the role of the pedal, and wrote on the subject to his publisher [Jacques Durand], who remembers the dazzling use Debussy made of it, especially in mixing and contrasting the *ff* and *pp* pedals' (M. Long, p. 75).

123   For information on the mechanism and sound quality of the *una corda* in Pleyel pianos of the time, see Marmontel, *HP*, pp. 355–6.

124   **Marmontel**, Antoine-François (1816–98); pianist, teacher and writer on music. He succeeded his teacher Zimmermann in taking the advanced classes at the Paris Conservatoire, where for forty years he was the conscientious guide of generations of pianists (Bizet, Planté, Diémer, d'Indy, Albéniz and Debussy were among his most renowned pupils). Marmontel did not study with Chopin but did hear him often from

1832 on; subsequently he lived very near the composer's home at the Square d'Orléans (see *HP*, p. 251). Marmontel's ear promptly discerned the characteristics of Chopin's playing; he published four volumes of selected Chopin works (*Oeuvres choisies*) as part of his *Ecole classique du piano* (Paris, Heugel, [1859]). The famous oil portrait of Chopin by Delacroix belonged to Marmontel before his son Antonin Marmontel bequeathed it to the Louvre.

125   Both op. 15/1 and the mazurka within the *Andante spianato* op. 22 (bars 67–96) bear the indication *semplice*. The OFE (no autographs are known) gives only very sparse pedal markings in the first instance and none in the second; the same applies to the outer sections of the Mazurka in C op. 33/3, also marked *semplice*. Kleczyński's assertions in this passage are confirmed by no other known source. I believe the author is quoting information from Czartoryska, Dubois and Mathias (who all prefaced the French edition of *FCI*) rather than just stating personal views.

126   This type of notation is somewhat rare in Chopin; it appears notably in the *Allegro de concert* op. 46 bars 130 and 206, in the Mazurka op. 7/1 bar 50, in the Nocturne op. 62/1 bars 68ff (succession of trills), and in the Polonaise op. 53 bars 33, 34, 37, 38, 65, 66, 69, 70, 155, 156, 159 and 160. The reading suggested by Viardot/Saint-Saëns is certainly correct; it is contrary to the assertions by Dunn (pp. 1, 23) but in agreement with the editors of the *CW* (I, p. 70). From Viardot/Saint-Saëns's account – confirmed by Mikuli – it emerges that in the *majority* of cases Chopin began the trill on the *auxiliary note*, upper or lower. Here again he follows the Baroque and Classical tradition; the less conservative Hummel (pp. 403–4) preferred to abandon the old singing principles applied to the keyboard and begin the trill on the principal note.

Chopin's notation and the indications or fingerings marked in his students' scores suggest the following three categories:

   1. *Trill beginning on the upper auxiliary note:*
as indicated by Chopin's notation in the Nocturne op. 62/1 bar 74, and by the fingering in the OFE for the *Barcarolle* op. 60 bars 23–4. The annotations on the Dubois score also specify this reading: Concerto op. 21, first movement, bar 87, where the trill, preceded by a crossed appoggiatura on the upper major second, is marked $\widehat{1\ 3}$; similarly the *Etude* op. 25/7 bars 7, 37, 51 (no fingering) and the Nocturne op. 62/2 bar 69, where the *f♯'* is preceded by an appoggiatura *g♯'*.

This way of performing is specified elsewhere by Chopin's notation: *Barcarolle* op. 60 bars 70–1; Nocturne op. 62/1 bar 67, etc. It may also apply in places where the *tr* sign is over the principal note not preceded by a grace note: Waltz op. 34/3 bars 95 and similar, etc.

   2. *Trill beginning on the lower auxiliary note:*
the trill preceded by two grace notes, the former on the lower second, the latter on the same as the principal note, and terminating with the same notes. In many cases of notes below the trilling pitch, Chopin specifies that the first grace note should be played simultaneously with the bass: *Allegro de concert* op. 46 bars 53, 136, 212; Concerto op. 21, first movement, bar 97; Nocturne op. 32/1 bars 40 and 61. In the last case the Dubois score joins the first note of the trill to the bass with a vertical line. It is exactly this that demonstrates Chopin's affinity with Baroque practice: the notation corresponds exactly to the ornament called *Doppelt-Cadence und Mordant* by J. S. Bach in his *Explication unterschiedlicher Zeichen* . . . prefacing the *Clavier-Büchlein* for Wilhelm Friedemann. The Dubois score specifies this same ornament in the Nocturne op. 32/2 for the trill in bars 8 and similar:

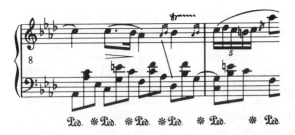

This is Chopin's most frequently used trill notation. It appears in the *Barcarolle* op. 60 bars 17, 19 and 106; Concertos: op. 11, first movement, bars 404–6 and 614; op. 21, slow movement, bars 7, 10, 25, 29, 78; Impromptu op. 36 bar 19; Mazurka op. 59/1 bars 8 and similar; Nocturnes: op. 32/2 bar 72; op. 37/1 bars 8 and similar; op. 48/2 bars 117–8, 131–4; op. 55/1 bars 14, 30, 46; op. 55/2 bar 1; Preludes: op. 28/9 bars 3 and 4; op. 28/24 bars 10 and 28; Sonata op. 35, 'Funeral March', bars 19–20 and similar; Waltz op. 34/3 bar 93; Variations op. 2, Introduction, bar 11. Although the performance specified in the music example above may not be suitable for some successions of trills, it is applicable to most of the cases mentioned above, also in several places in the Nocturnes where the Dubois score has a written grace note on the lower second preceding a *tr*, followed by a termination: Nocturnes: op. 15/2 bars 7, 15, 55, 56; op. 55/1 bar 6. The same applies to the Nocturne op. 9/2 bars 7 and 15, where the Dubois and Franchomme scores both carry this indication (bar 7 only in the Stirling score):

In his recording of this piece (see pp. 151–2 below, note 184) Koczalski plays the trill as indicated above, making the auxiliary note coincide with the bass – proof that this tradition was maintained through some of the pupils of Chopin's own pupils.

3. *Trill beginning directly on the principal note:*
as indicated by certain fingerings in the scores of students and associates, or as demanded by a musical context. This occurs in the Mazurka op. 7/1 bar 3, where the fingering specified is 3 5 (Jędrzejewicz); the Prelude op. 28/18, bar 18, r.h., 1 3 2 (Dubois); the Waltz op. 34/2 bar 5, 1 2 (Stirling); the Waltz op. 42 bar 1, 2 4 (Dubois) – by analogy the same would apply in the Waltz op. 64/1 bars 69ff.

In the Mazurka op. 30/4 bars 39 and similar, the trill begins on the principal note which is accented (in spite of the grace note preceding the g♯': an exceptional case according to Viardot/Saint-Saëns). In the Mazurka op. 68/2 bars 1 and similar, the trill is to begin directly on the d♯''', otherwise the characteristic augmented fourth would not form a dissonance with the bass.

Generally one has to be wary of hard and fast rules for trills in Chopin, but keep in mind that in most cases they should begin on an auxiliary note struck together with the bass. A comparison of similar notations used by Chopin in various contexts usually helps to show which of the above-mentioned categories applies.

127 A revealing passage from one of Chopin's letters describes Konstancja Gładkowska's singing in Rossini's *La Gazza Ladra*: 'She is admirable when she sings:

She does not clip it short like Mme Mayer, but gives the notes their full value:

i.e. not rapid *gruppetti*, but every one of the eight notes fully sung' (*SC*, p. 59). In order to give the *gruppetto* its full expressive value, and to specify the performance he has in mind, Chopin much prefers to write it out in full – in small or large characters – rather than use the customary signs ⌣ or ~.

In a similar way the Nocturnes, compositions of an essentially vocal character, present only four examples of the notation ~ (op. 9/2 bars 2 and 26; op. 27/2 bar 7; op. 32/2 bars 5 and similar) as against dozens of examples where the *gruppetto* is written out in full: op. 9/2 bars 10, 18, 27, 30; op. 15/1 bars 14, 18 and similar; op. 27/1 bars 22 and 89; op. 32/1 bars 4, 7 and similar, 16, 28 and similar; op. 32/2 bars 9 and similar; op. 37/1 bars 1 and similar (to be started simultaneously with the bass third beat, according to the Dubois score), 10, 12 and similar; op. 48/1 bar 15; op. 55/2 bars 30, 32, 33, 41, 49 (in the last case to be started simultaneously with the bass *c'*, according to the Dubois score); op. 62/1 bar 12; op. 62/2 bar 13 (to be started simultaneously with the bass, according to the Dubois score). See also the Concertos: op. 11, first movement, bars 168, 523, 618; op. 21, first movement, bars 142, 207, 211, 290; Preludes: op. 28/15 bars 11, 15, 17; op. 28/21 bar 12; Waltz op. 69/1 bars 7 and similar (autograph version intended for Maria Wodzińska), and many other examples.

When combined with other *fiorituras* or passing notes, a *gruppetto* is even more logically written out in full: Nocturnes: op. 15/1 bars 20, 54, 68; op. 15/2 bars 10, 12, 22, 50; op. 27/2 bar 50; op. 32/2 bars 6 and similar, 14 and similar. See also Concerto op. 21, first movement, bar 273; Impromptu op. 29 bars 45 and 48, etc.

128 In the Dubois score an appoggiatura is frequently linked by a line to the corresponding bass-note, indicating that the appoggiatura is to be played on the beat. Some examples:
 – Single appoggiatura
    Barcarolle op. 60 bar 34, first beat; Concerto op. 11, first movement, bar 403; Nocturnes: op. 15/2 bars 12 and 52; op. 27/2 bar 66; op. 48/1 bar 20; Prelude op. 28/13, bar 9
 – Appoggiatura in double notes and chords
    Barcarolle op. 60 bar 51; *Berceuse* op. 57 bar 31; Concerto op. 11, first movement, bar 255; Mazurka op. 24/4 bars 24 and 32; Nocturnes: op. 27/2 bars 12, 33, 36; op. 48/1 bar 67

– Groups of appoggiatura notes

Ballade op. 47 bars 116, 118, 120, 122, 231, 233; Concerto op. 21, slow movement, bars 7, 9, 26, 75; Impromptu op. 29 bars 58 and 74; Mazurka op. 33/3 bar 33; Nocturnes: op. 9/2 bars 13 and 21; op. 15/1 bar 49; op. 15/2 bar 8 (with a manuscript appoggiatura anticipating the low r.h. *a♯*, to be sounded together with the bass); op 37/1 bars 5 and 21, third beat; bars 37–8:

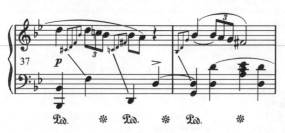

op. 48/1 bar 10; op. 48/2 bar 123

This way of giving the appoggiatura its full worth and, in certain cases, of augmenting the harmonic tension, is again related to the aesthetic of *bel canto* and its instrumental application in the Baroque era.

Note 82 (pp. 113–15 above) has shown the appoggiatura that pianistically stylizes the vocal '*portamento*' properly called *cercar della nota*.

In slow to moderate tempi Chopin still makes use of the long appoggiatura, indicated by a small uncrossed crotchet, which figures notably in the Concerto op. 21, first movement, bar 208, and in the Preludes op. 28/13 bars 7 and 9 (coinciding with the first beat of the bass part, according to the Dubois score); op. 28/15 bars 39 and 55 (altered to a crossed appoggiatura in CW, I, p. 36). When this appoggiatura appears in the melodic line (op. 21; op. 28/13 bar 7), there is reason to assume that it usually takes half the value of the note which it precedes.

129 **Reber**, Henri (1807–80): composer, theoretician and teacher. His *Traité d'harmonie* (Paris, Colombier, 1862) is still used, though his compositions (comic operas, ballets, symphonies, chamber music, songs) have fallen into oblivion. Chopin must have admired Reber for his formal classicism, which issued directly from the Viennese school, Rejcha having been his teacher. Of Chopin's pupils Reber taught composition to, among others, Mikuli and Tellefsen. He orchestrated the 'Funeral March' of the Sonata op. 35 for Chopin's funeral ceremony in the Madeleine; the manuscript score of this unpublished orchestration is now in *F-Pn*: Mss. 10471–10472. According to a letter from Grzymała (*SC*, pp. 374–5), one of Chopin's last requests (unfulfilled) was that his *PM* be bequeathed to Alkan and Reber. Marmontel (*PC*, p. 122) also recalls: 'When Chopin died, many of his dearest pupils chose Alkan to continue the late master's tradition.'

130 Chopin's indications to Lenz about the structure and style of the Nocturne op. 9/2 (see pp. 77–8 above) are a vivid example of these analytic precepts. Fontana/Kleczyński's remarks (see above) about the Nocturne op. 27/2 follow a similar line of thought.

131 That is, commencing with studies involving many black keys (thus in keys with many sharps or flats), and finishing with C major.

132 This study appears in pp. 34–5 of the one-volume Peters edition. In the older two-volume edition it formed the first study of the second volume.

133 Chopin frequently used this image to describe the abruptness of an uncontrolled sound; it is quoted also by A. Michałowski (see p. 56 above).

134 Cramer's name hardly appears in any other account. It appears in one of Chopin's letters of 1830 from Warsaw (*CFC*, I, p. 161) with reference to a lesson, and in Friederike Streicher's memoirs, but only at second hand: 'In Paris people had made me afraid, and told me how Chopin caused Clementi, Hummel, Cramer, Moscheles, Beethoven, and Bach to be studied, but not his own compositions' (Niecks, II, p. 341). If Clementi seems to occupy a primary place in the repertoire of studies prescribed to Chopin's students, Cramer does not. In his catalogue of the teaching works used by Chopin, Mikuli grades them in order of difficulty; Cramer comes first on the list and was therefore probably reserved for the less advanced players – which serves to indicate the general standard among students who approached Chopin.

Liszt says of Kessler's *Etudes*: 'Chopin and I had a special liking for them in the thirties' (Jerger, p. 143). No pupil of Chopin mentions them, however.

135 Of the contemporary authors of pedagogical piano compositions, Chopin gives his preference to Moscheles (see note 171, below). Mikuli's word is corroborated by Bedřich Thun-Hohenstein (Simonides, p. 77), Mme Rubio (Niecks, II, p. 189), Solange Sand (*CGS*, VII, p. 9) and Mathias (p. 6) who relates: 'He accepted me, telling me to begin with Moscheles's *Etudes* (Chopin himself played the third one of the second book wonderfully [no. 15 in A♭ from op. 70]) and the Concerto in A minor (Hummel's, naturally).'

136 Mikuli is the only one to give this information, which lays it open to doubt. Among Bach's harpsichord works – with the exception of one Concerto for three keyboards (probably *BWV* 1063) from which he performed an Allegro with Liszt and Hiller on 15 December 1833 – the '*48*' is the only work Chopin is positively known to have played – and how! Only exceptionally would the Suites appear in a programme of study. The Romantics (Beethoven, Moscheles, Mendelssohn, Schumann, Liszt, etc.) traditionally used the Fugues of the '*48*' for developing polyphonic playing; many of them are included for this purpose in piano methods of the time (Adam, Fétis–Moscheles, etc.). Nonetheless, Chopin certainly knew other of Bach's works, scattered among various anthologies – Clementi's and others. The opening theme in the first movement of Chopin's Sonata op. 4 is based on the main motif of Bach's (two-part) Invention no. 2.

As for the Partitas and the English and French Suites, they were then accessible in the Peters collected edition, in the new Peters edition revised by Czerny, and in France in the *Collection complète pour le piano des oeuvres de J.-S. Bach* (Paris, Launer, 1843, 10 vols, also edited by Czerny).

137 This is not the place to expound upon the immense and constant influence of Bach on Chopin, whom Liszt described as an 'enthusiastic pupil of Bach' (Niecks, I, p. 30). But we may note that Chopin's long preoccupation with the '*48*' is reflected in both his musical and aesthetic ideals, in his work as both composer and teacher. Regarding this aspect of his general aesthetic see Liszt (pp. 187–99), George Sand (*HV*, II, pp. 421–2; *Impressions et souvenirs*, pp. 80–1) and above all Delacroix's *Journal* (I, pp. 283–4), which relates a famous conversation on counterpoint, and notes elsewhere: 'My dear little Chopin took up the cudgels strongly against the school that regards part of music's beauty as coming from the sonority' (III, p. 99; see also III, p. 290). This effectively sets Bach up against Berlioz! As for the Leipzig Kantor's influence on Chopin's writing, already perceptible in his Sonata op. 4, it asserts itself continually in the independence of the melodic lines weaving through his polyphony, culminating in the imitative passages, canons and fugatos of his last works; the Sonata op. 65 is its high point.

In his piano practice Chopin regarded the '*48*' as his daily bread. It was the only score he took with him to Majorca; several months later in Nohant, he corrected the misprints in his Parisian edition (*SC*, pp. 181–2; *CFC*, II, pp. 283 and 349). His answer to Lenz, when the latter asked him how he prepared for concerts, speaks for itself: 'For a fortnight I shut myself up and play Bach. That's my preparation, I don't practise my own compositions' (Lenz, *GPV* 1872, p. 36). Friederike Streicher in turn relates: 'One morning he played from memory fourteen Preludes and Fugues of Bach's, and when I expressed my joyful admiration at this unparalleled performance, he replied: "Cela ne s'oublie jamais"' (Niecks II, p. 341). Finally Jane Stirling, returning to the piano a year after the death of her teacher, wrote: 'I started with some Bach Preludes, as he always advised' (Ganche, *DSFC*, p. 123). There are many other sources similarly demonstrating Chopin's veneration for Bach, and the important place he gave it in his teaching.

138   That is, at their first lessons with Chopin. As a rule Chopin did not teach children or beginners.

139   This passage corroborates Mathias who, however, lists Field instead of Hummel. The latter took a larger place than Field in the repertoire studied by Mme Dubois (see pp. 61–2).

140   That is, in the course of thirty-three lessons taken by this pupil (see *List of Chopin's pupils*, pp. 164–6 below).

141   That is, in the course of eighteen lessons taken by this pupil (see *List of Chopin's pupils*, p. 178 below).

142   To this list, the most complete we possess, can be added almost the totality of Chopin's works studied under his direction by Mme Dubois, as her annotated scores show, together with a handwritten note from Julien Tiersot by way of a posthumous confirmation (see p. 212 below). Mme Dubois's list is of exceptional documentary value, as much for its detailed character as for the personality of its author, Chopin's best French pupil, whom he taught over a period of five years (see *List of Chopin's pupils*, p. 164 below).

Mikuli's catalogue is less helpful: his Preface mentions Clementi, *Mozart*, Bach, *Handel*, *Scarlatti*, *Dussek*, Field, Hummel, *Ries*, Beethoven, Weber, Moscheles, Mendelssohn, Hiller, *Schumann* and Chopin (the names italicized here are not corroborated by any other sources). In this case one fears Mikuli's memory may have been defective, and that his list became confused with names of composers whose works he himself had taught, without necessarily having studied them with Chopin (or heard Chopin teaching them).

As for Mozart, Niecks had already observed (II, p. 189) that no pupil (except Mikuli) claimed to have worked with Chopin on any Mozart compositions. The gap is puzzling; could the veneration in which Chopin held Mozart have prevented him from entrusting Mozart's music to his own students – was he afraid his pupils would betray its stylistic purity? – or alternatively, might all his pupils except Mikuli simply have forgotten to mention Mozart? It is difficult to answer. On the other hand we know that Chopin listened respectfully to the remarks of Camille Pleyel, who had learnt the Viennese tradition from his father. Legouvé (I, p. 375) relates a little-known statement: 'Chopin often said, "There is only one man today who knows how to play Mozart, that's Pleyel, and when he feels like playing a duet sonata with me, it's a lesson for me."' In fact Pleyel was renowned in Parisian musical milieux for his playing of the Viennese masters, as Marmontel describes (*VC*, p. 141): 'I'll repeat that through his father, Ignaz Pleyel, the famous and very popular composer of chamber music, for years the favourite pupil and lodger of Haydn; through the special training he received from the most famous teachers; through his artistic contacts and a life entirely spent in exceptionally musical surroundings: through all these Camille Pleyel had acquired a truly extraordinary knowledge of the traditions, style and methods particular to each renowned master.'

As for Handel and Domenico Scarlatti, we are reduced to conjecture. We know from a letter (*SC*, p. 17) of Chopin's early enthusiasm for the *Ode for Saint Cecilia's day* which he heard in the Singakademie during his journey to Berlin in September 1828. He reacted similarly seven years later when Mendelssohn (II, p. 100–1) showed him the splendid volumes of Handel's music which he had just received. The harpsichord fugues are extensively represented in Clementi's anthology (*Selection of Practical Harmony for the Organ or Pianoforte*, London, printed by Clementi, [1801], repub. 1833, 4 vols) which Chopin certainly knew. Scarlatti's music he may have known from the edition of 200 sonatas published by Czerny (Vienna, T. Haslinger, [1839]).

Dussek and Ries do seem to be two cases that probably figured in Mikuli's teaching rather than in Chopin's; true, there is a mention of the *Trois Sonates* op. 19 by Dussek written on a score in the Zaleska-Rosengardt collection (see p. 235 below), but since it is not in Chopin's writing it proves nothing here. (Some of Dussek's sonatas suggest a possible influence on Chopin.)

The name of Hiller – dedicatee of the Nocturnes op. 15 – is mentioned only in Streicher's account (Niecks, II, p. 341) – which adds also Thalberg and Liszt, in partial contradiction of Mme Dubois. Mme Dubois in turn is firm about Schumann – that Chopin never set her any of Schumann's music to study (see pp. 138–9 below, note 148).

Speaking elsewhere of Chopin's repertoire (p. 3), Mikuli specifies: 'Of the virtuoso music of the kind that was running pianistic riot at the time, I hardly ever saw any on his desk.' Such an affirmation must go even more for Chopin's teaching, and it finds some confirmation in Mme Dubois's comment about Liszt's transcriptions that '*ce genre de musique ne lui allait pas.*' It could happen, though, that Chopin would stretch his principles to allow a pupil who so desired to study some novelty then in vogue. This might explain Thalberg's name in Streicher's memoirs, as well as those of Herz, Pixis and Hünten in other little known or unpublished documents. An autograph note (now in the Vienna Gesellschaft der Musikfreunde) sent to the Thun-Hohenstein sisters reads: '<u>H.</u> <u>Herz.</u> La dernière pensée de Weber. Variations br[illantes op. 51] en la♭ m[ajeur]. C^sse Juža'; on the verso in the hand of J. Thun: 'Chopin Paris November 1834'. A second note, previously unpublished, specifies the following programme for the two sisters:

<u>Hummel.</u> Nocturne à 4 mains [op. 99] C^sse Juža.

_____. Sonata en <u>mi</u> ♭ à 4 mains [op. 51] C^sse Anna.

<u>Pixis.</u> Robert le diable à 4 mains C^sse Juža.

<u>Moscheles.</u> Rondo brillant en <u>la</u> majeur [piano duet, op. 30] C^sse Anna.

(This document was kindly made available by the antiquarian H. Schneider of Tutzing/ Munich.) Another note – not in *SC* or *CFC* – addressed by Chopin to an assistant of the publisher Schlesinger reads: 'Kindly send me the Variations by <u>Hunten</u> on <u>Il Pirata</u> (piano duet)' (Nicolas Rauch Catalogue, no. 13 of the new series *Autographes. Vente aux enchères à Genève* (23 November 1955), p. 31, No. 118 and Plate 9).

To sum up, if Mikuli's catalogue requires to be treated with some caution, Mme Dubois's list gains in reliability, if one remembers that it is not complete. While it is certain that Chopin made all his regular pupils study a certain number of key works, like all teachers he would flexibly adapt a variable repertoire to the needs and capabilities of each pupil, a repertoire whose broad outlines we now know.

143 Another pupil, Emilie von Gretsch, who played much Beethoven for Chopin, studied, notably, the Sonata op. 31/2 (Grewingk, p. 10); Lenz (*B*, pp. 306–7) heard Chopin playing the Sonata op. 14/2, which Lenz may then have been studying with Chopin. Early in 1844, that is, while he was probably still Chopin's pupil, Georges Mathias performed in public the first movement of the 'Emperor' Concerto (*RGMP*, 1844/8, 25 February, p. 68). He may therefore have studied it with Chopin. Delacroix also wrote from Nohant:

'Chopin played me some Beethoven divinely' (*CFC*, III, p. 237; 19 August 1846), and, eight years later in his *Journal*, again referring to Beethoven: 'Why not play these beautiful concertos, like the one to which Chopin introduced me?' (II, p. 161, 9 April 1854).

These statements add, even if only a little, to our knowledge on the subject, since Lenz (*GPV* 1872, p. 40) maintains that Chopin was not familiar with Beethoven's last works, and Liszt recalls Chopin's unfavourable reaction to op. 106 one day when he played it for him in Paris (Stradal, p. 108). It seems that Chopin's sybaritism in this regard extended even to compositions of a much earlier period, according to an anecdote by Hallé (p. 35): 'One day, long after I had emerged from my retirement and achieved some notoriety as a pianist, I played at his request, in his own room, the Sonata in E flat, Op. 31, No. 3, and after the finale he said that it was the first time he had liked it, that it had always appeared to him very vulgar. I felt flattered, but was much struck by the oddity of the remark.'

144   Chopin also made his pupils study the *Concertstück* op. 79 and the *Invitation to the Dance* op. 65. Mathias (p. 5) recalls studying the *Concertstück*, and Tellefsen made his own two-piano arrangement of the work, which he once played with Chopin (Karłowicz, p. 198).

Chopin played the *Invitation to the Dance* with Mlle de Rozières (*CFC*, III, p. 80), and once asked Lenz (*GPV* 1872, p. 42) to perform it at George Sand's house.

145   It is surprising, as Niecks points out (II, pp. 108–9), that no pupil mentions – apart from the sonatas – the Impromptus and *Moments musicaux*, parts of which are quite Chopinesque in their writing.

In a letter of 1843 to her brother Maurice, Solange Sand writes: 'Tell [Chopin] also that I am again working on Schubert's serenade [*Ständchen*, no. 4 of *Schwanengesang*] to play it for my mother when I go to Berry' (*CFC*, III, p. 132). She may have been referring to Liszt's transcription (which includes an *ossia più facile* version), or perhaps to Stephen Heller's or Czerny's, all of them published around 1840.

146   'He did not admire Mendelssohn's *Lieder ohne Worte*, with the exception of the first of the first book [op. 19/1], which he called a song of the purest virginal beauty,' recalled Hallé (p. 35), who was not a Chopin pupil.

147   Niecks prints 'Septuor'; this erroneous title probably refers to Liszt's transcription (*c*. 1840) of the vocal sextet closing the second act of Donizetti's *Lucia*: *Andante final de Lucie de Lamermoor* [*sic*], *2e acte* [for piano solo by F. Liszt] (Paris, Bernard Latte, B.L. 2207).

148   Chopin remained quite closed to Schumann's art, his dedication of the *Ballade* op. 38 in the OGE ('A Monsieur Robert Schumann') being merely a courteous formality, an official acknowledgement of Schumann's dedication to him of the *Kriesleriana* op. 16. Schumann's literary orientation, his creation of a personal mythology after Jean-Paul Richter, and its extension into several piano compositions and his critical writings: all these were foreign to Chopin's aesthetic ideal, which was opposed to explicit programme music and the *Charakterstück*. We know Schumann's enthusiastic article (*GS*, I, pp. 3–5) saluting Chopin's Variations op. 2 as a work of genius and constructing a complete imaginary dramatic programme for them. Chopin's response was characteristic: 'Concerning [my Variations in B flat] I received a few days ago a ten-page review from a German in Cassel who is full of enthusiasm for them. After a long-winded preface he proceeds to analyse them bar by bar, explaining that they are not ordinary variations but a fantastic *tableau* [there follow facetious examples of this subjective and picturesque analysis]. I could die of laughing at this German's imagination' (*SC*, p. 99). His later meetings with Schumann and the latter's affectionate display of admiration do not seem to have altered Chopin's coolness towards the music of Florestan-Eusebius. Mathias relates

a sad anecdote (p. 6): 'Another day when Chopin, who was ill [. . .] was kind enough to receive us, I saw on his bed-side table a copy of Schumann's *Carnaval*, in the first Breitkopf edition with the title illustrated in lithograph. When my father asked him what he thought of it, Chopin answered with unusual coldness, and as if Schumann's music were hardly known to him. This was in 1840; yet *Carnaval* dates from 1834 [in fact it was published in 1837] and, as I have just said, not merely did Chopin seem not to know Schumann's opus 9, but he appeared not to have even the slightest desire to know it.' This is confirmed in Stephen Heller's reminiscences (Niecks, II, pp. 112–13), recalling particularly Chopin's alleged declaration that 'the *Carnaval* was not music at all'. There is no knowing what the Polish composer thought of the evocative portrait of him etched by Schumann in the impassioned cantilena of his op. 9! On the other hand, it is Schumann (*GS*, II, p. 343) who informs us that some of Chopin's *Ballades* were written under the influence of poems by Mickiewicz; while Chopin himself decided, at the last minute, not to put a literary epigraph at the head of his Nocturne op. 15/3, saying, 'Let them guess for themselves' (see p. 79 above, and p. 153, note 187). On the subject of Chopin's and Schumann's personal and musical relations, see Bronarski (*EtC*, II, pp. 71–140) and Egert (pp. 1–10).

149   This list appears (in numerical order of opus number) in the autograph declaration by Jane Stirling bound in the first volume of her collection (see Appendix II, p. 200 with note 5, below). The opus numbers indicated here in parentheses were added in pencil to the original, of whose first page a duplicate copy (without the pencilled additions) exists in *PL-Kjm* and is reproduced in facsimile in Vol. III of *OXF*.

150   When playing piano duets, at any rate with colleagues, Chopin always took the bass, the *secondo* part. At a grand soirée at the composer's house on 13 December 1836, 'they sat at the piano to play Moscheles's Sonata: Liszt played the *prima parte* and Chopin the *seconda*', wrote Brzowski in his diary (Czartkowski and Jeżewska, p. 215). Similarly, at a concert given before the court of Louis-Philippe at Saint-Cloud on 29 October 1839, where Chopin and Moscheles performed the latter's *Grande Sonate* op. 47: 'We both sat down at the piano, with Chopin again at the bass – the place he invariably takes,' related Moscheles (II, p. 44). Stephen Heller in turn 'remembered hearing [Chopin] play a duet with Moscheles (the [same *Grande Sonate*] of which Chopin was so fond), and on this occasion the Polish pianist, who insisted on playing the bass, drowned the treble of his partner, a virtuoso well known for his vigour and brilliancy' (Niecks, II, p. 96). Finally, Liszt recalled to Lenz a sonata by Onslow (op. 22) 'performed in public one day in Paris; it was quite *curieux*. Chopin played the top part, I myself forced him to' (Lenz, *GPV* 1872, p. 27).

151   There exist three collections of piano duets by Weber: opp. 3, 10 and 60. In a letter from Nohant to Grzymała [end of June 1839] Chopin writes: 'Ask Fontana to pass you the volume of Weber *Pièces faciles* for piano duet' (*KFC*, I, p. 351), and reiterates the request in a missive to Fontana [Thursday 8 August 1839]: '[. . .] if Grzymała comes here [. . .] send me the Weber duets if you have them' (*SC*, p. 182). Given the relative simplicity of these pieces, Chopin may have wished to give them as sight reading to George Sand, unless they were intended for Solange, then almost eleven years old.

152   For more complete enumeration of the concertos Chopin taught, see the list Mme Dubois made up for Niecks (pp. 61–2 above).

153   Chopin preferred to teach the Concerto in E minor, op. 11 – whose first movement was, in his opinion, the most finished – associated in his memory with the occasion when he himself premiered it in public (see pp. 142–3, note 158): '"How I loved the piece! And how I played it in the past!" he would say as though to himself' (Lenz, *UB*, p. 282).

On the subject of Chopin's rendering of orchestral accompaniments on the piano, see Lenz's text on pp. 66–7 above.

154 This title cannot apply to the Nocturne in G, op. 37/2, completed in Nohant only in summer 1839 (*SC*, p. 181). It must refer to the *Andante spianato*, whose composition lasted until 1834–5, thus preceding Chopin's meeting with Mendelssohn in Leipzig at the beginning of October 1835. It is not certain whether by that date the title of 'Andante spianato' had been definitely chosen for the piece; the designation 'Nocturne' is not necessarily Mendelssohn's or Schumann's interpretation but may have been contemplated by Chopin himself. Discussing the similarities of structure and especially of piano writing between the two op. 27 Nocturnes and the *Andante spianato*, Belotti (*DC*, p. 706–7) suggests that Chopin may initially have conceived op. 27 as a triptych – like the two preceding groups of Nocturnes opp. 9 and 15 – to include the piece in G, eventually published with the *Grande Polonaise brillante* as op. 22. This theory gains support from a letter of Mendelssohn to his family: '[Chopin] also has a quite delightful new Nocturne, a good part of which I have memorized in order to play it to Paul for his pleasure' (Mendelssohn, II, p. 100, 6 October 1835). There is a good chance that the exact phrase he uses – 'gar zu niedliches neues *Notturno*' – applies more aptly to the *Andante spianato* than to the two practically contemporary Nocturnes of op. 27.

155 This finds some confirmation in the account by Hipkins who remembers hearing Princess Marcelina Czartoryska in the 1850s playing this *Ballade* in the form of 'an extended version of the first section only' (Hedley, *C*, p. 174).

156 **Hallé**, Sir Charles (1819–95); originally Karl Halle, German pianist, teacher, conductor and composer, naturalized as British after settling there in 1848.

After studying music in Darmstadt with Rinck, Hallé came to Paris in 1836 to polish his musical education and piano playing. For some time he studied with Osborne, Kalkbrenner's assistant, under the latter's supervision. During his twelve years in the French capital Hallé was in contact with the most prominent musicians: Chopin, Liszt, Moscheles, Cherubini, Meyerbeer, Wagner; he became a close friend of Berlioz and Stephen Heller. During the 1848 revolution he went to England and settled in Manchester, where he soon became the centre of musical activity, founding the symphonic association which still bears his name. A sober and refined pianist, Hallé is thought to have been the first to perform in public (London 1861, in eighteen recitals) the complete cycle of Beethoven's 32 sonatas, in which he specialized. He introduced the English public to many works of the symphonic and choral repertoire, particularly those of Berlioz.

It was at the home of the Baron d'Eichtal, a financier who held a salon – and whose daughter, dedicatee of the Waltz op. 34/3, was certainly a pupil of Chopin – that Hallé first heard Chopin play, at the end of November 1836. It was for him a decisive revelation (see p. 271 below). From then on, and up to Chopin's tour of Britain, a cordial relationship existed between the two men; although Hallé never took lessons with Chopin, he heard him play often between 1836 and 1848, both in public and in private. Thus he can be trusted as a privileged and authoritative witness of Chopin's playing; his observations also coincide remarkably with those of another pianist-composer, Ferdinand Hiller (dedicatee of the Nocturnes op. 15), Chopin's close friend up to 1836 (see p. 270 below).

Hallé's autobiographical notes and artistic correspondence, prime documents of the history of nineteenth-century musical life, were assembled and edited by his son and daughter (see Bibliography).

157 **Filtsch**, Carl (1830–45): musical prodigy, pianist-composer, born in Transylvania; he died prematurely in Venice after a brilliant series of concerts in Paris, London and Vienna (1843–4). As a child he was taken in hand by a Hungarian countess and spent three

6   Carl Filtsch. Lithograph by Menut-Alophe, 1843.

years in Vienna, where he studied with Friedrich Wieck in the winter of 1837–8, and then with August Mittag (one of Thalberg's teachers). Accompanied by a brother who was also a pianist, Filtsch arrived in Paris at the end of November 1841, armed with a letter of recommendation to Chopin from Friederike Müller (Karłowicz, p. 141). Chopin gave Filtsch an average of three lessons weekly from December 1841 to April 1843 – that is, for a full year, since the summer of 1842 was spent at Nohant. That summer Liszt himself offered to teach Filtsch free; we do not know the reaction to this of Chopin, who had taken a jealous care in nurturing the gifts of this, his only student of real genius. Normally so punctilious about the exact interpretation of his music, Chopin respected Filtsch's musical individuality when the latter diverged from his own: 'Chopin, who gives him lessons, generally allows him to play according to his own feelings. He merely tells him: "we both understand that in different ways, but play it your way, do as you feel, it can go like that as well"' (Denis, p. 125; dated 20 April 1843). In any case, Filtsch's playing and personality were so close to Chopin's own that these differences must have been trifling. Chopin, deeply struck by the similarities, exclaimed: '*Mon Dieu, quel enfant!* Never has anybody understood me like this child, the most extraordinary I have ever encountered. It's not imitation, it's an identical feeling, instinct, which makes him play without thinking, with all simplicity as if it could not be any other way. He plays me almost all my own compositions without having heard me, without my showing him the least thing – not completely like me (for he has his own style) but certainly no less well' (*Der Humorist*, VII/37, Vienna, 22 February 1843, p. 155). These similarities are also noted by the *RGMP* critic (1843/9 and 18, pp. 69 and 150); while Ferdinand Denis recalls (p. 125): 'I went to hear the young Filshs [*sic*] at Mme Kreutzer's – a marvel who says the most beautiful things effortlessly, with a sobriety of means, a depth of feeling which makes him already a great artist – something like what Mozart must have been at the same age of twelve.' Chopin accompanied Filtsch several times in private performances of the Concerto op. 11. After one of these, at Chopin's home, Chopin, enraptured by his pupil's interpretation, took him to Schlesinger's music shop and gave him a vocal score of *Fidelio* in memory of the occasion.

Hedley has published excerpts of nine letters from the Filtsch brothers to their parents, relating various episodes and observations about the brothers' contact with Chopin and George Sand between February 1842 and April 1843 (*SC*, nos. 186, 187, pp. 216–17; 192, pp. 221–2; 194, p. 223; 196, pp. 223–4; 197, p. 225; 200, pp. 226–7; 201, p. 227; 203, pp. 227–8). In spite of Hedley's habitual extreme circumspection, I have doubts about the authenticity of this correspondence, which no article or other work has reproduced in facsimile. The general tone is somewhat surprising, and does not at all resemble that of the letters published by Klein in her article on Filtsch (obviously unknown to Hedley). Also, the letters published by Hedley refer to musical events involving Filtsch which, astonishingly in view of some of the important names mentioned, go completely untraced in the French musical press of the time. Above all, some of the letters (no. 187 in particular) show disturbing similarities, even down to the details of expression, to many previously published and well-known texts, such as Moscheles, Marmontel (*PC*), Mikuli, Lenz (*GPV* 1872), Denis and even George Sand (*HV*). A search for the autographs of these letters and comparisons with the texts published by Hedley merit a separate study, one beyond the scope of the present book. For these reasons I have refrained from quoting these letters, whose content in any case reveals nothing fundamentally new about Chopin's teaching or playing, except perhaps this passage: '. . . great executant though he is, [Liszt] cannot equal Chopin as a teacher. I do not mean that Liszt is not an excellent teacher: he is the best possible – until one has had the good fortune of knowing Chopin, who is, in the matter of method, far ahead of all other artists' (*SC*, p. 221).

For more information on Filtsch see Gajewski (*NC*), Klein, Lakatos, Lindenau, Sydow (*KF*).

158 One motive for composing the Concerto op. 21 (1829), and especially op. 11 (1830), was probably Chopin's aim of earning a reputation as a pianist-composer by performing them in various European cities. In fact, however, Chopin performed them in public on only a very limited number of occasions. After the première of his Concerto op. 21 in Warsaw on 17 March 1830 (repeated on 22 March), he did not perform it again. As for op. 11, which he premièred in Warsaw on 11 October 1830, Chopin then played it in

Vienna (11 June 1831), Munich (28 August 1831) and Paris (26 February 1832; 30 May 1832, first movement only; 25 April 1833, the Romance and final Rondo; 14 December 1834, the *Romance* only; and 5 April 1835). Several biographies refer to the concert in Rouen on 12 March 1838 as Chopin's last appearance with orchestra in op. 11 – despite the flattering invitation he received in 1848 from the London Philharmonic Society. It seems highly unlikely that he played with orchestra in Rouen. Referring to disagreements between the beneficiary, Orłowski, and the management of the Théâtre des Arts, the *Journal de Rouen* (13 March 1838) reported: 'In spite of all previous assurances, [the Théâtre management] yesterday staged a major opera, and thus deprived M. Orłowski of the presence of his orchestral musicians. This caused the cancellation of many important items on the programme, such as the symphony by Schubert, arranged for large orchestra by M. Orłowski; an overture by Ries, which had been prepared with fifteen rehearsals; and finally a Polonaise [op. 22] by M. Chopin.' The same article, which does not mention any other work by Chopin, records the appearance of an amateur singer: evidently the concert, following the fashion of the time, had been a recital interspersed with vocal music. Apropos of the Rouen concert see Goubault and Prod'homme (*CCR*); for the Parisian concert of 25 April 1833, previously unknown, see Eigeldinger (*CICP*).

Chopin's early retirement from the concert platform, together with the affecting circumstances in which the E minor Concerto was composed, may help to explain Lenz's remark that 'Filtsch [. . .] was never allowed to play the movement right through, since it would affect Chopin too powerfully.' On the other hand, Chopin continued to play his concertos in two-piano form with some of his pupils, who would take the solo part (Filtsch, Mme Dubois, Friederike Streicher-Müller, Mme Peruzzi) either in lessons or in private matinée performances.

159 This outburst of lyricism is quite exceptional; Chopin's letters very rarely comment on the emotional side of his works.

160 Despite Niecks's opinion (I, pp. 279 and 282), Berlioz's poetic paraphrase does not convincingly fit the *Larghetto* of the Concerto op. 21. Like Boschot, I suggest rather the *Romance* of op. 11, published in June 1833. This finds support in the reviews of that concert in *Le Pianiste* (II/4, 20 December 1834, p. 32) and especially in the *Gazette musicale* (I/52, 28 December 1834, p. 426) which characterizes the movement as being '*fort riche en nuances délicates.*' It seems very probable that this description refers to the *Romance* of op. 11, which Chopin played at the second performance of Berlioz's *Harold in Italy*, on 14 December 1834, in the concert hall of the Paris Conservatoire.

161 Delfina **Potocka**, *née* Komar (1807?–77). In the salons of the Parisian and Polish aristocracy, the Countess was celebrated as much for her beauty and her vocal talent as for her long liaison with the poet Krasiński. Chopin, who had met her on his arrival in Paris, felt a keen admiration for this lady, the subject of portraits by Scheffer and Delaroche. She was one of his pupils; he dedicated to her the Concerto op. 21 and the Waltz op. 64/1. Some biographers and commentators, following the publication of salacious letters allegedly addressed by the composer to Delfina Potocka, have assumed the existence of a violently sensual affair between the two. That these texts are forgeries has been definitely established by a graphological examination carried out by the Polish criminal police department (see *Ruch muzyczny* XIX/19, 1975, pp. 10–14).

According to Sowiński (p. 464), Delfina Potocka's excellent soprano voice had been trained in the purest *bel canto* tradition. The last music to be heard by Chopin, two days before his death, was an aria sung at his request by the Countess, the B minor Largo, *Dignare Domine*, from Handel's Dettingen *Te Deum*. A manuscript copy of this '*Fragment du Te Deum de Haendel*' in Delfina Potocka's writing was given by her to

Mikuli, who later gave it to Ferdinand Bischoff. Bischoff later documented this in a short article which, however, has escaped the attention of Chopin's biographers who persist in attributing the said aria to Marcello, Stradella, Pergolesi or Bellini. The version of this story from the composer's niece, Ludwika Ciechomska-Jędrzejewicz (see Bibliography), may be disregarded.

162 '. . . as I intended it' means helping by the lateral movement of the hand described above (see Mikuli, p. 37 above); the wrist must be perfectly free, the elbow passively following the hand's movement. A purely digital approach to this *Etude* can only result in stiffness. The expression 'bow strokes' underlines Chopin's conception of the ascending and descending arpeggios in this *Etude* as a pianistic adaptation of up and down bow-strokes (⌐ V) on the violin.

Chopin's caution about practising this *Etude* may, to a degree, result from the critic Rellstab's infamous comment: 'Those who have distorted fingers may put them right by practising these studies; but those who have not, should not play them, at least not without having Messrs von Gräfe or Dieffenbach [Berlin surgeons famous around 1830] at hand' (Niecks, II, p. 253).

163 See Higgins (*TCC*, p. 111–14) and Steglich (*CEdE*) regarding the divergences of tempo and mood indications in the two autographs of the *Etude* op. 10/3 (*US-NYpm* (Lehman); *PL-Wtifc*).

164 In his study edition of the *12 Etudes op. 25* (Paris, Salabert, 1977, p. 7) Alfred Cortot mistakes this poetic commentary for an evocation of Chopin's playing of the *Etude* op. 25/1, whereas in Schumann's panegyric it applies generally to several *Etudes* from the second book which Chopin had played to Mendelssohn, Clara Wieck and Schumann during his second visit to Leipzig, in mid-September 1836.

165 Chopin, who had a predilection for the *Etudes* op. 25/1 and 2, liked to play them in that order because of their tonal relationship (A♭ major – F minor). From programmes and press reviews we know that this was the case at his Parisian concert on 21 February 1842, in London on 23 June and 7 July and in Glasgow on 27 September 1848; also at his Edinburgh recital on 4 October and in his last public appearance on 16 November that year at the Guildhall in London, at a charity ball for Polish immigrants.

The autograph of the *Etude* op. 25/1 (*PL-Wn*) does not specify any *attacca* into the next *Etude*, as does the fair copy of op. 10/3 (*PL-Wtifc*), where the word *fine* is followed by the indication *attacca il presto con fuoco* [op. 10/4] – an indication absent from the first editions. The two pairs of *Etudes* op. 25/1–2 and op. 10/3–4 share the same major/relative minor sequence, and both lead from a moderate tempo into a very rapid one.

166 Victor Gille (p. 92) recalls hearing Paderewski: 'He started with the *Fantaisie* in F minor. After the opening prelude, faithful to Chopin's tradition, he played with ceaseless fermatas [bars 43–57]. He later told me in confidence that he counted up to twenty in each pause [*sic!*]. My father was a little surprised, as he had heard Chopin play the same piece with shorter fermatas.'

167 This refers to two celebrity concerts given at Pleyel's on 26 April 1841 and 21 February 1842, in which Chopin apparently performed the four (?) Mazurkas op. 41, plus three Mazurkas unidentified except by their keys of A♭, B major and A minor (according to a review in *RGMP*, 1842/9, 27 February, p. 82).

168 This passage is taken from an article announcing Hiller's concert on 15 December 1833, at which Liszt and Chopin participated, performing notably an Allegro from a J. S. Bach concerto for three keyboards (*BWV* 1063?). Berlioz's article, which describes the various talents of these three pianists, is of value in various ways. First, it comes from the only non-pianist genius of Chopin's contemporaries to have given a detailed description of his playing – one which confirms, despite Berlioz's non-pianistic perspective, the accounts of many pianist-composers or composer-pianists. Berlioz notices particular agogic fluctuations, which he implicitly attributes to the shifting rhythm of Polish folk dances (see note 169 below). Further on he remarks upon the extreme delicacy of Chopin's dynamics in the Mazurkas, this at a time when Chopin's health had not yet deteriorated. Thus Berlioz's comments, on pre-1833 Mazurkas, must refer to a conscious aesthetic of refinement on Chopin's part, independent of his health and constitution. Finally, it is striking to hear Berlioz, the creator of large symphonic frescoes, recognize Chopin's quintessence so promptly in these miniatures, the Mazurkas.

169   Here are a few concise indications as to rhythm, metre, accentuation and tempo in the Polish dances stylized by Chopin (or by his immediate predecessors) in order to aid recognition of the 'main rhythmic notes' [*eine starke Akzentuirung einzelner Noten*] to which Koczalski refers. He mentions Polonaise, Krakowiak, Kujawiak and Mazurka; these last two particularly involve his reference to the mobility of the accent or of held notes bearing the accent. With a few noted exceptions, the Polonaise and the Krakowiak (used in rondo form by Chopin in his op. 14 and the finale of the Concerto op. 11) have a fixed accent. The Polonaise (3/4; moderato), as it appears in its pianistic stylization at the beginning of the nineteenth century, carries an accent on the first beat, and, in cadences marking the end of a long period or section, on the second beat. The instrumental version of the Krakowiak developed at the same time and in the same conditions (2/4; $\quarternote = 104$ specified by Chopin for op. 14 and the finale of op. 11), and is characterized by a syncopation on the weak beat and/or weak subdivision of beats (that is, on the second and/or third quavers), and by two-plus-two bar structure.

The generic name 'mazurka' covers three popular dance forms, all in fact quite distinct: the Kujawiak, the Mazur and the Oberek. All three are in triple time, with the principal accent on the weak beats (second and occasionally third). They differ in their geographical origin, their choreography, their melodic shape, their rhythmic accentuation and their tempo. On the folkloric level they present the following characteristics:

– The **Kujawiak**, originating from Kujawy (south west of Toruń), is the slowest form, either sung or a relatively smooth turning dance for couples, in 3/4 ($\quarternote = 120$–160), adhering to four-bar construction and usually in minor keys. Strong accents are rare, the principal one falling on the second beat of every fourth bar. There is frequent use of agogic rubato.

– The **Mazur** (diminutive: Mazurek), originating in Mazovia (near Warsaw), is a more energetic song or stepping and turning dance, again for couples in a circle, in 3/4 or 3/8 ($\quarternote$/ $\quarternote = 160$–184), characterized by a constant shifting of the accent, which falls principally on the second and third beats, according to the whim of the original instrumentalists, who observe as a general rule a strong accent on the second beat, or on the first and second beat, of every fourth bar. For prosodic reasons, when the Mazur is sung the cadential accent falls on the longest note of every fourth bar: it may therefore strike the third beat (crotchet), the second and third beats (two crotchets), or all three beats (three crotchets).

– The **Oberek**, whose name has no particular regional origin, is a purely instrumental dance in 3/8 ($\eighthnote = 180$–240), with very rapid turns, frequent changes of direction, and moments at which the dancer lifts up his partner – as in the Voltas of the Renaissance. Because of the rapid tempo, it has a vigorous accent on the second beat at the end of each period; often in the major, the dance is accompanied by the dancers' shouts and stamping of feet.

It is very rare indeed for Chopin to include near-literal quotation of a popular tune in his Mazurkas; to my knowledge this occurs only in two compositions not intended for publication (trios of op. 68/2 and 3). In their miraculous variety the Mazurkas constitute a stylization and synthesis carried out on the basis of constant reference to the folkloric models described above. Zofia Lissa writes: 'Metric division into three parts, specific displacement of accents to the second and third beat of the bar, their variability, then the typical triplet motifs alternating with dotted rhythms and equal divisions of note values: these are the characteristic traits of the metre and rhythm in the popular music which Chopin transposed directly to the piano' (*SNOC*, p. 131). The distinctive feature of the Kujawiak, Mazur or Oberek appear rarely in their pure state in the Mazurkas, but rather in various combinations. The characteristics of the Kujawiak, and above all of the Mazur, are always predominant, since Chopin was and felt himself 'such a real blind Mazovian' (*SC*, p. 249, July 1845); it is their influence, too, that lies behind Chopin's type of accentuation when performing Mazurkas (see pp. 72–3 above). Among the Mazurkas containing definite folkloric features – not necessarily only in terms of accentuation – are op. 17/4 (Kujawiak), and the opening and closing sections of opp. 24/2, 33/2 (D major), 59/3 and 68/1 (Oberek). The 'long-held accented notes' to which Koczalski refers can be found in opp. 6/4 (opening phrase), 33/3 (C major, excluding the trio), 50/1 (bars 17–24 and similar), 56/1 (bars 6–12 and similar), 56/2 (opening and final sections), 56/3 (*idem*), and also in the momentary mazurka set inside the *Andante spianato* op. 22 (bars 67–96).

For Polish folk music and its influence on Chopin's works, see particularly Biegański, Bielawski, Bronarski (*ETC*, I, pp. 117–61), Hławiczka, Miketta, Pilipczuk, Sobiescy, Windakiewicz.

170 Henselt, Adolf (1814–89): Bavarian pianist-composer, pupil of Hummel, established in St Petersburg from 1838 as court pianist. After that date Henselt appears hardly ever to have left Russia, where he was inspector of music teaching at the 'Imperial Establishments for the education of noble young ladies'; he thus trained generations of students. Because of extreme fear of public appearances, he gave no more concerts after 1838; but Lenz (*GPV* 1872, pp. 85ff), who heard him play in private, has left a remarkable description of his musical individuality. Henselt, who suggests several analogies with Alkan, submitted his fingers to incessant gymnastics and played Bach daily while reading the Bible! Among other characteristics of his playing were a strict *legato*, inherited from Hummel, and a legendary technique for finger extension, which is notably illustrated in his *12 Etudes* op. 2 and his Concerto op. 16, works whose pianistic content may be compared with some of Liszt's productions of the same period. Henselt's musical output include 39 opuses and another fifteen or so unnumbered compositions, most of them for piano but some of them chamber music.

171 Moscheles, Ignaz (1794–1870): pianist, composer, conductor and teacher famous throughout Europe. Moscheles is by far the most important pianist of that transitional period between the last Classically trained generation (Hummel, Field, Cramer, Kalkbrenner, etc.) and the young Romantics. In its extent and variety, Moscheles's musical culture is comparable with that of his pupil and friend Mendelssohn – though specializing more in piano literature. Moscheles earned the unanimous praise of his contemporaries, who esteemed the man as highly as the artist. Chopin, no exception, wrote to a mutual friend: 'You know how much I love and admire Moscheles, so you will understand better than anyone my regret at not being able to come to Paris immediately [to hear him]' (*SC*, p. 229); and, a fortnight later: 'I heard [. . .] all about Moscheles's success at Erard's – and deeply regretted not having been there. It would have revived me a little and pulled me out of the wide ruts of the modern mostly commonplace school' [*l'école moderne généralement quelconque*] (*CFC*, III, p. 139). Such praise is rare from Chopin, so exclusive in his taste and musical judgements. Among the compositions he valued most are Moscheles's [24] *Etudes* op. 70 (Paris, Schlesinger, [1828]), the [12] *Nouvelles Grandes Etudes caractéristiques* op. 95 (Paris, Schlesinger, [1837]), and especially the *Grande Sonate* in E♭ for four hands, op. 47, which he performed several times with various partners, including Moscheles himself at the concert held at the court of Louis-Philippe in Saint-Cloud on 29 October 1839. It was that autumn that the two artists first met and that Moscheles had the revelation of hearing Chopin play, having admired Chopin's *Etudes* but without, until then, having found the proper way to perform them. It was probably at Moscheles's request that Chopin that same autumn composed the three *Etudes* (wrongly called posthumous) included in the second part of Fétis and Moscheles's famous *Méthode des méthodes* (Paris, Schlesinger, [1840]). One of Moscheles's daughters, whose married name was Emily Roche, took a few lessons with Chopin during his stay in London in 1848 (see *List of Chopin's pupils*), pp. 176–8 below). The fragments of Moscheles's diaries and correspondence compiled by his widow are a valuable source of nineteenth century musical history.

172 This text and the preceding ones (Lenz and Hallé) coincide remarkably over the delicate question of Chopin's accentuation in his Mazurkas. It transpires generally that in Chopin's hands some of these gave the impression of being in duple time (2/4 or 4/4) – at least to non-Polish ears. Chopin himself told Hallé that his accentuation reflected traditional Polish national rhythm. Belotti (*ARMC*) sought to explain Chopin's accentuation by maintaining that his folkloric models were characterized by a rhythmic asymmetry of the 7/8 type, not commonly notated during the last century. In support, Belotti invokes the example of Bulgarian folk music, quite ignoring the rich Polish heritage itself (such as the 60 volumes of melodies and dances collected by Oskar Kolberg). Tempting though Belotti's conclusions may seem, they are not shared by modern Polish ethnomusicologists, according to whom the Mazurka remains essentially in triple time.

To attempt here a reconstruction of Chopin's individual way of accentuation would probably be fruitless and out of place, and I limit myself to some points in the texts of Hallé, Lenz and Moscheles/Bülow. If Chopin's accentuation (as taught by him) could be heard in terms of duple metre, the reason lies mainly in a combination of two effects: the constant shifting of accents characteristic of the Mazur (see note 169 above) with, above all, Chopin's frequent lengthening of the first beat (without accent unless otherwise specified – and rightly so, since the mobile accent of the Mazur falls principally on the second beat). On this point we remember the critic of the *Wiener Theaterzeitung*, who remarked on the young Chopin's 'inobservance of the accent marking the beginnings of new musical ideas' (p. 288 below – a dynamic rather than a *tenuto* accent here). Lenz's comment on the Mazurka in C op. 33/3 is equally informative: '*though the third beat loses some of its value, submerged as it is in the flow of the melody*, it still does not cease to exist' (my italics). And indeed the principal motif of op. 33/3 has precisely this characteristic of a regularly accented second beat. To the extent that the accented notes are lengthened at the expense of those immediately before or after, one may speak of agogic rubato – one of whose effects is to produce a more or less general impression of duple time (this was not the case in Henselt's interpretation: according to Lenz, he alternated dynamic accents within a strict tempo, as a German not knowing the natural Polish folk rhythm).

In general, Chopin's musical editing is nowhere as constantly detailed as in the Mazurkas, where agogic punctuation, dynamics and articulation are indicated with extreme precision. Note how often, at the reappearance of a melodic motif, Chopin takes care to write in the rhythmic variants with attached articulation indications, among them

the *legato* slur, the *portando* (see pp. 113–15, note 82), and the *détaché* dot, which he differentiates from the 'dagger' indicating a dry *staccato* – a sign which still appears in his autograph of op. 63/1 (*F-Pn*). Last and most important, the dynamic accent indicated by *sf* (*sforzando*, printed *fz* in the OFE) should be distinguished from the agogic accent which lengthens the note, indicated by >. Chopin graphically differentiates between these two accents, sometimes taking the trouble to mark both signs on the same note or the same beat (see Mazurkas: op. 6/1 bars 42, 44, 46, 48, 50, 52, 54; op. 6/2 bar 40; op. 6/4 bars 4, 8, 16, 20, 24). There is reason, therefore, to respect the distinction, and not automatically to reinforce a dynamic accent by an agogic one, as all too often happens. In addition, Chopin uses two ways of writing the agogic accent, depending on whether it is to be short or long. In his prefaces to the Wiener Urtext edition in progress of Chopin's works, Jan Ekier specifies: 'For Chopin, the short accent (>) denotes a louder dynamic, whereas the long accent (⇒) implies an expressive stress.' (Another proof of the lengthening value of the sign ⇒ is its appearance over seven consecutive notes in the Mazurka op. 6/2 (bars 29–30); the return of this same melodic line towards the end (bars 69–70) bears the indication *portando*.)

Chopin's notation includes here and there alternating agogic accents, making an undisguised duple metre pattern (Mazurkas: op. 6/3 bars 2–4; op. 68/3 bars 35–6). The second section of op. 24/1 (bars 17–32) is an outstanding example:

The coupling here of triplets with the following crotchets is significant: the dot under the crotchet shortens its value while the accent on the first quaver of the triplet lengthens it, following a compensatory system. Notated so precisely, this example gives a graphic idea of the deliberate rhythmic ambiguities which Chopin implanted in his Mazurkas.

173   Ought this assertion to be questioned? – given that the ornamental variants passed on by Chopin's pupils and associates are far more numerous and significant in the Nocturnes than in any other of his genres (see pp. 122–3, 150–2, notes 105, 183 and 184). That would be to exaggerate the importance of a statistical point whose value is only relative, and to put too little trust in Koczalski's memory. Koczalski was in a good position to know about the Nocturnes, having recorded op. 9/2 adorned with all the variants from the edition of his teacher Mikuli (see p. 152, note 184). The answer to this apparent contradiction is to be sought elsewhere. Given the restricted framework of the Mazurkas, and Chopin's purity of taste, their embellishments had to be discreet and could not afford the luxuriance of those in the Nocturnes, which entailed the use of the Baroque-type *tempo rubato*. With only a few exceptions, Chopin did not see fit to write down these ornaments: perhaps he felt it would corrupt their improvisatory character; perhaps he wanted to keep these light ornaments to himself; or perhaps he trusted his more gifted students to be able to reproduce them by ear. Whatever the case, only five small ornamental variants have come down to us for the Mazurkas, three of them affecting op.

7/2. The embellishment given by the Stirling score for bar 11 occurs in a slightly different version in bar 27 of the Dubois score:

At bar 23, the latter source joins the *ab"* to the *bꞏ'* by this sign:

which indicates a descending chromatic *glissando*

similar to those printed in small notes in the Nocturne op. 15/2, bars 18 and 20. Finally, the Dubois score of the Mazurka op. 24/1 has the following delicate embellishment in bar 60 (the Stirling score has almost exactly the same version):

This variant felicitously answers the ornamented version in bar 58, in this final appearance of the principal motif.

174 I deliberately use here Sowiński's somewhat distorted French translation of Schindler's original German, because of Sowiński's own involvement, and his having had more opportunities than Schindler to hear Chopin's playing. Schindler's original – which once again berates Czerny! – reads: '*Gebildete Spieler erkannten bei der schon im zweiten Jahrzehend erreichten Tonfülle jene Anmerkung für störend, und gebrauchten das bereits vordhandene Pedal [forte] mit weiser Mässigung. Czerny aber, der diese Verbesserung des Instruments alsogleich in solchem Übermasse gebrauchte wie späterhin Chopin in seinen Mazurkas, sagt [. . .]*' (*BLB*, p. 477).

175 In fact the OFE gives inconsistent phrasing indications in the bass of bars 34–8 and 50–7. In the absence of an autograph, we have to reconstruct Chopin's probable intention with the help of the harmonic and agogic context – phrasing, articulation and r.h. accentuation being carefully specified in the OFE. Mikuli – who possibly had the use of a source now lost – starts his phrases consistently on the third beat, to end on the second beat of the following bar. This solution is adopted in the CW (X, no. 6) and Henle edition. On the other hand neither of these editions, nor Kobylańska (*K*, I, p. 55, no. 62), mentions that in the Dubois score the printed *Fine* in bar 16 is deleted and carried over to bar 32; the word is not in Chopin's hand.

176 Julius **Seligmann** (d. 1903), president of the Glasgow Society of Musicians. He attended Chopin's concert in Glasgow on 27 September 1848, and wrote down his remembered impressions of it in 1893 (45 years later!) at Hadden's request.

177   This indication is equally valid for other Mazurkas containing unison passages where *sotto voce* is required: op. 41/1 in C♯ minor (bars 45–9); op. 41/2 in E minor (bars 7–8, 15–16, 66–8), op. 56/3 (bars 17–23, 41–7, 153–9).

178   This text (there is no reason to doubt its reliability, given its author's reputation) is the more valuable for establishing an interpretative tradition not in any musical source. The autograph (*PL-Wn*), the OFE and Mikuli (and since then all modern critical editions) reproduce the third section (bars 74–121) as identical with the first, with the dynamics *f-pp*, *f-pp*, *ff-pp*. These pairs of dynamic contrasts stress the decidedly popular character of the first section but take no account of the subtle nuances introduced by Chopin in the reprise. As for the words used to describe these contrasting characters, (tavern – salon) they are comparable, *mutatis mutandis*, to the term Lenz uses for the C♯ minor Mazurkas opp. 41/1 and 50/3: that 'they begin on the organ, and end in a pure salon atmosphere' (*GPV* 1872, p. 41).

179   A cut from bar 87 to bar 110 is indicated in the Stirling, Dubois, Jędrzejewicz and Zaleska-Rosengardt scores; this very remarkable concordance among such different owners of the score must reflect the composer's will. Neither Mikuli nor any modern edition mentions this cut, except for the *CW* (X, p. 214) which mentions only *OXF* and Jędrzejewicz. The cut in the Stirling and Dubois scores also eluded Kobylańska's notice (*K*, I, p. 226, no. 546).

180   I tacitly correct Lenz's original text which, misreading the left hand in the bass clef, gives *B-E-B-E*! Also, in the *Kritischer Bericht* to the Mazurkas (p. 6), the editor of the Henle edition is misled by a pencilled cross over the first two beats of the final bar in the Dubois score, and reads this (impossibly) as a cut of these first two beats! Probably the sign has the simple meaning that Lenz points out: 'When Chopin was satisfied with a pupil['s performance], he marked a cross under the spot concerned with his finely sharpened pencil' (*GPV* 1872, p. 42). Apropos of the ballad-like, narrative character of this Mazurka – emphasized by this reference to a 'cohort of ghosts' – George Sand saw in Chopin 'all the superstitious fancies of Slavic poetry. Polish, he lived in the nightmare world of legends. Ghosts called to him and embraced him, and [. . .] he would thrust their emaciated faces away from his own, and struggle from under the grip of their icy hands' (*HV*, II, p. 446). A good many of Chopin's works besides this beautiful Mazurka can suggest a supernatural interpretation from the rich sources of Polish poetry.

181   Lenz mentions here a 'modulation to E♭' – a key which in this Mazurka is suggested only for the space of three beats (bars 44–5), fleetingly and in no way structurally. This tonal inflection, which serves as a bridge between C minor (bars 41–3) and G minor (bars 46–8), has no significance in itself. Lenz probably had in mind the beginning of this modulating episode (bars 41ff), introducing, without transition, the key of C minor, from which a nostalgic melody develops in the bass. He may have hastily misread the three flats in that bar as the key of E♭.

182   Kleczyński takes up a similar argument: 'By a thorough and correct comprehension of the Nocturnes, one can acquire a key to unlock the mysteries of the other and more magnificent works of the master. The manner in which he conducts a cantilena with so delicate a perception of the effects of the instrument, is a peculiar characteristic of Chopin's' (*CGW*, pp. 25–6).

183   Under the variant given by Lenz I reproduce the one noted down by Mikuli for the same passage (separate edition of op. 9/2). The Stirling and Dubois scores join the B♭ (last quaver of bar 4) to the following G″ (first beat of bar 5) by this sign:

which undoubtedly indicates an ascending run – either diatonic as in Lenz, or more probably chromatic as in Mikuli – joining the two notes and launching itself with a turn on the Bь. At the same place the Jędrzejewicz score has this sign:

which may well carry the same meaning – certainly in this context it cannot mean a break between the two notes! Chopin probably prized this variant since it appears under these various guises in six different sources (including the Stirling score and Franchomme's manuscript corrections for the Breitkopf & Härtel *Erste kritisch durchgesehene Gesammtausgabe*).

184   The 'figuration' in question, claimed by both Lenz and Gutmann/Niecks for this final cadenza, does not appear in any of the presently traced annotated scores. However, the separate edition of op. 9/2 published by Peters (No. 8522, edited by H. Scholtz) '*mit des Autors Varianten*' (that is, those published in Mikuli's separate edition, plus, as an *ossia*, the Tellefsen/Kleczyński variant reproduced here on p. 79 above) gives the following version of the cadenza, which may be that of the combined claims of Lenz and Gutmann's descriptions:

Scholtz's source was in all probability the score of Mlle R. de Könneritz (dedicatee of the Nocturnes op. 62; later Mme von Heygendorf) whose scores, corrected and annotated in Chopin's hand, were used for the Peters edition, according to Scholtz's preface: he affirms having had access to '3 Bände seiner Compositionen, u.a. sämmtliche Notturnos in der ältesten französischen Ausgaben, in denen sich von Chopin's Hand Verbesserungen, Berichtigungen von Druckfehlern und Ergänzungen dynamischer Zeichen vorfanden'. This variant is neither quoted nor mentioned in existing critical editions.

There are no less than fifteen known variants for this Nocturne op. 9/2 alone. Apart from that quoted above and the two given by Lenz and Tellefsen/Kleczyński (reproduced here on pp. 78–9 above), the Stirling score presents three and Mikuli eight, all included in the critical notes of the *CW* (VII, p. 118); to those can be added another indicated by Franchomme (see edition of the Nocturnes by Jan Ekier, Wiener Urtext, p. 13, bar 14, variant 7b). With the exception of the variant for the last two bars, given almost identically by Stirling and Mikuli, all the other ornaments have in common the *bel canto* style, their performance consequently entailing *tempo rubato* as understood and practised in the Baroque era. The *ad libitum* character of these ornamental variants becomes apparent in the five versions given near-identically in two sources for, respectively, bars 4–5 (Lenz; Mikuli); bar 14 (Franchomme; Mikuli); bar 22 (Stirling; Mikuli); bar 24 (Tellefsen/Kleczyński; Mikuli); bars 31–2 (Stirling; Mikuli). Given their complexity, it is not surprising that Chopin's pupils noted down these ornaments (or that he wrote them into their scores).

One may add that the eight variants published in Mikuli's separate edition are performed with extreme taste and suppleness by Koczalski in his recording of op. 9/2, reissued on the record *The Great Chopin Interpreters*, Veritas Records (VM 115).

Finally, the question arises, why should these variants occur in such quantity in the Nocturne op. 9/2 rather than elsewhere? Certainly this one represents a highly accomplished example of Chopin's conception of pianistically stylized *bel canto*; yet this is equally the case for opp. 9/1, 15/2, 27/2, 32/1 and 37/1. I see two reasons for this wealth of ornamentation, both equally plausible and in no way contradictory. Op. 9/2 particularly reflects Field's influence (see his Nocturnes nos. 1 and 9, Peters edition). Their contemporaries had noticed this debt, and Chopin himself recognized it (see p. 116 above, note 84). He may then have wished to impart a more personal stamp to this work, by means of these ornamental clusters which form part of a pianism and an *improvisando* conception transcending some of Field's somewhat fixed stereotypes. Also, op. 9/2 immediately on publication made such an impression on the public and on pianists, whether dilettantes or professionals, that its popularity finally began to irritate Chopin (see Lenz, GPV, p. 301; GPV 1872, pp. 41–2). By including these ornaments, beyond the powers of any mediocre player, Chopin may have been acting to prevent the piece from labelling him a salon composer, since it was in the salons that his Nocturne too often ran the risk of being, in his own word, *sentimentalisé*.

Appendix III below (pp. 257–61) reproduces this Nocturne complete, without the above-mentioned variants but with the fingerings of the OFE and the Stirling, Dubois, Jędrzejewicz and Franchomme scores, plus details of dynamics and realization of ornaments, taken from these various sources.

185 Below the variant noted by Kleczyński, I reproduce that given for the corresponding passage in Mikuli's separate edition.

186 The reliability of this passage appears to me debatable in spite of the 'tradition' Pugno could rightly claim. Even more questionable than the liberties taken with the original metronome marking is his postulation of a 4/8 time signature. In addition to the pendular movement of the bass, which precludes such treatment, one recalls Chopin's reported advice '[*not to*] *play by too short phrases*; that is to say, do not keep continually suspending the movement and lowering the tone on too short members of the [musical] thought' (see Kleczyński extract on pp. 43–4 above) – which is precisely what a 4/8 conception would cause, as indeed can be heard from Pugno's own recording of op. 15/2 (*Welte Mignon* 1905, Telefunken SLA 25057-T/4, side 8).

Among other annotations in this Nocturne, the Jędrzejewicz score contains several indications worthy of mention, even though they are obviously not in Chopin's or his sister's hand. Bars 12, 18 and 58 have the indication *i due Ped.*, while the final bar is provided with an interesting variant, reproduced in the critical notes of the CW (VII, p. 122). The Dubois score specifies that the trills in bars 7, 15, 55 and 56 should begin on the lower auxiliary note, that is, *f♯♯'*, and that the appoggiaturas in bars 12 and 52 and groups of appoggiatura notes (bars 8 and 9) should sound simultaneously with the bass. In bar 49 the reprise of the first theme is rhythmically altered from

to

(observed by Pugno in his recording). The high *a♯'''* at the beginning of the run in bar 54 is marked *pp*.

187 This information, also given by Szulc (*Echo muzyczny*, 1880/20, p. 159) and Hoesick (C, III, p. 414), can be neither confirmed nor discarded through study of the sources since no autograph contains the first page of op. 15/3. In a letter from Warsaw on 21 August 1830, Chopin writes: 'Today, *Hamlet*; I am going' (*KFC*, I, p. 131). But the chronology of this Nocturne indicates that it could not have been written directly following this performance. An incomplete preliminary draft of the Nocturne – from bars 85–6 onwards – was sold at Stargardt's (*Autographen, Auktion am 25. und 26. Februar 1975, Katalog 605*, p. 168, no. 698) and is now at *US-NYpm* (Lehman); it occupies the second recto page of a double sheet also containing a sketch for the *Etude* op. 10/9, followed by the mention *Paryż* (Paris). Chopin arrived in Paris at the end of September 1831; and op. 10 having been published in the OFE in June 1833, this autograph must date from 1832 or early 1833. Chopin's correspondence has no mention of a Parisian performance of Hamlet around that time. But it was precisely in 1832–3 that Chopin met Berlioz and enjoyed a brief close friendship with him. We know how Berlioz worshipped Shakespeare, whose plays he would frequently recite at artistic gatherings; this was also the time when he was struggling to marry the Irish actress Harriet Smithson, one of whose Parisian triumphs in 1827 had been in the role of Ophelia. Might Chopin have heard her in the performance of *Hamlet* on 15 and 19 January 1833, or Berlioz declaiming scenes of it in private? There is no confirming evidence, but the chronological coincidence is remarkable.

From a strictly musical point of view, the Nocturne op. 15/3 is in many respects unique within its genre. The bipartite A-B form is exceptional, as are the indications *languido e rubato* and *religioso* heading these two respective sections. The opening section combines a cantilena of Ukrainian character with the accentuation of a languid Mazur; the structure is punctuated in 12-bar periods, consisting of irregularly grouped sub-phrases; and the chromatic progressions introducing the second section are equally innovatory. This latter section, *im Orgelton*, imitates a four-part homophonic chorale, whose modal character is stressed by the absence of leading notes to minor resolutions (in the Stirling score the g♯' on the second beat of bar 113 appears to be amended to ♮, an emendation repeated in the Jędrzejewicz score but not mentioned in any critical editions). Then the chorale, muted, emerges only intermittently, covered by quiet brass calls in octaves – a rare type of writing in such a context, except for certain passages in some Mazurkas. Altogether the composition leaves a powerfully enigmatic impression, tinted with Nordic colour. Saying this is not an attempt to postulate a programme for it – a procedure Chopin had no time for. Yet, the fragmented, plaintive and hesitant soliloquy of the first section can well suggest a soliloquy of Hamlet – a character very near Chopin's Polish side. For the record, one might add that in Shakespeare's tragedy Ophelia's funeral cortège is accompanied by a procession of priests (V/1), and that the drama ends to the sound of bugle calls (V/2).

In the autograph sketch mentioned above, the second (B) section (notated with only one flat in the key signature) closes not with the printed final cadence but with four bars leading to the indication *da capo*! So at that early stage Chopin was still thinking of a ternary form. Although this sketch is otherwise musically very near the final version, the removal of the *da capo*, musical masterstroke though it is, might suggest an extra-musical motive, again inviting speculation.

As though not content with just having erased the (alleged) literary reference from his manuscript, Chopin also scored out the *languido e rubato* in Jane Stirling's score.

188 **Fontana**, Julian (1810–69): Polish pianist and composer, Chopin's fellow-student at high school, and then at the Warsaw Conservatory in Elsner's style and composition class. After the Polish insurrection of 1831 – in which he participated – Fontana emigrated to Paris where he once again met Chopin. From 1836 to the end of 1841 he worked as

Chopin's main copyist, his secretary in charge of dealing with publishers, and his factotum. In acknowledgement of services rendered, Chopin dedicated to him the two Polonaises op. 40. After living in Havana and New York from 1842 to 1852, Fontana returned to Paris. We are indebted to him for having contravened Chopin's formal wish – though with the consent of the composer's mother and sisters – in publishing the 'posthumous' works under the op. nos. 66–73 (Paris, Meissonnier [1855]; Berlin, [Adolf] Schlesinger [1855]), and then op. 74/1–16 (Berlin, Schlesinger [1857 and 1859]; Warsaw, Gebethner & Wolff [1859]). Numerous copies by Fontana of Chopin works have often been mistaken for Chopin autographs because of an extraordinary similarity in their writing; the Kobylańska catalogue (K) contains valuable elucidations on this.

Fontana, despite his long familiarity with Chopin, seems never to have assimilated the characteristics of Chopin's playing, according to Teofil Lenartowicz, Mickiewicz's brother-in-law: 'Fontana played some pieces by Chopin which he had published as posthumous works. Adam was listening to him from the doorway of the salon. But he visibly found the performance unpleasing; every note hit with force irritated him. On the other hand the playing of Princess Marcelline [Czartoryska], who went to the piano at his request, made a totally different impression on the audience.

– There, that's Chopin! The Princess can still always hear him, remember his way of playing and make it ever more her own: one cannot play the music of the masters except by following their tradition. Notes are mere notes, but music lives by whoever reads the notes, and you can hear at once if someone is just spelling out ABC or really speaking' (quoted in Gaillard, p. 661).

189 These indications are exactly corroborated by those of Koczalski (p. 98) and above all by the annotations in the Stirling, Dubois and Jędrzejewicz scores (in all three cases in Chopin's own hand). These three sources all have an added *pp* at the second appearance of the theme in bar 26. The printed *diminuendo* at bar 45 is scored out in all three scores and replaced by *cresc.* in Stirling and Jędrzejewicz. At the third appearance of the theme, bar 46, Stirling and Jędrzejewicz indicate *fff*, Dubois *ff*. At bar 50, all three scores specify *pp*; at bar 52, the *con forza* is erased in Stirling and Jędrzejewicz and replaced in the latter by a scarcely legible marking, interpreted in the critical notes of the CW as a possible *riten*. [?] (VII, p. 123). This edition mentions the annotations in the Stirling and Jędrzejewicz scores but not those in the Dubois score. Mikuli reports none of them; the Henle edition merely follows the autograph (*PL-Wn*) and the OGE, completely ignoring these important author's corrections.

For the second half of bar 21 Fontana supplies an ornamental variant (see CW, VII, p. 123) almost identical with the one which Mikuli gives for the upbeat to bar 4 of the Nocturne op. 9/2 (see p. 78 above). Note 82 (p. 114 above) describes the reading from the Dubois score for the first half of bar 28. The bass is doubled at the lower octave by 8va or 8 on the first beat of bar 49 (Dubois), the first and fourth beats of bars 58–9 (Jędrzejewicz), and bar 59 (Stirling and Dubois).

190 Although no autograph copy is traced, an anonymous copy corrected by Chopin (*PL-Wn*: Mus. 223) in fact shows an indication of tempo or mood at the beginning of the central section which has been scored out to the point of illegibility. In any case, the first editions and the scores of Chopin's pupils, as well as the Mikuli edition, have no change of tempo marked.

Before the return of the first motif, at bar 66, the four r.h. *d''*s have an added hairpin *crescendo* above them in the Dubois score. The indications from that source for playing ornaments are given here in notes 127–8 (pp. 133–4 above). The Stirling score in turn takes the piece's first l.h. *G* down an octave by the indication *8*, and gives an important correction in the arrangement of the final bar (see facsimiles on pp. [238] and [240] of Eigeldinger–Nectoux).

191   This text's exceptional value need hardly be emphasized, as the most detailed of those known to us – comprising also Lenz's indications for the Nocturne op. 9/2 (see pp. 77–8 above) – concerning Chopin's requirements on the subject of performance. These two special cases illustrate all the importance which Chopin attached to the study of his Nocturnes, with a view to the learning of pianistic declamation, the keystone of his teaching. The detailed character of these two texts is because they were intended for a professional pianist, Tausig, who, fascinated by Chopin's pianism, interrogated Lenz on the subject at Berlin in 1868. The annotations in Jane Stirling's scores, and even more those in the Dubois and Jędrzejewicz scores, provide a valuable complement to Lenz's remarks. Particularly telling details are the fingerings, and the indications for phrasing, breathing and for the interpretation of ornaments and nuances. Appendix III below (pp. 264–6) reproduces these for bars 1–36 (see p. 206 below, for the same bars in the Dubois score). In the second half of bar 48, Dubois has the annotation *les 2 mains* – written twice, in two different hands – above the octaves notated in the bass clef. For bar 70 Dubois gives the following simplified version of the first two beats, r.h.; this version may be considered as an *ossia*, for small hands that would have difficulty playing the passage *legato* without stiffening or hindering the crossing of parts:

Here is how the last bars are amended for the l.h. in the Stirling score, as *OXF* also prints in a footnote:

It corresponds approximately to the handwritten markings in the Jędrzejewicz score, which similarly stress the melodic progression and the anchoring notes of the lowest voice in the l.h. Dubois specifies *ff* in bar 72 from the r.h. octave semiquaver.

192 The OFE prints *Molto più lento* at the beginning of this middle section; in Dubois the entire indication is deleted, while in Stirling and Jędrzejewicz only the *Molto* is scored out. The indication *tempo primo* at the return of the first theme (bar 101), in ink and in Chopin's hand in the Jędrzejewicz score, corrects an omission in the OFE and confirms the intention of *più lento* for the middle section. The *tempo primo* at bar 101 is given in the Mikuli and Henle editions; as usual, the latter limits itself to using the text of the OFE and OGE supplemented by some readings from a manuscript copy by Fontana (*PL-Wtifc*). For more information on the newly rediscovered autograph of op. 48/1–2, see Eigeldinger *ACI*.

193 These refusals were motivated by Lenz's limited pianistic ability. But why, then, did Chopin declare to him of the Waltz op. 34/2: 'Never in your life will you play it' (Lenz, *GPV* 1872, p. 37) – when he had apparently shown himself capable of mastering the Polonaise op. 26/1 and various Mazurkas or Nocturnes of no less difficulty than this Waltz? Chopin, who was particularly fond of this Waltz (see Heller's remarks quoted in note 201 below), no doubt feared that the Russian dilettante would give a sloppy rendering of this iridescent pastel of Polish *żal* [= wistfulness]. Chopin's reaction also demonstrates his refusal to dissociate technical agility from the cultivation of touch, the one being invalid without the other. Lenz eventually managed to satisfy Chopin with the Nocturne op. 9/2: 'I received a *premier chevron* for the Nocturne [indicated by a cross marked on the score], returned with it again and received a second one. Back I came again with it. "No, don't trouble me with that piece again", said Chopin [. . .] "you've already had an additional cross; for you (!) it's now perfect; enough of it"' (*GPV*, p. 301).

I return to the Polonaise op. 26/2 for two textual details. Mikuli's edition gives a different reading for the run in bar 10, which he claims is from Mme Rubio's annotated score: the *d″* and *d‴* have an added natural. The document used by Mikuli now belongs to Prof H. Federhofer; it consists of a manuscript copy (probably in Mme Rubio's hand) of bars 9–12, with the two relevant naturals present and the annotation *corrigé ♮ par le crayon de Chopin même dans mon cahier*. The Chopiniana in Federhofer's possession, mentioned in his article (pp. 87–8), eluded the notice of Kobylańska (*K*), whose catalogue does not mention musical copies made by Mme Rubio-Kologrivoff and by Mme Streicher-Müller (*Ballade* op. 23, bars 6–8).

In the last bar of op. 26/2, the *ppp* of the OFE is altered to *fff* in the Stirling score and to *ff* in Jędrzejewicz.

194 Elsewhere, Pozniak generalizes with this assertion (p. 62): 'I know reliably that for practising the Polonaises Chopin expressly advised his pupils to count 3/4 *in quavers*. This would ensure that the tempo could not be different from that taken in the actual dance.' The tradition which Pozniak knew was in fact that carried on by Marcelina Czartoryska, and by Mikuli in Lwów, Pozniak's native town. Those two names give some reliable weight to Pozniak's repeated assertion (to determine the tempo of the Polonaises by counting aloud in quavers), not corroborated by any other sources. One thing beyond doubt is that Chopin wanted his Polonaises to be played at a tempo appropriate to their intrinsically majestic character. Hallé's remarks (p. 82 above) are unarguable, as is the statistical observation that of the eight Polonaises for solo piano published in Chopin's lifetime with opus numbers, two are headed *maestoso* (op. 26/2 and 53), two others *allegro maestoso* (op. 40/2 and 61), while the lyrical op. 26/1 is marked *allegro appassionato* and the triumphant op. 40/1 *allegro con brio*. Only the *Grande Polonaise*

brillante op. 22 has the instruction *allegro molto* by reason of its decorative character (op. 44 has no indication).

195   This has continued to be the sad fate of op. 54. Kleczyński also observes: 'The quick tempo, which the majority of players (even the most celebrated ones) give to this work, is entirely inappropriate' (*CGW*, p. 86).

196   The OFE erroneously prolongs the 8va up to the end of bar 79. In the corresponding bars 47–8, the Scherbatoff score has a manuscript annotation '————*loco*' to the same effect (the printed 8va ends here on the penultimate quaver of bar 47). But the printed version there is clearly the correct one; contrary to Gajewski (*NZM*, p. 4), I do not recognize Chopin's hand in this annotation, which seems to me a case of mistaken correction.

197   This testimony is corroborated by Koczalski's advice (p. 175) about giving the eleven bass A♭'s equal strength, like bell strokes – to which Mikuli naïvely added a twelfth (not printed in his edition) to make it midnight!

The autograph of op. 28/17 (*PL-Wn*) and the OFE confirm Dubois/Paderewski and Mikuli/Koczalski: the bass A♭'s are marked *fz* (*sforzando*) while the nuance *pp sotto voce* indicated at bar 65 remains in force until the *perdendosi* of bar 84 to the end. In passing, one notes that the Dubois score accentuates several of the low A♭'s with a line and also specifies that the r.h. ornament in bars 43 and 47 is to be started on the beat.

Under Chopin's fingers, this Prelude earned the praise of both the Moscheles family and of Meyerbeer: on 21 October 1839 the latter noted in his diary: 'Monday, at Leo's: Chopin played some new Mazurkas magnificently, and then once again that sublime [*himmlisch*] piece with the A♭s, which I so love' (III, p. 207). Moscheles, who was also present at this performance, wrote that his wife and eldest daughter were 'particularly moved by the A♭ major prelude in 6/8, with the A♭ pedal which keeps returning' (II, p. 39). Chopin also noted a fragment of the coda (bars 65–72) in Moscheles's album, dated that same day and signed: *Paris. 9. Novembre 1839/de la part de l'ami F. Chopin* (pr. coll.). Mendelssohn's exclamation about one of the op. 28 Preludes is traditionally attributed to this same piece: 'I love it, I cannot tell you how much or why; except, perhaps, that it is something which I could never have written at all' (Niecks, II, p. 332).

198   The principal motif of this middle section (bars 305–20 and similar, the melody played by the r.h. thumb) quotes the melody of the Polish Christmas Carol *Lulajże Jezuniu* [sleep, infant Jesus]. The custom of 'rocking the infant Jesus' to this popular lullaby goes back to the eighteenth century; in Poland the carol is still traditionally sung during the ritual Christmas Eve dinner. Knowing Chopin's attachment to the customs of his native country, one can imagine the 'indescribable' [*indicible*] impression created by his playing of this middle section of op. 20.

199   See p. 166 below for Lenz's very disrespectful judgement of Gutmann. Although partly justified in fact, Lenz's feelings also appear affected by jealousy over Gutmann's intimate rapport with Chopin, which Lenz never shared.

200   The succession of two fourth fingers in bar 31 comes from the Stirling score. The adaptation of this to 3–3 in bar 33, and the repetition of both fingerings at the corresponding bars 39 and 41, make perfect sense, and all appear in Mikuli's edition.

201   This adjunction figures also in the Stirling, Dubois and Jędrzejewicz scores and in Mikuli's edition. Such concordances give grounds for considering this as an intended correction by Chopin rather than just a variant *ad libitum*. It appears also in the CW (IX, no. 3) and in the Cortot and Peters (ed. Pozniak) editions; Henle, however, follows without comment the text of the first French and German editions, though claiming here to follow Mikuli. The fingerings from this example come from the Stirling score – a fine specimen of Chopin's logic, following the melody's pendular movement and ensuring a perfect equality of tone, with the thumb on each minim including the one with the trill in bar 5.

Chopin had a special fondness for this Waltz, one of the richest in Polish folkloric elements: 'One day when Stephen Heller – my informant – was at Schlesinger's music-shop in Paris, Chopin entered. The latter, hearing Heller ask for one of his waltzes, inquired of him which of them he liked best. "It is difficult to say which I like best," replied Heller, "for I like them all; but if I were pressed for an answer I would probably say the one in A minor." This gave Chopin much pleasure. "I am glad you do," he said; "it is also my favourite"' (Niecks, II, p. 249).

Kobylańska (*K*, I, p. 547, No. 1321) postulates, from this passage of Lenz's, the existence of an unidentified autograph of a *Valse mélancolique*, not necessarily even one by Chopin. She evidently misunderstood that Lenz was simply referring to the Waltz op. 34/2 by the title *Valse mélancolique*. Last century this title was often used for a slow waltz in a minor key: for example, Chopin's opp. 70/2 and 69/2 were issued posthumously (before the Fontana edition) by the Kraków publisher J. Wildt under the title *Deux Valses Mélancoliques* (see note 206 below).

202   These four initial bars have a prelude-like function and can, to a certain point, be treated in a freer tempo before launching the proper tempo. The Waltz op. 34/3, bars 9–16, and the Mazurka in A♭ copied by Chopin into Maria Szymanowska's album (*CW*, X, No. 58) are analogous situations: in all three cases the whirling introductory figure derives directly from the melodic forms of the Oberek (see pp. 145–6 above, note 169).

In the Dubois score the opening *a♭'* has the pencilled annotation 4 *mesures* above it (not in Chopin's hand), and underneath the note is pencilled similarly *tr*. Are we to understand that these four bars have the musical value of a trill, or should they in fact be preceded by four bars of trill? The second possibility seems more likely, given that this would give a symmetry to the four-plus-four (or eight-plus-eight) bar construction generally observed by Chopin in his Waltzes: bars 70–7 of the same Waltz do indeed contain a four-bar trill propelling the initial figure into the theme's return (see also the introductory trill of bars 1–8 of the Waltz op. 42). It should be noted that this *tr* indication at the opening of op. 64/1 does not occur in any of the four complete autographs of the Waltz nor the *incipit* in an album page, nor in Mikuli's edition, nor Pugno's edition of the Waltzes.

While Koczalski's recording (Replica RPL 2462; Milan) follows the printed text, Michałowski (a pupil of Mikuli) interestingly precedes the opening bars by a trill of almost four bars' length, not only in his late recording of the original text (*Great Virtuosi of the Golden Age*, Vol. VIII, Pearl Records: GEM 108) but also in his two earlier recorded arrangements (*The Great Chopin Interpreters*, Veritas Records: VM 115), the second of which approaches the furthest extremes of *café-concert* style!

The Dubois score contains numerous hand-written fingerings for the l.h. part; none of them, nor various right-hand fingerings at the reprise of the first theme after the trio, are in Chopin's hand.

203   Coeuroy, in his monograph, writes of the Waltz op. 64/1: 'We know from Mathias, a pupil of Chopin, that the latter, despite the fast tempo marking, would begin with a moderate tempo up to the B♮ of the ninth bar; then he would accelerate and maintain the tempo in the *poco più tranquillo*' (p. 125). I have not traced any original source for these indications, which seem questionable not only because they contradict what Lenz says but also because they do not tally with Pugno (*V*, pp. 46–51) – who was also a student of Mathias. None the less, it is known how much Chopin was wont to vary

his interpretation from one occasion to the next; so any attempt to establish *the* tradition here rests on very slippery ground!

204 The concern implied by the *unique* is to give full value to the first quaver in bars 3 and 4 (and in parallel passages), taking care not to cut it to a semiquaver as in the following beat. The warning has lost none of its relevance.

205 Schiffmacher's didactic theory is based, among other things, on a pianistic adaptation of the up-bow and down-bow of the violin (we have seen Chopin's similar conception for the *Etude* op. 10/1 in note 162 on p. 144 above). These *lancés* and *retirés* – to use Schiffmacher's terminology – are described by his pupil Aline Tasset (p. 49), but in a manner that inadvertently inverts normal violin bowing and follows instead that of the viol family: 'The *retiré* movement is designed to produce an exhaling sound analogous to the French silent *e*. In our examples it is represented by the sign ⊔ used in violin teaching to indicate the down-bow [*tiré*]. While the *lancé* movement [○] produces a sound one could compare to the bold down-stroke in writing, that of the *retiré* corresponds with the thin up-stroke [. . .] In the *lancé* movement, you strike the keyboard from outside to inside; in the *retiré*, on the contrary, the finger starts from the inner extremity of the key, slides over it without pressure [. . .] and produces the sound only upon leaving it, by an imperceptible pressure.'

A parallel may be drawn between imitating a violin up-bow (the proper equivalent of Tasset's *retiré*) on every third bass beat, and Chopin's advice, passed on by Franchomme: 'Never let the wrist fall on the last repeated chord in the bass'; or again: 'A third beat inappropriately accented [. . . suffices] to unbalance the composer's poetic work' (Picquet/Anonyme, pp. 38, 40).

The advice to anticipate the F double-sharp of bar 2 seems somewhat dubious – the more so since neither the sketch (*F-Po*) nor the autograph version given to Baroness Rothschild (*F-Pn*) gives the g♯♯′ as an anacrusis, but both begin directly on the first beat.

206 This Waltz belongs to a category of somewhat private works (like op. 69/1 and 2 notably) which Chopin did not intend for publication but with which he liked to pay tribute to his pupils and friends by copying them into their albums. In a letter accompanying an autograph present of the Waltz op. 70/2 (the latter now in the collection of Jacques Samuel, Vienna), Chopin wrote to Caroline Oury [Paris, 10 December 1842]: 'As for the little Waltz which I have had the pleasure of writing for you, please, I beg you, keep it for yourself: I should not like it to be made public' (*SC*, p. 225). Mme Peruzzi, who similarly received an autograph of the Waltz op. 69/1 (now at Harvard University, Dumbarton Oaks Research Library), recalled: 'He said it would not be published because they would play it . . . Then he would show how they would play it, which was very funny' (Niecks, II, p. 339). With his usual sagacity Chopin knew well which of his compositions would suffer worst by *un jeu sentimentalisé* (a fate which these Waltzes certainly have not escaped) and therefore preferred to keep them to a limited circle of initiates – a characteristic trait of his eminently aristocratic nature.

As for the title *Malinconia* proposed by Lenz for op. 70/2, it is hardly original and reflects the contemporary fashion whereby editors and students liked to dress up their favourite pieces with titles. In any case this Waltz, together with op. 69/2, was first published in 1853 by J. Wildt in Kraków, precisely under the title *Deux Valses Mélancoliques . . . écrites sur l'album de Mme la Comtesse P xxx* [Plater] *en 1844*.

List of Chopin's pupils whose recollections are quoted in this book

Anonymous Scottish lady

Descended from a distinguished Scottish family, this person identified herself only as a distant cousin of Jane Stirling, who introduced her to Chopin in March 1846. A relative beginner, she none the less received a few lessons from Chopin: 'The majority of his pupils, I always understood, were already excellent and even distinguished musicians before they went to him [. . .] whereas I was but a young amateur with only a great natural love for music, and very little previous training,' she wrote in a letter of reminiscences, dated 27 March 1903, to J. C. Hadden who published it in his monograph (pp. 157–9). These detailed reminiscences are corroborated in various respects in the accounts by other eminent pupils of Chopin, such as Gretsch, Mikuli and Streicher. There seems no reason, therefore, to dismiss their trustworthiness in the way that Hedley does (C, p. 106). In her biography of Jane Stirling, A. E. Bone, quoting from these same recollections, makes no attempt to establish the identity of this student, who from the first wished to remain anonymous, as Hadden reported.

Cheriemietieff, Countess Elizavieta Serguëievna

Chaperoned by her elder sister Anna, this young Russian aristocrat spent the winter of 1842–3 in Paris, where she was introduced as a listener to Chopin's lessons by Marie de Krudner, a compatriot pupil of Chopin. Cheriemietieff describes her first impression in a letter to her mother: 'He is very highly-strung. When Marie, sight-reading, was about to play a wrong note, he caught his breath even though nothing had happened. There were only the three of us in the room. As a teacher he is very pleasant. He explains each note scrupulously but with great delicacy. It is impossible to feel uneasy in his presence' (9 November 1842). It was at the home of the Countesses Cheriemietieff that Chopin played the first movement variations of Beethoven's sonata op. 26 in the presence of Lenz (see pp. 277–8 below), of whom

Elizavieta noted in her *Journal*: 'Mr Lenz; a great chatterbox; plays the piano [;] pupil of Chopin' (2 November 1842). Thus the Countesses found themselves involved in the Russian community then gravitating around Chopin: Mme Peruzzi (née Eustafiew), Mme Rubio (née de Kologrivoff), Mme Obreskoff, her daughter Princess Catherine Souzzo (dedicatee of op. 49), Marie de Krudner and Elizavieta Tschernischeff – or Czernicheff (dedicatee of op. 45). Overcoming her timidity, Elizavieta Cheriemietieff brought herself to ask Chopin for lessons in place of Marie de Krudner, who was leaving Paris: from 16 December 1842 to 20 January 1843 she received twelve lessons (two and later three hours weekly) in the afternoons at his home. After these lessons Chopin would go to the piano, as he had done after Marie de Krudner's lessons, and play Mazurkas, Nocturnes and other works: 'Chopin played exquisitely his *Valse mélancolique* [op. 34/2? 69/2? 70/2?], his *études*. His playing is out of this world, something airborne, misty: one imagines angels when listening to this music' (*Journal*, 17 November 1842). Besides Clementi and various exercises, Cheriemietieff studied a Beethoven sonata, as well as a Waltz and some Nocturnes and Preludes of Chopin's. On the page dated 8 December 1842, Chopin wrote into the young girl's album the first sixteen bars of the future Nocturne op. 55/1, written here in F♯ minor and marked *Andante*. This autograph is now in the Central Archives for Literature and Art in Moscow, together with the diaries of Anna and Elizavieta and some of their family letters. Fragments of these documents (originally written in French) are published in Russian translation in Niesmieyanova–Siemienovski and in Siemienovski. The short passages from Elizavieta's *Journal* quoted here are taken from the unpublished original.

Courty, Mme de (General de Courty's widow)

There is little information on the identity of this pupil, who describes some aspects of Chopin's teaching in a letter of recollections written for Louis Aguettant, who published it for the first time in his chapter on Chopin (pp. 195–6). Simplicity and naturalness in piano playing emerge as the essentials. According to Aguettant, Mme Courty 'readily spoke of her honoured teacher and played for me, with a talent unspoiled by age, some of the pages she had once studied under the composer's guidance' (p. 195).

Czartoryska, Princess Marcelina, née Radziwiłł (1817–94)

Descended from one of the most distinguished Polish families, she personi-fied the type of aristocratic, highly talented pupils whose social status forbade them a professional career. Lenz observes: 'Princess Czartoryska, a dedicated and intelligent pupil of Chopin, is living proof of how sometimes, no doubt in exceptional cases, an amateur too may reach the highest summits and be at home in the sanctuary of great masters' thoughts' (B, pp. 303–4). The Princess worked in Vienna with Czerny before studying with Chopin in Paris. Her contemporaries – from Liszt and Delacroix to the critics of the *RGMP* – unanimously acclaimed her playing as the most faithful reflection of her teacher's. Sowiński remarks: 'Princess Marcelina Czartoryska, a marvellous performer, seems to have inherited Chopin's manner, especially in phrasing and accentuation' (pp. 121–2). In later reminiscences, one of her listeners recalled: 'Some of [Chopin's] works, notably the Polonaises, were played by her with a startling yet most beautiful originality, which the listeners who had heard the master himself declared to be the most perfect of all readings of the composer' (Diehl and Mangold, p. 28).

Under the reign of Louis-Philippe, the Hôtel Lambert, where the Princess held her salon, became the rallying point for the expatriate Polish nobility and artistic community: Chopin felt at home there and played frequently for his compatriots; Delacroix and Franchomme were regular attenders, even after Chopin's death. Thoroughly devoted to her teacher, Marcelina Czartoryska took care of him during the end of his stay in Britain and was present by his death-bed. Charles Gavard claimed that some of Chopin's last words were to the Princess: 'Je vous recommande Franchomme, vous jouerez du Mozart ensemble, et je vous écouterai' (Janin, I, p. 602). Indeed, in the years following the composer's death Czartoryska regularly invited Franchomme, Tellefsen and the young Gounod to her '*Club des Mozaristes*' [*sic*], as repeatedly recorded in Delacroix's *Journal*. Her relatively few public appearances (Paris, London, Poznań, Lwów, Kraków) all attracted much attention and Lenz has described the emotion aroused by her playing during a musical evening in St Petersburg (*UB*, pp. 289–90). Princess Czartoryska had no real teaching career, but in 1846 she taught a young guest at the Hôtel Lambert, Emilia Borzęcka, who subsequently took a few lessons with Chopin. Later on, still in Paris, she provided information on Chopin's playing for Kleczyński (who dedicated the *FCI* monograph to her) and for Cecylia Działyńska (see p. 99, note 28), who codified some of Chopin's fundamental precepts. In her retirement at Kraków, she handed her tradition on to a Natalia Janotha and gave the pianist A. Michałowski some advice (see p. 94, note 13).

Dubois, Camille, *née* O'Meara (1830–1907)

Along with Mathias, she was Chopin's best 'French' pupil (albeit of Irish ancestry) and the only one to take up a professional career, apart from Pauline Viardot. Having worked from the age of nine to thirteen with Kalkbrenner, Camille O'Meara then studied with Chopin for five years (1843–8). According to Mikuli, Chopin took particular care over the training of this young pupil, and Marmontel writes: 'Mme Dubois [. . .] is also one of his favourite pupils, among those whose talent has best preserved her teacher's most characteristic traditions and methods' (*PC*, p. 7). This was also the opinion of Jane Stirling: 'I've heard Melle Meara, whose playing is as good as ever. I ardently wish her to preserve the tradition' (letter to Ludwika Jędrzejewicz, dated 26 November 1851; copy by Edouard Ganche among the Papiers E. Ganche in *F-Pn*). Mlle O'Meara, indeed, was Chopin's assistant around 1847–8. She made her public début under the sponsorship of Alard and Franchomme (Chopin's partners at his last concert in Paris, on 16 February 1848): 'These two skilful instrumentalists served as sponsors for this new and young virtuoso, whose playing is fine, delicate and distinguished like that of her illustrious teacher,' noted an *RGMP* critic (1852/6, 8 February, p. 42), also praising her 'calm bearing'. Although not belonging to the official teaching circles of Paris, Mme Dubois (married under this name in January 1853) applied herself to perpetuating her teacher's tradition with scrupulous fidelity. Paderewski, who visited her around 1890, relates that she was like a mother to all the pianists of the best Parisian society (Paderewski–Lawton, pp. 154–5). Liszt, explaining his concept of the *Berceuse* op. 57 during a masterclass in Weimar (1884), took care to add: 'Mme Dubois, in Paris, understands this quite differently from myself, and naturally she is the authority: go and see her!' (Jerger, p. 37). Mme Dubois's own printed scores of Chopin, used at her lessons with Chopin (now in *F-Pn*), constitute the most important source presently accessible of *performing* indications in Chopin's music. As such they call for a systematic study and detailed commentary beyond the scope of the present book (see pp. 212–19 below for some outlines for such a study).

Gretsch, Emilie, *née* von Timm (1821–77); twice married, under the names of von Brülow and then von Gretsch

Brought up in very musical surroundings, she started learning the piano with Dorn (one of Schumann's teachers) in her native town of Riga – where she later performed with Liszt and Henselt – and then continued her studies in St

7   Camille O'Meara (later Mme Dubois). Oil painting by Ary Scheffer,
1851.

Petersburg with Henselt. For almost two years (1842 to May 1844) she stayed
in Paris with her brother (who had come to work in the painter Horace
Vernet's studio), and took precisely 33 lessons with Chopin. He made her
study principally Bach, Beethoven, and his own works. Chopin highly
appreciated her interpretations of Beethoven, according to her recollections,
telling her after her performance of the Sonata op. 31/2:

You understand Beethoven marvellously, just as he should be understood and as nobody at present seems able to do, except for a small number of people, to which you belong. The technical side of it is no longer any trouble to you; having played it once you know it – so you have only to wish it in order to express many wonderful things very admirably.

(Grewingk, p. 10)

Chopin often prolonged the lesson so that eventually Emilie had heard him play almost all of his works. He apparently took leave of his pupil with regret: 'Eh bien! Dans ce peu de temps vous avez fait des progrès que c'est un charme!' (Grewingk, p. 13). Emilie's letters to her father (unfortunately only parts of the correspondence survive) give detailed accounts of these lessons; apart from their valuable technical information, these accounts shed quite unusual light on Chopin's psychological perceptiveness. What survived of this correspondence was compiled and commented on in a brochure by Emilie von Gretsch's niece, Maria von Grewingk. Apparently Emilie rarely performed in public but played in private circles, particularly in the duchy of Bade-Würtemberg and in St Petersburg.

Gutmann, Adolf (1819–82)

Chopin's favourite pupil, if hardly his best one! With Emile Gaillard (see p. 276, note 12), he was the only male pupil to have a composition dedicated to him (op. 39: 'A son ami Adolphe Gutmann') in appreciation of his première performance of it in front of Moscheles. He seems also to be the only one to have received several letters from Chopin, rather than just brief notes. Having arrived in Paris from Heidelberg in 1834, Gutmann is one of the first recorded pupils of Chopin's Paris years. He worked for five years with Chopin and came to know him the most intimately of all his pupils: Chopin, most unusually, addressed him as 'tu'. Nevertheless his playing was quite different from Chopin's, according to various witnesses: 'According to the connoisseurs, his style follows Thalberg's rather than that of the skilful teacher who gave him lessons', observed the *RGMP* critic (1844/12, 24 March, p. 104). Mikuli admitted later in his life that Chopin 'seemed to him far more lenient and understanding with other students [than with himself, Mikuli]. Gutmann, for example, never took account of his teacher's tastes, slashing and thumping the piano unconcernedly' (A. Michałowski. p. 76). Such liberties provoked the indignation of other students, and Lenz recalls:

With his robustness he impressed Chopin, who praised him as his favourite interpreter of his own compositions. He himself had raised him, he would say [. . .] Filtsch and myself loathed Gutmann and made fun of him: he had nothing of Chopin's art, yet the latter had gone to incredible pains to try and shape an image from this block of wood. And that was enough to blind him [. . .] This student was Chopin's invention!   (GPV, p. 302)

Nevertheless Chopin would occasionally even entrust him with some of his own pupils. Given the inaccuracies and boasting in Gutmann's recollections, his supposed presence at Chopin's death-bed has often been questioned, and was categorically denied by Chopin's niece, Ludwika Ciechomska-Jędrzejewicz, though at a much later date. None the less, contemporary documents expressly record Gutmann's presence: see letters from Grzymała and Pauline Viardot (*SC*, p. 375; *CFC*, III, pp. 443, 451), and Charles Gavard's description (Niecks, II, p. 318). Gutmann, having given several concerts in Paris and gone on tour (with letters of recommendation from Chopin) in 1845–6 to Berlin, Dresden, Warsaw and St Petersburg, subsequently devoted himself mostly to composition, and left about sixty salon pieces. His reminiscences of Chopin, conveyed through the intermediary of Stavenow, should be read with maximum caution; Niecks long ago pointed out their obvious inaccuracies when put beside other writers' accounts.

Harder, Maria Alexandrowna von (1833–after 1880)

This young Russo-German pianist travelled from St Petersburg to Vienna at the age of fourteen to consult Meyerbeer about her future studies. The latter recommended her to Chopin, although she had expected him to advise her to go to Liszt in Weimar. On arriving in Paris in (autumn?) 1847, she met first with a refusal: 'Je ne donne pas de leçons à des enfants,' Chopin informed her mother. But Maria Alexandrowna soon managed to charm Chopin to the point of receiving almost daily lessons (exceptional for him) until his departure for London in April 1848.

> Her talent developed with astonishing rapidity under [Chopin's] attentive and uncompromising tuition. Indeed, he made enormous demands on her capabilities, often forgetting he was dealing with an adolescent. (Adelung, p. 122)

Owing to his poor health, Chopin often taught lying down, from the study adjoining the drawing room:

> But this did not prevent him from attentively following her playing; even from a distance, and out of her sight, not the slightest detail of her playing escaped him. 'Fourth finger on F♯!', he would call out; his ear, sensitive to the slightest nuance, knew immediately, from the sound, which finger had played each note. (*Ibid.*)

Some of her musical reminiscences were written down by a friend, Sophie von Adelung, who describes Maria von Harder's playing as

> almost plain [. . .] None of these murmurings or ghostly sighings, those sudden changes of tempo usually to be heard in concert halls [. . .] Luminous and wholly concentrated, the wonderful melodies emerged like a magnificent swan-song [. . .] while the accompani-

ment, played lightly and gracefully, with an astonishing technique, remained a simple accompaniment without attracting undue attention to itself.   (Adelung, p. 123)

In a letter to Liszt (dated 5 November 1853), Bülow mentions a well-known pianist's passion for Maria von Harder: 'Charles Mayer is roaming the streets, mad with love for a young Russian pianist, Mlle de Harder, a *soi-disant* pupil of Chopin, who is going to perform his *Concerto symphonique* in a charity concert' (La Mara, *CLB*, p. 42). (Bülow's mistrust ('soi-disant') is unfounded.)

Lenz, Wilhelm von (1809–83)

Of Baltic origin, he was a Counsellor of State to the Russian Imperial Court, a passionate amateur musician, and author of the monograph *Beethoven et ses trois styles*. A cultured individual of an inquisitive and somewhat whimsical mind, he is sketched thus in a letter by Stephen Heller: 'This gentleman is a Russian agent by the name of Lenz, that's all we know. He is the most enthusiastic lover of music and has "intimate connections" with Liszt, Prince Choknosowski, Chicardinsky, Henselt, the late Field, and other distinguished Kalmouk and Siberian personalities. At his home he played us several pieces fit to make nature quiver, accompanying the whole with gestures and grimaces enough to make you roll around the floor' (dated 2 September 1842; Heller, p. 108). Lenz had indeed worked with Liszt, and it was thanks to the latter's recommendation that he was able to introduce himself to Chopin at the beginning of October 1842. He does not fail to mention this in a letter to Balzac: 'I am at home until one o'clock, then I go to Chopin's to play the piano, and I return at three, in time to *faire* Paris' (10 October 1842, in Balzac, *C*, IV, p. 498). Lenz himself describes this first meeting:

> The servant told me Monsieur Chopin was not in Paris. I did not fall for this and retorted: 'Hand him my card and I'll take care of the rest.' With my card in his hands, Chopin came to meet me – a young man of medium height, slender, lanky, his face worn and expressive and his dress of the greatest Parisian refinement. Never since have I encountered a spectacle of such natural, seductive elegance. Chopin did not invite me to sit down and I remained standing, as in the presence of a sovereign. 'What can I do for you? Are you a pupil of Liszt? an artist?'
>
> 'A friend of Liszt – may I be allowed the happiness of studying your Mazurkas, which I treat as a Bible [*für eine Literatur*], under your guidance? I have worked on a few of them with Liszt' – I realized, too late, that I had blundered.
>
> 'Ah?' said Chopin in a drawling though most polite tone – 'How can I be of any help to you, then? Do play me what you have worked on with Liszt, I still have a few minutes' – he extracted a small elegant watch from his waistcoat pocket – 'I was just about to leave and had asked my servant not to let anybody in, please excuse me.'

As with Liszt thirteen years before, I felt myself in the most awkward of situations. Was this an examination? But *after* Liszt, I should no longer be frightened, and then, I come from St Petersburg – without further ado I made my way to the piano and opened it as though I were at home. It was a Pleyel; I had been told that Chopin played on no other instrument. Among the French makes it was the one with the lightest touch. Before sitting down, I played a chord, 'to try the *gué* [depth]', I said. The precaution and the expression seemed to please Chopin; he smiled, leaned wearily on the instrument, and looked me straight in the face with his penetrating gaze. Hardly daring to cast a glance in his direction, I launched into the B♮ Mazurka [op. 7/1] which is so typical and for which Liszt had written me some variants.

I managed quite well and the flight over two octaves came out better than ever; the instrument responded more easily than my Erard.

Chopin courteously whispered: 'This run isn't yours, is it? *He* showed it to you – he has to put his stamp on everything; well, he may, he plays for *thousands* of people and I rarely play for *one*! All right, I'll give you lessons, but only twice a week, that's my maximum; it will be hard for me to find three-quarters of an hour.' He looked at his watch again – 'And what do you *read*, how do you spend your time in general?' This was a question for which I was well prepared. 'I prefer George Sand and Jean-Jacques above all other writers,' I said too hastily; he smiled and was a beautiful sight at that moment.

'So Liszt has prompted you; I see you're initiated, so much the better. Be punctual, my house is like a dovecote [*pigeonnier*] and my time is planned by the minute. I can see already that we'll become better acquainted; a recommendation from Liszt says something, and you're the first pupil he has sent me; from mere acquaintances we are now friends.'   (GPV, p. 300, GPV 1872, pp. 34–5)

This account well reflects the general tone of Lenz's recollections, which often require a certain degree of interpretation; once cleared of a certain amount of rather cumbersome *mise-en-scène* advantageous to the author, however, they constitute a mine of information through his keenness of observation and the vividness of his impressions. Moreover, there is no reason to doubt their accuracy – as some have done – particularly since they are often confirmed by other sources. Dilettante though he was, of all Chopin's pupils Lenz provides the most abundant and detailed information on Chopin's wishes as to interpreting his works. For Lenz, these lessons were as much an occasion for aesthetic conversation as for pianistic improvement. Impatient at times with his pupil's impetuosity and theorizing, Chopin nevertheless appreciated the aptness of his remarks and his extensive musical knowledge; it seems that Lenz introduced him to some works of Weber and Beethoven that were then little or not known in Paris. But Chopin remained implacable in his teaching requirements, refusing Lenz permission to work on compositions exceeding his pianistic capabilities (Polonaise op. 26/2; Scherzo op. 31). On the other hand Lenz was allowed to sit in at Filtsch's lessons, and to accompany Chopin to the home of the Countesses Cheriemietieff where Chopin played the first movement variations from

Beethoven's Sonata op. 26 (see pp. 55 above and 277–8 below). Lenz records his reminiscences in two sources, *UB* and *GPV* (*GPV* 1872 is a revised version in book form).

Mathias, Georges-Amédée-Saint-Clair (1826–1910)

Of German descent on the paternal side and Polish on the maternal side, Mathias made a triple career as pianist, composer and teacher. After working with Kalkbrenner, he studied with Chopin from around 1838–9 (for five years according to Niecks; seven years according to Fétis and Pougin; seven or eight years according to Marmontel); he is therefore one of those who profited the longest from Chopin's teaching. Clara Wieck met the young Mathias during her stay in Paris, and in a letter to her father (19 March 1839) describes him with unusual enthusiasm:

Yesterday I visited a Mr Mathias, whose son is a second Liszt (twelve years old, I believe) in terms of genius. You should hear this child, an immense talent, a pupil of Chopin. How can I describe his gifts? You know about child prodigies; I should only add that this one has received an excellent education, has wonderfully flexible fingers, plays all of Chopin, and that there is nothing he cannot do. In fact he outshines all the keyboard strummers around here. Remarkably, he has never worked more than one hour [per day], is very sickly (just like Chopin) and has never been healthy. His father, an extremely reasonable man, does not make him play in public and is not one of those fathers who deify their children. I was to give him lessons, but I told him he had no need of a teacher. (You know, I would be too afraid to teach him, since his mental abilities exceed his physical abilities.) I played duets with him and I plan to visit this family often, especially as I shall be living quite near them.

(Litzmann, I, p. 302)

Coming from someone of Clara Wieck's training and insight, these observations on the accuracy of the playing, the small amount of time spent at the instrument and the intensity of the mental concentration are most significant. From 1862 onwards, Mathias taught for more than thirty years at the Paris Conservatoire, thereby introducing the Chopin tradition into official French musical circles. He trained Raoul Pugno and Isidore Philipp, among other particularly representative pupils – both strongly influenced by his teaching – and to a lesser extent, Ernest Schelling and Teresa Carreño (there is an interesting piano roll recording of the latter playing the Nocturne op. 48/1: *Welte Mignon*, 1905, on Telefunken SLA 25057-T/4, side 8). Marmontel describes Mathias's playing:

Under his agile and firm fingers, the most arduous passages retain their transparent clarity; one never senses fatigue, or is aware of the difficulties overcome. The expression, controlled by the principles of style and good taste, is never exaggerated. One recognizes

8   Georges Mathias. Lithograph by Cossmann, *c.* 1850.

clearly in Mathias's masterly playing the double influence of the two great artists [Kalkbrenner and Chopin] from whom he is descended.   (*VC*, p. 147)

As a composer Mathias left over fifty works, not only piano music but also chamber music, concertos, symphonic and sacred music – somewhat exceptional for one of Chopin's pianist-composer pupils. In a preface to Isidore Philipp's *Exercices quotidiens tirés des oeuvres de Chopin* he recorded some vivid memories of his teacher's personality, playing and teaching.

Mikuli, Karol (1821–97)

Pianist, pedagogue and composer of Armenian descent, born in Czernowitz (Bucovine). Of all the students of Chopin who took up the profession, he worked the hardest to hand down his teacher's tradition. Dedicating his life to the discipleship of Chopin, he refused to let himself be seduced by the music of such as Wagner or Brahms, for fear of betraying his teacher's musical aesthetic: 'As far as he was concerned, Chopin represented the supreme musical authority,' observes Koczalski (p. 9). Up to a certain point, one could say that Mikuli played Beethoven's Schindler to Chopin – though in a more reliable and effective way. Arriving in Paris in 1844 with the express purpose of studying with Chopin, he had to overcome the composer's habitual reserve – which melted immediately on hearing Mikuli play the Scherzo op. 31. From that year on he was Tellefsen's fellow-student under Chopin, who made them study composition with Reber. Both of them were then among Chopin's official copyists, according to Mikuli (none of whose copies of Chopin works have been traced, though), and the young Karol was given permission to attend other people's lessons, until the 1848 Revolution (Koczalski is mistaken in referring to 'seven years' of studies). Mikuli then undertook successful concert tours through Eastern Europe, and eventually settled in Lwów in 1858. For thirty years he enlivened the city's musical life as concert organizer and director of the Conservatory, where he principally taught piano, harmony and counterpoint. He composed about thirty works (piano music, songs, chamber music, and subsequently sacred music), sometimes drawing inspiration from Rumanian folklore which he carefully studied. In January 1880 Chopin's collected works were published (Leipzig, Kistner, 17 vols.) edited by Mikuli and based 'for the most part on the composer's own indications' – according to the heading. This immense task was conducted from the basis of the original French editions annotated by Chopin in the course of Mikuli's lessons, and on which the latter had himself recorded Chopin's remarks during the lessons of other pupils, and also the annotated scores of Countess Potocka, Princess Czartoryska and Friederike Streicher-Müller. For the musical text Mikuli also took the advice of Mme Dubois, Mme Rubio, Hiller and Franchomme – the last-named particularly as far as chamber music was concerned (part of their correspondence is in the hands of Prof. H. Federhofer, who kindly communicated it to me). Mikuli's edition, still authoritative, is criticized mostly for the liberties taken with fingerings. The author explained himself quite openly to Aleksander Micha-łowski: 'The question of fingering is inseparably tied up with the interpretative individuality of the pianist, the shape of his hand and the style of his

9   Karol Mikuli, Photograph by Mazur and Roszkiewicz, Lwów.

technique. Nobody can impose a fingering and this aspect should not be given prime importance among all the problems relating to the interpretation of Chopin's music. This explains why some of the master's own indications have been overlooked in Mikuli's edition. The latter openly admitted that in this regard he did not always follow Chopin's indications' (A. Michałowski, p. 76). Mikuli may be reproached more for not having taken the trouble to distinguish typographically between Chopin's fingerings and his own; with this reservation, Mikuli's approach, with its humanistic rather than philological emphasis, does seem valid – from which it follows that his fingerings cannot claim universal value. The preface accompanying his edition constitutes the most comprehensive surviving source – if not the most detailed – concerning the tenor of Chopin's teaching. Among Mikuli's principal pupils in Lwów were Aleksander Michałowski (who later taught Bronislaw von Pozniak), Maurycy Rosenthal, Heinrich Schenker, and particularly Raoul Koczalski, whom Mikuli to some extent instituted as his heir to the Chopin tradition.

Peru, F.-Henry (1829/1830?–1922)

Little is known of this pianist-composer except for what he himself says in his memoirs (see Bibliography) and in some interviews and articles all published much later (see Bertini; Hipkins, pp. 9–11; Montabré), also in detailed reminiscences of one of his pupils, Ludwika Ostrzyńska, who took some lessons with him in February–April 1914 and continued to receive his advice subsequently. According to these sources, Kalkbrenner, unable to subdue the eighteen-year-old Peru, entrusted him to Chopin in 1847. The latter is said to have taken a liking to him and taught him until 1849 – on the basis of which Peru, at the time of the First World War, described himself as Chopin's 'last pupil'. One might therefore be tempted to identify with his name the mysterious initial in the title *Plan de la méthode dicté à Mr. P. par Ch[opin]'* in Ludwika Jędrzejewicz's copy of the *PM* (see p. 90, note 1). Peru stresses as a particular characteristic of his teacher a constant variation in repeated performances of one work. He is the only one to single out, as a point of departure in Chopin's teaching, the infinitely varied types of attack on one individual key (perhaps Chopin's way of freeing him from the stiffness engendered by Kalkbrenner's teaching?). After Chopin's death Peru claimed to have travelled through Spain, Italy and Germany performing his teacher's works. On 11 December 1913 in the Salle Pleyel, Paris, he gave a 'Soirée Musicale et Conférence sur son Maître Chopin', in the course of which he played the *Etudes* op. 25/1, 2, 7, 9, 10, the Nocturnes opp. 15/2 and 37/1, and the Waltzes op. 34/1 and 3. A 'Dernière Séance Musicale de Peru' took place in the same hall on 30 April 1914. The programme states: 'Je jouerai les dernières oeuvres apprises avec mon maître Chopin à l'âge de vingt ans. Le piano sur lequel je les exécuterai est celui [*sic!*] où j'ai pris ma dernière leçon, place Vendôme, il y a de cela, hélas! 64 ans' – two further 'dernier' occurrences in this passage to add to his claim as the 'dernier élève' of Chopin. Except for two Preludes, the op. 35 'Marche funèbre' and an Impromptu which open the programme, this latter recital was identical with the preceding concert. It was on the initiative of Peru and Massenet that a monument by the sculptor Georges Dubois was erected in the Luxembourg gardens in Paris, to commemorate the fiftieth anniversary of Chopin's death. As a composer Peru published more than fifty genre pieces, all for piano.

Among the evidence presently known there is no outright proof or disproof of Peru's claim to be a Chopin pupil. Followed by other scholars less forthright in their opinions, Ganche was the first to distrust him: 'From 1910 to 1922 a *quidam* had the impudence to appear in Paris as a pupil of Chopin, trying to solicit *la charité publique*' (*DSFC*, p. 81, note 1), the *quidam* being Peru. The Papiers E. Ganche (*F-Pn*) include a dossier entitled *Affaire Peru*, with the mention 'imposteur'. In addition to the above mentioned programmes it includes press cuttings (but not, curiously, Peru's *S.I.M.* article) and an exchange of correspondence between the pianist (20 November 1913; 5 December 1913) and Ganche (2 December 1913): in response to a request from Peru to the Société Chopin to buy some tickets for his lecture-recital, Ganche asks for proof of Peru's claim to be Chopin's pupil, and meets a polite refusal in the form of an evasive and resignedly dignified letter – on which Ganche drew his conclusion.

There is no doubt that if the ageing Peru decided to announce his two concerts as from an *ancien élève* of Chopin, it was for pecuniary purposes. He was then in some poverty, as is attested to by something of a press campaign in his support between 1911 and 1914, the time of publication of his own *souvenirs* in the *S.I.M.* So the question is one of whether circumstances tempted Peru into an imposture, as Ganche believed, or whether he had indeed worked with Chopin – as his pupil Ludwika Ostrzyńska did not doubt for a moment – and only then used it for publicity purposes, under financial pressure. The only evidence is in the documents themselves. Certainly the various reminiscences of the pianist contain manifest inexactitudes of date, place and deed (such as the matter of Chopin's piano, Place Vendôme, to take just one example). It is difficult to know whether to ascribe such errors to deliberate confabulation or to the lapses of an octogenarian memory. More troubling, no early contemporaries mention the name Peru, whose career appears to have occurred without their knowledge. Gille's listing of him (Gille, pp. 180, 191) among Chopin's pupils is anything but proof (see p. 98, note 21, above), and neither is Marie Roubaud's statement confirming Peru as a friend of hers (unpublished letter to Ganche, 27 July 1916). On the other hand, Elie Poirée's monograph *Chopin* (Paris, Laurens [1907], p. 59) uses Peru's reminiscences, though it was published well before the press campaign of 1911–14. Particularly, various traits related by Ostrzyńska are well in keeping with Chopin's teaching and aesthetic: disapproval of tempo change inside a piece unless indicated (p. 2), of excessively prolonged *forte* playing (p. 3), and of adding spurious virtuosic cadenzas to the printed text (p. 4). Finally, the remarkable constancy with which Peru returns to Chopin's own varieties of ways of performing one work is striking (and attested to by others), a characteristic through which, he relates, he himself suffered in lessons. There his tone is more convincing – whence the interest and credit given to that aspect of his *témoignage*. Such an assertion would have been hard for an octogenarian impostor to fabricate in detail. In view of that, and perhaps also on the principle of innocent unless proved guilty, the present writer is inclined to accept Peru's claim to be a Chopin pupil, suggesting nevertheless that his reminiscences be treated with caution.

Peruzzi, Countess Elise, *née* Eustafiew

Mme Peruzzi, friend of both Liszt and Herz, met Chopin around 1836 and became more closely acquainted with him during the following year, as is documented at that date by an autograph copy of the Waltz op. 69/1 with a dedication by the composer. Chopin, who valued Mme Peruzzi's sight-reading skill, enjoyed playing the piano duet and two-piano repertoire with her; occasionally they would also improvise dialogues at the piano in the form of questions and answers. She twice performed Chopin's concertos in matinées: op. 21 and op. 11 respectively; the *RGMP* (1843/5, 29 January; 1844/16, 21 April) describes these occasions in highly laudatory terms. Of Mme Peruzzi's playing, Gustave Chouquet declared to Niecks: 'This *virtuosa* had no less talent than the Princess Marcelline Czartoryska. I heard her at Florence in 1852, and I can assure you that she played Chopin's music in the true style and with all the unpublished *traits* of the master' (Niecks, II, p. 177). She was one of the first to whom Chopin showed his *Berceuse*. At Niecks' request, Mme Peruzzi set down in writing some vivid reminiscences of her teacher (Niecks, II, pp. 338–9 – a new Appendix VIII incorporated in the third English edition).

Roche, Emily, *née* Moscheles (1827–89)

Eldest daughter of the pianist Moscheles (see pp. 146–7, note 171), she was trained principally by her father. While on tour with him she heard Chopin for the first time in autumn 1839, at the house of her uncle, the banker Auguste Leo. A few days later she accompanied her parents to Chopin's house, where she was profoundly moved by his performance of the Prelude op. 28/17. But there was no mention of lessons at that stage. At the age of fifteen Emily already possessed scores of Chopin's opp. 10, 12, 13, 14, 18, 20, 21, 22, 23, 25, 28, 31, 32, 33, 34, 35 and 36 (plus perhaps one or two works without opus numbers, among them certainly the *3 Nouvelles Etudes* published in her father's *Méthode des Méthodes*). This list, giving a glimpse of her Chopinean repertoire and pianistic level at the time, can be inferred from an unpublished letter from Moscheles to Maurice Schlesinger, dated London, 2 November 1842 (*F-Pn*):

. . . may I ask you [*dich*] at the first convenient opportunity to send the following Chopin works for my Emily, who is very fond of his compositions. She wants to add to those she already has, to make up the complete collection to bind together. / Op. 1. Rondeau / –2. Var. "la ci darem" / –3. Introd. et Polonaise / –4. ? [Sonata, published only posthumously] / –5. Rondeau à la Mazurka / –6. Mazurkas / –7. [*idem*] / –8. ? [Trio] / –9. Notturnos / –11. Premier Concerto / 15. Notturnos / –16. Rondo / –17. Mazurkas / –19. Bolero / –24. Mazurkas / –26. Deux Polonaises / –27. Notturnos / –29. Impromptu / –30. Mazurkas / –37. Notturnos / –38. Ballade / –39. Scherzo / –40. 2 Polonaises / –41. Mazurkas / Everything from then on.

On the autograph letter (kindly drawn to my attention by Dr Jeffrey Kallberg), Schlesinger or an assistant has deleted the op. nos. 1, 2, 3, 6, 7, 8, 9, 11, 15, 16, 17, 24, 26, 27, 29, 30, as well as the final phrase ('Von hier alle folgenden') which would cover opp. 44–49. The numbers left undeleted are those not published or stocked by Schlesinger, so presumably all the others were sent. Even as early as 1842, then, Mlle Moscheles was planning to make up a complete collection of Chopin's works. On returning to Paris in 1843 she studied briefly with Stephen Heller, according to one of his unpublished letters: 'Miss Moscheles is a young person of sixteen [. . .] She is also an advanced musician, and I am to get up at nine o'clock tomorrow morning to give her a lesson; her father asked me to make her work on my Scherzo [op. 24]' (letter addressed to Eugénie de Froberville [Paris, October 1843], private collection). As a tribute to her budding talent, Heller dedicated to Emily the fifth of his *Pensées fugitives* op. 30. In September 1846 Emily Moscheles married J. A. Roche. In spring 1848 she also took some lessons with Hallé, who had recently arrived in London. On 3 May of the same year Moscheles wrote to Chopin, asking him to teach his daughter (*CFC*, III, p. 340). Bülow's testimony confirms that Emily then received some lessons – Belotti (*ARMC*, pp. 662–3, note 19) reasonably estimates ten or perhaps twelve at the most. It can be noted in passing that in 1845 Kalkbrenner had similarly requested '*quelques conseils*' from Chopin for his son Arthur, who was learning the Sonata op. 58 (*SC*, p. 260).

Roubaud, Marie, *née* de Cournand, (1822–1916/17?)

Born in St Petersburg but of French descent, she studied in Paris with Osborne (pupil and occasional assistant of Kalkbrenner). During winter 1847–8 she had the benefit of Chopin's tuition; he gave her precisely eighteen lessons, one hour per week on Thursdays at one o'clock (documented in the Papiers E. Ganche, *F-Pn*). Ganche (*DSFC*) collected the reminiscences of this pupil, who confided to him that she did not know her own exact year of birth. Marie Roubaud mentioned particularly that Chopin 'paid special attention to sound quality and *legato*, did not write annotations on the score, and always demonstrated at the piano' (*DSFC*, p. 86). Chopin allowed her to copy for her own personal use an unpublished manuscript of the [*Fantaisie-*] *Impromptu* (published, with the '*Fantaisie-*' added to the title, by Fontana as op. 66 in his edition of *Oeuvres posthumes*). After Chopin's death, this pupil played in public on rare occasions. Her first appearance, sponsored by Alard and Franchomme (who accompanied Miss O'Meara a few days later in her début performance!) was thus described in the *RGMP* (1852/5, 1 February, p. 37):

We feel that Mme Roubaud de Cournand [she played under this name] needs only to gain more assurance in order to take her place among the most distinguished pianists. Two serious classical pieces by Beethoven and Mozart, played with Alard and Franchomme, had shown how well she understands and can convey the intentions of the great masters. Nothing, therefore, can justify the excess of emotion which compelled her to leave the piano at the very moment when she had the audience spellbound by her expressive and delicate rendering of some beautiful *Etudes* by Chopin, her teacher.

In fact, as Jane Stirling wrote to Ludwika Jędrzejewicz: 'She was so nervous at playing in public for the first time that she was unwell. She had great success. Franchomme and Alard were in this concert' (letter of 20 January–10 February 1852, Wróblewska-Straus, *LSJ*, p. 131). Six years later, she gave another concert, described by the *RGMP* critic as 'one of the most beautiful of the season' (1858/13, 28 March, p. 107).

Rubio, Vera, *née* de Kologrivoff (1816–80)

Russian musician of precocious talent (she gave her first concert at the age of eight), she was recommended to Chopin by the violinist Artôt, in a letter dated 10 May 1841 (*CFC*, III, p. 49). An unpublished letter from London, dated 12 July 1842, from Charlotte Moscheles to Maurice Schlesinger (*F-Pn*) also recommends Mlle de Kologrivoff, who was then arriving in Paris 'pour y étudier la musique sous la direction de Chopin'. This excellent pupil's lessons therefore would not have started before autumn 1842; they continued until 1846, the year of her marriage to the painter Luigi Rubio. According to a letter she wrote to Chopin, summarized by Karłowicz (p. 138), Rubio was to paint a miniature oil portrait of the composer, but this picture remains unknown: either it was never painted, or it has disappeared, or it has gone to ground in a private collection. On the other hand, Rubio painted an excellent portrait of René Franchomme, son of the cellist, around 1847 (collection of M. Laurent Pénicaud, Tonneins/Lot-et-Garonne). It was Mme Rubio whom Chopin enjoined, 'You must sing if you wish to play' (Niecks, II, p. 187). She was his assistant in 1846 and then again (after a long and complicated journey) in 1849, a year in the course of which she taught Jane Stirling. Having taught piano in Paris, Mme Rubio ended her days in Florence where her husband was teaching at the Academy of Fine Arts. The magnificent portrait of Chopin by the Polish painter Teofil Kwiatkowski (*c.* 1844), formerly in the possession of Alfred Cortot, was wrongly attributed by the latter to Luigi Rubio.

Schiffmacher, Joseph (1827–88)

Pianist-composer and teacher from Alsace. He studied the piano in turn with Rosenhain, Schulhoff, Gottschalk and Chopin, and harmony with Reber. It is not known precisely when and for how long he studied with Chopin (probably around 1847, the year of publication of the Waltz op. 64/2 which he mentions). Delacroix is supposed to have said of him, in a Parisian salon, that 'he's the only one who reminds me of Chopin' (Tasset, p. 4). Up to 1887 Schiffmacher published more than 130 genre pieces exclusively for the piano. As a teacher he earned a substantial reputation in Strasbourg, Lyon, Geneva and Paris, by the originality of his conception of artistic studies. The notes he wrote in preparation for a didactic work were published and augmented after his death by one of his students, Aline Tasset. Schiffmacher was one of the piano teachers of the child André Gide, whose *Notes sur Chopin* make some good reading – but with no explicit mention of Schiffmacher.

Stirling, Jane Wilhelmina (1804–59)

Descended from a distinguished Scottish family, this pupil remains famous for her devotion to the person, the works and the memory of Chopin. Many actions inspired by this devotion have established her in the eyes of posterity, to some extent, as the first Chopin 'musicologist'. She did indeed carefully preserve the complete works of her teacher in (mostly) the OFE, furnished with numerous inscriptions, variants and autograph annotations – doubtless with a view to a complete revised and corrected edition, probably projected by Chopin during his stay in Scotland (see Appendix II, pp. 200–11 below). From Karasowski (II, p. 7) and from Jane Stirling's letters to Ludwika Jedrzejewicz (Ganche, *DSFC*, pp. 103–49; Wróblewska-Straus, *LSJ*) we know that this generous Scotswoman bought most of Chopin's estate, also gathering and sorting out many more autographs, letters, papers, drawings and various other objects – which she then either gave to close friends, kept for herself, or forwarded to Chopin's family in Warsaw (such as the last piano he had hired, which she bought from Pleyel after the sealing of the Place Vendôme apartment – information kindly supplied by Mr H. Musielak).

It is well known that Jane Stirling's relations with Chopin were tinged with an unreciprocated love. When did master and pupil meet? The answer is not definitely established. In a book containing some original documents but otherwise incoherent in its argumentation and singularly devoid of scientific rigour, Jane Stirling's biographer, A. E. Bone, traces the beginnings of this relationship back to 1832 (p. 39). However no existing documents in any way confirm this hypothesis. The English pianist Lindsay Sloper, a pupil of Chopin, who lived in Paris from 1841 to 1846, told Niecks (II, p. 291) that he had given lessons to Miss Stirling prior to introducing her – at her request – to Chopin. On the other hand the first mention of Jane Stirling's name from Chopin's pen is dated 3 January 1844, in the form of an autograph dedication on the score of the Nocturnes op. 9. This constitutes a *terminus post quem non*, 1841 a *terminus a quo* – if we are to trust Sloper's accuracy. In addition, August 1844 was the publication date in Paris of the Nocturnes op. 55, dedicated to Jane Stirling, and the Mazurkas op. 56, dedicated to her friend Catherine Maberly – also Chopin's pupil. From these dates and facts we may reasonably infer that the composer probably met Miss Stirling around 1843 or, at least, on the 3rd of January 1844 – an opinion held by Harasowski.

Chopin seems to have thought well of this pupil's talent, for he told her: 'Vous jouerez un jour très, très bien' (Ganche, *DSFC*, p. 135). Nevertheless he entrusted her to Mme Rubio in 1849; after her teacher's death, Jane continued her studies with Tellefsen, to whom she was particularly close. It was she who organized Chopin's stay and concerts in Scotland, with the help of her elder sister, Mrs Erskine, from whom she was inseparable. Solange Clésinger-Sand sketches these two characters in her memoirs: 'During lesson-times at the master's house, one would often come across two long persons, of Scottish origin and size, thin, pale, ageless, solemn, dressed in black, never smiling. Under this rather lugubrious surface were concealed two lofty, generous and devoted hearts. The one who took lessons was called Miss Stirling; the other lady accompanying her was her sister Mrs Erskine' (Eigeldinger, *SCFC*, p. 238). Chopin, who in his correspondence first refers to them as 'mes braves Ecossaises', eventually grew somewhat exasperated with their over-solicitude and their tendency towards religious proselytism (*SC*, 324, 326, 344–5, 349, 351–3). Miss Stirling discreetly helped the composer out of a difficult financial situation in the year of his death. It was she who supervised Clésinger's work for the Père-Lachaise funeral monument, and who argued with the touchy Fontana over the publication of the posthumous works. She remained on particularly close terms with Mme Dubois, Franchomme, Tellefsen, and above all with Ludwika Jędrzejewicz – whom she constantly consulted about everything concerning Chopin's estate. Her correspondence with the latter is a mine of information, still partly unexplored; Karłowicz (pp. 189–98) has summarized the content of 46 of these missives (dating from 1849 to 1854); Ganche (*DSFC*, various pages) reproduces long extracts from them, but tacitly modifies several turns of phrase. His manuscript copy of these fragments is now in the Papiers E. Ganche, *F-Pn*; at present *PL-Wtifc* holds the originals of 25 of these letters, now published through the work of Hanna Wróblewska-Straus (*LSJ*).

Streicher, Friederike, *née* Müller (1816–95)

One of Chopin's best professional students, she gave up her career after 1849, the year of her marriage to J. B. Streicher of the famous Viennese piano-making family. Arriving in Paris in 1839 with the express purpose of working with Chopin, Friederike Müller called on him with a letter of recommendation from the Countess Appony (dedicatee of the Nocturnes op. 27) whose musical salon was frequently honoured with the presence of Chopin and his best pupils. Friederike Müller received lessons from Chopin for a year and a half without interruption (end of October 1839 to spring 1841), taking two hours of lessons a week:

Many a Sunday I began at one o'clock to play at Chopin's, and only at four or five in the afternoon did he dismiss us. Then he also played, and how splendidly; but not only his own compositions, also those of other masters, in order to teach the pupil how they should be performed. One morning he played from memory fourteen Preludes and Fugues of Bach's, and when I expressed my joyful admiration at this unparalleled performance, he replied: 'Cela ne s'oublie jamais.'   (Niecks, II, p. 340–1)

A little later she mentions this significant trait:

I heard him often preluding in a woderfully-beautiful manner. On one occasion when he was entirely absorbed in his playing, completely detached from the world, his servant entered softly and laid a letter on the music-desk. With a cry Chopin left off playing, his hair stood on end – what I had hitherto regarded as impossible I now saw with my own eyes. But this lasted only for a moment.   (Niecks, II, p. 341)

For Chopin to have entrusted her from the start with his *Etudes* and Preludes, this student must have been exceptionally advanced. According to Marmontel, Friederike Müller was counted among his 'disciples affectionnées'; and indeed, Chopin dedicated to her his *Allegro de Concert* op. 46 – which inspired Liszt to nickname her 'Mademoiselle opus quarante-six'. The fact that she met Ludwika Jędrzejewicz (see *SC*, p. 241) in Vienna, and Pauline Viardot (see Marix-Spire, pp. 177–8), shows that she was familiar with Chopin's friends and family. In her last lesson, in spring 1841, Chopin paid tribute by giving her the autograph of the *Etudes* op. 10/3 and 4. Having moved back to Vienna, she returned to appear in public a year later, according to the *RGMP*:

Yesterday [17 April] Mlle Frédéricque Mueller, a native of Brunn (Moravia) and pupil of Chopin, gave her first *public* concert. This young lady combines in her elegant playing all the beauties and all the depth universally acknowledged in her great teacher. That is enough to place Mlle Mueller among the *coryphées* of her art, and it will not be long before her name shines at the side of those whose talent has aroused the just enthusiasm of all Europe.   (*RGMP*, 1842/18, 1 May, p. 197)

It was she who, from Vienna, recommended Filtsch to Chopin (see Kar-łowicz, p. 141). Between the end of 1844 and February 1845, Friederike met her teacher again in Paris and delighted him with her performance of his op. 46. For the text of his edition Mikuli made use of (among other sources) scores annotated by Chopin during Friederike Müller's lessons. She, in answer to Mikuli's request, wrote to him (8 January 1879):

In some of my scores there are corrections in his hand; I can also remember many more. In the letters I wrote from Paris to my aunts in Vienna there are some observations which could prove useful [to Mikuli's edition]; these letters are with me and I shall look through them straight away. They also give the order in which I studied his works, even though I think I can remember that myself.   (Federhofer, p. 96, note 30)

These scores and letters are not to be found in any of the libraries or public archives in Vienna. The memoirs of Friederike Streicher-Müller, quoted by Niecks as extracts from her diary between 1839 and 1841, are in fact probably a reworking of a text she originally intended for Mikuli (a fragment of whose Preface is quoted), made on the basis of material from the above-mentioned letters, and therefore subsequent to 1880. Niecks, contrary to his usual practice, does not specify that this testimony was drafted at his request. In

10 Friederike Müller (later Mme Streicher). Lithograph by Anton
Hähnisch, 1847.

any case it constitutes a living source of information on Chopin's teaching.
The German edition of Niecks (II, pp. 366–70) possibly quotes the original
German of Frau Streicher's text.

Tellefsen, Thomas Dyke Acland (1823–74)

A Norwegian pianist-composer and teacher who settled in Paris in 1842, he was born into a family of musicians and received a sound musical education rooted in Bach and the Baroque masters – which would not displease Chopin (in a private concert Tellefsen played some Bach Fugues on an early eighteenth-century harpsicord: see *RGMP* 1853/52, 25 December, p. 447). Arriving in Paris with the aim of studying with Chopin, Tellefsen had to wait two and a half years before his hopes were realized. In the meantime he took lessons with a compatriot pupil of Kalkbrenner, and later (beginning of 1843) attended the latter's classes without much enthusiasm. Thanks to the intervention of Henri de Latouche, a literary man friendly with George Sand, the young Norwegian was introduced to Chopin in December 1844; as he was giving vent to his enthusiasm, Chopin observed, 'Vous êtes un peu *schwärmerisch*, mais c'est bien, comme tous les gens du Nord' (Tellefsen, p. 79). Tellefsen then received three lessons weekly, two of them free of charge; he appears then to have been one of Chopin's copyists, according to Mikuli, his fellow student in Reber's composition class. Tellefsen accompanied Chopin on the journey to Britain, by which time his own pianistic education seems to have been completed – he himself made a tour of England in the first half of 1849. In a letter to his mother (28 December 1849) Tellefsen relates:

Before his death [Chopin] told his sister [Ludwika] that I should be the one to teach her daughter [Ludka, later Mrs Ciechomska]: you can imagine what that means to me. He also expressed the wish that I should finish his Pianoforte Method; I am working at it already, with great enthusiasm.   (Tellefsen, p. 117)

Such an assignment demonstrates Chopin's trust in this pupil, of whom one wonders whether he was equal to the responsibility: the completed piano method (to which Jane Stirling refers in June 1850: see Ganche, *DSFC*, p. 116) was never published nor even completed. (See p. 90, note 1, above.) The above letter suggests that he returned the original to Ludwika Jędrzejewicz before the latter passed it to Marcelina Czartoryska in 1850; he could also have had later access to it via Czartoryska. Tellefsen remained on close terms with Marcelina Czartoryska, Franchomme, and Jane Stirling to whom he gave some lessons in the years after Chopin's death. Having become a highly respected teacher in Paris, he performed there as a concert pianist in the decade 1850–60; the *RGMP* more than once reports his successes, notably in the following passage:

Another pianist, M. Tellefsen, hailing from the depths of Norway and guided by that star which leads all artists to Paris, gathered around him last Tuesday a select audience for an evening concert at the famous Hôtel Lambert. M. Tellefsen was pupil, friend and faithful admirer of Chopin. He has inherited the master's tradition and has become imbued with his spirit. His style is moulded on that of the master with whom he felt close affinities of sentiment and soul. Suffice it to say that this artist does not play the piano like everyone else. Many others will astonish or dazzle more than he; but very few will know how to make the keyboard speak a better articulated, or more confidential, delicate and profound language. Few will be able to interpret better the hazy, slightly mystical poetry whose gentle breath the Polish composer has imparted to all his works. M. Tellefsen proved this the other evening, interpreting with quite extraordinary talent a Nocturne and a Waltz by Chopin, as well as a Polonaise for piano and 'cello by the same composer. He also managed his part to perfection in a quartet by Beethoven, with Alard, Franchomme and Casimir Ney. He was then heard both as composer and executant in a set of variations on an original theme, and in three Mazurkas, for which he gained well-deserved applause for both skills.   (*RGMP*, 1851/18, 3 May, p. 141)

In 1860 Tellefsen published through Richault a twelve-volume *Collection des Œuvres pour le piano par Frédéric Chopin*, with an introductory note: 'Monsieur Tellefsen, a pupil of Chopin, himself equipped with all the qualities necessary to ensure good performance and fortunate enough to possess a collection of scores corrected by the composer's hand, has kindly agreed to undertake this work.' Mikuli was to take over the torch; in his Preface (p. 1), he refers to the Richault edition as incomplete owing to the editor's poor state of health – probably a tactful euphemism, as the text is unsatisfactory. As a composer Tellefsen left 44 opus numbers, consisting of piano pieces, chamber music and two concertos; about ten of these works are dedicated to students and friends of Chopin. As often happens in these cases, Tellefsen's letters to his family are full of references to Parisian musical life but devoid of any detail about Chopin's teaching methods.

Thun-Hohenstein, Count Bedřich (1810–81)

Descended from illustrious aristocratic Bohemian lineage, he arrived in Paris in autumn 1834 in the company of his parents and four brothers and sisters. The family met Chopin at the home of the secretary to the Saxon embassy Thomas Albrecht (dedicatee of the Scherzo op. 20). From then on the Thun family befriended the composer, who was described as 'maître de clavecin [!] des enfans [*sic*] à Paris' by the senior Countess in a letter a year after their arrival in the capital (Simonides, p. 80). Of the five children three in all had the privilege of Chopin's teaching. The two youngest, Anna (1812–85) and Juža (1815–95), took some lessons in October–November, as shown by two short autograph letters from Chopin (see p. 137, note 142). The Count Bedřich, who remained longer in Paris, received just under twenty lessons, between the end of November 1834 and March 1835, of one hour weekly, happily prolonged, at least at first. 'Il est très attentif et donne toujours presque une heure et demie', he wrote of Chopin in a letter of 17 December 1834 (Simonides, p. 77). He is the only pupil except for Mme Peruzzi to mention sessions of sight-reading duets as part of Chopin's teaching. He also briefly reports his impressions of Hiller's concert on 22 February 1835, where his teacher participated in a Duo for two pianos by Hiller. In mid-September 1835 Chopin stayed at the Thun-Hohenstein family château in Děčín. It was then that he copied into the album of one of Bedřich's sisters a first version of the Waltz op. 34/1, dedicated, as is the final autograph fair copy, to the young Countess Juža who felt a tender attachment to him. The last epistolatory document, a letter headed Prague, 8 May 1845, from Bedřich to Chopin, recommends a young compatriot wishing to perfect his piano playing, and bears witness to the former pupil's happy memories (Karłowicz, p. 181).

Viardot, Pauline, *née* García (1821–1910)

Daughter of the famous Spanish singer and teacher Manuel García, and the younger sister of Malibran – whose dazzling appearances on European stages unjustly overshadowed Pauline's early career, especially in France – this exceptionally talented and cultured musician was as remarkable a pianist as singer. As a child, she was taught for two years by Liszt who predicted a virtuoso career for her. Later, Chopin was to interrogate her intensely about these two years of teaching, 'to the point that Pauline, to make him happy, noted on paper the programme of studies which Liszt had elaborated for her', according to a statement by Alice Viardot (Desternes–Chandet, pp. 244–5). It was shortly after her first successes as a singer, during the winter of 1839–40, that Pauline Viardot formed a friendship with George Sand, and served as the model for the character of *Consuelo* – a novel in which some thoughts on popular songs and the evocative powers of music (Chapter 55) reflect Chopin's views, on Sand's own admission (*HV*, II, p. 421 note). Pauline and Chopin were soon brought closer together by their musical affinities: their worship of Mozart, their love for *bel canto*, as much of the eighteenth century as of the Romantic period, and their taste for folk music, particularly that of Spain (*SC*, pp. 249, 335) and Berry (see Sand, *CGS*, IX, pp. 839 and note 1, 840; XII, p. 264; they both made transcriptions of Berry songs). Pauline Viardot seems not to have received lessons from Chopin in the strict sense so much as informal pianistic advice, in Paris, and above all in Nohant during her summer visits in 1841, 1842, 1843 and 1845. These were the sessions that inspired the drawing by Maurice Sand (see Fig. 11; the handwritten date is wrong) showing Chopin exclaiming 'Ça c'est le jeu de "Listz" [*sic*]! Il n'en faut

11   Chopin teaching Pauline Viardot: 'That's the "Listz" [*sic*] way of playing! You mustn't play like that when accompanying the voice.' Ink drawing by Maurice Sand, from his first album, Nohant, June 1844 (the date does not tally with Viardot's visits to Nohant).

pas pour accompagner la voix.' These joint visits to Nohant often provided opportunities to sight-read favourite composers: 'Pauline and Chopin read entire scores at the piano', wrote Sand in 1841 (*CGS*, V, p. 401). As a singer Pauline Viardot participated, together with Franchomme, in one of Chopin's most important Paris concerts (21 February 1842), at which Chopin himself accompanied her in a song of her own composition on La Fontaine's *Le chêne et le roseau*. She subsequently adapted Spanish and French lyrics to several Mazurkas which she sang in London, apparently to Chopin's great pleasure (*SC*, pp. 316, 318–19, 324–5). (However, a bone of contention in that regard emerges from a letter from Chopin to Marie de Rozières, headed London, 30 June 1848: 'In Viardot's programmes [. . .] there is no longer the item: "Mazurkas of Chopin" but merely "Mazurkas arranged by Mme Viardot" – it appears that it looks better. It is all the same to me; but there is a pettiness behind it. She [. . .] is afraid of a certain newspaper which perhaps does not like me. It once wrote that she had sung music "by a *certain* Mr Chopin" whom no one knows, and that she ought to sing something else. Don't mention it to [name illegible] for it might come back here and be taken as another example of my ingratitude' (*SC*, p. 322).) From then on she often included these transcriptions in her programmes, earning the approval of Delacroix (II, p. 316) and also Ferdinand Hiller (*ATZ*, II, p. 54). The Parisian editor Gérard published [1866] *Six Mazourkes de F. Chopin arrangées pour la voix par Mme Pauline Viardot. Paroles de Louis Pomey* (opp. 50/2, 33/3, 6/1, 7/1, 68/2, 24/1); in 1899 Gebethner & Wolff published, in Warsaw, fifteen adaptations – five of them duets – of lyrics of the same writer with Polish translation: *Mazurkas. Arrangées pour voix par Mme Pauline Viardot* (opp. 50/2; 33/3; 6/ 1; 7/1; 68/2; 24/1; 6/4; 7/3; 24/2; 33/2; 50/1; 67/1; 7/3 – duo – ; 17/1; 59/1). We know that Viardot took part in the performance of Mozart's *Requiem* at Chopin's funeral at the church of La Madeleine. Saint-Saëns, a regular visitor to Pauline Viardot's salon, compiled various fragments of her recollections of Chopin's playing and teaching (*EV*, *QM*).

Zaleska, Zofia, *née* Rosengardt (1824–68)

A pianist from Warsaw who settled in Paris in 1843, she married the Polish poet Bohdan Zaleski (1802–86) there three years later. Having come to Paris in order to study with Chopin, Zofia Rosengardt immediately became part of the literary circle of Polish émigrés, represented principally by Mickiewicz, Słowacki, Zaleski, Witwicki and Klementyna Hoffman-Tańska. It was through Witwicki's introduction that her lessons with Chopin began, ten in all, early in November 1843. Between then and mid-March 1844, Zofia Rosengardt's diary (the passages referring to Chopin and the Polish émigrés are published in Hordyński) mentions eight lessons, normally one a month, but two in November 1843 and three in March 1844. The reason for this scarcity lay not in the financial difficulties that troubled this gifted pupil, but in her nervous disposition: her somewhat manic and disordered attitude was not conducive to Chopin's peace of mind, and some of his own fluctuations of mood may have been precipitated by this pupil. 'He has plenty of wit and natural wisdom, also some wild, painful, nasty and angry moments when he breaks chairs and stamps his feet. He is as capricious as a spoilt child, scolds his pupils, treats his friends coldly. This happens mostly on days when he's ill, physically weak, or has argued with Madame Sand', she wrote to her parents between 24 December 1843 and 6 January 1844 (Hordyński, pp. 156–7). In December 1844, Bohdan Zaleski had to intercede with Chopin to resume Zofia's interrupted lessons (CFC, III, pp. 184–5). Zofia's diary mentions one of these in April 1845, and another in May 1846. Among the works studied, in addition to studies by Clementi and Moscheles, she mentions one Impromptu, the Nocturne op. 9/2 and possibly a Polonaise. Nevertheless, the clashes of temperament did not prevent Chopin from being a witness at his pupil's marriage to Zaleski, on 28 November 1846 at the church of Saint-Roch; indeed, quite uniquely, he even composed for this occasion two religious pieces, including a *Veni creator* – the unknown and unpublished autograph is thought to be in the possession of the Bourbon-Parme family. A dedication dated 16 January [18]48 written on the title page of the first edition of the Sonata op. 65 (*F-Ppo*) shows that contact was maintained thereafter. After Chopin's death Jane Stirling occasionally encountered this pupil whom she familiarly named 'la Sophisette' in her letters to Ludwika Jędrzejewicz (Wróblewska-Straus, *LSJ*, pp. 138, 145). Kleczyński, during his stay in Paris (1859–66), sought the advice of, among others, Zofia Zaleska. Her scores, deposited in *F-Ppo*, raise some sticky problems concerning identification of the annotations they contain, which are in a number of different hands (see Appendix II, pp. 234–8 below).

Appendix I

TRANSLATED TRANSCRIPT OF CHOPIN'S
'SKETCH FOR A METHOD' (*PROJET DE MÉTHODE*)

This text is reproduced here in full for the first time; a number of Chopin's deletions and alterations are included inside curved brackets { }. The translated transcript follows the page order of the autograph – paginated by a hand different from Chopin's – as it appears in its present binding, in the Pierpont Morgan Library, New York. A horizontal line marks the beginning of each new sheet of paper. For the history and the drafting principles of the *PM*, see p. 90, note 1.

The elbow level with the white keys, the hand [pointing] neither in [*dedans*] nor out [*dehors*].

Notes and their keys on the piano

Each sound relative to another is low or high, deep or shrill. – In order to write down sounds, it is therefore natural to use lines superposed one above another like steps of a ladder.

Let's make a supposition and imagine a ladder composed of as many steps as are necessary to fit all the sounds from the deepest to the highest. Music notated on such a large number of lines would of course be indecipherable.

To guide the eye, we write down on one of the central lines of this long ladder the sound which all voices are able to sing and [which] all instruments modelled on the voice are able to play, being consequently in a region of sounds neither too high nor too low. We obtain a note which we conventionally call *do* or *ut* like the Italians, or *c* or *da* like the Germans. As one never sings {a sound/deleted} too low or too high, we start

---

Notes and their keys on the piano

One sound relative to another is low or high (deep or shrill). – In order to write down sounds, we therefore use lines superposed one above another.

Because the distance from the lowest possible to the highest sound is too large to make it easy to identify all the intermediary sounds visually, when notated on the corresponding lines, we do as follows.

Let's imagine a ladder composed of as many steps as would be necessary to contain all the sounds from the deepest possible to the highest. Music written on such a vast number of lines would be indecipherable. To guide the eye and make reading possible, we notate the step corresponding to the sound that all voices can sing and that all principal instruments can play. This notated step will give us a note which by *convention* is called a C [*un* do – *ou un* ut].

With this central note as our starting point, we shall find high notes as we go up and low notes as we go down. So by suppressing this middle step for the convenience of the eye, we will divide this ladder of sounds into high and low; and in numbering them, in the high part we will find that one rarely writes for the voice above the 5th line, and descending we will find that one rarely sings lower than the 5th line.

Thus we will help our eye immensely if we omit the lines above those five marked in the high region and below the five in the low region – except to add them when required.

For learning notes and the keys on the piano

Sound, one relative to another, is low or high (deep or shrill). To notate different sounds we therefore use a certain quantity of lines superposed one above another.

Since the distance from the lowest possible sound to the highest would be too great, the ladder upon which we would have to notate this series of sounds would be too vast for the eye to be able to grasp. And besides, since we seldom use very low or very high sounds, we have placed in the middle of the ladder the note that a man, a woman, a child can sing and that all string and wind instruments can play as the middle of

———

Intonation being the tuner's task, the piano is free of one of the greatest difficulties encountered in the study of an instrument. One needs only to study {the most comfortable (that is the most natural)/deleted} a certain positioning of the hand in relation to the keys to obtain with ease the most beautiful quality of sound, to know how to play long notes and short notes and [to attain] {comprehensive/deleted} unlimited dexterity.

———

One cannot overpraise the genius who presided over the construction of the keyboard, so well adapted to the shape of the hand. Is there anything more ingenious than the higher [= black] keys – destined for the long fingers – so admirably serving as points of pivot. Many times, without thinking, minds who know nothing about piano playing have seriously proposed that the keyboard be levelled: this would eliminate all the security that the pivot points give to the hand, [and] consequently make the passage of the thumb in those scales involving sharps and flats extremely difficult {If levelling the keyboard, one should logically remove a joint from each finger/deleted}: legato thirds and sixths, and generally all legato playing, enormously difficult. And as the intonation is looked after by the tuner, the mechanical difficulty presented by the piano – with the keyboard that so assists the hand – is less difficult than one imagines. – I am not, let it be understood, dealing here with musical feeling or style but *purely* with the *technical* aspect of playing, what I call the *mechanism*.

I divide the study of piano mechanism into three parts:

1st   Teaching both hands to play adjacent notes (notes a tone and a semitone apart), that is, scales – *chromatic* and *diatonic* – and *trills*. Since there cannot be devised any *fourth* theoretical combination of adjacent notes, whatever we invent to be played using tone and semitone intervals has to be a combination or selection of scales and trills.

2nd   Notes further than a tone or semitone apart, that is, intervals of a tone and a half upwards:
The octave divided in minor thirds, with each finger thus occupying a key, and the *common chord* with its inversions. (Disjunct notes [*Les notes sautées*]).

3rd   *Double notes* (in two parts): *thirds*, *sixths*, *octaves*. When you can play your thirds, *sixths* and octaves, you are then able to play in three parts – as a result [you have] chords, which you will know how to divide from your knowledge of disjunct intervals.

The 2 hands together will give 4, 5, 6 parts – and there is nothing more to be invented as far as mechanism of piano playing is concerned.

To those who are studying the art of piano playing I suggest {not just some more or less brilliant and debatable theories but/deleted} some practical {easy to verify/deleted} and *simple* ideas which I know from experience to be really useful. As art is infinite within the limits of its means, so its teaching should be governed by the same limits in order to give it boundless potential.

People have tried out all kinds of methods of learning to play the piano, methods that are tedious and useless and have nothing to do with the study of this instrument. It's like learning, for example, to walk on one's hands in order to {make an entrance in a salon/deleted} to go for a stroll. Eventually one is no longer able to walk properly on one's feet, and not very well on one's hands either. It doesn't teach us how to play the *music* itself {nor what one calls difficulties/deleted} – and the kind of difficulty we are practising is not the difficulty encountered in good music, the music of the g[reat] masters. It's an abstract difficulty, a new genre of *acrobatics*.

So we are not dealing here with {infinitely stretching/deleted} more or less ingenious theories, but with whatever goes straight to the point and smoothes the technical side of the art.

We know lines, piano keys, signs and tones; we have some idea of hammers and dampers.

[I]. Position yourself so as to be able to reach both ends of the keyboard without leaning to either side. The right foot on the sustaining pedal without operating the dampers.

II. Find the right position for the hand by placing your fingers on the keys E, F♯, G♯, A♯, B: the long fingers will occupy the high [= black] keys, and the short fingers the low [= white] keys. Place the fingers occupying the high [= black] keys all on one level and do the same for those occupying the white keys, to make the leverage relatively equal; this will curve the hand, giving it the necessary suppleness that it could not have with the *fingers straight* {curving it to the degree most comfortable to its shape, a suppleness that it could not have with the *fingers straight*/deleted}. A supple hand; the wrist, the forearm, the arm, everything will follow the hand *in the right order*.

III. Intonation being the tuner's task, this great difficulty no longer existing for the pianist, it is useless {would be absurd/deleted} to start learning scales with C major, the easiest to read, and the most difficult for the hand as it has no pivot. Begin with one that places the hand at ease {with 3 keys/deleted}, with the long fingers on the black keys like B major {F♯ major/deleted} for instance.

Dear Child: you've had excellent lessons in music. You've been taught to love Mozart, Haydn and B[eethoven]. You sight-read [the works of] the great masters, you {feel and understand them as much as possible/deleted}. You lack only what one calls *fingers*, in order to play more easily {without wasting a lot of time/deleted} as you feel it, [the music of] the great masters of which you've been given the taste.

About notes

Music proceeds by sounds. As soon as there are two sounds, one is higher, the other lower. It's therefore logical that we should use lines placed one above the other to notate the sounds. One can imagine sounds going infinitely high, as well as low. In this infinity of sounds there must be a region in which vibrations are more easily discernible to us. Let's take from the middle of this region one of the sounds which can comfortably be sung by everybody – men, women, children – and which we *call ut* or *do*, or *c* or *da*: this note is found almost at the middle of the piano keyboard, on the white key before a group of 2 black keys; moving from this key, to the right we shall find higher and higher sounds, and to the left lower and lower. To write down these sounds, it is simplicity that the lines above the one where we have notated the *ut*, or *do*, or *c* serve to mark the higher, shriller sounds, and the lines underneath this same line of *ut* to mark the lower, deeper sounds.

No one will notice the inequality of sound in a very fast scale, as long as the notes are played in equal time – the goal isn't to learn to play everything with an equal sound. A well-formed technique, it seems to me, [is one] that can control and vary [*bien nuancer*] a beautiful sound quality. For a long time we have been acting against nature by training our fingers to be all equally powerful. As each finger is differently formed, it's {evident that we shouldn't/ deleted} better not to attempt to destroy the particular charm of each one's touch but on the contrary to develop it. Each finger's power is determined by its shape. The thumb has the most power, being the broadest, shortest, and freest; the fifth [finger] as the other extremity of the hand; the third as the middle and the pivot; then the second [a few words illegible], and then the fourth, the weakest one, the Siamese twin of the third, bound to it by a common ligament, and which people insist on trying to separate – which is impossible and, fortunately, unnecessary. As many sounds as there are fingers – everything is a matter of knowing {how to use the fingers/deleted} good fingering. Hummel was the most knowledgeable [?] on this subject. {Fingering, by these principles, isn't difficult/deleted} Just as we need to use the conformation of the fingers, we need no less to use the rest *of the hand*, the wrist, the forearm and the arm. – One cannot try to play everything from the wrist, as Kalkbrenner claims.

Cadences, trills:

The art that manifests itself through sounds is called music.
The art of expressing one's thoughts through sounds.
The art of handling [*manier*] sounds.
Thought expressed through sounds.
The expression of our perceptions through sounds.
The expression of thought through sounds.
The manifestation of our feelings through sounds.
The indefinite (indeterminate) language [*parole*] of men is sound.
The indefinite language [*langue*] music.
Word is born of sound – sound before word.
Word [:] a certain modification of sound.

We use sounds to make music just as we use words to make a language.

1. One abstract sound doesn't make music, just as one word doesn't make language.
2. In order to have music, there must be several sounds.

3. As soon as there are 2 sounds, one is higher and the other lower.
4. To write music, it is logical to use lines graded by height.
5. The relationship between two sounds indicating which one is higher and
    which one is lower, we can imagine sounds rising infinitely high and
    descending infinitely low.
6. In this immensity of sounds we find a region in which the vibrations are
    more easily perceptible to us.
7. Choosing from the central part of this region one of the sounds which
    can comfortably be sung by everybody – women and men, young and
    old; by an adolescent as well as by a mature man – that we call *ut*, *do*,
    C or *da* (situated almost in the middle of the keyboard, on a white key,
    before two black keys),
8. leaving this note on the keyboard, on the right we find higher and higher
    sounds, and on the left of it, lower and lower sounds.
9. To write down these sounds, all the lines on top of the one where we have
    placed our *ut* will be for the high sounds, and all those below will be for
    the low notes.

The values of modern notes and rests

One rarely encounters in modern music the note ⊟
whose value is that of two semibreves ♦ ♦

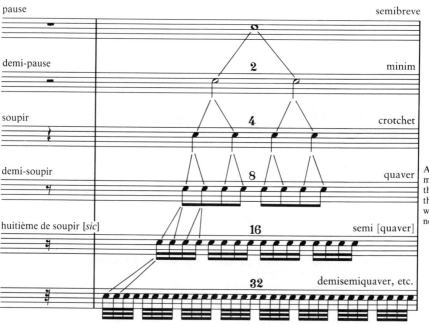

pause		semibreve
demi-pause	2	minim
soupir	4	crotchet
demi-soupir	8	quaver
huitième de soupir [*sic*]	16	semi [quaver]
	32	demisemiquaver, etc.

A dot
means ha
the value
the note t
which it i
near.

About bars
in which each beat has the value of a crotchet

[1] A bar in quadruple time
appears as follows

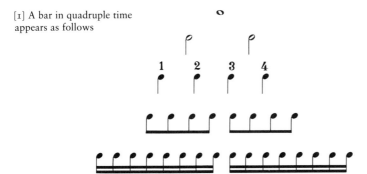

indicated by **C**, or, with a dot added to each crotchet, by $\frac{12}{8}$

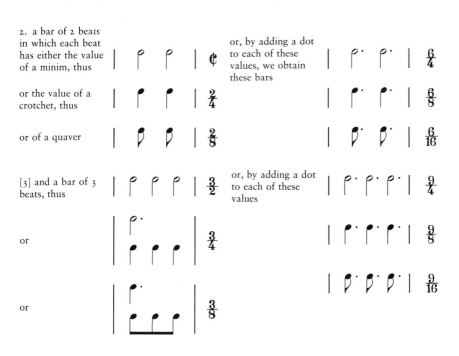

Appendix II: Annotated scores belonging to pupils and associates of Chopin

This appendix is not so exhaustive that it could constitute a separate study independent from the orientation of the present book. Its purpose here is, on the one hand, to provide fuller information on the sources and topics quoted from in the above notes; and, on the other hand, to project outlines for a properly specialized study that has yet to be carried out. Indeed, the thorny problems raised by the annotated scores of Chopin's students and associates have not hitherto been subjected to any systematic or comparative approach. The present appendix, as up-to-date as possible, makes no claim to definitive conclusions, particularly since other annotated scores, at present unknown, inaccessible or presumed lost,[1] may well surface in the course of time.

Of the seven sources examined, the first three (Stirling, Dubois-O'Meara, Jędrzejewicz) are of prime importance, as much by virtue of their provenance as of their contents. The specific character of each one, together with the different working conditions under which each of them was marked, have sometimes made it convenient to present them here in different ways. If this study has managed to solve some hitherto unsolved problems, it has also inevitably raised some new ones, or had to suggest probabilities in some cases rather than definite answers.

Fingerings are by far the most abundant material in these sources; one can immediately guess the order of difficulties confronting the researcher. If, as a rule, a person's handwriting is more identifiably marked by that person's alphabetical script than by his or her numbers, then how have we any certainty of identifying fingerings, marked in pencil (sometimes ink), by various hands, in various circumstances, often within the same copy? In one place, we find fingerings evidently jotted down hastily at the piano, during a lesson or at practice; in another place fingerings tidily copied out from another score – or, perhaps, even dictated? In view of these complications, it seems unlikely that even specialized graphological study would manage to elucidate the more doubtful examples. For those familiar with Chopin's writing, and with those of his entourage and pupils, the main possibility is that of making comparisons with autograph documents containing numbers noted in the most varied conditions possible.

For Chopin autographs, we have at our disposal proofs, corrected in ink, of the *Etude* op. 10/2 (see Fig. 12, p. 199), a chart of scales and arpeggios drawn up and fingered by him (see Fig. 5, p. 35) and numerous autograph musical manuscripts. His pocket diaries and a

---

[1] Between the last third of the nineteenth century and the first decade of the present one, the existence was attested of annotated scores formerly belonging to Delfina Potocka, Marcelina Czartoryska, Friederike Streicher-Müller, Vera Rubio-Kologrivoff, Aleksandra Faucher-Wołowska, R. von Heygendorf-Könneritz, our Anonymous Scottish lady, Karol Mikuli, Thomas Tellefsen, Wilhelm von Lenz and others.

12 First page of the *Etude* op. 10/2, proof for the original French edition
containing inked corrections, all by Chopin.

few hastily written notes (*PL-Wtifc*) help in the matter of pencilled numbers. Jane
Stirling's script is fairly easily identifiable thanks to two written declarations heading the
seven volumes of her collection, the list of pupils compiled by her (see Fig. 2, p. 8), and
the dates in her letters to Ludwika Jędrzejewicz (*PL-Wtifc*). The facsimile reproductions
in the Kobylańska Catalogue (*K*, II) can equally help to identify numbers probably written

by Franchomme through the time signatures in pieces he copied out; the same goes for the tables of incipits in his hand in the Jane Stirling scores. On the other hand, there are no known available autographs of Mme Dubois-O'Meara that might aid possible identification of her script – probably present in the scores which she used during her lessons with Chopin.

We shall not enter here into the problems posed by non-verbal and non-numerical markings such as accidentals, hairpin dynamics, etc., even though some of them may be attributed fairly certainly to Chopin's hand, and some of them even to that of Jane Stirling.

The Stirling scores

Provenance

Paris, Bibliothèque Nationale, Music: Rés. Vma 241 (1–7). Bequeathed in 1979 from the estate of the late Marthe Ganche, née Bouvaist (d. 1971), they were the property of Edouard Ganche until his death in 1945, having been given to him in 1927 by Anne D. Houstoun, who received them directly from her great-aunt Jane W. Stirling (d. 1859), Chopin's pupil.[2]

Description

Virtually all Chopin's works engraved in his lifetime[3] – including the posthumously issued opp. 66–73 – are present, in the OFE,[4] bound in seven volumes. On the collection's arrival at *F-Pn* the following autograph declaration in the hand of Jane Stirling[5] was tipped in at the beginning of Vol. I:

Pour les Oeuvres complètes de Chopin en 7 Volumes
J'ai joué avec Chopin les Oeuvres suivantes:
Op. 7, 9, 10, 15, 21, 24, 25, 26, 28, 29, 32, 33, 34, 35, 36, 37, 38, 47, 48, 49, 51, 55, 56, 58, 64, 65.

---

[2] See *List of Chopin's pupils*, pp. 179–81.

[3] The following compositions without opus numbers are missing: *Polonoise* in G minor; [Two Mazurkas in G and B flat – limited lithographed edition]; *Grand Duo Concertant sur des thèmes de Robert le Diable*; Variation VI (Largo) from *Hexameron*, a collective work by Liszt, Thalberg, Pixis, H. Herz, Czerny and Chopin; Mazurka published in the album *Notre Temps No. 2*'.

[4] Op. 5 is the German edition of F. Hofmeister. The following are in reprints or re-editions of the OFE: opp. 3, 10, 16, 17, 25, 3 *Etudes composées pour la Méthode des Méthodes* [without op. no.]. Two posthumous publications, the Sonata op. 4 and the *Variations sur un Air national allemand* [without op. no.] are in the Austrian Haslinger edition.

[5] A partial duplicate, now in *PL-Kjm*, is reproduced at the beginning of OXF Vol. III. It differs from the first part of the attestation reproduced here ('*Pour les Oeuvres complètes de Chopin en 7 Volumes*') on just two points: opp. 34, 51 and 56 – added in pencil in our attestation – are absent. On the other hand the indication of volumes – absent in our attestation – is given in pencil: 3, 4, 5, 6.

Les doigtés au crayon sur ces Oeuvres sont de sa Main, ainsi que tout ce qui
est *écrit*.

Les doigtés à l'encre ne sont pas écrits de sa Main. Plusieurs m'ont été
indiqués par lui, et d'autres ont été pris sur des Morceaux doigtés par lui
pour ses Elèves.

La Table des Matières a été écrite par Chopin et par Franchomme.

Volumes [ ][6]

par M.A. [Sigismund] Neukomm.

J.W.S.

Pour le recueil des Oeuvres de Chopin en 2 Volumes[7]

Vol. Ier J'ai joué avec Chopin tout ce que ce Volume contient excepté Op. [ ].
Les doigtés sont copiés d'après ceux qu'il m'a faits.

Vol. 2 de même.

(Les exceptions sont, pour les 2 Volumes:

Op. 3, 8, 11, 19, 22, 34, 40, 57, 63.)

For the complete Works of Chopin in 7 Volumes

I have played with Chopin the following Works:

opp. 7, 9, 10, 15, 21, 24, 25, 26, 28, 29, 32, 33, 34, 35, 36, 37, 38, 47, 48, 49, 51, 55, 56, 58, 64,
65.

The fingerings in pencil in these Works are from his Hand, as is everything that is *written
out*.

The fingerings in ink are not in his Hand. Several were indicated to me by him, and others
have been taken from Pieces fingered by him for his [other] Pupils.

The list of Contents was written by Chopin and by Franchomme.

Volumes [ ][6]

by Monsieur A. [Sigismund] Neukomm.

J.W.S.

For the selection of Works by Chopin in 2 Volumes[7]

Vol. 1 I have played with Chopin everything that this Volume contains except op. [ ].
The fingerings are copies from those which he gave me.

Vol. 2: the same.

(The exceptions are, for the 2 volumes:

opp. 3, 8, 11, 19, 22, 34, 40, 57, 63.)

At the head of each of the volumes I–VII is a table of *incipits* of the works
contained, in Franchomme's hand for Vols. I, II and VII, and in that of
Sigismund Neukomm for Vols. III–VI. At the end of Vol. VII there is a

---

[6] Indication left blank: *cf.* last sentence of note 5 immediately above.

[7] These two volumes are now unknown, possibly destroyed. They were probably made up of
duplicate copies of what the seven volumes contain and would have contained only Stirling's own
annotations, copied from Chopin's own in the large collection.

cumulative table of *incipits* for all seven volumes (the 'Table des Matières' mentioned by Stirling), in Chopin's writing and initialled *Ch* in the following cases: opp. 1, 37/1, 38, 48/1–2, 49, 50/1–2 [without the initials], 55/1–2, 57, 58. The others without exception are in Franchomme's hand.

The following works bear an autograph dedication by Chopin:[8]

- op. 9   *à Mlle Sterling* [sic] / *le 3 Janvier 1844* / *Chopin* (pencil)
- op. 35   *à Mlle Stirling* [or Sterling?] / *F. Chopin* (ink)
- op. 37   *à Mlle J.W. Stirling.* / *Chopin* (ink)
- op. 64/1   *à Mademoiselle JW Stirling* / *8 Decembre 1847. Chopin* (pencil)
- op. 65   *J.W. Sterling* [sic]. *5 Janvier 1848* (pencil)
- Mazurka for E. Gaillard, no opus number (*CW*, X, no. 42):
             à Mlle JW Stirling / *F. Chopin* (pencil).[9]

Among the annotations by Chopin having nothing to do with performance, there are dates on a title page (op. 24: *1845*) or at the top of pieces (op. 25/7: *7 Juin 1845*; op. 10/6: *1847*).[10] On the title page of op. 34/2 is written *à jouer* [to be played]; under the last system of op. 10/2 we see × *6me* [= op. 10/6], and at the top of op. 10/9 *prelude en re mineur* [= op. 28/24]. The title page of op. 11 sports the annotation *Adagio* [= *Romance*], which Stirling none the less claimed not to have studied with Chopin. Finally a precious programme of work for her is listed on the back of the second cover page of op. 9:

Préludes.   *2me* Cahier

Ier Cahier <u>mi</u> <u>majeur</u>   × re♭   <u>majeur</u>
              <u>mi</u> <u>mineur</u>   si♭   <u>majeur</u>
              <u>si</u> <u>mineur</u>   × sol♭ majeur [= op. 28/13]
              <u>la majeur</u>[11]   la♭   majeur – 2e Polonaise à Dessauer [= op.
                                      26/2] Maz [or Mar[che]?]

---

[8] To this can be added the dedication present on the title page of op. 1 until it was cut out for an autograph album by Anne D. Houstoun, according to Ganche: *A Melle J.W. Stirling/Fr. Chopin/ Paris. 7 juin 1845.*

[9] A score survives in *PL-Kj*, bound in velvet with Jane Stirling's monogram, of op. 55, whose title page bears the inked inscription *à Mlle J. W. Stirling./F. Chopin/Paris 1845* (see Belotti, *FCU*, III, plate 116). Jane Stirling therefore owned at least two copies of this work (which Chopin dedicated to her); the copy in *PL-Kj* (from the former Ganche collection) carries no other annotations.

[10] Do these dates all carry the same significance? That on the title page of op. 24 could, at a pinch, be considered in lieu of a dedication. But despite the coincidence of the date *7 June 1845*, common to op. 1 (title page) and op. 25/7 (heading the piece), the other dates entered inside collections of pieces seem to refer to a period of work or to one particular performance – unless of course they had some commemorative significance no longer traceable. Whatever the answer, these dates and those others accompanying the dedications are valuable pointers for tracing relations between Chopin and Stirling, as well as the latter's periods of study with him.

[11] This key, corresponding to op. 28/7, is probably an error. In fact the four Preludes concerned are marked, in the Stirling score, with a pencilled cross (= to be studied) and a numbered order; the number 4 is given to op. 28/11, that is, the B major Prelude – which gives the tonally more symmetrical and satisfying plan of E major – E minor – B minor – B major.

13   Autograph note in pencil, by Chopin, on the back of the cover of the
Nocturnes op. 9 in Jane Stirling's printed score, listing works to be studied
(8 Preludes from op. 28 and the Polonaise op. 26/2).

Preludes		2nd Book	
1st Book	E major	× D♭ major	
	E minor.	B♭ major	
	B minor	× G♭ major [=op. 28/13]	
	A major[11]	A♭ major – 2nd Polonaise for Dessauer [=op. 26/2] Maz [or Mar[che]?]	

Still in pencil, on the top right-hand corner of the first page of music of op.
47, appears, *C'est moi qui ai corrigé / toutes ces notes / Ch.*[12]

Content

Inside each volume the compositions are arranged by opus numbers:

Vol. I   opp. 1; 2; 3; 4 [posth.]; 5; 6/1–5; 7/1–4; 8; 9/1–3; 10/1–12
Vol. II   opp. 11; 12; 13; 14; 15/1–3; 16; 17/1–4; 18
Vol. III opp. 19; 20; 21; 22; 23; 24/1–4; 25/1–12; 26/1–2
Vol. IV   opp. 27/1–2; 28/1–12, 13–24; 29; 30/1–4; 31; 32/1–2; 33/1–4; 34/1,
             2, 3; 35; 36
Vol. V   opp. 37/1–2; 38; 39; 40/1–2; 41/1–4; 42; 43; 44; 45; 46; 47; 48/1, 2;
             49
Vol. VI   opp. 50/1–3; 51; 52; 53; 54; 55/1–2; 56/1–3; 57; 58; 59/1–3; 60; 61;
             62/1–2

[12] This phrase has inspired the wastage of much ink from recent commentators and editors of the
third *Ballade*, op. 47. The Stirling score's corrections in this work consist of corrections of two
wrong notes and one wrong rest, plus the addition of seven missing accidentals. These are all
printer's, not author's errors (as is shown by the facsimile edition of the now-lost autograph and by
the OGE, more accurate than the OFE), and so the corrections are therefore not 'author's
corrections' in the technical sense. Since the corrections in question also mostly appear in the
Dubois score, and are hardly more numerous (apart from the accidentals) than in plenty of other
pieces in the Stirling collection, there are no grounds for attaching excessive significance to
Chopin's phrase. Its purpose here seems one of authentification, attesting to his participation in
Stirling's project of preparing a corrected and revised edition.

14   Beginning of the Mazurka op. 7/1 in Jane Stirling's score, with inked
fingering – sometimes inked over pencil – in Jane Stirling's hand.

Vol. VII opp. 63/1–3; 64/1, 2, 3; 65; *3 Etudes composées pour la Méthode
des Méthodes* [without op. no.]; *Variations sur un Air
national allemand* [without op. no., posth.]; *Nouvelle
Mazurka* (dedicated to E. Gaillard) [without op. no.]; opp.
posth. [66; 67/1–4; 68/1–4; 69/1–2; 70/1–3; 71/1–3; 72/1, 2, 3–
5; 73]

The works for piano and orchestra (opp. 2, 11, 13, 14, 21 and 22) are all in the reduction for one piano, and the early chamber music (opp. 3 and 8) includes only the piano part (that is, with the other line(s) not printed above the piano staves as the 'cello line is in op. 65).

Nature of the musical annotations[13]

- – Corrections of misprints
- – Textual modifications (deletions, additions, changed notes[14])
- – Fingerings
- – Indications of tempo and mood[15]
- – Phrasing, articulation, agogics[16]
- – Instructions for ornaments[17]

[13] A certain number of them (in particular those correctly reproduced in OXF) appear in the present book's Notes, *passim*. This Appendix lists a few characteristic ones, under the appropriate rubrics.
   The compositions not containing any annotations (including crosses, whose meaning is discussed below (p. 207, note 21) are as follows: opp. 2; 5; 6/2–5; 7/4; 8; 9/3; 10/7, 10, 12; 13; 14; 16; 17/2–4; 20; 22; 23; 24/2 and 4; 25/3–5; 28/5, 8, 10, 12, 16, 18, 19; 30/2–4; 31; 32/2; 33/3; 40/1–2; 41/1–4; 42; 43; 45; 46; 50/1–3; 52; 54; 56/2; 59/1 and 3; 61; 62/1–2; 63/1 and 3; 64/3; 3 *Etudes composées pour la Méthode des Méthodes* [without op. no.] (D♭, A♭); *Nouvelle Mazurka* [without op. no.] (dedicated to E. Gaillard); all the opp. posth. except 68/3 (its opus number not marked).

[14] *Cuts and deletions:* op. 10/3 bars 32–3, 36–7 and 45–53 (cuts *ad usum delphini*); op. 33/4 bars 87–110 (author's correction; the same cut in the Dubois, Jędrzejewicz and Zaleska-Rosengardt scores); op. 37/1 bar 19, deletion of the r.h. *gruppetto*; op. 37/2 bar 29 (probably author's correction). Some other deletions, intended as facilitated versions for pupils, are listed below on p. 207, note 20.
   Insertions: ornamental variants introduced in op. 7/2 bar 11 (another variant for the parallel bar 27 in the Dubois score: see p. 148–9, note 173), op. 9/2 bars 4–5, 22, 31 and last bar (partly analogous variants in other collections: see notes 183–5, pp. 150–2), op. 11 (*Romance*) bar 59 (variant never published), op. 24/1 bars 58 and 60 (the latter almost the same as a variant in the Dubois score: see pp. 148–9, note 173), op. 34/2 bars 8, 160, 196 (author's correction: see p. 157, note 201), op. 35 ('Funeral March', bar 30).
   Modifications: op. 7/1 bars 56–8 (alternative version, in Jane Stirling's hand); op. 21 (second movement) bars 45–72, l.h. part for solo performance (given virtually correctly in OXF, *Concertos*, pp. 82–5).

[15] There are no handwritten metronome indications. Op. 15/3, the indication *languido e rubato* is deleted (see p. 153, note 187); op. 28/14, *Allegro* is replaced by *Largo* (see p. 125, note 112); op. 33/1 the misprinted *Presto* is corrected to *Lento* (same correction in the Jędrzejewicz score; Dubois has *Mesto*, as has the autograph). For op. 48/2, bar 57, see p. 156, note 192.

[16] Break marked in op. 9/2, middle of bar 12 after the B flat cadence (same indication in the Dubois and Jędrzejewicz scores); crotchet stems added to bring out the r.h. countermelody *e″-d″-f″-e″-d″/f′-e′-d′-e′* in op. 25/1 bars 15–16; pauses above the two dotted crotchets at the opening of op. 25/7. In op. 28/15 bars 23–4, the fourth beat ornament is slurred over the next bar; the same in op. 37/1 bars 82–3, for the r.h. repeated *d″*s; op. 28/21 bar 47, upward stem to bring out the last three l.h. quavers; op. 33/4, *rall.* is specified in bar 144, and accents indicate the summit of the melodic line, bars 181–2; op. 48/1 bars 72–4, the l.h.'s melodic range is marked out by added stems (analogous indications in the Jędrzejewicz score; op. 49 bar 44, oblique stroke indicating a break.

[17] In this respect Jane Stirling's scores are much less rich in annotation than the Dubois collection. In op. 9/2 bar 7, the trilled r.h. *f″* is preceded by *e♮″-f″-g″* in small notes (the same correction in the Dubois, Jędrzejewicz and Franchomme scores, indicating it clearly as Chopin's desired reading);

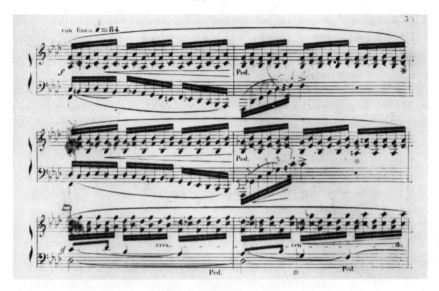

15   Nocturne op. 15/1, bars 25ff, in Jane Stirling's score, with musical modifications and pencilled fingering in Chopin's hand.

- Dynamics[18]
- Pedalling[19]
- Various performing indications[20]
- Crosses ('X' marks)[21]

at bars 13 and 21 the arpeggiated r.h. figuration in small notes is preceded by an additional *g'* (likewise Jędrzejewicz); op. 17/1 bar 51, the third beat r.h. mordant has ♭ inked in above it; op. 21, second movement, bar 39, the r.h. *tr* takes off from a small-note *b♭''* (= same effect as for op. 9/2 bar 7 just mentioned); op. 48/1 bar 10, a line indicates the r.h. *g♭'* to be played together with the l.h. second beat.

[18] The varied dynamic indications are numerous, ranging through every stage from *ppp* to *fff* but also including the indications *cresc.* and *dim.* as well as ⟨ and ⟩ indications. There are grounds to take as definitive authorial corrections the numerous dynamic corrections in op. 27/2 (bars 25–6, 45–6, 50 and 52), since they are corroborated by those in the Dubois and Jędrzejewicz scores (see p. 154, note 189); the same goes for op. 32/1 (bars 8–9, 12, 27–9, 48–9, end), although these recur only in the Jędrzejewicz score, into which Jane Stirling copied some of them. In bar 1 of the second movement of op. 21 there is an inked *p*; also in the final bar of op. 26/2 the printed *ppp* is replaced by *fff* (*ff* in Chopin's hand in the Jędrzejewicz score), offering the possibility of a diametrically opposed interpretation to that of the OFE.

[19] In an apparently unique type of indication, the simultaneous use of both pedals (we know of Chopin's use of this from pp. 57–8 above) is prescribed in op. 15/2 bars 12, 18, 20 and 58 by a 2 (Chopin's hand), explained by *i due Ped.* in the same place (except bar 20) in the Jędrzejewicz score. In addition, missing pedal indications have been restored in op. 36 bars 61, 67, 68 and 73; op. 47 bars 49–53 (similarly in the Jędrzejewicz score); op. 58, third movement, bar 4. There are modifications to the printed pedalling in op. 25/2 bars 18–19; op. 34/1 (the pedal is held on during the last six bars); op. 37/1 bar 16. Pedal indications are also inserted in op. 25/7 bars 1, 2, 3 and 5 (not reproduced in *OXF*), probably in Jane Stirling's hand.

Remarks and problems

Among the annotated scores – known at present – having belonged to pupils or associates of Chopin, those of Jane Stirling constitute in all respects source *alpha*. It was they that served as the basis for Ganche's edition (*OXF*). Comparison between it and the originals shows up many omissions and weaknesses in *OXF*. The absence of the chamber music in *OXF* remains inexplicable. If Ganche considered Stirling's annotated and corrected scores as the definitive version *ne varietur* of Chopin's *oeuvre* (a debatable conclusion in view of the complexity of the manuscript tradition and the

[20] *Arpeggiations:* op. 32/1 bar 12 (r.h. 4th beat), bar 30 (l.h. 1st beat); op. 55/2 bar 60 (r.h. 3rd beat). *Ensemble of attack* between the two hands: op. 27/2 bar 8 (*eb'''* and *bbb''* of the r.h. small-note ornament simultaneously with the l.h. 3rd beat *db'* and *eb*); bar 51, r.h. run starts simultaneously with the l.h. *cb'*, last beat; op. 28/9 bar 8, the semiquavers in the 2nd, 3rd and 4th beats coincide with the last triplet quaver (similar version in the Jędrzejewicz score); op. 32/1 bar 28, r.h. quintuplet spread over the 2nd and 3rd l.h. quavers (*a♯*, *e♯'* – the same in the Jędrzejewicz score). *Redistribution between the hands:* r.h. takes over l.h. notes: op. 25/7 bar 45, *e'*; op. 27/1 bar 27 (4th–5th, 9th–10th quavers) and bar 28 (3rd–4th, 9th quavers); op. 28/15 bars 9 (last l.h. *f'*) and 50 (*e*); op. 28/21 bars 4 and 12 (last *eb'*) – partly analogous indications in the Jędrzejewicz score in the cases of opp. 27/1 and 28/21. *Facilitations for performance:* modifications of texture in op. 15/1, r.h., bars 25–30 and 37–44; deletion of l.h. runs in op. 25/7 bars 21, 24 (reduced to the last four notes, taking the value of semiquavers – similar version in the Jędrzejewicz score) and 52; op. 28/7 bar 12, *e'-f♯'* deleted from the l.h., which takes over the r.h. *a♯'* instead. *Bass doublings* at the lower octave with the sign 8 or *8va*: op. 27/1 bar 84, 1st beat; op. 27/2 bar 59, 1st and 4th beats (analogous version in the Dubois and Jędrzejewicz scores); op. 37/1 bar 1, 1st beat (= as printed in bar 67); op. 55/1 bars 73–4, on each 1st and 3rd beat.

[21] Single, double, sometimes triple crosses, drawn in pencil, are generously scattered through the Jane Stirling scores – as well as those of Mme Dubois-O'Meara and Ludwika Jędrzejewicz. They reveal various meanings according to their positioning and context. On a title page or top of a piece, they indicate a work to study, as seen in those designating four Preludes from op. 28, each accompanied by a number indicating their order (see note 11, p. 202, above). Placed at the end of a piece, they indicate that the pupil's work on the piece is considered satisfactory or finished: they appear after a good many works listed by Jane Stirling in her attestation of works studied with Chopin. The crosses that frame off the opening section of op. 38 specify that that introduction may be played by itself (see pp. 65–6 above and p. 140, note 155). In the course of a piece, two separate crosses isolating a section or groups of bars indicate cuts to the musical text (opp. 33/4; 10/3). Elsewhere a cross marks the place to interpolate a variant reading (op. 7/1) or ornament (op. 9/2) or correction. In other places it can define the placing of a simultaneous attack of the two hands (when grace notes are involved – op. 27/2 bar 51). Finally, Lenz provides a possible key for some remaining crosses, sometimes double, which appear in various places in the music:

'When Chopin was satisfied with a pupil[s performance], he marked a cross under the spot concerned with his finely sharpened pencil. I received one (a *premier chevron*) for the Nocturne [op. 9/2], returned with it again and received a second one. Back I came again with it. "No, don't trouble me with that piece again," said Chopin [. . .] "you've already had an additional cross, I don't give more than three, and *you're* not going to play it any better now!"'

(*GPV* 1872, p. 42)

Apart from that, a cross might very rarely indicate the thumb, following the old English fingering system of + , 1, 2, 3, 4; this happens notably in opp. 34/2 (bars 81–3) and 34/3 (bars 17–20) of the Jędrzejewicz collection, where Jane Stirling indicates the 'translation' into the continental system in op. 34/3.

derivation of the various editions that appeared during the composer's life), he none the less reproduced its various annotations far from completely or correctly. OXF makes no typographical distinction between the handwritten fingerings and those tacitly taken from the OFE, nor between Chopin's pencilled annotations and Stirling's pencil or ink ones. Although he claimed to have added nothing besides his listed sources,[22] Ganche took fingerings appearing only once in the Stirling scores and tacitly repeated them in parallel passages within the same pieces – a permissible procedure if it is explained and consistent. Moreover, he equally tacitly interpolated various indications taken from the Dubois-O'Meara scores,[23] to which he had access before coming into possession of the Stirling collection. The absolute faith he had in his source led him on occasion to choose readings suggestive more of bias than of scientific examination. Therefore that long-authoritative edition should be treated with caution, now that its primary source is once again accessible.

The Stirling scores assume exceptional significance not merely because of the many corrections and annotations that they contain, but above all because they constitute a unique *corpus* of Chopin's *oeuvre*, probably assembled and corrected under Chopin's supervision with a view to a collective edition to improve on the first French editions. In that regard the composer's participation in preparing the final index of *incipits* stands as some surety, as does his autograph attestation in op. 47 – 'C'est moi qui ai corrigé toutes ces notes' – which otherwise would imply an inexplicable exclusive preoccupation with the third *Ballade*. At the end of his stay in Scotland, his health very unstable, Chopin wrote to Grzymała: 'I have put my affairs into some kind of order, in case I should happen to expire somewhere' (*CFC*, III, p. 396). It seems probable that it was during that summer of 1848, when he was in almost daily contact with Jane Stirling, that the composer put his works 'into some kind of order' – with the help of his devoted and possessive student, and perhaps even at her instigation, since it was she who undertook the preparatory work for having them bound and for supplying

---

[22] Ganche described his edition as one
  'whose text would be in exact accordance with the autograph manuscripts available to us and with this original edition, which had been so carefully supervised by the composer himself. The proposed new edition was, we decided, to be entirely free from additions and alterations'.
                                                                    (*OXF*, Preface, p. [1])
[23] These cases are mostly fingerings (opp. 9/1–2; 25/1, 8; 27/2; 34/2; 37/1; 48/1). A notable example occurs in op. 32/1 where bars 58–9 in the Dubois score give r.h. fingering 4–4 and 1–1, which is however reproduced by Ganche in the similar bars 37–8. Other such interpolations are indications for playing ornaments (opp. 15/1; 37/1; 48/1–2) and one simplified reading (op. 48/1). Finally, in op. 64/1, the very first beat has *tr* above it, clearly borrowed from the *non-autograph* inscription 4 *mesures/tr* at the same place in the Dubois score.

incipits at the beginning of each volume, helped by Neukomm. Even if it is clear that the final cumulative index at the end of Vol. VII can have been completed by Franchomme only after the appearance of the *Oeuvres posthumes* (1855, in the edition prepared by Fontana) which form part of the Stirling collection, the question still remains as to when it was that Franchomme collaborated with Chopin in the initial preparation of the index. The earliest possible time would have been 1847, but it was most probably after Chopin's return from Britain, in the summer of 1849 when Chopin was relatively isolated at Chaillot, and Franchomme was a frequent visitor (see *CFC*, III, pp. 415, 433). As for the incipits in Vols. I–VII, by Franchomme and Neukomm, they certainly postdate the composer's death[24] and were drawn up at the request and following the indications of Jane Stirling. The seven volumes cannot have been bound until after August 1855 – when the posthumous works in Vol. VII first came off the press – but were probably bound before 1857, when the posthumous op. 74/1–16, excluded from the collection, came out (Berlin, A.M. Schlesinger) – although Jane Stirling had in fact been closely involved with Fontana's dealings to collect these Polish songs, as her letters to Ludwika Jędrzejewicz confirm.

Jane Stirling's autograph declaration, heading the seven volumes, raises some questions about the constitution of the collection and the provenance of the copies comprising it. Assembled certainly by the Scotswoman – one can hardly imagine Chopin carrying out the operation – the collection up to op. 65 includes a certain number of scores formerly belonging to the pupil (those with Chopin's dedications) and used in her lessons (indications such as 'à jouer'). But this is not the case for them all. If we take literally her list of the twenty-six opus numbers she studied with the composer, several pieces fingered only in Chopin's hand had no part in Jane Stirling's lessons. In any case we have to broaden the scope of the affirmation according to which 'the fingerings in pencil in these Works [the twenty-six opus groups] are from his Hand', because some other works are also annotated exclusively by Chopin.

---

[24] It is not possible that Neukomm's work could have been done in the three days he spent in Chopin's and Stirling's company at the end of August 1848, in the home of Mr and Mrs Schwabe at Manchester. Apart from social obligations, in these three days he had to give a concert, and in addition he was suffering at the time from cataract trouble – not reflected in his clear writing in the Stirling scores – which was operated on just over a month later. On the other hand, on 26 December 1849 Neukomm composed a piece which was published shortly after under the title *A la mémoire de notre ami Fr. Chopin / Elégie harmonique pour l'Orgue Expressif ou Piano* (Paris, Richault; Vienna, Diabelli). From 1850 onwards, he had plenty of time to be in contact with Jane Stirling, either in Britain or in Paris, according to his numerous journeys documented in his *Verzeichnis meiner Arbeiten in chronologischer Ordnung* (facsimile in R. Angermüller, *Sigismund Neukomm. Werkverzeichnis – Autobiographie – Beziehungen zu seiner Zeitgenossen*, Munich and Salzburg, 1977).

Moreover, the 'fingerings in pencil' are far from being all in his hand: there is no mistaking the characteristic script of the Scotswoman in numerous pencilled numbers, written mostly with great care and legibility. The fingerings in ink, however, are all in Stirling's hand. The reason, if there is one, for these two different treatments is not evident; but it gives us all the more grounds to assume that her task of collating extended over several months. She explicitly acknowledges two distinct provenances by affirming: 'Several [of the fingerings in ink] were indicated to me by him, and others have been taken from Pieces fingered by him for his Pupils.' If the term 'indicated' remains ambiguous (possibly meaning 'dictated' during a spell of editorial revision), one source she used is known: the scores which eventually were to belong to Chopin's older sister, Ludwika Jędrzejewicz (described on pp. 220–7 below). The fingerings and various indications from that source are recopied, sometimes in ink, sometimes in pencil, in the Stirling scores. The works involved are opp. 27/2, 29, 33/4, 34/2, 34/3, 47, 48/2(?). Most often the indications from the Jędrzejewicz scores go with other annotations (ink and/or pencil) taken from sources now lost or unknown. In fact the scores of those of Chopin's pupils and associates who kept in touch with Stirling then copied into the Jędrzejewicz scores, are listed on page 225 correspond closely enough with these extra annotations to qualify as possible sources for her task of collation. The same applies to Tellefsen's edition, allegedly prepared from 'a collection corrected by the composer's hand.'[25] The autograph annotations by Chopin in the Stirling collection, which Jane Stirling then copied into the Jędrzejewicz scores, are listed on page 225 below.

In total, 63 pieces in the Stirling collection are annotated with handwritten fingering (each piece or movement within an opus number being counted here singly); 22 contain inked annotations (i.e. by Stirling), 16 of them exclusively inked ones; 57 contain pencilled annotations (i.e. by Chopin and/or Stirling), 41 of them exclusively pencilled ones. It should be added that ink is occasionally used for corrections of accidentals, but also of notes and sometimes of dynamics.

Facsimile edition

Eigeldinger–Nectoux.

---

[25] Ganche had already observed: 'Tellefsen, authorised by Jane Stirling to consult these volumes, paid them little attention' (*VAFC*, p. 124 n. 3).

Further reading

Ganche, OXF, Preface
Ganche, VAFC, pp. 117–46
Kobylańska, PC
Ekier, FCB, passim
Ekier, WWN, pp. 108–11, 118–19, and passim
Kobylańska, K, I, pp. 31–2 and passim
Kobylańska, TBWV, p. xv and passim
Eigeldinger, 'L'exemplaire Stirling. Présentation historique et analytique', in Eigeldinger–Nectoux, pp. xvii–xlv

Critical editions[26]

OXF; CW.
Chopin, Ballady, ed. J. Ekier, PWM-TiFC, 1967
Chopin, Etudes op. 10, op. 25, 3 Nouvelles Etudes, ed. P. Badura-Skoda, Wiener Urtext Edition, 1973, 2 vols. (UT 50030–50031)
Chopin, Impromptus, ed. J. Ekier, Wiener Urtext Edition, 1977 (UT 50058)
Chopin, II Koncert fortepianowy f-moll op. 21. Wersja na jeden fortepian [reduction for one piano], ed. J. Ekier, PWM-TiFc, 1980
Chopin, Nocturnes, ed. J. Ekier, Wiener Urtext Edition, 1980 (UT 50065)

---

[26] The text of OXF is the only source of Stirling for all the editions listed, none of whose editors had access to the Stirling collection itself. This dependence inevitably calls for prudence, given Ganche's lapses already described.

The Dubois-O'Meara scores

Provenance

Paris, Bibliothèque Nationale, Music; Rés. F. 980 (1–4). Bequeathed in 1919 (Vols. I–III), and in 1923–5 (the remainder, consisting of loose scores later bound together to form Vol. IV), to the Library of the Conservatoire National de Musique, Paris, whose contents have been deposited since 1964 in *F-Pn*.

Description and content

The following note, in the hand of Julien Tiersot (Conservatoire librarian at the time of the bequest) is glued to the verso of the front flyleaf of Vol. I:

Ces trois volumes d'oeuvres pour piano de Chopin (n°s 34.324$^{a\ b\ c}$) ont été légués à la Bibliothèque par Louis Diémer à qui ils avaient été confiés, sous réserve de cette destination dernière, par Mme Dubois, née O Méara,[27] élève de Chopin, aux leçons de qui ces exemplaires avaient servi. Maintes pages portent la trace de fines annotations au crayon de l'auteur, nuances, doigtés, corrections, même additions (v. par exemple un contre-chant ajouté p. 7 de la 2me Grande Valse brillante, op. 34, dans le 3me vol., et plus loin, à la p. 2 des 4 Mazourkas op. 33, la correction de 'Presto' en 'Mesto'). En d' autres endroits, des coups de crayon indiquent la correspondance de l'attaque d'un dessin d'agrément ou d'une petite note avec celle de la basse, témoignant de la volonté de Chopin que ces dessins ou notes d'ornement soient attaqués sur le temps même et non avant ou après (voir plusieurs exemples de ce cas dans les Nocturnes, op. 32 et suiv., reliés dans le 2me volume).

[These 3 volumes of piano works by Chopin (nos. 34.324$^{a\ b\ c}$) were bequeathed to the Library by Louis Diémer, to whom they had been entrusted specifically on that condition by Mme Dubois, née O Meara,[27] a pupil of Chopin, at whose lessons these scores were used. Several pages bear the trace of fine annotations in pencil by the composer, nuances, fingerings, corrections, even additions (see for example a counter-melody added on p. 7 of the 2nd *Grand Valse brillante*, op. 34, in the 3rd volume, and later, on p. 2 of the 4 Mazurkas op. 33, the alteration from 'Presto' to 'Mesto'). Elsewhere, pencil markings indicate to attack an ornament or a grace note together with the bass note, showing that Chopin wanted those embellishments or ornamental notes played on the beat and not before or after (see various examples of this in the Nocturnes, from op. 32 onwards, bound in the second volume).]

None of the scores has any autograph dedication. However, the top right hand corner of the title page to op. 55 bears the following pencilled inscription not in Chopin's hand: *donné par l'auteur / à Melle C. Meara*. At the beginning of Vol. III, the title page to op. 29 has this inked indication to the binder: *Mme Dubois / 1 Vol. Voir / la couverture.*

---

[27] See *List of Chopin's pupils*, p. 164.

The four volumes contain the following works – grouped by musical genre – of which nearly all are in the OFE or its subsequent reprinting:[28]

Vol. I   opp. 10/1–12; 25/1–12; 28/1–12, 13–24; 11; 21; 58; 35.

Vol. II opp. 9/1–3; 15/1–3; 27/1–2; 32/1–2; 37/1-2; 48/1, 2; 55/1–2; 62/1–2; 57; 23; 38; 47; 20; 31; 54; 22; 26/1–2; 40/1–2; 44; 61.

Vol. III opp. 29; 36; 51; 18; 34/1, 2, 3; 42; 64/1, 2, 3; 6/1–5; 7/1–4; 17/1–4; 24/ 1–4; 30/1–4; 33/1–4; 41/1–4; 50/1–3; 56/1–3; 59/1–3; 63/1–3; 59/2 (supplement to *RGMP*, 24 May 1846); 43; 19; 60; 14.

Vol. IV opp. 34/1, 2; 64/2; 18; 46; 11; 38; 47; 51 (supplement to *RGMP*, 9 July 1843); 9/1–3.

The scores in this last volume – all duplicates, except for op. 46 – all retain their original coverings of coloured paper; only opp. 18 and 46 contain annotations. The works for piano and orchestra (opp. 11, 14, 21 and 22) are all in the reductions for one piano. Generally, the compositions containing the most annotations (all in pencil – purplish-blue pencil being quite frequent) are the Nocturnes, *Etudes* and Concertos; next come the Waltzes, Preludes and Mazurkas. The *Ballades*, Scherzos and Polonaises have the fewest markings.

Nature of the musical annotations[29]

- Corrections of misprints
- Textual modifications[30]

---

[28] Opp. 7/1–4, 10, 11 (the copy in Vol. IV), 17/1–4, 18 (the copy in Vol. III), 25 and 28/1–12 are all the French re-editions made from the plates of the OFE.

[29] The following compositions contain no musical annotations (if we discount the written fractions $\frac{1}{2}$ and $\frac{1}{4}$ which appear mechanically and with no musical relevance in the margins of some scores): opp. 6/3–4; 7/4–5; 9/1–3 (the copy in Vol. IV); 10/2 and 10; 11 (the copy in Vol. IV); 14; 15/3; 17/1–3; 19; 24/2; 25/5; 28/2, 5, 8, 14 and 19; 30/2–3; 33/2; 34/1–2 (the copy in Vol. IV); 38 (the copy in Vol. IV); 40/1; 41/3–4; 44; 47 (the copy in Vol. IV); 50/1; 51 (the copy in Vol. IV); 56/1; 59/3; 63/1 and 3; 64/2 (the copy in Vol. IV).

[30] Op. 7/2, the word *Fine* printed in bar 16 is deleted and moved to bar 32. (Mikuli indicates *Fine* in both these bars, as if there were some doubt in his mind!) Op. 21, first movement, bar 220, the last two l.h. quavers are corrected to $c\natural'$ and $d\flat'$. Op. 27/2 bar 28, the r.h. dotted crotchet is changed to three quavers on this same $b\flat''$. Op. 32/2 bar 1, a c completes the beginning of the r.h. arpeggio (the same addition in the Franchomme score and the Mikuli edition; it is in this form that the arpeggio is reproduced in the OFE, in the penultimate bar of the Nocturne). Op. 33/4, bars 87–110 are deleted. Op. 46, bars 12–83 are deleted. Op. 58, first movement, bar 186, the l.h. arpeggio on the third beat begins on $F\sharp$ and not B (the same correction in Franchomme and the Mikuli edition). Op. 62/1 bar 72, the initial r.h. $c\sharp''$ is changed to $d\sharp''$, probably to preserve the analogy with the figure of bar 6 (3rd beat), which appears here in a trilled form.

The textual modifications affecting opp. 15/2, 33/4, 34/2, 48/1 and 64/1(?) are pointed out respectively in notes 186, 179, 201, 191 and 202 above, and also in note 23 on p. 98–9.

The ornamental variants added in opp. 7/2, 9/2 and 24/1 are reproduced in notes 173, pp. 148–9, and 183, pp. 150–1. See also pp. 122–3, note 105.

- Fingerings[31]
- Metronome markings, indications of tempo and mood[32]
- Phrasing, articulation, agogics[33]
- Instructions for ornaments[31]
- Dynamics[34]
- Pedalling[35]
- Various performing indications[36]
- Crosses[37]

---

[31] Many examples can be found in the present book's notes dealing with this subject. Ganche (*DSFC*, pp. 205–7) reproduces some indications of how to play ornaments, which are omitted from the present book.

[32] At the top of the *Andante spianato* op. 22 we read ♩.[=]63 – whereas the OFE specifies ♩. = 69. Op. 32/2 bar 3, ♩ = 88[?]. Op. 33/1, the erroneous printed *Presto* is altered to *Mesto* (similarly in Mikuli; in the Stirling and Jędrzejewicz scores it is altered to *Lento*. Op. 48/2 bar 57, *Molto più lento* is deleted (see p. 156, note 192).

[33] See note 79, pp. 112–13, concerning indications of breaks in the phrasing. Elsewhere an added slur prolongs the span of a shorter phrase (op. 10/12 bars 73–7, l.h.), or specifies the beginning of a melodic phrase (op. 48/1 bar 15) or of a new harmonic sequence (op. 32/1 bar 8, l.h.). In other places, a continuous line joins the notes of a hidden melodic figure, whose intervals are to be embraced *legatissimo* (op. 36 bars 71–2, l.h. *e-g♯-a-e-d-f♯-A-D*; op. 60 bars 34–5, l.h., *c♯'-c♯'-c♯'/ c♯-f♯-g♯-a♮-b*).

Agogic markings: op. 6/1, the *rit.* in bar 69 is deleted and moved to bar 71. Op. 10/5 bar 64, 2nd beat, the *poco rall.* is deleted. Op. 29, *rit.* at the beginning of bar 24. In several places the accent > appears, which generally indicates the lengthening of a note.

[34] Op. 10/3 bar 61, *pp* (2nd beat). Op. 10/5 bar 65, the printed *pp* is deleted. Op. 10/7 bar 25, *f* (5th–6th beats); bar 27, the printed *cresc.* is deleted and replaced by *dim.* for bars 27–8. Op. 10/12 bar 83, *ff* (not in the OFE). Op. 11, first movement, bar 470, hairpin *decresc.*; bars 472–3, hairpin *cresc.* Op. 15/1 bar 36, printed *dim.* deleted. Op. 15/2 bar 54, r.h. *pp* on the top *a♯'''*. Op. 18 bars 171 and 175, *p*. Op. 21, first movement, bar 146, the printed *cresc.* is moved to the last beat; bar 151, *f*; bar 153, *p*; bar 155, *f*. Op. 25/3 bar 29, r.h., *f*. Op. 25/8 bar 28, *p*. Op. 27/2, see note 189, p. 154. Op. 28/15 bar 26, r.h., *p* (4th beat); bar 44, *pp*. Op. 28/17 bar 53, *p*. Op. 28/20 bar 12, *f* (2nd beat). Op. 32/1, 'recitativo' section, beginning of the last line, *f* on the small notes. Op. 32/2 bar 55, *pp*. Op. 33/4, bar 224, *f* (1st beat). Op. 36 bar 39, *pp* (not in the OFE); bar 88, *pp*; bar 100, *ppp* (4th beat). Op. 37/1 bar 66, hairpin *cresc.* Op. 37/2 bar 68, *f*; bar 74, *p*; bar 107, *pp*. Op. 43 bar 32, *p* (3rd–4th quavers); bar 48, *p* (*idem*). Op. 48/1 bar 72, r.h., *ff* (3rd beat). Op. 48/2 bar 91, *p* (1st beat). Op. 55/1 bar 72, r.h., *p* (1st beat). Op. 55/2 bar 2, r.h. *p* (2nd dotted crotchet); bar 47, r.h., *p* on the rising *e♭'–d♭''*. Op. 57 bars 66–8, hairpin *decresc.* Op. 58, first movement, bar 21, l.h., hairpin *cresc.*; bar 27, hairpin *cresc.* in both hands; slow movement, bar 59, l.h. hairpin *cresc.* Op. 61 bar 93, r.h., *p* at the end of the run.

[35] Op. 18 (the copy in Vol. III) bar 291, *ped.* at the beginning of the run. Op. 58, *scherzo*, bar 55, *ped.*

[36] *Simultaneous attack of notes:* Op. 64/1, penultimate bar, the *a♮'* of the r.h. run is marked to be sounded with the bass A♭ (as printed in bar 35).

Redistribution between the hands: Op. 28/15 bar 9, r.h. takes the l.h. *f'* (as in Stirling). Op. 31 bar 180, final turn of the double trill is marked *m.g.* Op. 48/1, second half of bar 48, the octaves are to be shared by the two hands as indicated by *les deux mains* (written twice, the lower version not in Chopin's writing).

Facilitation for performance: Op. 48/1 bar 70, the first eight semiquavers for the r.h. thumb are deleted.

Bass doublings at the lower octave indicated by *8* or *8va*: op. 9/2 bars 11–12, on F, G, C, F: op. 27/2 bar 49 on the first D♭, bar 59 on F, G♭ (this example also in Stirling); op. 29 bar 81, on the first

Remarks and problems

The special interest of this collection – although it has its gaps – is that Mme Dubois is generally acknowledged as one of Chopin's best pupils. Subsequently she was one of the few female pupils to continue her teacher's tradition, in private lessons that were regarded as authoritative in the second half of the nineteenth century.

These annotated scores have been the object of various considerations in the literature listed below, but still await a systematic and exhaustive study. Moreover, the scores bound in Vol. IV (with numerous indications – mainly of fingering – for op. 18) have eluded the attention of recent researchers into the subjects, such as Holland (pp. 252 and 255–300) and Kobylańska (*CBKP*; K, I, p. 45).

The Polish complete edition (*CW*), whose critical apparatus regularly takes into account many indications from *OXF* or the Jędrzejewicz scores, refers only in exceptional cases to the Dubois scores (mainly op. 57). The *Urtext* Henle editions mention this source at the head of the critical commentaries to their most recent publications, but hardly take it into account in the details of their editing. In this respect Ekier's *carnet critique* on the *Ballades* (*FCB*) is much more satisfactory. The same editor scrupulously reproduces the annotations from the Dubois scores in his recent critical editions of the Impromptus, Scherzos and Nocturnes (see p. 219 below, *Critical editions*). In spite of certain errors and omissions, the same can be said of Badura-Skoda's critical edition of the *Etudes* opp. 10 and 25 and the *3 Nouvelles Etudes* (see p. 219 below, *Critical editions*).

Ganche was the first to draw attention to the existence of the Dubois scores (*DSFC*, pp. 202–10). The pages on the subject by Holland (pp. 255–300) are inadequate and riddled with approximations, misreadings and copying errors – the author having evidently worked from microfilms when the original itself poses sticky problems of legibility! Thus in Holland's transcription of the Waltz op. 64/1 (pp. 297–300) an average of one in three of

---

beat *c*; op. 32/2 bars 50–1, $B\flat$, $A\natural$, $A\flat$, $G\natural$, $A\flat$. In each case this bass reinforcement coincides with a musical climax.

  Octave extension of a run or arpeggio: op. 25/2 bar 67, r.h., 8va---- marked from the top c'''. The same thing (also notated 8va----) appears at two other musical climaxes: op. 48/2 bars 113–14; op. 62/2, second half of bar 68, r.h. For these two cases Ekier (*Nocturnes*; see under *Critical editions* on p. 211) proposes interpreting this as an octave extension of the figure, started from the top octave.

[37] For the various meanings of Chopin's crosses, see p. 207, note 21, which discusses crosses in the Stirling scores. Though less numerous in the Dubois scores, the crosses assume the same functions, according to their various positions.

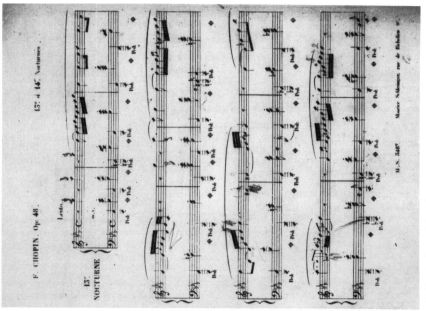

16   Beginning of the Nocturne op. 48/1 in Camille Dubois-O'Meara's score, with pencilled fingering and annotations by Chopin.

her readings is faulty – besides which that choice of piece is debatable, since many of the fingerings there are not in Chopin's hand.

The abundance of agogic indications and of instructions on playing ornaments is what particularly characterizes the Dubois scores – apart from the fingerings and just two metronome indications. Are *all* these annotations attributable to Chopin, as Tiersot's note at the head of Vol. I assumes? This has so far been tacitly and almost unanimously accepted. Only Holland (p. 296) and Kobylańska (*K*, I, p. 343) rightly voice serious doubt about the l.h. fingerings in the Waltz op. 64/1 – the same problem arises with most of the r.h. fingerings in the reprise of the first part after the trio. (It is not impossible that these numbers are the work of Mme Dubois, because the same characteristic 5 reappears in Franchomme's score of op. 58 – first movement, bar 201 – and Mme Dubois gave lessons to Cécile Franchomme: see page 232 below.) Also Ekier, in the critical commentary to his edition of the Impromptus (pp. xiii–xvi; see page 211 above, under *Critical editions*), slightly questions the authenticity of certain indications, though he reduces his suspicions in his subsequent editions of the Scherzos and Nocturnes. Even if a very large majority of the fingerings in the Dubois scores seem positively attributable to Chopin's hand, this cannot be automatically assumed for them all. In op. 25/8, bar 27 r.h., the figures are assuredly not in the composer's hand; the script of some fingering in opp. 25/3 (bar 69), 25/6 (bar 5, r.h.) and 28/23 may also appear suspect. But in all these cases the writing is not the same as that incriminated above in op. 64/1; there may therefore be *two* different hands present apart from Chopin's. Mme Dubois's own writing of either words or numbers is unfortunately not preserved elsewhere, or that might have permitted comparison and possible attribution. As for annotations in letters and words, the word *Fine* written at bar 23 of op. 7/2 is not Chopin's; at the very beginning of op. 64/1 the expression *4 mesures* is of uncertain authenticity, though the *tr* also present, between the staves of the opening bar,[38] is very similar in writing to that in bar 72 of op. 62/1.

We have already seen that some amendments in *OXF* were taken from the annotations in the Dubois scores (see page 208 above); but these latter also show some concordances with the annotations in other scores belonging to Chopin's pupils and associates. The most striking concordances are mentioned in the list below:

Textual modifications: op. 33/4, bars 87–110 are cut (*idem* in Jędrzejewicz and Zaleska-Rosengardt). Addition of an ornamented variant in op. 7/2 bar 27 (a very slightly different version in Stirling at the parallel passage in bar

---

[38] See p. 158, note 202.

11), op. 9/2 bars 4–5 (*idem* in Jędrzejewicz, Lenz, Mikuli, Franchomme), op. 24/1 bar 60 (almost identical version in Stirling, which additionally gives an added mordant in small notes in bar 58). Addition of notes to the r.h. of op. 34/2 bars 8, 160 and 196 (*idem* in Stirling, Jędrzejewicz, Lenz, Mikuli).

Identical fingerings occurring either as isolated figures or in groups: op. 9/1 bars 67–9, l.h.; op. 9/2 bars 4, 7, 30, 32, r.h.; op. 18 bars 76–7, r.h. (Stirling: parallel bars 109–10); op. 24/1 bar 17, r.h. (Stirling: parallel bar 21), bar 24 r.h.; op. 25/8 bars 9–10, r.h.; op. 28/15 bars 3, 11, r.h.; op. 34/1 bars 39–40, r.h.; op. 55/1 bars 69–70 r.h., bar 71 l.h.; op. 57 bar 1 l.h., bars 44, 48–9, r.h.

Tempo indication: op. 48/2 bar 57, *Molto più lento* scored through (only the *Molto* deleted in Stirling and Jędrzejewicz).

Performance of an ornament: op. 9/2 bar 7, the *tr* is preceded by a small e♮" (*idem* in Stirling, Jędrzejewicz and Franchomme).

Dynamics: op. 27/2, corrections to bars 25–6, 45–6, 50 – see note 189 on page 154 above (*idem* in Jędrejewicz; confirmed by Fontana and Koczalski).

Other performing indications: op. 28/15, bar 9, the l.h. f' to be taken by the r.h.; op. 28/15, bar 19 l.h., upward crotchet tails are added to the g♭ and a♮ to emphasize the countermelody they form; op. 27/2 bar 59, bass octave added to the first and fourth beats (*idem* in Jędrzejewicz, where they also occur in the previous bar).

In spite of these concordances, there is no evidence to suggest direct contact between the Dubois scores (where the manuscript additions never look as if they have been *copied* in and where there is no sign of Jane Stirling's writing) and those of other pupils and associates of Chopin – with the exception of Franchomme's scores where we have already seen one concordance of fingering and of its calligraphy (see also p. 232 below). Given that they occur analogously in *several* other sources, the modifications to the musical text can be reliably considered as corrections (opp. 9/2, 33/4, 34/2). The same applies to the indications of tempo (op. 48/2) and dynamics (op. 27/2). As for the fingerings, they are too sporadic to suggest a contact with the Stirling scores.[39] In some cases the concordances result from the fact that only

---

[39] Among the fingerings common to both sources, only those of opp. 24/1 (bar 21) and 57 (bars 1, 44, 48–9) are in Stirling's inked writing in her collection – even though op. 57 contains many concordances, also in ink. With all the other fingering concordances mentioned, Chopin's hand is recognizable in the Stirling scores.

one fingering is practicable (op. 18; op. 34/1; op. 57 bar 44); elsewhere they can be accounted for by Chopin's consistency in teaching his own fingerings, which formed the integral part of his approach to the keyboard.

Facsimile edition

Drath, pp. 45–53 (op. 18),[40] 70–80 (op. 34/1), 111–19 (op. 34/2), 138–46 (op. 34/3), 156–64 (op. 42), 229–33 (op. 64/1), 265–71 (op. 64/2), 283–9 (op. 64/3).

Further reading

Ganche, *DSFC*, pp. 202–10
Kobylańska, *CBKP*, pp. 159–61
Ekier, *FCB, passim*
Holland, pp. 255–300
Ekier, *WWN*, pp. 107–8
Kobylańska, *K*, I, p. 45 and *passim*
Kobylańska, *TBWV*, pp. xv–xvi and *passim*

Critical editions

CW, XI, pp. 25–30, 47–8.
Chopin, *Ballady*, ed. J. Ekier, *op. cit.*
Chopin, *Etudes op. 10, op. 25, 3 Nouvelles Etudes*, ed. P. Badura-Skoda, *op. cit.*
Chopin, *Impromptus*, ed. J. Ekier, *op. cit.*
Chopin, *Scherzi*, ed. J. Ekier, Wiener Urtext Edition, 1979 (UT 50061)
Chopin, *II Koncert fortepianowy f-moll op. 21. Wersja na jeden fortepian*, ed. J. Ekier, *op. cit.*
Chopin, *Nocturnes*, ed. J. Ekier, *op. cit.*

---

[40] The author unfortunately reproduces the copy from Vol. III which contains virtually nothing except the indication *ped.* at bar 291, whereas the Vol. IV copy (*OFE*, first printing) contains a host of fingerings and agogic indications, as well as some dynamic ones.

The Jędrzejewicz scores

Provenance

Warsaw, Museum of the Fryderyk Chopin Society: M/174–M/176. Purchased in Warsaw in 1936 from Ludwika Ciechomska, the great-granddaughter of Ludwika Jędrzejewicz, Chopin's older sister. Deposited until 1959 with the musicologist Ludwik Bronarski (Fribourg, Switzerland), who used it to establish the critical commentary of the *CW*, this collection of scores is believed to have belonged to Chopin before it became the property of his sister Ludwika (see Kobylańska, *K*, I, p. 40; *TBWV*, p. xiv).

Description and content

These scores, in the OFE or its subsequent reprinting,[41] are bound in three volumes marked with a letter C. On the recto of the blank page between the title page and the first page of music, op. 1 carries the inked signature *Louise Jędrzejewicz*. At the top of its title page, the Concerto op. 11 has a pencilled inscription in Bronarski's hand: *z /egzemplarza siostry/Chopina* [in Chopin's sister's score]. The collection is arranged numerically by opus numbers except for opp. 25 and 28, as follows:

Vol. I: opp. 1; 2; 3; 6/1–5; 7/1–4; 8; 9/1–3; 10/1–12; 25/1–12; 11

Vol. II: opp. 12; 13; 14; 15/1–3; 16; 17/1–4; 18; 21; 22; 23; 24/1–4; 26/1–2; 27/
          1–2; 29; 30/1–4; 32/1–2; 33/1–4; 34/1, 2, 3

Vol. III: opp. 38; 39; 40/1–2; 41/1–4; 42; 43; Mazurka for E. Gaillard
          [without op. no.]; 44; 45; 46; 47; 48/1, 2; 49; 50/1–3; 51; 52; 54; 28/
          1–12, 13–24.

The opening of the Nocturne op. 15/1 bears the pencilled date $\frac{4}{5}$ *1833*; the Mazurka op. 24/3, after the final double bar, bears the pencilled date $\frac{22}{9}$ *1835*, in the latter case at least, and possibly both, in a hand other than Chopin's. The copy of the *Tarentelle* op. 43 is incomplete, the works for piano and orchestra are in the reduction for one piano, and the chamber music (opp. 3 and 8) consists of only the piano part. Third in importance by the number of compositions it contains, the Jędrzejewicz collection is no less intriguing for its complete lack of opp. 55–65.

---

[41] Opp. 3, 16 and 17 are in M. Schlesinger's edition (M.S. 2447, M.S. 1703 and M.S. 1704 respectively). Opp. 10, 18 and 25 are in H. Lemoine's edition (2775 H.L., 2777 H.L. and 2776 H.L. respectively).

Nature of the musical annotations[42]

- Corrections of misprints
- Textual modifications[43]
- Fingerings[44]
- Indications of tempo and mood[45]
- Phrasing, agogics, accentuation
- Instructions for ornaments[44]
- Dynamics[44]
- Pedalling[46]
- Various performing indications[47]
- Crosses[48]

---

[42] The works bearing annotations are: opp. 3; 7/1; 9/2–3; 10/1, 3, 5, 6 and 8; 15/1–3; 16; 18; 21; 25/6, 7 and 9; 26/1–2; 27/1–2; 28/4, 6, 9, 11, 15, 17, 21; 29; 32/1; 33/1–4; 34/2–3; 38; 39; 41/1 and 3; 42; 45; 46; 47; 48/1–2; 49; 51; 52; Mazurka for E. Gaillard [CW, X, no. 42].

[43] In op. 10/3, bars 32–3 and 36–7 are deleted (as in the Stirling score); perhaps there are grounds to envisage a cut to bar 54, marked by a cross (the end of the cut in the Stirling score). Op. 15/1 bars 27, 29, 39 and 41, the first semiquaver (double notes) in the r.h. is deleted and replaced by a semiquaver rest, the only element of correction there carried over by Jane Stirling from her own copy. Op. 15/2, the final bar is embellished with an arpeggiated figuration reproduced in the critical commentary of the CW, VII, p. 121, and in that of the edition by Ekier of the Nocturnes, p. xxi (see under *Critical editions*, p. 211). Op. 28/15 bar 33, the fourth crotchet in the bass, C♯, is corrected to E (presumably to apply also in bar 49). Op. 33/4, bars 87–110 are cut, as in Stirling, Dubois and Zaleska. Op. 34/2 bars 8 and 160, notes are added to the top voice (see text and music example, pp. 86–7 and note 201, pp. 157–8).

[44] A number of these indications are reproduced in the present book's notes, *passim*.

[45] At the head of op. 33/1 the faulty printed indication *Presto* is corrected to *Lento*. Op. 48/2 bar 57, at the beginning of the middle section, the *Molto* is deleted from *Molto più lento*; at the return of the first theme, bar 101, *tempo primo* is added in ink, in Chopin's hand.

[46] Op. 15/1, the *Ped.* marked in the middle of bar 72 is extended to the second small note of the final arpeggio and resumed immediately after. Op. 15/2, bars 12, 18 and 58 bear the indication *i due Ped.*, not in Chopin's hand (probably Stirling's). Op. 28/6 bar 13, the 4th c♮" in the r.h. is linked by a vertical line to the ✲ indicating the release of the pedal; the note is thus to be isolated between two pedals (see Appendix III, p. 248). Op. 47 bars 52–3 (at the beginning of the second group), the pedalling (absent from the OFE) is indicated as in CW, III, p. 40 (3rd edition onwards), also as in the edition of the *Ballades* by Ekier, p. 37 (see under *Critical editions*, p. 211).

[47] Op. 28/9 bar 8, r.h., a vertical line specifies the simultaneous attack of each semiquaver with the third quaver of the triplet groups. Op. 48/1 bars 34–6, the melodic line at the top of the l.h. chords is emphasized (see Appendix III, p. 266); bars 71–5, the bass figure is underlined more or less as in the Stirling score (see p. 155, note 191).
Arpeggiation of chords: op. 18 bar 309; op. 51, final bar, where the l.h. d♭ is linked to the r.h. g♭'.
Facilitations for performance: op. 25/7 bars 22 and 24, the l.h. run is reduced to just its last four notes, changed to semiquavers. Op. 27/1 bars 27–8, the r.h. takes over the top notes of the four arpeggios: d', a-d, a-d'-f♯'-d'-a, a. Op. 28/21 bar 4, the last top e♭' in the l.h. is taken by the r.h. Op. 48/1 bars 27–38, some notes are deleted and some l.h. chords and arpeggios are rearranged (see Appendix III, p. 266).

[48] At the beginning of the piece: op. 28/6. At the end of the piece: opp. 9/2; 29; 34/3; 51. Within the piece, at the end of a section: op. 38 bar 46 (double cross isolating the first section); op. 47 bars 47 and 156; op. 48/1 bar 24. For the significance of these crosses, see p. 207, note 21.

17   Nocturne op. 15/1, bars 25ff, in the Jędrzejewicz score, with musical
modifications and pencilled fingering copied by Jane Stirling from those
of Chopin in her own score (*cf.* Fig. 15).

Remarks and problems

The manuscript markings in the Jędrzejewicz scores have been partially
included in the critical commentary of *CW* by Bronarski, who then had the
originals. Ekier takes them into account systematically in his *carnet critique*
on the *Ballades* and in his editions of the Impromptus, Scherzos and
Nocturnes (see pp. 211 and 219 above, under *Critical editions*).

The markings in these scores have much in common with those in the
Stirling collection. Significant correspondences are to be found in the
following cases:

Textual modifications and corrections: opp. 9/2; 10/3; 15/2; 15/3; 28/15; 29;
33/4; 34/2 (for details see note 43 on page 221).

Fingerings: op. 15/1, bars 8, 14, 26, 28; op. 15/2, bars 3, 14, 54; op. 26/1, bar 68;
op. 26/2, final bar; op. 27/1, bars 13–14; op. 27/2, bars 8–9; op. 28/4, bar 12; op.
28/6, bars 1, 3, 5, 6, 7–8, 9, 10, 13, 19–20, 22, 23; op. 28/21, bar 4; op. 29, bars 9,
10, 22–3, 27, 30, 38, 40–3, 60, 61, 64–5, 93, 94, 97 (see Appendix III, pages 245–7
below); op. 32/1, bars 12, 19, 27–30, 37–8, 39, 48, 58, final section (see
Appendix III, pages 262–3 below); op. 33/4, bars 124–5, 161–2, 170; op. 34/2,

18 Nocturne, op. 27/2, bars 44ff, in the Jędrzejewicz score, with pencilled modifications of dynamics in Chopin's hand.

bars 14, 67, 82–4, 150, 173–4, 176–7, 179, 181, 183; op. 34/3, bars 17–20; op. 47, bars 116, 159–61; op. 48/1, bars 4, 8, 9, 12, 22 (see Appendix III, pages 264–5 below).

Tempo indications: opp. 33/1, beginning, and 48/2, bar 57: correction of a printer's error and a printer's omission (for details see note 45 on page 221).

Phrasing, agogics, accentuation: op. 9/2, middle of bar 12, break after the cadence in B♭; op. 33/4 bar 124, accent on third beat; op. 48/1 bars 72–5, countermelody emphasized in the bass (see note 191, pp. 155–6).

Dynamics: op. 15/2, bar 11, *p*; op. 26/2, final bar, printed *ppp* altered to *ff* (*fff* in Stirling); op. 27/2, additions and alterations at bars 25–6, 45–6, 50 (see note 189, page 154 above); op. 32/1, bars 8–9, 'hairpin' *cresc. – decresc.*, bar 12, 'hairpin' *decresc.*, bars 27–8, *f–p*; op. 47, bars 115–16, 'hairpin' *cresc.*

Pedalling: op. 15/2, bars 12, 18, 58; op. 47, bars 52–3 (for details see p. 221, note 46).

Performing indications: op. 27/2, bar 59, bass doublings at the lower octave (see note 189 on page 154 above); op. 28/9, bar 8 (see note 47 on page 221).

Indications facilitating performance: op. 15/1, bars 27ff and 39ff, modifications to the r.h. pattern; op. 25/7, bars 22 and 24; op. 27/1, bars 27–8; op. 28/21, bar 4 (for details in the last three cases see note 47 on page 221).

There are two particularly illustrative cases in which these similar indications are the only ones to appear in a particular composition in the two collections (opp. 26/1; 34/3), and other cases where the shared indications appear in conjunction with only one or two other annotations peculiar to one of the two sources (opp. 10/3; 15/1–3; 26/2; 27/1; 28/4, 9, 21; 33/1, 4; 47; 48/1–2). As a statistic, roughly two-thirds of all the written fingerings appearing in opp. 29 and 32/1 are common to both Jędrzejewicz and Stirling.[49]

There is more. In various places equally densely annotated in the Dubois or Franchomme copies, Jędrzejewicz and Stirling seem to enter into a 'coalition', adopting a common reading different from the two others. Thus the printed *Presto* heading of op. 33/1 is corrected in the latter two to *Lento*, as opposed to *Mesto* in Dubois. The *Molto più lento* at bar 57 of op. 48/2 is entirely scored through in Dubois, whereas only the word *Molto* is deleted in Jędrzejewicz and Stirling. Similarly, neither of the latter adds a *c* at the beginning of the r.h. arpeggio, bar 1 of op. 32/2, as has been added to Dubois and Franchomme. These last two carry the fingering 4 on the r.h. *d‴* in bar 64 of op. 29, whereas Jędrzejewicz and Stirling have 5 (see Appendix III, p. 246 below). Finally, in op. 48/1 bar 22, 3rd and 4th beats r.h., Dubois indicates 4–5

---

[49] The similarity, between *OXF* and Jędrzejewicz, of numerous fingerings for op. 29, had already attracted the attention of the *CW* editor (IV, p. 41, 9th edition onwards).

on the notes $g''-b\flat''$, while the two others prescribe the crossing over of 5–4 (see Appendix III, page 265 below). (This list is not exhaustive, but illustrates characteristics of the Stirling–Jędrzejewicz concordances.)

To consider these various coincidences as fortuitous is asking rather much of chance! They must imply the existence of a contact between the Jędrzejewicz and Stirling collections – at least for a certain number of scores, which were then not yet bound. That said, from which direction did these contacts come, and under what circumstances?

While examining the annotations in the Jędrzejewicz scores at *PL-Wtifc*, I was immediately struck by the variations of calligraphy in the annotations from one composition to the next, and sometimes even within a single work. Some fingerings and worded indications were written in a quick running hand, while others had been entered steadily and carefully – copied, almost without doubt. For example, Chopin's hand was immediately recognizable in the inked *tempo primo* in op. 48/2, in the fingerings of opp. 34/3 and 51, the fingerings and dynamics of op. 27/2 and the dynamics of op. 26/2. The numbers carefully written out ('copied'), on the other hand, offered a perfect similitude to Jane Stirling's script just as it appears in the autograph sources mentioned at the beginning of this Appendix (the writing of the figures 3, 2 and, secondarily, 5 being particularly characteristic). This script is notably that of the fingerings appearing in opp. 15/1, 26/2, 27/1, 32/1, 48/1 and elsewhere. The *f* and *p* marked in op. 32/1 correspond equally to Jane Stirling's alphabetical script. The inescapable conclusion even then was that Jane Stirling had deposited annotations at various points in the Jędrzejewicz collection. The acquisition of the Stirling collection – previously inaccessible – by the Bibliothèque Nationale, Paris, in November 1979, made it possible to confirm and elaborate that conclusion.

A detailed survey of the annotations in each collection proves indeed that at least part of the Jędrzejewicz collection passed through Jane Stirling's hands. She introduced into Chopin's sister's scores a quite considerable number of annotations marked in her own collection by Chopin's hand: opp. 15/1–3; 25/7 (?); 26/2 (fingering in the last bar); 27/1–2; 32/1; 33/4; 34/2; 48/1; 48/2 (bar 1, ♯ to the r.h. *d'*). As a corollary, she found autograph annotations by Chopin in the Jędrzejewicz scores which she then carried over – in ink and pencil – into her own collection: opp. 27/2; 29; 33/4; 34/2; 34/3; 47; 48/2 (?). Finally, for some works which Chopin had annotated sporadically and in different places in each collection, she copied in both directions: opp. 27/2; 33/4; 34/2; 48/2 (?).

At the same time some isolated annotations, common to both collections, do not form part of Stirling's task of collation. This is the case with opp. 26/1;

26/2 (dynamics in the last bar); 28/4, 6, 9 and 21. The writing, sometimes showing the use of pencils of different quality within a single piece (therefore presumably entered at different times), is manifestly Chopin's in both sources. That finding leads one to believe that some scores from both collections were equally used by Chopin in his lessons. As a conclusion, it is not impossible that the scores concerned from the Jędrzejewicz collection might be considered as his working copies (corrections of dynamics in op. 27/2; the inked *tempo primo* in op. 48/2).

The manuscript intervention of Jane Stirling in the Jędrzejewicz scores clashes with the 'tradition' attached to their provenance, for reasons of chronology. According to the said tradition the Jędrzejewicz scores, having belonged in the first place to Chopin, were taken to Poland by Ludwika on her return from France at the beginning of September 1844 – a date said to explain the lack of opp. 55–65. However, at that time Jane Stirling had hardly entered Chopin's personal life, having been his student for only a few months: this effectively excludes the possibility of her having put her hand to scores in her teacher's possession. There is an equally strong objection to the argument about the missing opp. 55–65: in September 1844 there would have been every reason for Ludwika to have returned to Warsaw *particularly* with Chopin's two *derniers-nés*, the opp. 55 and 56 (not in the collection, though), which came off the press in August 1844, precisely when the Jędrzejewicz family was on holiday at Nohant, before spending a few days again in Paris on their return journey to Poland.

The presence of Stirling's writing in the Jędrzejewicz scores makes it fairly certain that it was not until after summer 1844 that her annotations were written in her teacher's scores,[50] which could not have been taken to Poland until a later date. It seems probable, then, that these scores were part of the collection of music, manuscripts and papers (including the *PM*) removed by Ludwika before the affixing of the Place Vendôme seals on the day of Chopin's death. Since there is no mention of them in the very detailed correspondence from Jane Stirling to Ludwika between 1850 and 1854, there are grounds to believe that the latter took them away on her departure from Paris on the 2nd January 1850. At the latest, they could have been sent to Warsaw in '*la petite malle de musique*' to which the Scotswoman alludes in a letter of 31 January 1850.[51] Between the end of October 1849 and January

---

[50] Before taking possession of these scores, Ludwika must have held her brother's works mostly in the OGE (essentially Kistner, then Breitkopf & Härtel), as evidenced by a letter of 12 December 1845 from Chopin to his family: 'My new Mazurkas [op. 59] have been published by Stern in Berlin, so I don't know whether they will reach you, since in Warsaw you usually receive your music from Leipzig' (*SC*, pp. 257–8).

[51] Wróblewska-Straus, *LSJ*, p. 81.

1850 Jane Stirling, who was in daily contact with Ludwika, would have had all the time necessary to carry out her work of collating the two collections – unless indeed she had already begun the work while Chopin was alive, from the time when she was putting together the *corpus* of her teacher's works. This last hypothesis, however, is rendered implicitly less plausible by the willingness and gratitude which she always showed to Chopin's family, and to Ludwika in particular.

Further reading

Ekier, *FCB*, *passim*
Wróblewska–Gendaszek, pp. 133–40
Ekier, *WWN*, p. 107 and *passim*
Kobylańska, *K*, I, p. 40 and *passim*
Kobylańska, *TBWV*, p. xiv and *passim*
Eigeldinger–Nectoux, pp. xlii–xliii

Critical editions

CW
Chopin, *Ballady*, ed. J. Ekier, *op. cit.*
Chopin, *Impromptus*, ed. J. Ekier, *op. cit.*
Chopin, *Scherzi*, ed. J. Ekier, *op. cit.*
Chopin, *Nocturnes*, ed. J. Ekier, *op. cit.*

The Franchomme scores

Provenance

Collections of Antoinette Couturier-André (Paris), the late Yvonne Faure-André (La Croix-en-Touraine), and Laurent Pénicaud (Tonneins/Lot-et-Garonne). Great-granddaughters of Chopin's 'cellist friend Franchomme,[52] Mmes Couturier and Faure received these scores in 1956 on the death of their mother.[53] M. Laurent Pénicaud, son of Georges and Elisabeth (née André), received his collection in 1982 on the death of his mother.

Two volumes formerly belonged to Adèle Forest (see below), daughter of the lawyer Jules Forest who resided at Le Côteau (near Azay-sur-Cher), a relative of Franchomme and also a friend of Chopin. In all probability, some scores contain annotations in Franchomme's hand, while others may have been used by his eldest daughter Cécile (1838–1903), who in 1850 was a pupil of Mlle O'Meara (later Mme Dubois).

Description and content

A total of 52 opuses (ten of which are duplicated in various editions) plus two compositions published during Chopin's life without opus number, most of them in the OFE or its reprinting,[54] are divided as follows among the three collections:

---

[52] See pp. 101–2, note 32.

[53] Claire André-Le Mire, wife of René-Edouard André (1867–1942), himself the son of Edouard André (1840–1911) and Louise Franchomme (1844–73), who was Auguste Franchomme's third and last child.

[54] The OGE is represented by opp. 3 (Mechetti: piano solo arrangement by Czerny), 5 (Hofmeister), 65 (Breitkopf & Härtel), and also op. 4 (Haslinger), published posthumously.

The following are notably in reprints or re-editions of the OFE: opp. 3 (Brandus, M.S. 2447), 16 (M. Schlesinger, M.S. 1703), 18 (Lemoine, 2777 H.L.), 28/1–12 (Brandus, 4594), 34/2 (Richault, 4353R), 53 (M. Schlesinger, M.S. 3958 – new title: 8e Polonaise), 64/1–2 (Richault, 4353 R), 3 Etudes composées pour la Méthode des Méthodes (M. Schlesinger, M.S. 4102).

Certain works for piano and orchestra are in the first collected French edition, issued by Brandus et Cie around 1852, using the plates of the OFE and entitled Edition Originale / Oeuvres complètes pour le piano / de / Frédéric Chopin / Seule édition authentique / sans changements ni additions d'après les épreuves corrigées par l'auteur lui-même. These include opp. 2, 11 (Pénicaud collection), 21 (Pénicaud collection) and 22 (Pénicaud collection). A copy of op. 13 (Faure collection) is in the later reprint by Brandus et Dufour.

In addition, the embossment of Brandus figures on the title pages of opp. 6, 11 (Faure collection), 12, 14 (Couturier collection), 21 (Faure collection), 26, 27, 29, 32, 34/2, 47, 49, 51, 53 and 55. Reprints or not, these scores cannot have been acquired until after January 1846, when the Brandus brothers bought out M. Schlesinger. Also, the embossment 'G. Brandus, Dufour et Cie' or 'G. Brandus et S. Dufour' appears on opp. 24 and 54 (M. Schlesinger), 64/3 (Brandus), 35 and 39 (Troupenas); these scores cannot have been sold before 1854 or 1858, the two years in which Brandus associated with Dufour for various titles. Similarly, op. 57 (Meissonnier) – Faure collection – carries the embossment of Gérard, successor of Meissonnier: this score was therefore bought after 1860.

Opp. 2; 5; 10/1–12; 12; 14; 18; 19; 22; 24/1–4; 27/1–2; 32/1–2; 35; 38; 42; 43; 45; 51; 58; 64/1 and 3; 65; *Grand Duo Concertant sur des thèmes de Robert le Diable*; *3 Etudes composées pour la Méthode des Méthodes* – collection of Antoinette Couturier-André.

Opp. 3 (two versions); 4; 6/1–5; 7/1–4;[55] 9/1–3; 11; 13; 14; 16; 21; 28/1–12; 29; 39; 48/2; 49; 52; 53; 55/1–2; 57; 64/2; 64/1 and 2 – collection of the late Yvonne Faure-André.

Opp. 1; 4; 8; 11; 13; 21; 22; 26/1–2; 28/13–24; 33/1–4; 34/2 (two different edns); 36; 37/1–2; 44; 46; 47; 54; 57; 59/1–3; 60; 61; 64/1 – collection of Laurent Pénicaud.

The *Etudes* op. 10 in the OFE bear the double autograph dedications in ink: *à mon Ami chéri Au. Franchomme / FF. Chopin* (cover) and *au plus grimacieux et gracieux Franchomme. / le plus attaché FF. Chopin* [to the most grimacing and gracious Franchomme from the most devoted FF. Chopin] *le* $\frac{6}{6}$ [18]33 (title page). Similarly, the title page of Nocturnes op. 9 in the OFE has: *A mon cher ami chéri et bien chéri Aug. Franchomme / FF. Chopin* [to my dear, dearest and well endeared Aug. Franchomme]. This title page and that of the *Grand Duo Concertant* both bear the signature in ink of *A. Forest* – dedicatee of the latter work. One guesses from this that Franchomme probably gave his copy of op. 9 to this young lady (later Mme Adolphe de Lauverjat) who, according to family tradition, was a pupil of Chopin.

The scores of the Franchomme collection are not bound; several of them still retain their original covering of coloured paper. Op. 2, exceptionally, includes separate parts for the orchestral accompaniment; opp. 3 (Brandus edition) and 65 include the separate 'cello part. Pages 11–18 are lacking in op. 8, which also includes the parts for violin (two copies; one, annotated, is signed *A. Franchomme* at the top right of the first page) and 'cello. None of the works published posthumously by Fontana figures in the collection.

---

[55] The catalogue of the exhibition *Frédéric Chopin, George Sand et leurs amis* (Paris, Bibliothèque Polonaise, July–October 1937) lists as belonging to R.-E. André a copy of op. 7 – in M. Schlesinger's edition – bearing the autograph dedication *A l'ami Franchomme* (p. 33, no. 276), and one of op. 28 in the Breitkopf edition (p. 16, no. 103). No trace of these two scores remains in the collections mentioned here. Similarly, there is no trace of op. 65 in the OFE; one might have expected it to be present, with an autograph dedication, given the close collaboration of the two musicians in the preparation of that work.

Nature of the musical annotations

- Corrections of misprints: opp. 2; 3 (Brandus edition); 8; 9/1–3; 10/3; 11 (Schlesinger and Brandus editions); 13 (Brandus–Dufour edition); 14 (Couturier collection); 21 (Brandus edition); 22 (Brandus edition); 28/7; 29; 42; 47; 55/1; 58; *Grand Duo Concertant*
- Textual modifications: op. 9/3, bar 79; op. 32/2;[56] op. 58, first movement;[57] *Grand Duo Concertant*[58]
- Fingerings: opp. 8; 9/1 and 2; 11 (Brandus edition); 18; 21 (Brandus edition); 22 (Schlesinger edition); 27/2; 29; 42; 46; 47; 55/1; 57 (Pénicaud collection); 58; 64/2; *Grand Duo Concertant*
- Phrasing, articulation: opp. 8; 9/1; 29; 64/2
- Instructions for ornaments: op. 9/2, bars 7 and 15[59]
- Dynamics: opp. 8; 11 (Brandus edition); 21, second movement[60] (Schlesinger edition)
- Indications of various kinds[61]
- Crosses: op. 27/2, bar 33

Remarks and problems

The scores containing annotations have been listed immediately above in the main text, because the ensemble of the Franchomme collection has not so far been the object of any study. The editors of the *CW* did not take it into consideration, nor did the editors of more recent critical editions. Kobylańska (*CiFC*, p. 18) fleetingly mentions their existence, but elsewhere

---

[56] Bar 1, a *c'*, not printed in either the OFE or OGE (no autograph copy traced), is added at the bottom of the r.h. arpeggio. The same addition appears in the Dubois score and in Mikuli's edition.

[57] Bar 104, the last l.h. *c* is replaced by *e*. Bar 186, the bass *B* on the third beat at the beginning of the l.h. arpeggio is replaced by the *F♯* a fourth below; likewise in the Dubois score and the Mikuli edition. Note that this corrected reading is that printed in the OFE at the reprise of the same figure at bar 190.

[58] Bars 57–8, each of the octave *B*s is preceded by a *c♯'-c♯''* octave appogiatura with the indication *m.g.* for the latter and *m.d.* for the *B*s. Bars 59–62, the corrected text corresponds more or less with the *CW* version (XVI, p. 71), which reproduces here the reading of the Breitkopf edition, in whose preparation Franchomme himself participated. The only difference is that the middle note of each of the third r.h. chords in bars 59 and 61 is not *f♯''* but *d♯''* in the annotated copy, which also deletes the last chord of bar 62. It might be added that Franchomme's score is valuable in various respects – by virtue of its autograph corrections and annotations, in Chopin's hand, and the rarity of this OFE, which remained unknown to the *CW* editors. Bar 226, the notes of the *tremolo* are replaced by *D♯-d♯* (l.h.) and *f♯'-b*, *f♯* (r.h.), marked in ink.

[59] See Appendix III, pp. 257–8.

[60] Bar 1, *pp* is added (in Chopin's hand), absent from the piano reduction in the French edition. The Stirling score has *p* (ink).

[61] *Grand Duo Concertant*, bars 87–8 of the piano part: the third and then first beat bass notes are doubled at the bass octave.

(*K*, I, pp. 66–7, 68–9, 70–1; *TBWV*, p. 18) deals only with op. 9/1–3. This source, therefore, with its specific problems,[62] remains to be explored.

Relatively complete in its present state, the Franchomme collection was partly put together quite late, as is shown by the fairly high proportion of scores in reprints and re-editions (see note 54 on p. 228). Manuscript intervention by Chopin is therefore excluded in some cases. Besides, apart from fingering, performing indications here are rarer than in the Stirling, Dubois or Jędrzejewicz collections. Even apart from the absence of any tempo or pedal indications, the total of annotations pertaining to phrasing, performance of ornaments, and dynamics is very low – except for dynamics in op. 8. This collection has a very different make-up, therefore, from (notably) Mme Dubois's scores.

If Chopin's hand can be identified with near certainty in the *Grand Duo Concertant*, in several corrections of the Nocturnes op. 9,[63] and in the inked *pp* at the head of the slow movement of op. 21 (Faure collection), the same does not hold for the majority of other cases. Franchomme's hand is easily identifiable in the Trio op. 8, through numerous indications of agogics, dynamics, phrasing and articulation in the separate violin part (where his signature helps to identify their authenticity), the 'cello part and the piano part (finale). As well as the very firm tracing of *f* and *p*, that of instructions like *rit.* or *riten.*, *a tempo, cres., dol[ce]*, etc., corresponds exactly to the script of the 'cellist in his numerous ink autographs.[64] Without doubt Franchomme on various occasions, in private, played the Trio with Chopin,[65] who did not disown that early work in his mature years.[66] If this hypothesis is reliable, then Franchomme's score is an important source for interpreting op. 8,

[62] The compositions bearing no annotations are the following: opp. 1; 3 (Mechetti edition); 4 (Faure and Pénicaud collection); 5; 6; 7; 10/1–2 and 4–12; 12; 13 (Pénicaud collection); 14 (Faure collection); 16; 19; 24; 26; 27/1; 28/1–6, 8–12 and 13–24; 32/1; 33; 34/2 (both editions); 35; 36; 37; 38; 39; 43; 44; 45; 48/2; 49; 51; 52; 53; 54; 55/2; 57 (Faure collection); 59; 60; 61; 64/1 (the three scores of the Couturier, Faure and Pénicaud collections); 64/2 (Richault edition, Faure collection); 64/3; 65; 3 *Etudes composées pour la Méthode des Méthodes.*

[63] A variant for bar 79 of op. 9/3, written on a small card attached to the score, appears not to be in Chopin's hand.

[64] See Eigeldinger-Nectoux, pp. [1, 53, 343, 345, 377–80] for the *incipits* in Franchomme's hand in the Stirling collection. Facsimiles of musical autographs of Franchomme appear also in Kobylańska, *K*, II, pp. 26–8, 114, 124–5, 128–9, and *CBKP*, between pages 152 and 153.

[65] Delacroix notes in his *Journal*, 1 July 1847: 'Music [*Séance*] at Chopin's at three o'clock. He was divine. They played him his trio with Fauchon, etc., then he played it himself and with complete mastery [*de main de maître*]' (I, pp. 233–4). It is possible that the editor of the printed *Journal* misread the written abbreviation Franch[omme], since no instrumentalist called Fauchon is otherwise known, and since Franchomme's name appears complete and correctly spelt at the earlier date of 21 February 1847.

[66] See note 65 immediately above. In 1840 Chopin set Friederike Streicher to work on his trio, according to her memoirs (see Niecks, II, p. 342).

whose autograph and OFE are sparser in performing indications. Franchomme also appears to be the author of the corrections (clefs, notes, accidentals, slurs, ties, dynamics) in opp. 2, 11, 21 and 22 – possibly also opp. 13 and 14 (?) – in the posthumous editions listed in note 54 (p. 228 above). Apart from their resemblance to the 'cellist's musical script, these corrections show the hand of an experienced musician who has mastered problems of notation. In this connection we know that Franchomme, in the years immediately after Chopin's death, not only made copies of unpublished works but also copied out, even made piano reductions of, some *tutti* and orchestral accompanying passages from op. 11 (second and third movements). It seems probable that it would have been then – or on other analogous occasions – that he corrected the scores just mentioned; at the same time we would then have a *terminus a quo* date of around 1852 for his work as copyist.

As far as fingering is concerned, in addition to Chopin's hand one can distinguish mainly two scripts, coexisting notably in opp. 27/2, 47 and 58 (first movement). One of them, smaller, more rectilinear and studied, disconcertingly recalls some of Jane Stirling's markings in her own collection (*cf.* op. 10/3 bars 39 and 41–2, in Eigeldinger–Nectoux). It is harder to attribute to her the other script, bigger and less characterized, as it appears, alone, in opp. 42 and 58 (scherzo). Finally, the two 5s at bar 201 of the first movement of op. 58 (first two r.h. semiquavers) feature also at the same place in the Dubois score but with the script of these same figures as they appear in the Dubois score of op. 64/1, beginning, where, as already mentioned, they cannot be in Chopin's hand. This parallels another striking concordance between these two collections: the few fingerings in op. 57 in one of the Franchomme scores (Pénicaud collection) recur in the Dubois score, notably with the characteristic slide 2–2 on the first bar's $d\flat'-c'$. We have already seen (p. 224 above) the Dubois–Franchomme coalitions in the adoption of a common reading contrary to Stirling–Jędrzejewicz.

Some of Franchomme's scores were probably used by his daughter Cécile during her lessons with the future Mme Dubois: 'Young Cécile Franchomme is a great credit to her teacher Mistress O'Méara, she has exactly the right touch; she played me my Nocturne [probably op. 55/1] surpassingly well [*supérieurement*]. I went to compliment Mlle Méara on it,' reports Jane Stirling in a letter of 13 June 1850 to Ludwika Jędrzejewicz (manuscript copy by Edouard Ganche, among the Papiers E. Ganche, now in *F-Pn*; *cf.* also Ganche, *DSFC*, p. 115). With this connection in mind, one notes that, in statistical terms, the fingerings in the Franchomme scores are corroborated in Dubois and Stirling twice as often by the former as by the latter. One also notes the exact concordance of the Franchomme score with Stirling, Dubois and Jędrzejewicz for the fingerings added to opp. 9/2 (bars 3 and 4), 27/2 (bar 8) and 29 (bar 65). Whatever the connection linking these four sources, such unanimity constitutes a guarantee of authenticity for many of the annotations in the Franchomme scores. Nevertheless, these last appear a secondary source by comparison with the three other sources just mentioned, because of the scarcity of annotations attributable to Chopin's hand.

The Zaleska-Rosengardt scores

Provenance

Paris, Bibliothèque Polonaise: F.N. 15811–44 (six items included in these numbers bear the additional reference (a) or (a) and (b); they were added after the cataloguing of the collection). Exceptionally, op. 58 is numbered F.N. 14610. Bequest of Maryla Bohdana Okińczyc (d. 1949), adopted daughter of Dionizy Zaleski, himself the son of the poet Bohdan Zaleski and of Zofia Zaleska-Rosengardt, to whom these scores belonged; she was Chopin's pupil from November 1843.[67]

Description and content

This collection of scores, catalogued approximately by opus number, is not bound. A few scores retain their original covering of coloured paper; apart from a few exceptions, about two-thirds of them are in the OFE or its reprintings, and the remaining third in the OGE or its reprintings. 35 opuses are represented (with three duplications), plus two works without opus number and one in Fontana's posthumous numbering: op. 1 (Meyer edn, Braunschweig); 2 (OFE); 10/1–12 (OGE); 10/1–12 (OFE); 13 (OGE); 14 (OGE); 15/1–3 (OFE); 17/1–4 (OFE); 20 (OFE); 21 (OGE); 23 (OGE); 25/1–12 (OGE); 25/1–12 (Lemoine edition); 27/1–2 (OFE); 28/1–12 (Brandus edition) and 13–24 (OFE); 29 (OGE); 30/1–4 (OFE); 31 (OFE); 32/1–2 (OGE); 33/1–4 (OGE); 36 (OGE); 38 (OGE); 40/1–2 (OFE); 40/1–2 (Richault edition, edited by Tellefsen [1860]); 43 (OGE); 45 (OFE); 47 (OGE); 51 (OFE); 53 (OFE); 55/1–2 (OFE); 57 (OFE); 58 (OFE); 59/1–3 (OFE); 60 (OFE); 62/1–2 (OFE); 63/1–3 (OFE); 64/2 (OFE); 65 (OFE); 3 *Nouvelles Etudes* [without op. no.] (OGE); Mazurka *Notre Temps* No. 2 [without op. no.] (OGE); op. posth. 66 (Meissonnier edition, succeeded by Gérard, edited by Fontana).[68]

The distribution between OGE and OFE, gradually tending more towards OFE, is easily explained. The OGE scores (three of which bear the stamp of the Spiess music shop in Warsaw) were taken by Zofia Rosengardt from Poland to Paris, whereas those in the OFE were bought or received after her arrival in the French capital in May 1843.

[67] See *List of Chopin's pupils*, pp. 188–9.
[68] The compositions bearing annotations are the following: opp. 10 (both copies); 15; 20; 21; 23; 25 (both copies); 28; 29; 31; 32; 33; 36; 43; 47; 57; 63; 3 *Nouvelles Etudes*.

The title pages of two compositions bear an autograph dedication in pencil by Chopin: op. 58, *Pani Zofii Rosengart/Chopin* [to Mme Zofia Rosengardt]; op. 65, *Pani Zaleskiej/16 Stycznia 48/Ch* [to Mme Zaleska, 16 January 1848]. Outside the musical text appear various inscriptions definitely not attributable to Chopin. On the cover of op. 10 (OGE) is written in ink '*Concerto en la bémol – Hummel*[69]*/Trois Sonates de Dusseck* [sic] *op. 19*'. The last cover page of op. 25 (OGE) is covered with annotations in Polish about theoretical notions: intervals, major and minor scales, flat and sharp tonalities, regularly based around C and A. The first cover page of op. 25 (Lemoine edition)[70] displays a written staff with diminished seventh chords, notated in semibreves and ascending chromatically from C to G.

Nature of the musical annotations

- Corrections of misprints
- Textual modifications (op. 33/4, excision of bars 87–110)
- Fingerings
- Indications of tempo and mood
- Phrasing, agogics, accentuation
- Dynamics
- Pedalling
- Various performing indications
- Crosses

Remarks and problems

The scores of the Zaleska-Rosengardt collection, with their mixture of sources, present quite a singular make-up, and stand out from the other sources studied here as much by the tenor of their various annotations as by the multiplicity of different hands supplying these. Judging from the co-existence of at least three or four different hands in the numerical writing – little of it seems attributable to Chopin – these copies must have been used by Zofia Rosengardt mostly for her personal work or her teaching, or maybe even by her friends and progeny, rather than for her own lessons with Chopin – which were rather sporadic anyway. Therefore the present pages make no

[69] It is known that Chopin regularly assigned his students Hummel's Concertos in A minor and B minor, opp. 85 and 89, in preference to Hummel's other concertos.

[70] This is also the edition of the Stirling, Dubois and Jędrzejewicz scores. The plates of opp. 10, 25, and 18 having been surrendered by M. Schlesinger to Lemoine in December 1842, it was in the latter's edition that these works were sold in Paris from 1843 (information kindly supplied by J.-M. Nectoux).

attempt to embark on clearing up the problems raised by these scores (these problems are doubtless the reason why Kobylańska omits them from her catalogue, K), especially since their content is of lesser interest to the purpose of the present book.

Among the characteristics peculiar to the Zaleska scores, we find an abundance of continuous fingerings: on practically every note of the r.h. in op. 29 (first section) and op. 57, as also in certain pages of op. 47 (bars 116–36, r.h.; bars 157–64, l.h.; bars 173–83, r.h.). Other unusual traits are the profusion of agogic and dynamic markings on the one hand, as against the almost total absence of indications of how to play ornaments on the other. Even more characteristic of this collection is an abundance of expressions written out in full or in abbreviated form, in Polish as well as French, concerning technique, character, nuances, agogics, touch, pedalling, and so on (notably in opp. 25/9, 28/6, 47, 57, 63/2–3). Thus, at the beginning of op. 25/9 (Lemoine edition) one reads: *tenir le poignet bas* [keep the wrist low]. Op. 57 contains the following in succession:[71] *2ᵉ partie très douce* [2nd voice very soft] (end of bar 10); *rall.* (end of bar 12); *doux* (end of bar 13); *coulé, petite Péd.* (bar 19); *régulier* (bar 20); *Rit.* (end of bar 26); *Petite Péd.* (beginning of bar 27); *dolcissimo* (bars 27–28); *les 2 péd.* (bar 35); *net* (bar 36); *petit péd., léger* (bar 39); *petite péd., égal* (bar 43); *Rit.* (end of bar 62); *petite péd.* (bar 63). Op. 28/20 is even provided with a title: *Stabat Mater*! Another peculiarity – more captivating – is the pencilled Polish adjective *Deszczowy* [of rain falling; rainy] at the head of op. 28/15. I have shown elsewhere (Eigeldinger, *PGE*, pp. 86–90) that this marking is in all probability in Chopin's hand, thus tipping the balance of the long debate over the identity of the 'raindrop' Prelude in favour of this no. 15. As for Chopin's possible manuscript contributions to the Zaleska scores, they may be recognized with reasonable certainty in the fingering added to *Etudes* 2 and 7 from op. 25 (Lemoine edition), as well as in fingering and other annotations in the middle section of op. 29 and notably in the first two sections of op. 36 (we know that Zofia Rosengardt had begun working with Chopin on an Impromptu, but without seeing it through: see text on page 28 above).

Further reading

Kobylańska, *NDC*
Eigeldinger, *PGE*, pp. 86–90

[71] This list omits annotations of dynamics, which are indicated by the usual signs.

ADDENDUM

Virginia Fortescue's article has recently revealed the whereabouts of a score of the Nocturnes op. 9 used at Zofia Zaleska-Rosengardt's lessons with Chopin, bearing a dedication and important annotations by Chopin. Her article and the two accompanying facsimiles (title page and page 7 of the music) are the source behind the following remarks.

Provenance

Collection of Virginia Fortescue, University of Port Elizabeth, Cape Province, South Africa. The score was received by its present owner at an unspecified date from Joseph Okińczyc (Dordogne), a relative of the Zaleskis. It had therefore become detached from the rest of the Zaleska-Rosengardt collection before the latter's bequest to *F-Ppo* and was thought lost up to 1981, its existence attested to only by express mention in the diary of Zofia Zaleska-Rosengardt.

Description

The score is the OFE of op. 9 (imprint: M.S. 1287) with the embossment of Maurice Schlesinger and bearing the pencilled dedication at top right title page: *Pannie Rozengardt / za to że bardzo wielkie dziecko / F. Ch* [To Mlle Rosengardt because she is a great child]. Another hand – probably that of the dedicatee – has added to the left the date *2 janvier/1844*. Zofia's diary (see Hordyński, pp. 149–51) confirms that as the day of a 'leçon orageuse', at the end of which Chopin noted, perhaps as a peace offering, the dedication which the young girl reproduced exactly in her autobiographical notes, relating the circumstances of the lesson when the teacher's sarcasm confronted the pupil's wilfulness. In contrast to the scores now in *F-Ppo*, this score stands out through the indisputable authenticity of its annotations and by the interest of the variant inscribed at the end of the cadenza of op. 9/2, the only Nocturne to carry any manuscript indications.

Content

Textual modifications:
On the r.h. rising sixth of bars 4–5, a sign (similar to those observed in the Stirling, Dubois, Jędrzejewicz and Franchomme scores) followed by an $f[\sharp]''$ (as in Jędrzejewicz) just before the g'' of bar 5 is interpreted by Fortescue (p.

47) as an arpeggiation sign. This is probably the symbol reproduced in the present book's note 183 (pp. 150–1 above), signifying a chromatic rising *glissando* which launches itself from an initial turn. It would thus be interpreted as Mikuli directs in his separate edition of op. 9/2 with ornamental variants (see music example on p. 78 above).

The end of the cadenza is embellished, from the thirteenth semiquaver group (whose last two notes, *d''''–c♮''''*, are deleted), by a figuration unknown elsewhere, but which confirms the statements by Lenz (*UB*) and Gutmann (in Niecks) quoted on page 78 above. Its transcription by Fortescue (p. 48) seems problematic at the beginning and the end. I propose the following reading, based admittedly on a somewhat mediocre facsimile:

The final bar is replaced by a large arpeggio identical with that in the Stirling score (see transcription in Eigeldinger–Nectoux, p. xxxii).

Fingering: bars 2–4, r.h. (confirmations in Stirling, Dubois, Jędrzejewicz and Franchomme for bars 3–4).

Phrasing and articulation: a slur covers all of bar 21 up to the first note (*g''*) of bar 22, which is followed by a break.

Further reading

Hordyński, pp. 149–51
Zamoyski, pp. 239–40
Fortescue

The Scherbatoff scores

Provenance

Harvard University, the Houghton Library: fMus. C 4555. B 846c.
Bequeathed in 1933 by a former Harvard student, John B. Stetson Junior, of
Philadelphia.

Description and content

The compilation is miscellaneous; it was bound in one volume towards the
last quarter of the last century, bearing the initials *M.T.*, that is, Marie
Tcherkassky, née de Scherbatoff.[72] On the inside of the front cover is glued an
ex-libris specifying the origin of the donation:

Harvard College Library / In Memory of / Aleixo de Queiroz Ribeiro / de Sotomayor
d'Almeida / e Vasconcellos / Count of Santa Eulalia / The Gift of / John B. Stetson Junior /
of the Class of 1906.

The recto of the inside cover page is occupied by a table of contents in Marie
de Scherbatoff's hand entitled *Catalogue écrit l'année 1875*:

24 *Préludes*	Chopin
2e *Impromptu*	Chopin
Sonate avec la marche funèbre qu'il m'a / jouée avant	
qu'elle ne soit imprimée et qu'on / a jouée à son	
enterrement	Chopin
Deux Nocturnes	Chopin
Grande Polonaise	Chopin
3me Ballade	Chopin
Walse	Chopin
Mazurka	Chopin
Mazurka	Goria
Fantaisie et Variations sur le Cor / des Alpes de Proch	Fesca
Allegro de Bravoure	Cavalcabo
Eloge des larmes de Schubert arr. par	Heller

[72] Maria Nikolaïevna de Scherbatoff (?–1892), wife of prince Alexeï Borissovitch Cherkassky – or
Tcherkassky. She was born and died in Moscow, and performed there in public from 1834.
Gajewski's discovery of her collection of dedicated and annotated scores identifies de Scherbatoff
as a hitherto unknown pupil of Chopin. From the indication concerning the 'Funeral March',
'which he played for me before it was published', Gajewski deduces that Maria de Scherbatoff
must have first met Chopin between 1837 (presumed date of composition of the 'Funeral March')
and the spring of 1840 (date of publication of opp. 35 and 36, both bearing an autograph
dedication). If, as I am inclined to believe, the annotations in the *Ballade* op. 47 are Chopin's own,
Maria de Scherbatoff was still (or once again) his pupil in 1841–2 (op. 47 having appeared in
November 1841).

The title page of op. 36 bears the autograph dedication in ink: *à Mademoiselle la Princesse Marie de Scherbatoff / de la part de F. Chopin*. Similarly, op. 35 is dedicated to *Mademoiselle Marie de Scherbatoff / de la part de / F. Chopin*. In both cases, the dates in autograph, figuring between the mention *Paris* and the signature, have been cut out.

The Chopin works in the list above – OFE, OGE or issues of album leaves then printed in Russia – correspond with the following opuses: 28/1–24 (OFE); 36 (OFE); 35 (OFE); 55/1 (album) and 48/1 (OFE); 53 (OFE); 47 (OFE); 42 (OGE); 6/1 and 7/1 (album).

Nature of the musical annotations

- Corrections of misprints
- Cut in the text (op. 35, finale)[73]
- Fingerings (opp. 28/11 and 16; 35, 'Funeral March'; 47; 53; 55/1)
- Tempo indication (op. 36)[74]
- Octave displacement (op. 53)[75]
- Instructions for ornaments (op. 55/1)
- Crosses (op. 47)

Remarks and problems

In his list of Chopin's works contained in the Marie de Scherbatoff collection, Gajewski repeats Marie de Scherbatoff's omission of a tenth and last composition, the Mazurka op. 7/1 which follows op. 6/1 in the album *Le Salon. Nouvelle Revue musicale* (published by Odéon, Moscow, as no. 7 (19 April 1846).)

The expression '*de la part de*' figuring in the dedications of op. 35 and 36 suggests that these scores were sent, rather than signed on the spot, by the composer – especially since these two opuses appeared simultaneously in the OFE. Chopin used the same formula in addressing to Maria Wodzińska, then in Poland, a dedicated copy of the Waltz op. 18 '*de la part de son ancien professeur*' dated '*Paris, 18 Jui[llet] 1834*' (see Bory, p. 104). In any case this conjecture does not preclude the possibility that Marie de Scherbatoff did work with Chopin.

[73] Between bars 46 and 47 of CW (VI, pp. 69 and 128). See also OXF (II, *Sonatas*, p. 60); Ganche (*VAFC*, p. 144); Mikuli (VII, p. 34), on the basis of the Czartoryska and Streicher-Müller scores. The Scherbatoff scores of opp. 35 and 36 show the OFE in its earliest form, shortly before its reprintings incorporated corrections by Chopin.

[74] Bars 59–60, *in tempo* – an indication appearing in the OGE but absent from the OFE.

[75] Cf. p. 157, note 196.

The manuscript fingerings are in two different hands, though not easy to differentiate. One of them (mostly in op. 53) is smaller, more pressed and less cursive than Chopin's numbers. The other hand (opp. 28/11; 35; 47), plus the pen marking '*in tempo*'[76] in op. 36, can safely be attributed to Chopin.

The fact that most of the annotations in the Scherbatoff scores are not corroborated literally in other students' scores does not in fact undermine the authenticity of this new source. One example suffices to demonstrate this: the l.h. fingering 5–5 (so characteristic of Chopin!) in the trio of the 'Funeral March' in op. 35 (first two quavers of bars 31, 34, 36, 46) figures in Stirling and Jędrzejewicz at analogous passages in the Nocturnes opp. 27/1 and 32/1.[77]

Further reading

Gajewski, *NZM*
Jaeger, p. 83
Kobylańska, *TBWV*, pp. xvi, 87 and 88

---

[76] This recalls the analogous annotation *Tempo primo*, also in ink and undoubtedly in Chopin's hand, in the Jędrzejewicz score of the Nocturne op. 48/2, bar 101.

[77] Cf. p. 116, note 85.

The Orda scores

Provenance

Warsaw, Museum of the Fryderyk Chopin Society: M/610. Purchased in 1962 from the antiquarian Nicolas Rauch in Geneva. These scores were the property of Napoléon Orda,[78] as is shown by Chopin's autograph dedication quoted below.

Description and content

Now bound in one volume, the scores are preceded by an inked manuscript table of contents; the hand appears like that of a man of the nineteenth century (Orda?):

Etudes op. 10 [1–12]
Trois Nocturnes op. 9 [1–3]
Trois Nocturnes op. 15 [1–3]
Trois [sic] Mazourkas op. 6 [1–5]
Trois [sic] Mazourkas op. 7 [1–4]
Quatre Mazourkas op. 17 [1–4]
Grande Valse op. 18
Variations s[ur] Ludovic op. 12
Rondo op. 16
Bolero op. 19
Duo Piano et Violoncelle s[ur] Robert le Diable [without op. no.]

Grouped by musical genre and by opus number, these scores are those of the OFE[79] and were therefore printed in 1833–4. A print of the Chopin lithograph portrait after Vigneron, edited by Maurice Schlesinger, is attached to the copy of the Etudes op. 10, whose title page carries an inked dedication in Chopin's hand: 'Napoleonowi Ordzie [to N.O.] /FF. Chopin'. We know this to be a copy of the first printing of op. 10, as its printed dedication is still to J. [sic] Liszt – a misprint quickly corrected in the reprintings!

[78] Napoléon Orda (1807–83), Lithuanian pianist, composer, and theoretician who emigrated to Paris in 1831. It is probably in the immediately subsequent years that he worked with Chopin, judging by the opus numbers and publication dates of the works forming his collection. Sowiński (p. 444) does not mention Orda as a pupil of Chopin; on the other hand J. W. Davison (Niecks, I, p. 257, note 8) takes him as such. Chopin valued Orda's compositions no more (SC, p. 188) than he did Sowiński's! He was still in contact with his old pupil during the last months of his life (CFC, III, pp. 406 and 432; SC, pp. 368–9). Orda returned to his native land in 1856.
[79] With the exception of op. 17 (M. Schlesinger's edition).

Nature of the musical annotations

- Corrections of misprints (op. 19)
- Fingerings (opp. 12 and 19)
- Phrasing and agogics (opp. 12 and 19)
- Crosses (opp. 6/1; 7/1; 7/3; 7/4; 17/1; 17/3)

Remarks and problems

The annotations in op. 19 have some chance of being in Chopin's hand. The crosses all appear at the beginnings of pieces, in the Mazurkas only.

Among the annotated scores listed in this Appendix, those of Orda are by far the least rich in indications. But this overall observation does not exclude the possibility that the scores served at lessons with Chopin, bearing in mind their probable date suggested in note 78 (p. 242).

Further reading

Wróblewska–Gendaszek, pp. 140–2

Appendix III: Fingerings and annotations in the scores of pupils and associates

To maximize the scope of the musical examples given in the main text above, this Appendix offers some works and extracts furnished with the fingerings and other annotations from the most important scores used by Chopin's pupils and associates. The selection of these here has been dictated by the characteristics and frequency of the fingerings, as well as by their provenance; some of them illustrate correlations of ideas or correspondences between various sources. The four principal sources are represented by the symbols:

○	△	▽	□	◌
Stirling	Dubois	Jędrzejewicz	Franchomme	all 4 combined

Unless otherwise mentioned at the foot of the page, added indications other than fingerings (phrasing slurs, breathing points, attack of ornaments, 8ᵛᵃ signs and arpeggiation signs) are taken from the Dubois scores.

IMPROMPTU op. 29 (bars 35–82)

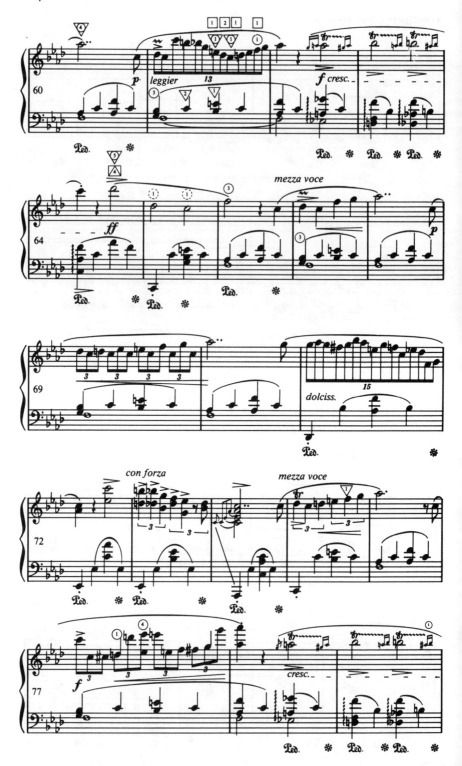

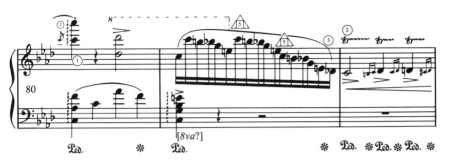

MAZURKA op. 7/3 (bars 56-72)

248

PRELUDE op. 28/6

(a) Pedalling and dynamics according to the Jędrzejewicz score.

MAZURKA op. 7/1 (bars 1-30)

Vivace ♩.=50

MAZURKA op. 24/1 (bars 1-33)

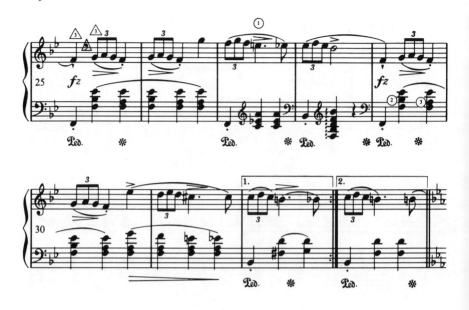

WALTZ op. 18 (bars 1-31)

(a) The '8' specifies a bass octave doubling of the b♭". The autograph at Yale University gives the same version (see facsimile in Janis, p. [30]).

254

WALTZ op. 18 (bars 124-150)

PRELUDE op. 28/15 (bars 1-27)

(a) L.h. f″ taken over by the r.h. in the Stirling and Dubois scores.

(b) *Crescendo* according to the Stirling score.
(c) Slur in the Stirling score.

NOCTURNE op. 9/2

(a) Dynamics according to the Stirling score.

(a) Dynamics according to the Stirling score.

(a) Dynamics according to the Stirling score.
(b) This accent, printed in the first editions, is deleted in the Dubois and Jędrzejewicz scores.

NOCTURNE op. 27/2 (bars 44-52)

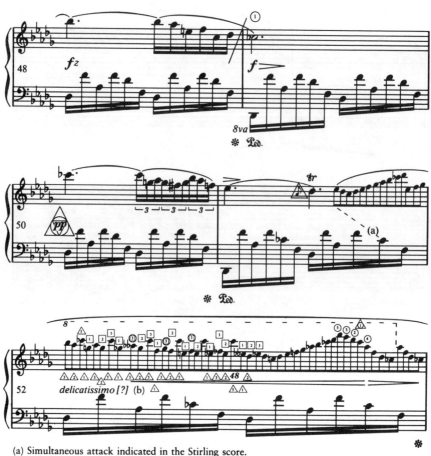

(a) Simultaneous attack indicated in the Stirling score.
(b) Annotation in the Jędrzejewicz score.

NOCTURNE op. 32/1 (bars 57-end)

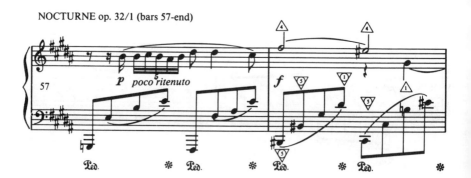

(a) Lines indicating respectively simultaneous attack with the l.h., and a break of silence, in the Stirling score.
(b) Slur added to the Stirling and Jędrzejewicz scores.

NOCTURNE op. 48/1 (bars 1-36)

Lento

(a) Simultaneous attack specified in the Stirling score.

(b) Dynamics according to the autograph.

266

(a) From here on, arpeggiation signs, note deletions, hairpin dynamics, etc., follow the annotations in the
Jędrzejewicz score.

Appendix IV: Chopin's playing described by his contemporaries

To complement the chapters on Chopin's teaching, the opportunity is taken here of quoting the main accounts of Chopin's own playing as described by his contemporaries: the teacher Chopin is indissolubly linked, after all, to the pianist, simply reflecting the latter in the didactic medium. The quotations are grouped under four headings, according to the categories (often flexible) to which their authors belong: *Composers and Pianists*; *Pupils*; *Associates*; *Music Critics*. Despite their diversity of date and origin, many of these accounts exhibit remarkable concordances, contributing generally towards a unified impression. Two sub-headings are entitled respectively 'Chopin playing Beethoven' (under *Pupils*) and 'Chopin as improviser' (under *Associates*). Liszt's main text on this subject has already been quoted virtually in its entirety (p. 51 above). The second main category of contributors is intentionally restricted here since it has already been the main subject of our book: it nevertheless includes passages which, except for a few fragments, have not been quoted above. The passages given in this Appendix may serve to fill out any somewhat mosaic feeling inherent in the main texts above, an unavoidable consequence of their reorganization of the source material. Here, however, the aim is purely descriptive; the texts are left to speak for themselves and for one another.

Composers and pianists

Mendelssohn

The next morning, the three of us [Mendelssohn, Hiller and Chopin] were at the piano, which afforded me great pleasure. They have both developed their skills even further, and as a pianist Chopin is now one of the greatest of all – doing things as original as Paganini does on the violin, and bringing about miracles that one would never have believed possible. Hiller too is a remarkable player, vigorous with a touch of coquetry. Both, however, labour somewhat under the Parisian tendency of overdoing passion and despair, and too often lose sight of calm, discretion and the purely musical; I on the other hand perhaps do this too little – and so we all three supplemented and, I believe, learned from each other, with myself acting a little bit the part of schoolmaster, and they the *mirliflores* or *incroyables*.

Letter to his mother (Düsseldorf, 23 May 1834), II, p. 41.

I cannot deny, dear Fanny,[1] feeling again that your opinion [of Chopin] does not do him sufficient justice; maybe he was not in the right mood for playing when you heard him, which with him can often be the case. But as for myself, his playing has enchanted me anew, and I am convinced that if Father and yourself had heard him play some of his better pieces as he played them to me, you would say the same. There is something entirely his own in his piano playing, and at the same time so masterly that he may truly be called a perfect virtuoso; and since I love and enjoy every kind of perfection, that day [in Chopin's company] was most pleasant [. . .]

Letter to his family (Leipzig, 6 October 1835), II, pp. 99–100.

Rebecka Dirichlet[2]

Rebecka's desire to hear [Chopin][3] was so great that she decided to try a request, or, as she herself writes, to try the trick of introducing herself to him as the 'soeur de Messieurs Paul et Felix Mendelssohn-Bartholdy'. The ruse failed miserably. Dirichlet went to him, saying a sister [would be overjoyed to hear] just one Mazurka – 'Impossible, nervous strain, bad piano,' was the response, – 'and how is our dear Mrs Hensel [Fanny], and Paul, is he married? Charming couple, etc. – Go and have a walk.'

Hensel, II, pp. 17–18.

Schumann

In the morning, Chopin . . . 'His Ballade I like best of all.' I am very glad of that; I am very glad of that. Doesn't like his works being discussed. Warmed me through and through . . . To Dr Härtel.[4] It was stirring just to watch him at the keyboard. New Etudes in C minor – in A flat major – in F minor – old Masurken in B flat – two new ones – a Ballade – Notturno in D flat. He tells extraordinary things of Liszt. He [Chopin] never seems to correct, never even to spot, misprints; Liszt does to an extraordinary degree, can thrill by playing on any old honkytonk . . . Wonderful playing on a new pianoforte, built to the French design. Etude in E minor, if I'm not mistaken, and two of the

---

[1] Fanny Hensel-Mendelssohn (1805–47) was the elder sister of the composer; a highly talented pianist, she composed several works in collaboration with her brother.
[2] Rebecka Dirichlet-Mendelssohn (1811–58) was Mendelssohn's younger sister, gifted with a beautiful voice.
[3] At Marienbad in August 1836.
[4] The lawyer Dr Hermann Härtel; with his brother Raimund proprietor of the firm of Breitkopf & Härtel.

above. [I] bring him Sonata and *Etudes* by me, [he] gives me *Ballade*. Pack things up. Post [stage coach]. Artist brought to Eleonoren.[5] Now *Notturno* played, *Etude* in pure arpeggios in C major. Farewell. Away. Away.

Personal diary (Leipzig, 12 September 1836), quoted in Eismann, I, p. 98.

From Chopin I [heard] a new *Ballade*.[6] It seems to me his most ingenious composition (though not of most genius); and I told him I liked it best of all. After a long pause for contemplation he said with great emphasis, 'I am glad, it's my favourite one also.' Besides this he played me a host of new *Etudes* [op. 25], *Notturnos*, *Mazureks* [*sic*] – all incomparable. Just to see him sitting at the piano is stirring [. . .] But Clara is a greater virtuoso and gives almost more meaning to his composition than he does himself. Imagine the perfection, a mastery that seems quite unaware of itself!

Letter to Dorn (Leipzig, 14 September 1836), *RSB*, pp. 78–9.

It was already an unforgettable picture to see him sitting at the piano like a clairvoyant, lost in his dreams; to see how his vision communicated itself through his playing, and how, at the end of each piece, he had the sad habit of running one finger [*glissando*] over the length of the plaintive keyboard, as though to tear himself forcibly away from his dream.

GS, II, p. 23.

Henriette Voigt[7]

Yesterday Chopin was here and played for an hour on my piano – a fantasia and new *études* of his [from op. 25] – interesting man and still more interesting playing; he moved me strangely. The over-excitement of his fantastic manner is imparted to the keen-eared; it made me hold my breath. Wonderful is the ease with which his velvet fingers glide, I might almost say fly, over the keys. He has enraptured me – I cannot deny it – in a way which hitherto had been unknown to me. What delighted me was the childlike, natural manner which showed in his demeanour and in his playing.

Personal diary (Leipzig, 13 September 1836), quoted in Niecks, I, p. 311.

[5] *Davidsbündler* nickname for Schumann's motherly friend Henriette Voigt; see note 7 immediately below.
[6] Probably an early version of op. 38.
[7] Henriette Voigt (1808–39) was the wife of a Leipzig merchant, whose salon welcomed artists, particularly musicians. Mendelssohn and Schumann were regular visitors; the latter enrolled Frau Voigt into his fraternity of *Davidsbündler* under the name of Eleonore, and dedicated to her his Sonata in G minor op. 22. The German edition of Niecks (I, p. 323) possibly reproduces the original German of this extract.

Hiller[8]

He disliked being without company – something that seldom occurred. In the morning he liked to spend an hour by himself at his grand piano; but even when he practised – or how should I describe it? – when he stayed at home to play in the evenings, he needed to have at least one of his friends close at hand [. . .]

But I must describe his wonderful playing, which will remain impressed on my soul until I draw my last breath. I have said that he rarely opened his heart out; but at the piano he abandoned himself more completely than any other musician I have ever heard – with such concentration that all extraneous thoughts simply fell away. Nobody before had stirred the keys of a grand piano like that, nor known how to release such countless sonorities from it. Rhythmic firmness was combined with freedom in the declamation of his melodies, so that they would seem to have occurred to him at that very moment. What in the hands of others was elegant embellishment, in his hands became a colourful wreath of flowers; what in others was technical dexterity seemed in his playing like the flight of a swallow. All thought of isolating any one quality – novelty, grace, perfection, soul – fell away; it was simply Chopin. Even the lack of that imposing sonorous strength familiar from Liszt, Thalberg and others, appeared as an element of charm – this vain combat between energy of mind and matter produced a feeling of nostalgia. Even the deepest understanding of his compositions and the most intimate familiarity with them can give no idea of the poetry of address that was his very own. All material considerations vanished – it was like the light of a wonderful meteor, bewitching us all the more with its unfathomable mystery.

BU, pp. 150–2.

---

[8] Ferdinand Hiller (1811–85); German pianist, composer and conductor. After studying with Hummel in Weimar he spent over seven years (1828–36) in Paris where he was friendly with all the important musicians. During these years Hiller was a close friend of Chopin (the Nocturnes op. 15 are dedicated to him); together with Liszt, Franchomme and Berlioz, they formed something of a coterie. 'Of our old romantic Parisian fraternity which, with Mendelssohn and Chopin, comprised five members, only we three, Berlioz and yourself, remain in this base world', wrote Liszt to Hiller on 15 February 1855 (Sietz, I, p. 106). On his return to Germany Hiller occupied various important posts, eventually settling in Cologne in 1850; highly active there, he became the most prominent musical personality in the Rhineland. His friendship with Chopin appears to peter out after 1836, for no known reason other than that of distance.

Hallé

The same evening [30 November 1836] I went to dine with Baron Eichtal, where I was very cordially treated, and where I heard – *Chopin*. That was beyond all words. The few senses I had have quite left me. I could have jumped into the Seine. Everything I hear now seems so insignificant, that I would rather not hear it at all. Chopin! He is no man, he is an angel, a god (or what can I say more?). Chopin's compositions played by Chopin! That is a joy never to be surpassed. I shall describe his playing another time. Kalkbrenner compared to Chopin is a child. I say this with the completest conviction. During Chopin's playing I could think of nothing but elves and fairy dances, such a wonderful impression do his compositions make. There is nothing to remind one that it is a human being who produces this music. It seems to descend from heaven – so pure, and clear, and spiritual. I feel a thrill each time I think of it.

Letter to his parents (Paris, 2 December 1836), pp. 224–5.

The same evening [30 November 1836] I heard him play, and was fascinated beyond expression. It seemed to me as if I had got into another world, and all thought of Kalkbrenner was driven out of my mind. I sat entranced, filled with wonderment, and if the room had suddenly been peopled with fairies, I should not have been astonished. The marvellous charm, the poetry and originality, the perfect freedom and absolute lucidity of Chopin's playing at that time cannot be described. It was perfection in every sense. He seemed to be pleased with the evident impression he had produced, for I could only stammer a few broken words of admiration, and he played again and again, each time revealing new beauties, until I could have dropped on my knees to worship him [. . .] Strange to say, the idea of taking lessons did not occur to me then; I felt that what I had to do could be done without a master; lessons of style might be more useful later on [. . .]

I can confidently assert that nobody has ever been able to reproduce [his works] as they sounded under his magical fingers. In listening to him you lost all power of analysis; you did not for a moment think how perfect was his execution of this or that difficulty; you listened, as it were, to the improvisation of a poem, and were under the charm as long as it lasted.

Autobiography [*c.* 1894–5?], pp. 31–4.

Berlioz

Chopin's talent is of an entirely different nature [from Liszt's]. In order to appreciate him fully, I believe he has to be heard from close by, in the salon rather than the concert hall, with all preconceived notions put aside, as these would be inapplicable to both him and his music. As interpreter and composer, Chopin is an artist apart, bearing no point of resemblance to any other musician I know. His melodies, all impregnated with Polish elements, have something naively untamed about them that charms and captivates by its very strangeness; in his *Etudes* one finds harmonic combinations of astonishing depth; he has created a kind of chromatic embroidery in several of his compositions, whose effect is so strange and piquant as to be impossible to describe. Unfortunately, virtually nobody but Chopin himself can play his music and give it this unusual turn, this sense of the unexpected which is one of its principal beauties; his playing is shot through with a thousand nuances of movement of which he alone holds the secret, impossible to convey by instructions.

There are unbelievable details in his Mazurkas; and he has found how to render them doubly interesting by playing them with the utmost degree of softness, *piano* to the extreme, the hammers merely brushing the strings, so much so that one is tempted to go close to the instrument and put one's ear to it as if to a concert of sylphs or elves. Chopin is the *Trilby* of pianists.

Le Rénovateur, II/345, 15 December 1833.

Chopin was impatient with the constraints of metre; in my opinion he pushed rhythmic independence much too far [. . .] Chopin *could* not play in time.

Mémoires, II, p. 296.

Moscheles

He played to me at my request, and only now do I understand his music, as well as the enthusiasm of the ladies. His *ad libitum* playing, which with other interpreters of his music tends to degenerate into a mere lack of rhythm [*Tactlosigkeit*], in his hands is the most graceful and original feature of the discourse; the harsh, amateurish modulations which I stumble over when playing his compositions no longer shock me, because his delicate fingers glide over them with elfin lightness; his *piano* is breathed forth so softly that he needs no vigorous *forte* to produce the desired contrasts; so one does not miss the orchestral effects which the German school demands from a pianist, but allows oneself to be carried away as by a singer who, untroubled by the accompaniment, gives full rein to his feelings; enough: he is unique in the piano world [. . .] He played me *Etudes* and his most recent work, the 'Preludes'.

[Letter; Paris, mid-October 1839], II, p. 39

Liszt

I remember some 25 years ago calling on Chopin, late one Sunday afternoon. I had already known him several years and my enthusiasm and admiration for his marvellously poetical talents had invariably, with each meeting, increased till I almost began to look upon him as 'a God amongst musicians'.

Well, when I arrived, I found him seated at the piano with a pen in his hand, and on a small table next to the piano a manuscript with the ink still wet. After a cordial greeting from him, I remarked that he looked as if he had been working very hard, as his face looked pale; his hair was in disorder, and there were several smudges of ink on his face and also on his long thin fingers. He pointed to the manuscript and said: 'You guess correctly; since 11 o'clock this morning have I [*sic*] been busy at that Nocturne (it was the beautiful one in G major in double notes [op. 37/2]),' and now I feel that it does not exactly suit me.' He thereupon played it to me and entranced me with its beauties, which under his ravishing touch and incomparably artistic use of the pedals, sounded if possible more divinely beautiful than it is possible to describe in words.

I sat beside him entranced, and when he had finished I found it impossible to tell him how beautiful I found this, his latest inspiration. Chopin, however, with that innate tact and delicacy which characterized him especially, immediately proposed to play me some of his other later compositions which I had not seen. Knowing how much I esteemed him as a pianist, and how I adored him as a veritable *God-gifted genius*, he played for me in succession some eight or ten of his latest works, in a style which was a 'revelation' of

9 There is some chronological confusion or fantasy here from either Liszt or his chronicler, since Chopin announced this Nocturne's completion in a letter to Fontana from Nohant [8 August 1839], and offered it, with op. 37/1, to Breitkopf & Härtel on 14 December the same year (SC, pp. 181 and 188). Liszt was in fact outside France all of that time. The reported encounter could have taken place in Paris in April 1840 (when the piece was still unpublished) or in April 1841, two occasions when Liszt was in Paris. One remembers Liszt's famous review of Chopin's concert of 26 April 1841, which lists Nocturnes and Preludes among the items played. But Liszt cannot have been present at either the gestation or the completion of op. 37/2.

him, both as a virtuoso and composer. Especially beautiful was the Prelude in F sharp minor,[10] a work replete with enormous difficulties, which he *wove* intricately under his fingers, [so] that at times a wailing melody was unravelled, and then again completely absorbed by wonderful arabesques and chromatic progressions. It was so enchanting that he complied with my earnest entreaty, and repeated it *twice*. Each time it seemed more beautiful, and each time he played it more ravishingly.

This performance is as vivid now in my memory as if it had happened only yesterday. I begged him to play me his favourite piece of his own, the 'Variations in B flat', and on my absolutely insisting, he complied. Such a poetic temperament as Chopin's never existed, nor have I ever heard such delicacy and refinement of playing. The tone, though small, was absolutely beyond criticism, and although his execution was not forcible, nor by any means fitted for the concert room, still it was perfect in the extreme.

Conversation quoted in Strelezki,[11] pp. 12–13.

Marmontel

As regards evenness of fingers, delicacy, perfect independence of the hands, Chopin clearly belonged to the school of Clementi, whose excellent studies he always recommended and appreciated. But where Chopin was entirely himself was in his marvellous way of leading and modulating the sound, in his expressive, wistful way of colouring it. He had a completely individual manner of touching the keyboard, a supple, mellow touch, creating sound effects of a misty fluidity whose secret he alone knew.

No pianist before him employed the pedals alternately or simultaneously with so much tact and skill. With most modern virtuosos, excessive, continuous use of the pedal is a capital defect, producing sonorities eventually tiring and irritating to the delicate ear. Chopin, on the contrary, while making constant use of the pedal, obtained ravishing harmonies, melodic whispers that charmed and astonished. A wonderful poet of the

---

[10] Liszt had a special predilection for this Prelude, which he wrongly identified in his book on Chopin (pp. 273–4) as the 'raindrop' Prelude. The influence of the piece on Liszt's piano writing is apparent notably in the coda of 'Au bord d'une source' (*Années de Pèlerinage, Vol. I: Suisse*), in the final version published in 1855. The same Prelude was later the topic of a seminar in which Liszt took part in Weimar in June 1884 (see Jerger, pp. 41–2).

[11] Anton Strelezki (real name Arthur Bransby Burnand, 1859–1907) was an English pianist and composer. As a pupil of Tausig and Nicolas Rubinstein he introduced himself to Liszt in 1869, and then studied with the latter for six months. His little known book contains reminiscences of Liszt including Liszt's views on, principally, Schumann, Mendelssohn, Chopin and Wagner. 'Strelezki' and Liszt met again in later years, the last occasion being during Liszt's final visit to Paris in 1886.

piano, he had a way of understanding, of feeling and expressing his ideas which others, with very few exceptions, have often tried to imitate without achieving anything more than clumsy parodies.

If we draw a parallel between Chopin's sound effects and certain techniques of painting, we could say that this great virtuoso modulated sound much as skilled painters treat light and atmosphere. To envelop melodic phrases and ingenious arabesques in a half-tint which has something of both dream and reality: this is the pinnacle of art; and this was Chopin's art.

PC, pp. 4–5

Pupils

Mikuli

Chopin played rarely and only reluctantly in public: to 'exhibit himself' was absolutely against his nature. Prolonged ill-health and nervous irritability did not always allow him to unfold the full range of his resources in the concert hall. Even in intimate circles he rarely played anything but his shorter compositions, and occasionally fragments from the larger ones. Thus Chopin was hardly in a position to acquire universal fame as a pianist.

And yet Chopin possessed a highly developed technique, one giving a perfect command of the instrument. In every kind of touch the evenness of his scales and passage work was unsurpassed, indeed phenomenal; under Chopin's hands the piano needed to envy neither the violin for its bow nor wind instruments for their living breath. The tones melted into one another, as wonderfully as in the most beautiful singing.

His hand was that of a born pianist, not so much large as extremely supple, permitting him to arpeggiate the most widely-spaced harmonies and to stretch wide spans in the sorts of passage he himself had most daringly introduced into piano playing. All this was without ever showing the slightest sign of fatigue, his playing being characterized above all by its radiant freedom and ease. In the process, the tone which he could *draw* from the instrument, especially in *cantabile*, was always immense [*riesengross*]; in this regard Field alone could be compared with him.

He gave a noble, manly energy to appropriate passages with overpowering effect – energy without roughness – just as, on the other hand, he could captivate the listener through the delicacy of his soulful rendering – delicacy without affectation. For all the warmth of Chopin's temperament, his playing was always measured, chaste, distinguished and at times even severely reserved [. . .]

In keeping time Chopin was inexorable, and some readers will be surprised to learn that the metronome never left his piano. Even in his much maligned *tempo rubato*, the hand responsible for the accompaniment would keep strict time while the other hand, singing the melody, would free the essence of the musical thought from all rhythmic fetters, either by lingering hesitantly or by eagerly anticipating the movement with a certain impatient vehemence akin to passionate speech.

Although Chopin played mostly his own compositions, he had all the great and beautiful works of the piano literature in his memory – a memory as highly developed as it was reliable. Above all he prized Bach, and between Bach and Mozart it is hard to say whom he loved more. His interpretation of their music was of unrivalled greatness [. . .] Naturally, Beethoven was also close to his heart. Chopin took particular pleasure in playing the works of Weber, particularly the *Concertstück* and the Sonatas in A flat major and E minor; Hummel's Fantasy, Septet and concertos; Field's Concerto in A flat major and his Nocturnes, to which he would improvise the most beautiful *Fioritures*. Of virtuoso music of the kind that was running pianistic riot at the time, I hardly ever saw anything on his desk, nor did anyone else.

Preface, pp. 2–3.

Emile Gaillard[12]

Thumping is not playing [. . .] Chopin never flattened his piano, and yet, under his fingers, everything came out wonderfully. While his left hand played a beautiful song, straight from the heart, his right hand would seem casually to unfold a magnificent lacework of sound. Virtuosity disappeared behind the emotion; one was less dazzled than moved. He appeared to caress the keyboard, while his sensitive and grieving soul rose and wandered freely among us. When he finished playing a Nocturne one wished only to be quiet so that the enchantment should not be broken. He himself, on finishing a piece, would often stay sitting at the keyboard in silence, pursuing a dream of his own.

Déchelette, *Journal des Débats*, 28 December 1934.

[12] Emile Gaillard (1821–1902), banker, friend and pupil of Chopin, was the dedicatee of the Mazurka in A minor [without op. no.], published in Paris by Chabal [1841] – CW, X, no. 42. Chopin also offered him an album leaf (*Paris, le 20 Juillet 1840*), published as No. 18 of the Waltzes in the Henle edition.

Mathias

Chopin as a pianist? First of all, those who have heard Chopin may well say that nothing remotely resembling his playing has ever been heard since. His playing was like his music; and what virtuosity! what power! yes, what power! though it would only last for a few bars; and the exaltation, the inspiration! the whole man vibrated! The piano became so intensely animated that it gave one shivers. I repeat that the instrument which one heard Chopin playing never existed except beneath Chopin's fingers: he played as he composed . . .

[. . .] Chopin, performer of genius, interpreted Mozart, Beethoven with the feeling of Chopin, and it was extremely beautiful, it was sublime. He was not of the category of critical or historic performers, which is not to say that the latter are unworthy: for not everybody can possess genius.

Preface, p. 5.

CHOPIN PLAYING BEETHOVEN

Anonymous Scottish lady

Chopin allowed me to finish the beautiful air, and then took my place and played the entire sonata [Beethoven op. 26]. It was like a revelation [. . .] He played that *Marche funèbre* of Beethoven's with a grand, orchestral, powerfully dramatic effect, yet with a sort of restrained emotion which was indescribable. Lastly he rushed through the final movement with faultless precision and extraordinary delicacy – not a single note lost, and with marvellous phrasing and alternations of light and shade. We stood spellbound, never having heard the like.

Letter to J. C. Hadden (27 March 1903), Hadden, pp. 157–8.

Lenz

Chopin had been called on[13] to play Beethoven's sonata (the variation movement). How then did Chopin play Beethoven's op. 26? He played it beautifully, but not as beautifully as his own compositions; not seizing it, not in relief, not like a story whose suspense is heightened from one variation to

[13] 9 November 1842 at the Parisian home of the Countesses Cheriemietieff, in the presence of Marie de Krudner.

the next. His *mezza voce* was whispered, but he was unrivalled in the cantilena, with an infinite perfection in the continuity of structure: ideally beautiful, but *feminine*! Beethoven is a *man*, and never ceases to be so! [. . .] Everyone was delighted, I too was delighted – but only by Chopin's tone, by his touch, by his elegance and grace, by his purity of style.

As we drove back together, I was quite honest when he asked my opinion. 'I indicate,' (*j'indique*) he replied, without a trace of touchiness, 'it's up to the listener to complete (*parachever*) the picture.'

GPV 1872, p. 39.

Elizavieta Cheriemietieff

At four o'clock Chopin arrived. His playing made a vivid impression to-day; after the lesson[14] he played his *masourques* [*sic*] and Nocturnes; he is so courteous and unassuming. I no longer know how to describe his playing. It is something so unique that the instrument becomes unrecognizable under his fingers. At last I have found the person who plays as I sometimes imagined playing should be, that is, perfection; he has discovered how to give the piano a soul. It's something so ethereal, so transparent, that delicacy, yet his sounds [are] so full, so large. Listening to him, one feels as though suspended somewhere between heaven and earth – as he expresses his thoughts. It's truly sublime; every note has a value, an idea which he knows how to convey perfectly. All possible eulogies are no exaggeration, I assure you. One sees how he senses all that he makes the piano say, one understands him. He's a genius far above all the pianists who dazzle and exhaust their listeners.[15] This one can play all day without one wanting to say 'enough'; every sound goes straight to the heart. I'm so sorry you won't hear him! [. . .] He played two Nocturnes, which took the breath from us, we were even in tears [. . .] It's a desecration, I find, to play his compositions; nobody understands them. He himself plays them sometimes far from in strict time, following his inspiration, and then it's beautiful.

Letter to her mother (Paris, 11 November 1842), Siemienovski, pp. 127–8.

[14] These were lessons given to Marie de Krudner in November–December 1842, which the Countesses Cheriemietieff attended as listeners before Elizavieta in her turn took lessons with Chopin.
[15] This recalls Auber's remark, reported by Baron de Trémont: '*Monsieur Chopin, vous me reposez du piano!* [you reconcile me to the piano]' (see p. 286 below).

Anonymous Scottish lady

And truly in his hands the piano *did* sing, and in many tones. I watched, I listened, but can find no adequate description of that thrilling music. One never thought of 'execution', though that was marvellous. It seemed to come from the depths of a heart, and it struck the hearts of listeners. Volumes have been written, yet I think no one who did not hear him could quite understand that magnetic power.

Letter to J. C. Hadden (27 March 1903), Hadden, p. 159.

Associates

Sophie Leo[16]

No one who has not known Chopin will ever be able to imagine a being like him or to conceive to what exaltation the soul, before its release from its mortal shell, can attain; no one who has not heard Chopin's compositions played by their composer will ever have an intimation of how, quite without regard to tradition, or to praise or blame, the purest inspiration may be carried along on the wings of the spirit. Chopin was *himself*, surely the first, probably the eternally unique manifestation of his species [. . .]

He appeared hardly to touch the piano; one might have thought an instrument superfluous. There was no suggestion of the mechanical; the flute-like murmur of his playing had the ethereal effect of Aeolian harps. Yet despite these gifts, to which there was nowhere in the wide world a parallel, Chopin was gracious, modest, and unassuming. He was not a pianist of the modern school, but, in his own way, had created a style of his own, a style that one cannot describe.

Whether appearing in the private salon or in the concert hall he stepped quietly and modestly to the piano, was satisfied with whatever seat had been provided, showed at once by his simple dress and natural bearing that all

---

[16] Sophie Augustine Leo-Dellevie (b. 1795) was the wife of Auguste Leo, a Hamburg banker based in Paris from 1817 to 1848. Apart from these anonymously-published reminiscences, she published a second volume: *Personen und Zustände aus der Restauration* (Berlin, 1853). The couple kept a musical salon of high repute, attended notably by German musicians staying in or passing through Paris: Meyerbeer, Mendelssohn, Hiller, Hallé, Clara Wieck, Heller, and Moscheles who met Chopin there in October 1839. For his entire stay in Paris Chopin was close to Auguste Leo, his financial advisor and intermediary on various occasions with English and German editors. The *Grande Polonaise brillante* op. 53 is dedicated to him.

forms of affectation and charlatanry were distasteful to him, and, without any sort of introduction, at once began his soulful and heartfelt performance. He was above setting off his talent by appearing before the public with long, dishevelled hair, or with a lorgnette, or with coquetry. He offered art, not artifice, and gave it a dignified setting, not a grotesque one.

'Musical Life in Paris (1817–1848)', pp. 401–3.

Solange Clésinger[17]

Whoever has not heard him, or, lacking that, one of his favourite pupils, such as the Princess Marcelline Czartoryska, Mlle O'Meara or Mlle de Rozières,[18] cannot know even what his music is about.

Certainly the printed edition does not adequately convey all the originality and charm his adepts were able to draw from it [. . .] The woman, the

[17] Solange Clésinger (1828–99) was the daughter of George Sand and Casimir Dudevant. She lived in Chopin's vicinity from the time of the journey to Majorca until after his separation from Sand, which indeed was precipitated by family quarrels at the time of Solange's marriage to the sculptor Clésinger in May 1847. Chopin, who had taken her part in the matter, remained loyal to the end. There have been some rather far-fetched attempts to prove a closer attachment between Chopin and the young girl, on the basis of her evident affection for him. During the summer visits to Nohant between 1839 and 1845 Chopin gave Solange some lessons in place of her regular teacher, Mlle de Rozières. A lazy and mediocre student, Solange seems nonetheless to have inherited something of her mother's musical sensitivity. Some aspects of her reminiscences are of particular interest in view of her privileged position.

[18] Marie de Rozières (1805–65); piano teacher in Paris. Chopin introduced her to George Sand in 1840 as a teacher for Solange. Mlle de Rozières was then receiving free lessons from Chopin, as Sand notes in a letter (CGS, V, p. 309); she seems to have continued receiving his advice, according to Chopin's letter to her of [winter 1844] (CFC, III, p. 186 – see also SC, p. 241). But she cannot be counted as one of Chopin's 'élèves préférées'; in 1846 she seems to have worked as supervisor for some of his less talented pupils. She interfered indiscreetly in Chopin's private life (embarrassing him by a flaunted affair with Antoni Wodziński, brother of Maria) and in his relations with George Sand and Solange. Having taken the Clésingers' side in the quarrels provoked by their marriage, she maintained contact with Chopin until the last months of his life. A portrait of Chopin having belonged to her – drawing heightened with crayon by N.-E. Maurin, now in PL-Wtifc – contains on its reverse the following unpublished manuscript explanation:

Note. The Comtesse de Rozières (by birth), whose parents were ruined in the Revolution, was a talented pianist and gave lessons. She dreamt, being an impassioned admirer of Chopin, of taking lessons with the Master, and put aside money for this purpose; she knew the price of his lessons was 50 francs [sic]. She sought out the great Pianist; he was content with her playing, but objected that his lessons were doubtless very costly for her – She insisted – 'Are you patient?' he asked. – Oui, Monsieur, je suis très patiente. – [']Well, come with me to see a friend (Mme G. Sand), whose daughter is un diable (Solange, later Mme Clézinger [sic]). If you can cope with her, fine, I'll give you a lesson for every lesson you give her.['] She coped and became close to the household; Chopin took a great affection for her [sic; see SC, pp. 201–2 and 204 for Chopin's contrary view in 1841]. When he found how well she could make chocolate, each morning he would order his chocolate 'chez Rozières' as he said and his valet would bring it to him. They were neighbours in the Cité d'Orléans. At that time nobody possessed better than her the Chopin tradition, her playing was special and admirable.

children (young Filtsch who died so young!) brought a finer sense than the masculine talents did to this celestial music, even when their fingers did not compare in strength and agility with the more practised and robust hands of the latter. For it was not a matter of hitting hard, of tough and dexterous performance. Liszt played these adorable melodies badly. He botched them. Without thumping, without hitting, without breaking, one had to bring out of an intractable instrument the vibrant and terrible accents of wrath, grief, victory or defeat. Under the flexible and responsive fingers of Chopin's pale and frail hand the piano became the voice of an archangel, an orchestra, an army, a raging ocean, a creation of the universe, the end of the world. What divine majesty! What elemental forces, what cries of despair! What triumphant hymns! What suave grace, what angelical tenderness, what infinite sorrows! What funeral marches and triumphal processions! What rays of sunlight on flowers in full bloom, on the glittering river, on the valley of scented lemon trees![19] What tears from the depths of the damp cloister! What impatient whinnyings of the war-horse, what duels of knights, what village or courtly dances (what minuets) interrupted by the jingling of arms or the cannon of the citadel! And what melancholy raindrops falling one by one on the tiles in the cell garden! George Sand gave a title to each of Chopin's wonderful Preludes; these titles have been preserved on a score he gave to us.[20]

'Frédérick Chopin',[21] in Eigeldinger, *SCFC*, pp. 226–7.

[19] This phrase, the next one, and the one beginning 'And what melancholy raindrops' [*quelles mélancoliques gouttes de pluie*] correspond very closely to some of those used by George Sand in her famous text on the Preludes op. 28 (*HV*, II, p. 420). Solange may have remembered this text or had it in front of her, or else may have recalled the titles noted by her mother on a copy of the score, or even have had this copy at her disposal. Whatever the case, the similarities are striking. Up to a point Solange's text – together with Sand's – could be used to reconstruct Sand's titles. Both texts contain circumstantial imagery some of which could be applied closely enough to the character of the following Preludes:
 – *Quelle marche funèbre* (no. 20) *ou triomphale* (no. 9)
 – *Quelles larmes au fond du cloître humide* (no. 4)
 – *Quelles mélancoliques gouttes de pluie tombant une à une* . . . (no. 15)
and so on with other examples.

[20] This copy is at present untraced. M. Georges Lubin has confirmed its absence from the various archives relating to George Sand. Precise knowledge of the titles invented by her would do much to clarify the controversial question of which Preludes were actually *composed* in Majorca.

[21] Manuscript title of a text conserved in *F-Pn*, Rés. Vmc. MS. 23, bequeathed by Roger de Garate who noted on the outer cover: 'Ce qui est coupé, c'est Aurore Sand [grand-daughter of George Sand and niece of Solange] qui l'a coupé devant moi.' Numerous sentences, even paragraphs, have indeed been cut away. The text can be dated around 1895. In their article 'Chopin et la fille de George Sand' (*Revue des Deux-Mondes*, Paris, December 1957, pp. 500–3), Suzanne and Denise Chainaye published a letter from Solange to Samuel Rocheblave, dated 19 January 1896. The end of this letter is missing there, its existence attested to by a colon at the end of a page; M. Georges Lubin has kindly supplied the missing words: 'Last year I wrote (in answer to a request) twenty

CHOPIN AS IMPROVISER

Fontana

From his earliest youth, the richness of his improvisation was astonishing. But he took good care not to parade it; and the few lucky ones who have heard him improvising for hours on end, in the most wonderful manner, never lifting a single phrase from any other composer, never even touching on any of his own works – those people will agree with us in saying that Chopin's most beautiful finished compositions are merely reflections and echoes of his improvisations. This spontaneous inspiration was like an inexhaustible torrent of precious materials in ferment. From time to time, the master would draw out of it a few cups to throw into his mould, and these were found to be full of pearls and rubies.

[Preface to] *Oeuvres posthumes de Fréd. Chopin*, pp. 1–2.

Delacroix

On our way back, Grzymała and I talked about Chopin. He was telling me that Chopin's improvisations were far bolder than his finished compositions. It was evidently something like comparing the sketch of a painting to the finished product.

Journal (20 April 1853), II, p. 22.

George Sand

Chopin is no longer listening. He is at the piano and does not observe that we are listening to him. He improvises as if haphazardly. He stops. 'Eh bien, eh bien', exclaims Delacroix, 'ce n'est pas fini!' 'It hasn't begun. Nothing's

pages about him. They were found to be too harsh (you will guess for whom [G. Sand]) and laboured.' Our manuscript, numbering 26 pages written on recto sides only, may be identified with the text mentioned in her letter and consequently dated 1895. Despite its cuts, Solange's script contains important details touching, among other things, upon Chopin's last illness and death. Only the passages relevant to our purpose are quoted here, with spelling and punctuation tacitly modernized (which they are not in the complete version given in *SCFC*).

coming to me . . . nothing but reflections, shadows, reliefs that won't settle. I'm looking for the colour, but I can't even find the outline.'[22]

'You won't find one without the other,' responds Delacroix, 'and you're going to find them both.'

'But if I find only the moonlight?'

'You'll have found the reflection of a reflection,' answers Maurice.

This idea pleases the divine artist. He resumes playing without seeming to recommence, so vague and hesitant is its musical outline. Little by little our eyes become filled with those soft colours corresponding to the suave modulations taken in by our auditory senses. And then the *note bleue* resonates and there we are, in the azure of the transparent night. Light clouds take on all the forms of fantasy; they fill the sky; they crowd round the moon which casts upon them large opal discs, awakening their dormant colours. We dream of a summer night: we await the nightingale.

A sublime melody arises.

Impressions et souvenirs, pp. 85–6.

Bohdan Zaleski[23]

At four o'clock I went to Chopin's. Witwicki was there [. . .] Chopin entered unexpectedly, pale, tired, but in good spirits and in an inspired mood. He greeted me affectionately and sat down at the piano. It's impossible to describe the form and subject of his playing. For the first time in my life the beauty of the music moved me so vividly that I could not hold back my tears. All the nuances, all the musician's emotions, I could grasp, and I remember in the most exact way the motives and the feelings I had while listening to each piece. First he played a magnificent Prelude, then the *Berceuse*, then a Mazurka, again the *Berceuse* – of which Mme Hoffman said that the angels in Bethlehem must have sung like that. There followed a splendid Polonaise, and finally, in my honour, an improvisation in which he evoked all the sweet and sorrowful voices of the past. He sang the tears of the *dumkas* and finished with the national anthem, 'Poland is not [yet] dead' [*Jeszcze Polska nie zginęła*] in a whole gamut of different forms and voices, from that of the

---

[22] This extract is a literary and poetic adaptation of a discussion on Ingres and Delacroix, on line, colour and reflection; the discussion took place in January 1841, first in Delacroix's studio, then continued at George Sand's house in the Rue Pigalle where Maurice (a pupil of Delacroix), Chopin and Mickiewicz joined the painter and the novelist.

[23] Polish poet (1802–86) whom Chopin knew before leaving Poland and whom he met again in Paris after the 1831 insurrection. With Mickiewicz, Słowacki, Witwicki, Klementyna Hoffman-Tańska – mentioned in this text – and others, Zaleski belonged to the literary circle of Polish immigrants in Paris. In November 1846 he married Zofia Rosengardt, Chopin's pupil. Chopin's songs op. 74/8, 11, 13 and [19] are based on poems by Zaleski.

warrior to those of children and angels. I could have written a whole book about this improvisation.

Personal diary (2 February 1844), quoted in Ganche, *DSFC*, pp. 24–5.

Ferdynand Dworzaczek[24]

One day Chopin was improvising. I was lying on the sofa; I was in ecstasy, listening to him and day-dreaming. All of a sudden his music rang out with a song which went to the heart of my soul . . . a well known song . . . a song from the homeland . . . beloved . . . from the family home . . . from childhood years . . . My heart throbbed with yearning, tears sprang to my eyes – I leapt up: 'Fryderyczku!' I cried, 'I know that song from the cradle . . . my mother used to sing it . . . I have it in my soul, and you just played it!' He looked round with a strange expression. His eyes shone; his fingers were moving delicately over the keys; 'You never heard this tune before!' he declared. 'But I have it here, here, in my soul!' I cried, pressing my hand to my breast. 'Oh!' – he rose and embraced me – 'you have just made me indescribably happy, there are no words for it! You never knew this song . . . only its spirit: the spirit of the Polish melody! And I am so happy to have been able to grasp and reveal it.'

Wilkońska, p. 154.

Heine

[. . .] he is not only a virtuoso but also a poet; he can reveal to us the poetry that lives in his soul; he is a composer, and nothing can equal the pleasure he gives us when he sits at the piano and improvises. He is then neither Polish nor French nor German: he betrays a much higher origin, from the land of Mozart, of Raffael [*sic*], of Goethe; his true fatherland is the dream realm of poetry. When he sits improvising at the piano, I feel as though a compatriot from the beloved homeland were visiting me and recounting the most curious things which have taken place there during my absence . . .

'Über die französische Bühne. Zehnter Brief' (1837), [25] in *Sämtliche Werke*, VIII, pp. 125–6.

---

[24] Ferdynand Dworzaczek (1804–77) was a renowned Warsaw doctor. From 1831 to 1835 he stayed in Germany, then in Paris where he met Chopin (information kindly suppled by Mme D. Turło, of the TiFC, Warsaw).

[25] The last two *Briefe* (9–10) from *Über die französische Bühne* (1837) were translated into French by the publishers Calmann and Lévy in *De tout un peu* (Paris, 1888). Letters 1–8 also appeared in French, in a translation allegedly by Heine, under the title *De La France* (Paris, Lévy brothers, 1857).

There is only one pianist I prefer [to Thalberg:] Chopin, who, it is true, is more a composer than a virtuoso. In the vicinity of Chopin I completely forget the playing of the past master, and I sink into the soft unfathomed depths of his music, into the sorrowful delights of his creations, as exquisite as they are profound. Chopin is the great poet of music, the artist of genius whose name should be mentioned only in company with those of Mozart, Beethoven, Rossini and Berlioz.

Lutèce (Paris, 26 March 1843), pp. 316–17.

Besides [Liszt] all other pianists are eclipsed, with a single exception, Chopin, the Raphael of the pianoforte.

Lutèce (Paris, 20 April 1841), p. 187.

Balzac

He found sublime themes on which he embroidered caprices, played sometimes with Chopin's Raphaelesque perfection and grief, sometimes with Liszt's Dantesque fire and grandiloquence, the two musical approaches closest to that of Paganini. The performance, having reached this degree of perfection, places the performer on the level of the poet: he is to the composer as the actor is to the author, a divine translator of divine things.

Le Cousin Pons, CH, VI, p. 743.

You should judge Listz [*sic*] only once you have had the opportunity to hear Chopin. The Hungarian is a demon; the Pole is an angel.

[Passy,] 28 May [1843], *LH,* II, p. 226.

Godefroid recognized a talent identical with Chopin's. It was a soul that expressed itself through divine sounds dominated by a melancholy gentleness.

L'Envers de l'histoire contemporaine, CH, VII, p. 396.

This beautiful genius [Chopin] is less a musician than a soul manifesting and communicating itself through all manner of music, even through simple chords.

Ursule Mirouët, CH, III, p. 384.

Marquis de Custine

[. . .] I rediscovered you and with you the piano, without its tiresome features, without its meaningless notes, but with the thoughts that you express in spite of the instrument itself. You do not play on the piano but on the human soul.[26]

Letter to Chopin [27 April 1841], *SC*, pp. 193–4.

You have gained in suffering and poetry; the melancholy of your composition penetrates still deeper into one's heart; one is alone with you in the midst of a crowd; it is not a piano that speaks but a soul, and what a soul![27]

Letter to Chopin [Paris, February 1848], *SC*, p. 307.

Baron de Trémont[28]

I would name him the *intimate* pianist, and by that I mean that one must have part of his exquisite musical sensibility to appreciate its scope. He is a musician apart, who has no connection whatever with any other. The unexpected, the originality, the pathos, and that kind of *irritabilité nerveuse* which alone leads to the sublime: those are the elements of a talent which either you cannot understand or else you have to enthuse over.

Auber, like all true musicians tired of the number of prodigies that the piano sends us every year, eulogized finely after the pleasure of hearing him play: 'Mr Chopin,' he said, 'you reconcile me to the piano [*vous me reposez du piano*].' In effect, what one hears is no piano; it is a succession of fresh, touching thoughts, often melancholy, sometimes tinged with terror; and to convey them the instrument undergoes a thousand transformations under his fingers through a *finesse* of touch, from what one can compare only to spider's webs up to effects of the most imposing strength; and yet Chopin is

---

[26] After Chopin's concert at Pleyel's, 26 April 1841.

[27] After Chopin's last concert in Paris, 16 February 1848.

[28] Louis-Philippe-Joseph Girod de Vienney, Baron de Trémont (1779–1852), godson of Louis-Philippe, was an *auditeur* to the State Council under the Empire, then made prefect of Aveyron and the Ardennes in 1814, finally prefect of the Côte-d'Or in 1831–2. Patron of the arts and an amateur violinist, he organized in his salon musical soirées in which the most illustrious artists, among them Chopin, participated. As well as the letter by Chopin (quoted in note 30 immediately below), another one exists, dated Wednesday 14 [February 1838], referring to an occasion two days later when Chopin was to play through his '*concerto* [op. 11?]' (*CFC*, II, p. 233). The Baron de Trémont has remained famous for his six-volume collection of autographs of celebrities, gathered by him and accompanied by written annotations; he bequeathed this in 1850 to the Bibliothèque Nationale, Paris.

frail and unwell; also he cannot show his range in public; he needs intimacy, a small number of friends, to whom his accents seem to say: 'comme je vous aime, je m'épuise pour vous plaire' (1843).[29]

He is too much *himself* to have had imitators, or to be considered as head of a contemporary *jeune école*; but it is certain that Thalberg, Liszt, Döhler, Dreyschock, Wolff, Henselt, Heller, Rosen, etc., studied him attentively; and that study could profit only from hearing him play his music, for the most exact performance of his compositions cannot convey what they became under his hands. Liszt, the pianist who can master the greatest difficulties, has often given that opinion. Chopin, immersed in his inspiration, is not halted by any *complication* of harmony, figurations or fingering, and many passages, perfectly clear under his fingers, sound confused and muddy when played by other pianists. Only the overconfident will *believe* they can convey his entrancing music, and then a part of its beauties has passed by them unnoticed. One has to forgo it unless one has very long, slender fingers [see p. 68 above for Mme Streicher's contrary view], as there are intervals up to twelfths; and an equal difficulty is that of often playing very *legato*. The arpeggios there are also very brilliant (1849).

> *Frédéric Chopin, Célèbre / pianiste et compositeur*, pp. 115 and 117–18 of an autograph script.[30]

---

[29] This sort of argument became something of a fixation in contemporary musical criticism, as evidenced by this unsympathetic piece by Henri Blaze de Bury after the concert of 21 February 1842:

> M. Chopin's talent appears publicly only at long intervals, even then surrounded by all kind of painstaking supervision and organization. M. Chopin admits only an elite audience of initiates to his exquisite, delicate, marvellous talent – but a fragile one which screens itself from analysis – needs a hall specially made up of responsive constitutions, of almost ethereal natures; there is in M. Chopin's playing something *perlé*, rare, Aeolian, that simple mortals could not grasp. The day a microscope is invented for the ear, that day M. Chopin will become deified. (*Revue des Deux Mondes*, 1 April 1842, p. 159; article signed H.W. [= Hans Werner, pseud. of Blaze de Bury]).

[30] Extracts are from the baron de Trémont's *Collection d'autographes / et de notices manuscrites*, Tome II, pp. 114–20 (*F-Pn*, dept. of manuscripts, Fr. 12757). The dates 1843 and 1849 (after Chopin's death in the latter case) are in Trémont's hand. The autograph note from Chopin to Trémont (apparently unpublished previously) reads: 'Je suis bien coupable de ne pas avoir / répondu de suite à Votre aimable invitation / et de ne pas Vous avoir dit encore, combien / j'aurai de plaisir à Vous revoir demain. / Votre devoué / Chopin / Samedi.' This is therefore evidently a different occasion from the one (on a Friday) mentioned in the letter quoted in note 28 immediately above.

Music critics

Anonymous[31]

Recently, at the Kärntnertor Theatre, was heard a concert by a young pianist, Herr Chopin, whose name was still completely unknown to the musical world. It was therefore the more astonishing to discover in him not merely a good but a really outstanding talent, in the originality of both his playing and his compositions; the mark of genius showed itself at least in his sense of form and outstanding individuality.

His playing, like his compositions – of which on this occasion we heard only the Variations [op. 2] – carries a certain modesty which indicates that this young man is not in the least concerned with impressive effects, although he sailed through difficulties which would raise eyebrows even here in the home of virtuoso pianism. Yet he did it with an almost ironical naïvety, apparently anxious only to feast his large audience with music for music's sake. And indeed he was successful: the fair-minded public rewarded him with sustained applause.

His touch, though clean and secure, has little of the brilliance of tone by which virtuosi proclaim themselves from the first bars; he accentuates only gently, like a person conversing in the company of cultured people, avoiding that rhetorical aplomb considered indispensable amongst virtuosos. He plays very calmly, without the fiery ardour which generally distinguishes artist from dilettante, and yet our discriminating and sensitive audience at once recognized a true artist in this unknown young foreigner [. . .]

The young man's playing revealed inadequacies, indeed significant ones, perhaps most noticeably his inobservance of the accent marking the beginnings of new musical lines [*Constructionen*]; nevertheless he was acclaimed as an artist promising of the very best, once he has had the opportunity to play more and further afield [. . .] he also displayed the most remarkable individuality in his composition [op. 2], in the novelty of forms, figuration and passage work in the Introduction and the first, second and fourth Variations, as also in the transformation of Mozart's theme in the *Polacca* finale. To end the concert, the young virtuoso good-naturedly agreed to improvise a free fantasy[32] before our public – a public before which very few improvisers, apart from Beethoven and Hummel, have found favour. If

---

[31] Unsigned, this review is sometimes attributed to Adolf Bäuerle, then director of the *Wiener Theaterzeitung*.

[32] On themes from the opera *La Dame blanche* by Boieldieu, then being produced in Vienna; also on the popular Polish song *Chmiel* [Hops].

the young man, multiplying the changes of theme, had wonderfully calculated the public's amusement, nevertheless the calm flow of ideas, the sureness of their sequence and the propriety of their development gave quite sufficient proof of his rare gift in this capacity. Herr Chopin gave such pleasure to this small audience that we must eagerly await his next appearance before a larger one.

Wiener Theaterzeitung, 20 August 1829.[33]

August Kahlert

At the time[34] I was personally able to hear Chopin playing and I was immediately astonished by his peculiar way of handling the instrument and by his exceptionally fully developed technique, which according to the opinion of friendly experts who have heard him in Paris recently, has been brought to a state of an even higher perfection. His manner of playing is a denial of all heaviness, based on a maximum reciprocal independence of the fingers and on the lightest touch which can be imagined, the fruit of constant practice. Thus we can only learn to perform these compositions after having mastered his *Etudes*, which have appeared of late. The sound is not great in the sense of quantity but it is excellent in quality. He avoids all shrill and glaring sounds which occur in usual piano technique, but he preserves an admirable melodiousness even in ephemeral passages. This is particularly noticeable in the most difficult *staccatos* and arpeggios and what this demands of the pianist is gained only after a full acquaintance with the new fingering. The third, fourth and fifth fingers of his right hand are extremely developed, and are thus raised to such an independence that it is possible for him to perform at the fastest rate with one hand the runs of sixths upwards and downwards in the chromatic scale. Thanks to this speed, to the lightness of his leaps, and to the great arpeggios, Chopin adds an admirable melodiousness which is often lacking at the piano.

All descriptions of such achievements are insufficient, and it is worthless

---

[33] Review of Chopin's first concert in Vienna, 11 August 1829 (a second concert took place on the 18th). Besides the op. 2 Variations the programme was originally to include the *Krakowiak Rondo* op. 14; but Chopin, after difficulties with the orchestra at the rehearsal, replaced this work at the last minute by an improvisation (see *SC*, pp. 32–3).

[34] The time of Chopin's trip to Wrocław (Breslau), where on 8 November 1830 he played in an impromptu concert (finale of the Concerto op. 11 and improvisation on Auber's *La Muette de Portici*). He was heard by Kahlert (then music critic at Wrocław), and subsequently told his parents, without naming him, that Kahlert had perhaps understood him better than any other listener (*SC*, p. 62). Poet and philosopher, Kahlert was from 1834 to 1843 one of Schumann's collaborators in the *Neue Zeitschrift für Musik*.

dwelling for long on Chopin's method of playing. It seems almost incredible that anyone could acquire more skill than Chopin in the sphere of technique, though he has said that this is true of Liszt. Chopin's method of playing is a little related to Clementi's, in which he was surely trained in the beginning. Chopin adds considerable difficulties which are not yet taken into account in Clementi.

> Quoted in translation in Musioł, E, pp. 6–7; originally 'Über Chopin's Klavier-Kompositionen', Der Gesellschafter oder Blätter für Geist und Herz, 1834/3, p. 165.

Fétis

In his concert which he gave at the salons of MM. Pleyel et Cie on the 26th of this month, M. Chopin performed a concerto [op. 11], which gave as much astonishment as pleasure to its audience, both by the novelty of melodic ideas and by the brilliant passages, modulations and general form of the movements. There is a soul in the melodies, fantasy in the passage work and originality in the whole. The modulations are too rich [trop de luxe], and there is some disorder in the sequence of phrases, so that sometimes the music seems more improvisatory than planned: these are the defects accompanying the qualities. But such flaws go with the composer's youth; they will vanish with experience. If M. Chopin's later works fulfil his early promise he will undoubtedly make himself a brilliant and deserved reputation.

This young artist also deserves praise as a performer. His playing is elegant, fluent and graceful, possessing brilliance and distinctness. He draws little sound from the instrument, resembling in this the majority of German pianists; but his present studies in this field, under the guidance of M. Kalkbrenner [sic!], cannot fail to give his playing the sinew it needs, and without which the colour of the instrument cannot be controlled.

Revue musicale, VI/5, 3 March 1832.[35]

---

[35] Review of Chopin's first concert in Paris, 26 February 1832. Besides op. 11 Chopin played the op. 2 Variations and participated in the performance of Kalkbrenner's Introduction, March and Grand Polonaise op. 92 for six pianos. Chopin writes of 'an immense pantaléon which, of course, Kalkbrenner will have, and the other [piano], which falls to my lot, is a monochord piano which is tiny, but its tone carries, like little bells on a giraffe. Add to these two the four large pianos which form the orchestra' (SC, p. 99).

Anonymous[36]

Kalkbrenner was the first of the many local pianists whom I heard, and I had the chance to hear a large number of pianists, among them one lady pianist who takes an honourable place among the others. She was Mme Pleyel, born Moke, next to Messrs Chopin, Liszt, Carl Schunke, H. Herz, Hiller, who played in various concerts and soirées all in the space of eight days.

Most of the famous pianists will already be known to you, and so you will perhaps be glad to hear something of Chopin and Liszt. First of all Chopin.

He played his Nocturnes and some of his *Etudes*. At a glance Chopin's scores look unplayable, so full are they of the most difficult figurations and chord formations; so one can only acknowledge him as a rare master when he plays them in such a way as to claim our complete wonderment. His playing is perfect in every respect. There we find tone, strength, infinite grace, sorrow, profound feeling, a cleanness and lightness in performance that leaves nothing more to wish for – and, most important of all, originality in his way of playing his multifariously original works. These all convey the impression of that youthful melancholy which every cultivated developing mind perceives. Where others sigh for love in nature, by hill and stream, Chopin composes instead; where others bring us to despair through their sorrowful sighing, he gladdens us. He is rightly the most beloved pianist. The opposite of Chopin is Liszt, about whom you will hear in a later report.

'Briefe aus Paris', Neue Leipziger Zeitschrift für Musik, I/15–16, 22 and
26 May 1834, pp. 60, 64.

Anonymous

The catalogue of pianists undoubtedly offers a few exceptions: we cite particularly M. Chopin, who prefers thought to the tour-de-force, and whose compositions and playing style are distinguished by a correctness of design which never becomes mean, narrow, or too predictable; by an originality without pretension, boldness without exaggeration, brilliancy without

---

[36] This unsigned article is probably by Joseph Mainzer, Heinrich Panofka or Franz Stoepel, all three of them Parisian correspondents for Schumann's *Zeitschrift* in 1834. Under the heading follows only 'Von einem andern Correspondenten', presumably meaning a different correspondent from the one who had written the Paris report for the early numbers of the *Zeitschrift*, whose first number (3 April 1834, p. 4) already speaks of Chopin and Liszt.

As for the pieces played by Chopin (Nocturnes and *Etudes*), they must have been played at a private or semi-private gathering, since no public concert in which he played solo piano works is known from that year, 1834.

tawdriness, energy without flying fists, and with an expression always clear, always sensed and profoundly gripping. M. Chopin has learned to make the piano sing, which is the rarest quality in this genre; above all he is able to soften the tone of the instrument, eliminating some of its dry, disjointed character. If I were to use a somewhat trivial but singularly apt metaphor, by which I have heard someone describing his particular type of sonority, I should say, with one of our most spiritual artists, that the notes which he plays are ripe, whereas those of most of his colleagues are green. Otherwise, M. Chopin's superiority is most incontestably apparent in his expression of tender feelings, which he can render with incomparable grace, delicacy and freshness of imagery.

Le Pianiste, II/15, 5 June 1835.

Schindler[37]

[. . .] These were my feelings upon once again hearing Chopin, whom I had met in Vienna ten years earlier.[38] *Chopin is the prince of all pianists*, Poetry in person at the piano. And as anything really good, genuine and right in Paris gathers its numerous admirers and supporters, Chopin's position in the Parisian artistic world is a recognized, well established fact! This suffices to spread the reputation of his playing in general; as to the details, however, it says little or nothing, and copious explanation would not suffice to elucidate further the essence of his being.

It is easy to capture and describe the way in which the so-called tyrant of the piano – Liszt – interprets a work of Beethoven, or whips through his 'Mazeppa' and the 'Galop chromatique'; but Chopin's playing must be heard for its uniqueness to be grasped. It does not impose itself through strength of attack, nor through the fiery brilliance used by others to secure the crowd's applause, for Chopin's health unfortunately forbids him all physical strain, and his mind and his body live in continual misunderstanding and feverish combat. The prime virtue of this great master of the keyboard lies in the complete *truth of expression of every feeling*, in which he excels and which cannot be imitated without lapsing into caricature. Devoid of display, his

---

[37] Anton Schindler (1795–1864), Beethoven's *famulus* in his last years, his principal converser in the *Conversation Books* (from 1819 onwards), and above all his first biographer. The work from which this extract is taken takes the form of a criticism of Parisian musical life under Louis-Philippe. The notes in Schindler's diary (see M. Becker, *Anton Schindler, der Freund Beethovens. Sein Tagebuch aus den Jahren 1841–3*, Frankfurt, n.d.) made in Paris in 1841 tell us nothing specific about Chopin's playing, beyond Schindler's high regard for it.

[38] Schindler visited Paris twice in 1841. He had probably heard Chopin in Vienna in 1830–1.

playing is not for the crowd, which wants to be dazzled because it is itself blind. Considering this, as also the fact that Chopin's nature could never be influenced by even the warmest applause from the noblest of audiences, things are well as they are. Given the present state of the keyboard world today, however, one is moved to bewail the physical conditions that limit Chopin's public appearances as well as his choice of programmes. With what authority he would play, complete with orchestral accompaniment, the great masterpieces of piano literature banned from the lecterns of all *Koryphäen* of the piano – particularly as his soul is of the purest artistic breed, far from any hint of ostentation: *to seek fame*, to specialize in show-pieces and tours-de-force, is the antithesis of artistic modesty! O Fate, how cruelly and malevolently you treat even this true genius of art!

BP, pp. 71–5.

Escudier[39]

Chopin played eight pieces.[40] This artist's compositions all share a perfect resemblance of forms; only the thought varies, and this is not one of their less brilliant qualities. A poet, and a tender poet above all, Chopin makes poetry predominate. He creates prodigious difficulties of performance, but never to the detriment of his melody, which is always simple and original. Follow the pianist's hands, and see the marvellous ease with which he performs the most graceful runs, draws together the width of the keyboard, passes successively from *piano* to *forte* and from *forte* to *piano*! M. Pleyel's magnificent instruments lend themselves admirably to these various shadings. Listening to all these sounds, all these nuances – which follow each other, intermingle, separate and reunite to arrive at the same goal, melody – one might well

[39] Léon Escudier (1816–81). In 1838, in collaboration with his brother Marie, he founded the weekly *La France musicale* (a rival paper to *RGMP*) and a publishing house. The two brothers, who together wrote several works of musicography, separated shortly before 1860, Léon Escudier taking over the publishing business to leave *La France musicale* to Marie, meanwhile founding a new periodical, *L'Art musical*; in addition he wrote *Mes Souvenirs* (Paris, 1863), which contains little information concerning Chopin.

[40] At his concert at Pleyel's (21 February 1842) with Pauline Viardot and Franchomme. Among Chopin's own works the programme specifies: *Andante suivi de la 3ᵉ Ballade*; *Suite de Nocturne, Préludes et Etudes*; *Nocturne, Préludes, Mazurkas et Impromptu* – nine titles in fact comprising perhaps about fifteen pieces. The *RGMP* review mentions three Mazurkas, in A flat, B major and A minor, three *Etudes*, op. 25/1, 2 and 12, the Prelude op. 28/15, the Impromptu in G [flat, op. 51 – if so, a pre-publication première], four Nocturnes including op. 27/2 in D flat and op. 48/2 in F sharp minor, and the *Ballade* op. 47. Since the programme twice mentions Preludes in the plural and Nocturne in the singular, it may be supposed that Chopin in fact played four Preludes grouped in pairs, and the two specified Nocturnes. As for the initial Andante, this could be that of op. 22, with which Chopin liked to begin.

believe one is hearing small fairy voices sighing under silver bells, or a rain of pearls falling on crystal tables. The pianist's fingers seem to multiply *ad infinitum*; it does not appear possible that only two hands can produce effects of rapidity so precisely and naturally. Do not ask Chopin to simulate grand orchestral effects on the piano. This type of playing suits neither his constitution nor his ideas. He wishes rather to astonish you with his light swiftness, with his *masurkes* [*sic*] with their novel forms, and not to give you nervous attacks and make you swoon. His inspiration is all of tender and naïve poetry; do not ask him for big gestures or diabolic variations; he wishes to speak to the heart, not to the eyes; he wishes to love you, not to devour you. See: the public is in ecstasy; enthusiasm is at its peak: Chopin has achieved his aim.

La France musicale, V/9, 27 February 1842.

George Hogarth[41]

There was a numerous and fashionable assembly, who were delighted with the entertainment provided for them.[42] M. Chopin performed an *Andante Sostenuto* and a Scherzo from [*sic*] his Opus 31, a selection from his celebrated studies, a Nocturne and a *Berceuse* and several of his own Preludes, Mazurkas and Waltzes.[43] In these various pieces he showed very strikingly his original genius as a composer and his transcendental powers as a performer. His music is as strongly marked with individual character as that of any master who has ever lived. It is highly finished, new in its harmonies, full of contrapuntal skill and ingenious contrivance; and yet we have never heard music which has so much the air of unpremeditated effusion. The performer seems to abandon himself to the impulses of his fancy and feeling, to indulge in a reverie and to pour out unconsciously, as it were, the thoughts and emotions that pass through his mind . . .

He accomplishes enormous difficulties, but so quietly, so smoothly and with such constant delicacy and refinement that the listener is not sensible of their real magnitude. It is the exquisite delicacy, with the liquid mellowness of his tone, and the pearly roundness of his passages of rapid articulation

---

[41] Hedley (C) and Belotti (*FCU*, III, pp. 1320–1), who quote this review, do not mention its author, a friend of Walter Scott who can be identified from a letter from Chopin to his family in August 1848, 'I have met many distinguished personalities [including] Hogarth, who was Walter Scott's beloved friend, etc. etc. He wrote a very nice article about me in the "Delinius" [*sic*] in connection with my second recital' (*SC*, p. 333).

[42] Chopin's second matinée in London, 7 July 1848, at the home of Count Falmouth in St. James's Square.

[43] The printed programme mentions a *Ballade* interposed between some Mazurkas and Waltzes.

which are the peculiar features of his execution, while his music is characterized by freedom of thought, varied expression and a kind of romantic melancholy which seems the natural mood of the artist's mind.

Daily News, 10 July 1848, quoted in Hedley, C, p. 107.

Anonymous

M. Chopin's Soiree Musicale – This eminent Pianiste gave a 'Soiree Musicale' on Wednesday evening, in the Hopetoun Rooms,[44] and we have rarely seen such a display of rank and beauty congregated at a similar entertainment. Most of the elite of our Edinburgh Society were present, as well as a considerable sprinkling of strangers. This speaks volumes for the increase of musical taste amongst us. The performances of M. Chopin are of the most refined description; nothing can equal the delicacy of his tone, or rival the lightness of his passages. They fall most deliciously on the ear accustomed to the 'hammer and tongs' work of the modern school. Our limits will not admit of our entering into lengthened description of his system, but we may mention that, while all other pianistes strive to equalize the power of the fingers, M. Chopin aims to utilise them; and in accordance with this idea, are his treatment of the scale and the shake, as well as his mode of sliding with one and the same finger, from note to note, and of passing the third over the fourth [i.e. the fourth over the fifth] finger. The gem of this performance, in our opinion, was the *Berceuse*, although the most popular were the Mazourkas and Valses, with which M. Chopin concluded one of the most delightful musical evenings we have ever spent.

Edinburgh Advertiser, Friday 6 October 1848.

[44] The concert took place in Edinburgh, 4 October 1848. *The Caledonian Mercury* of 2 October announced four solo groups by Chopin: 1. *Andante and Impromptu*; 2. *Etudes*; 3. *Nocturnes and Berceuse*; 4. *Prelude, Ballade, Mazourkas, Valses* – that is, the same sequence as his musical matinée at Glasgow on 27 September, of which a surviving programme (private collection) has an opus number added in ink under each title (see Bory, p. 189).

Bibliography

Abraham, Gerald, *Chopin's Musical Style*, London, Oxford University Press, 1968, 5th edition

Adam, Louis, *Méthode de piano du Conservatoire*, Paris, Imprimerie du Conservatoire, XIII [1805]; Geneva, Minkoff Reprint, 1974

Adelung, Sophie von, 'Chopin als Lehrer', *Neue Musik-Zeitung*, XLIV/8 (1923), pp. 121–3

Agoult, Comtesse d', *Mémoires (1833–1854)*, Paris, Calmann and Lévy, 1927, 11th edition

Agricola, Johann Friedrich, *Anleitung zur Singkunst* (Berlin, 1757) zusammen mit dem italienischen Original von Pier Francesco Tosi, *Opinioni de' Cantori antichi e moderni* (Bologna, 1723), facsimile, edited by Erwin R. Jacobi, Celle, Moeck, 1966

Aguettant, Louis, *La musique de piano des origines à Ravel*, Paris, Albin Michel, 1954

[Anonymous], *Conseils aux jeunes pianistes*, Paris, Fischbacher, 1904

Bach, Carl Philipp Emanuel, *Versuch über die wahre Art das Clavier zu spielen* (Berlin, 1753–62, 2 vols); facsimile, edited by Lothar Hoffmann-Erbrecht, Leipzig, Breitkopf & Härtel, 1957

Badura-Skoda, Paul, 'Schlanker, meine Herren!', *Chopin-Jahrbuch*, [I], Vienna, Amalthea-Verlag, 1956, pp. 17–27

CH   Balzac, Honoré de, *La Comédie humaine*, edited by Marcel Bouteron, Paris, Gallimard, Bibliothèque de la Pléiade, 1935–7, 10 vols

C   *Correspondance*, edited by Roger Pierrot, Paris, Garnier, 1960–9, 5 vols

LH   *Lettres à Madame Hanska*, edited by Roger Pierrot, Paris, Delta, 1967–71, 4 vols

Basso, Alberto, 'Chopin et l'esprit de la musique instrumentale baroque', *in* Lissa (ed.), pp. 271–4

ARMC   Belotti, Gastone, 'L'asimmetria ritmica nella Mazurca Chopiniana', *Nuova Rivista Musicale Italiana*, V/4–5 (1971), pp. 657–68, 827–46

FCU   *F. Chopin l'uomo*, Milan, Sapere Edizioni, 1974, 3 vols

DC   'Le date di composizione dell'op. 22 di Chopin', *Nuova Rivista Musicale Italiana*, I/4(1967), pp. 697–711

OIRC   *Le Origini Italiane del 'Rubato' Chopiniano*, Wrocław, Ossolineum, 1968

Saggi sull'arte e sull'opera di F. Chopin, Bologna, Centro Italo-Polacco di Studi Musicologici, 1977

Bérard, Jean-Antoine, *L'Art du Chant*, Paris, 1755; Geneva, Minkoff Reprint, 1972

Berlioz, Hector, 'Concerts', *Le Rénovateur*, II/345, 15 December 1833

Mémoires, Paris, Calmann and Lévy, 1919, 2 vols

Bertha, A. de, 'Ch. Valentin Alkan aîné', *Revue de la S.I.M.*, V/2 (1909), pp. 135–47

Bertini, Paolo, 'L'ultimo allievo di Federigo Chopin a Parigi' [F.-H. Peru], *La Nuova Musica*, XIX/274 (1914), pp. 15–16

Beu, Octavian, 'Carol Miculi. Un prieten romîn al lui Chopin', *Studi muzicologice*, VI (1957), pp. 45–56

Biegański, Krzysztof, 'Evolution de l'attitude de Chopin à l'égard du folklore (suivant ses Mazurkas)' *in* Lissa (ed.), pp. 95–9

Bielawski, Ludwik, 'Problem Krakowiaka w twórczości Chopina' [The question of the Krakowiak in Chopin's works], *in* Lissa (ed.), pp. 100–3

Binental, Leopold, *Chopin. Dokumenty i pamiątki* [Chopin. documents and souvenirs], Warsaw, Łazarski, 1930

Bischoff, Ferdinand, 'Delfine Potocka an Chopins Sterbelager', *Neue Musik-Zeitung*, XXXI/10 (1910), p. 211

Blaze de Bury, Henri, *Musiciens contemporains*, Paris, Lévy frères, 1856

Boissier, Mme Auguste, *Liszt pédagogue. Leçons de piano données par Liszt à Mademoiselle Valérie Boissier à Paris en 1832*, Paris, Champion, 1927; Geneva, Slatkine Reprint, 1976

Bolte, Theodor, *Die Musikerfamilien Stein-Streicher*, Vienna, Schönberger, 1917

Bone, Audrey Evelyn, *Jane Wilhelmina Stirling (1804–1859)*, Chipstead, the author, 1960

Bory, Robert, *La vie de Frédéric Chopin par l'image*, Geneva, Jullien, 1951

Boschot, Adolphe, *Un romantique sous Louis-Philippe. Hector Berlioz (1831–1842)*, Paris, Plon, 1908

Branson, David, *John Field and Chopin*, London, Barrie & Jenkins, 1972

Brisson, Adolphe, *Portraits intimes*, Paris, Armand Colin, 1897, Vol. 3

CI　　Bronarski, Ludwik, *Chopin et l'Italie*, Lausanne, La Concorde, 1947

EC　　'Les élèves de Chopin', *Annales Chopin*, VI (1965), pp. 7–12

EtC　　*Etudes sur Chopin*, Lausanne, La Concorde, 1944–6, 2 vols

Brown, Maurice J. E., *Chopin. An index of his works in chronological order*, London, Macmillan, 1972, 2nd edition

Bülow, Hans von, *Briefe und Schriften*, ed. Maria von Bülow, Leipzig, Breitkopf & Härtel, 1895–1908, 8 vols

Caswell, Austin, 'Mme Cinti-Damoreau and the Embellishment of Italian Opera in Paris (1820–1845)', *Journal of the American Musicological Society*, XXVIII/3 (1975), pp. 459–92

Chainaye, Suzanne and Denise, *De quoi vivait Chopin*, Paris, Les Deux-Rives, 1951

Chmara, Barbara, 'Das Problem der Agogik der Nocturni von Field und Chopin', *in* Lissa (ed.), pp. 275–80

Choisy, Frank, *Frédéric Chopin. L'homme, l'artiste, le compositeur, le pianiste, le pédagogue*, Geneva, Editions du Conservatoire Populaire de Musique, 1923

Chomiński, Józef (editor), *Słownik muzyków polskich* [Dictionary of Polish musicians], Kraków, PWM, 1964–7, 2 vols

CFC　　Chopin, Frédéric, *Correspondance*, [French edition, translated by] Bronisław Edouard Sydow, Paris, Richard-Masse, 1953–60, 3 vols

KFC　　*Korespondencja Fryderyka Chopina*, ed. Bronisław Edward Sydow and Janusz Miketta, Warsaw, PIW, 1955, 2 vols

Korespondencja Fryderyka Chopina z rodziną [Chopin's correspondence with his family], edited by Krystyna Kobylańska, Warsaw, PIW, 1972

'"Metoda" Chopina', Polish translation, signed A., *Ruch muzyczny*, XII/ 12 (1968), pp. 5–7

SC   *Selected Correspondence of Fryderyk Chopin*, edited and translated after Sydow, by Arthur Hedley, London, Heinemann, 1962

Ciechomska, Ludwika, 'Ostatnie chwile Chopina' [Chopin's last moments], *Kurier Warszawski*, no. 177, 26 July 1882

Coeuroy, André, *Chopin*, Paris, Plon, 1951

Cortot, Alfred, *Aspects de Chopin*, Paris, Albin Michel, 1949

Czartkowski, Adam and Jeżewska, Zofia, *Fryderyk Chopin*, Warsaw, PIW, 1970, new edition

[Debussy, Claude], *Lettres de Claude Debussy à son éditeur*, edited by Jacques Durand, Paris, A. Durand & fils, 1927

Déchelette, Albert, 'Le jeu de Chopin', *Journal des Débats*, 28 December 1934

Delacroix, Eugène, *Journal*, Paris, Plon, 1932, 3 vols

Denis, Ferdinand, *Journal (1829–1848)*, edited by Pierre Moreau, Fribourg, Librairie de l'Université, and Paris, Plon, 1932

Desternes, Suzanne and Chandet, Henriette, *La Malibran et Pauline Viardot*, edited in collaboration with Alice Viardot, Paris, Arthème Fayard, 1969

Diehl, A. M. and Mangold, Alice, *Musical Memories*, London, R. Bentley & Son, 1897

Dietschy, Marcel, *La passion de Claude Debussy*, Neuchâtel, la Baconnière, 1962

Drath, Jan Bogdan, *Waltzes of Fryderyk Chopin: Sources. Volume I: Waltzes Published During Chopin's Lifetime*, facsimile, Kingsville, Texas A & I University Publications, 1979

Drzewiecki, Zbigniew, 'L'interprétation de Chopin', *Perspectives polonaises*, 2 (1965), pp. 17–26

Dunn, John Petrie, *Ornamentation in the Works of Frederick Chopin*, London, Novello, [1921]; New York, Da Capo Press, 1971

Durand, Jacques, *Quelques souvenirs d'un éditeur de musique [I–II]*, Paris, A. Durand & fils, 1924–5, 2 vols

Egert, Paul, *Friedrich Chopin*, Potsdam, Akademische Verlagsgesellschaft Athenaion, 1936

CHB   Eigeldinger, Jean-Jacques, 'Chopin et l'héritage baroque', *Schweizer Beiträge zur Musikwissenschaft*, II (1974), pp. 51–74

'Deux élèves suisses de Chopin. Daniel Heussler et Bovy-Lysberg', *Revue musicale de Suisse romande*, XXIX/1 (1976), pp. 12–25

PGE   'Le prélude "de la goutte d'eau" de Chopin', *Revue de Musicologie*, LXI/1 (1975), p. 70–90

SCFC   'Solange Clésinger: Frédéric Chopin. Souvenirs inédits', *Revue musicale de Suisse romande*, XXXI/5 (1978), pp. 224–38

CICP   'Un concert inconnu de Chopin à Paris', *Revue musicale de Suisse romande*, XXXIV/1 (1981), pp. 2–9

ACI   'Autographes de Chopin inconnus: Deux Nocturnes op. 48, Polonaise-Fantaisie op. 61', *Revue musicale de Suisse romande*, XXXVII/4 (1984), pp. 154–71

Eigeldinger, Jean-Jacques and Nectoux, Jean-Michel, *Frédéric Chopin: Oeuvres pour piano. Facsimile de l'exemplaire de Jane W. Stirling avec annotations et corrections de l'auteur*, Paris, Bibliothèque Nationale, 1982

Eismann, Georg, *Robert Schumann. Ein Quellenwerk über sein Leben und Schaffen*, Leipzig, Breitkopf & Härtel, 1956, 2 vols

Ekier, Jan, 'Chopin jako pedagog' [Chopin as teacher], *Ruch muzyczny*, XVIII/10–11 (1974), pp. 15–17, 16–18

WWN   *Wstęp do Wydania Narodowego Dzieł Fryderyka Chopina. Część 1. Zagadnienia edytorskie* [Introduction to the National Edition of the works of Fryderyk Chopin. Part 1. Editorial problems], Kraków, PWM-TiFC, 1974

FCB   *Fryderyk Chopin: Ballady. Komentarze źródłowe* [Chopin's Ballades: Source commentary], Kraków, PWM-TiFC, 1970

Federhofer, Helmut, 'Der Chopinschüler Carl Mikuli in Rom und Graz', *Deutsches Jahrbuch der Musikwissenschaft*, X (1965), pp. 82–96

Fétis, François-Joseph, *Biographie universelle des musiciens*, Paris, Firmin-Didot, 1877–81, 2nd edition, 10 vols

Fétis, François-Joseph and Moscheles, Ignace, *Méthode des Méthodes de piano*, Paris, Schlesinger [1840]; Geneva, Minkoff Reprint, 1973

Fitzlyon, April, *The Price of Genius. A Life of Pauline Viardot*, London, Calder, 1964

Fontana, Jules, [Preface to] *Oeuvres posthumes pour piano de Fréd. Chopin*, Paris, Meissonnier, [1855], 8 vols

Fortescue, Virginia, 'The unknown Chopin. An alternative to the Cadenza of the Nocturne Op. 9 No. 2', *South African Journal of Musicology*, I (1981), pp. 45–51

Gaillard, Paul-André, 'Jugements portés sur Chopin par Mickiewicz d'après le Journal de Caroline Olivier', *in* Lissa (ed.), pp. 659–61

NZM   Gajewski, Ferdynand Jan, 'Nieznane źródło marginesowych notatek Chopina' [An unknown source of marginal annotations by Chopin], *Ruch muzyczny*, XXI/21 (1977), pp. 2–4

NC   Gajewski, Ferdinand, 'New Chopiniana from the Papers of Carl Filtsch', *Studi Musicali*, XI/1 (1982), pp. 171–7

DSFC   Ganche, Edouard, *Dans le souvenir de Frédéric Chopin*, Paris, Mercure de France, 1925, 6th edition

FC   *Frédéric Chopin. Sa vie et ses oeuvres*, Paris, Mercure de France, 1921

VAFC   *Voyages avec Frédéric Chopin*, Paris, Mercure de France, 1934, 6th edition

Gerig, Reginald R., *Famous Pianists & their Technique*, Washington and New York, Luce, 1974

German, Franciszek, 'Chopin im Lichte unbekannter Memoirenquellen gesehen', *in* Lissa (ed.), pp. 662–8

'O pamiątkach Chopinowskich na Górnym Śląsku' [Recollections of Chopin in Upper Silesia], *Chopin na Śląsku* [Chopin in Silesia], Katowice, Prace Archiwum Śląskiej Kultury Muzycznej, 1973, pp. 41–60

Gide, André, *Notes sur Chopin*, Paris, L'Arche, 1948

Gieseking, Walter, *So wurde ich Pianist*, Wiesbaden, Brockhaus, 1963, 2nd edition

and Leimer, Karl, *Piano Technique*, New York, Dover Publications, reprint, 1972

Gille, Victor, *Souvenirs romantiques*, Paris, Omnium Littéraire, 1954

Goubault, Christian, 'Un musicien polonais ami de Flaubert: Antoni Orłowski (1811–1861)', *Les Amis de Flaubert*, No. 54, Dieppedalle, 1979, pp. 19–25

Grewingk, Maria von, *Eine Tochter Alt-Rigas, Schülerin Chopins*, Riga, Löffler, 1928

Hadden, James Cuthbert, *Chopin*, London, Dent, 1934, 6th edition

Hallé, C. E. and Marie, *Life and Letters of Sir Charles Hallé Being an Autobiography (1819–1860) with Correspondence and Diaries*, London, Smith & Elder, 1896

Harasowski, Adam, *The Skein of Legends around Chopin*, Glasgow, MacLellan, 1967

Harding, Rosamund E. M., *The Piano-forte. Its History traced to the Great Exhibition of 1851*, Cambridge University Press, 1933; New York, Da Capo Press, 1973

C   Hedley, Arthur, *Chopin*, London, Dent, 1957, 4th edition

NUC   'Nieznana uczennica Chopina' [An unknown pupil of Chopin, Juliette de Caraman], *Ruch muzyczny*, XIV/4 (1970), pp. 6–8

Heine, Heinrich, *Sämtliche Werke*, Leipzig, Insel-Verlag, 1910–15, 10 vols

Heine, Henri [Heinrich], *Lutèce. Lettres sur la vie politique, artistique et sociale de la France*, Paris, Lévy frères, 1855, 2nd edition

Heller, Stephen, *Lettres d'un musicien romantique à Paris*, edited by Jean-Jacques Eigeldinger, Paris, Flammarion, 1980

Hensel, Sebastian, *Die Familie Mendelssohn (1729–1847)*, Berlin, Behr, 1886, 5th edition, 2 vols

CI   Higgins, Thomas, 'Chopin Interpretation. A Study of Performance Directions in Selected Autographs and Other Sources', unpublished Ph.D. dissertation, University of Iowa, 1966, Microfilm 67–02 629

'Znak łuku u Chopina' [The Phenomenon of Chopin's Slurs], *Rocznik Chopinowski* XII (1980), pp. 203–24

'Whose Chopin?', *19th Century Music*, V/1 (1981), pp. 67–75

TCC   'Tempo and character in Chopin', *The Musical Quarterly*, LIX/1 (1973), pp. 106–20

ATZ   Hiller, Ferdinand, *Aus dem Tonleben unserer Zeit*, Leipzig, Mendelssohn, 1868, 2 vols

BU   *Briefe an eine Ungenannte*, Köln, DuMont and Schauberg, 1877

Erinnerungsblätter, Köln, DuMont and Schauberg, 1884

FMB   *Felix Mendelssohn-Bartholdy. Briefe und Erinnerungen*, Köln, DuMont and Schauberg, 1874

Hipkins, Edith J., *How Chopin played. From Contemporary Impressions collected from the Diaries and Notebooks of the late A. J. Hipkins*, London, Dent, 1937

Hirt, Franz Josef, *Meisterwerke des Klavierbaus. Geschichte der Saitenklaviere von 1440 bis 1880*, Olten, Urs Graf-Verlag, 1955

Hławiczka, Karol, 'Ein Beitrag zur Verwandtschaft zwischen der Melodik Chopins und der polnischen Volksmusik', *in* Lissa (ed.), pp. 176–84

C   Hoesick, Ferdynand, *Chopin. Życie i twórczość* [Chopin's life and works], Warsaw, Hoesick, 1910–11, 3 vols; reprinted Kraków, PWM, 1962–8, 4 vols

Chopiniana, Warsaw, Hoesick, 1912

i Chopin. Z zagadnień twórczości [Słowacki and Chopin. Creative problems], Warsaw, Trzaska, Evert and Michalski, 1932

Holcman, Jan, 'The Labyrinth of Chopin Ornamentation', *The Juilliard Review*, V/2 (1958), pp. 23–41

Holland, Jeanne, 'Chopin's Teaching and his Students', unpublished Ph.D. dissertation, University of North Carolina, 1973, Microfilm 73–26 183

Hordyński, Władysław, 'Zofia Rosengardt-Zaleska, uczennica Chopina i jej pamiętnik' [A pupil of Chopin, Zofia Rosengardt-Zaleska and her diary], *Roczniki Biblioteczne*, I/4 (1961), pp. 139–58

Huldt-Nystrøm, Hampus, 'Thomas Dyke Acland Tellefsen', in *Norsk Musikkgranskning. Årbok 1956–58*, edited by O. M. Sandvik, Oslo, Grundt Tanum, 1959, pp. 80–198

Hummel, Johann Nepomuk, *Méthode Complète Théorique et Pratique pour le Piano-Forte*, French translation by D. Jelensperger, Paris, A. Farrenc, [1828?]; Geneva, Minkoff Reprint, 1981

Jaeger, Bertrand, 'Quelques nouveaux noms d'élève de Chopin', *Revue de Musicologie*, LXIV/1 (1978), pp. 76–108

Janin, Jules, *735 Lettres à sa femme*, edited by Mergier-Bourdeix, Paris, Klincksieck, 1973–9, 3 vols

Janine-Weill, *Marguerite Long. Une vie fascinante*, Paris, Julliard, 1969

Janis, Byron, *Chopin/Janis: The Most Dramatic Musical Discovery of the Age. Grande Valse Brilliante op. 18; Waltz in G♭ op. 70, No. 1*, facsimile and transcription, New York, Envolve Books Inc., 1978

Jerger, Wilhelm, *Franz Liszts Klavierunterricht von 1884–1886*, Regensburg, Bosse, 1975

Kalkbrenner, Frédéric, *Méthode pour apprendre le piano à l'aide du guide-mains*, Leipzig, Kistner; Paris, the author, new edition, no date

Kallberg, Jeffrey, 'The Chopin Sources: Variants and Versions in Later Manuscripts and Printed Editions', unpublished Ph.D. dissertation, University of Chicago, 1982

'Chopin in the Marketplace: Aspects of the International Music Publishing Industry in the First Half of the Nineteenth Century', *Notes*, XXXIX/3 and 4 (1983), pp. 535–69 and 795–824

Kałuża, Zofia, 'Chopin i Marcelina Czartoryska', *Ruch muzyczny*, XVIII/17 (1974), pp. 13–14

Kamieński, Lucjan, 'Zum "Tempo rubato"', *Archiv für Musikwissenschaft*, I (1918), pp. 108–26

Kapp, Julius, 'Chopin's "Préludes" op. 28. Aufzeichnungen von Laura Rappoldi-Kahrer nach Angaben von Liszt, W. von Lenz und Frau von Mouckhanoff', *Die Musik*, IX/10 (1909), pp. 227–33

Karasowski, Moritz, *Friedrich Chopin. Sein leben, seine Werke und Briefe*, Dresden, Ries, 1877, 2 vols

Karłowicz, Mieczysław, *Souvenirs inédits de Frédéric Chopin*, French translation by Laure Disière, Paris and Leipzig, Welter, 1904

CGW   Kleczyński, Jean [Kleczyński, Jan], *Chopin's Greater Works*, translated with additions by Natalie [*sic*] Janotha, London, William Reeves, 188?

FCI   *How to play Chopin. The works of Frederic Chopin, their proper interpretation*, translated by Alfred Whittingham, London, William Reeves, [1913], 6th edition

Frédéric Chopin. De l'interprétation de ses oeuvres, translated from Polish by Kleczyński (?), with letter-prefaces by M. Czartoryska, C. Dubois-O'Meara and G. Mathias, Paris, Félix Mackar, 1880

Klein, Marie, 'Karl Filtsch', *Ostland*, II (1920), pp. 604–8, 638–44, 663–71

CiFC   Kobylańska, Krystyna, 'Chopin in French Collections', *Polish Music*, V/4 (1970), pp. 16–19

CBKP   'Chopiniana w Bibliotece Konserwatorium Paryskiego' [Chopiniana in the Library of the Paris Conservatoire], *Annales Chopin*, IV (1959), pp. 136–71

TBWV   *Frédéric Chopin. Thematisch-bibliographisches Werkverzeichnis*, translated by Helmut Stolze, Munich, G. Henle Verlag, 1979

NDC   'Nieznane dedykacje Chopina w Bibliotece Polskiej w Paryżu' [Unknown dedications by Chopin in the Bibliothèque Polonaise, Paris], *Ruch muzyczny*, XII/15 (1968), p. 14

PC   'Prace Chopina nad zbiorowym wydaniem dzieł własnych' [Chopin's work towards a collected edition], *Ruch muzyczny*, XII/14 (1968), pp. 3–6

K   *Rękopisy utworów Chopina. Katalog* [Catalogue of Chopin's works in manuscript], Kraków, PWM, 1977, 2 vols

Korespondencja Chopina z George Sand i z jej dziećmi [Chopin's correspondence with George Sand and her children], Warsaw, PIW, 1981, 2 vols

Koczalski, Raoul, *Frédéric Chopin. Betrachtungen, Skizzen, Analysen*, Köln, Tischer & Jagenberg, 1936

Kreutz, Alfred, 'Das Tempo rubato bei Chopin', *Das Musikleben*, II/10 (1949), pp. 260–4

Lacassagne, Joseph, *Traité général des Eléments du Chant*, Paris, 1766; Geneva, Minkoff Reprint, 1972

Lachmund, Carl V., *Mein Leben mit Franz Liszt. Aus dem Tagebuch eines Liszt-Schülers*, Eschwege, Schroeder, 1970

Lakatos, István, 'Filtsch Károly, a Chopin-tanítvány (1830–1845)', *Zenetörténeti írások*, Budapest, Kriterion, 1971, pp. 56–66

CLB   La Mara (pseudonym of Marie Lipsius), *Correspondance entre Franz Liszt et Hans von Bülow*, Leipzig and Brussels, Breitkopf & Härtel, 1899

Franz Liszt's Briefe, Leipzig, Breitkopf & Härtel, 1893–1904, 9 vols

Legouvé, Ernest, *Soixante ans de souvenirs*, Paris, Hetzel, 1886–7, 2 vols

ACK   Leichtentritt, Hugo, *Analyse der Chopin'schen Klavierwerke*, Berlin, Hesse, 1921–2, 2 vols

Friedrich Chopin, Berlin, Schlesische Verlagsanstalt, 1920, 2nd edition

Leimer, Karl, *see* Gieseking, Walter and Leimer, Karl

B   Lenz, Wilhelm von, *Beethoven et ses trois styles*, St Petersburg, 1852; new edition with foreword and bibliography by M.-D. Calvocoressi, Paris, Legouix, 1909

GPV   'Die Grossen Pianoforte-Virtuosen unserer Zeit aus persönlicher Bekanntschaft. Liszt – Chopin – Tausig', *Neue Berliner Musikzeitung*, XXII/37, 38, 39 (1868), pp. 291–3, 299–302, 307–10

GPV 1872   *Die Grossen Pianoforte-Virtuosen unserer Zeit aus persönlicher Bekanntschaft. Liszt – Chopin – Tausig – Henselt*, Berlin, Behr, 1872

UB   'Übersichtliche Beurtheilung der Pianoforte-Kompositionen von Chopin', *Neue Berliner Musikzeitung*, XXVI/36, 37, 38 (1872), pp. 282–3, 289–92, 297–9

[Leo, Sophie], 'Musical Life in Paris (1817–1848). A Chapter from the Memoirs of Sophie Augustine Leo', *The Musical Quarterly* XVII, 2–3 (1931), pp. 259–71, 389–403 (annotated translation by W. Oliver Strunk from *Erinnerungen aus Paris (1817–1848)*, Berlin, Hertz, 1851)

Lindenau, Bernhard, 'Carl Filtsch', *Archiv für Musikforschung*, V/1 (1940), pp. 39–51

Lisowska, Agnieszka, 'Karol Kurpiński jako pisarz, działacz i organizator muzyczny w Warszawie' [Karl Kurpiński as composer and musical organizer in Warsaw], *Szkice o kulturze muzycznej XIX wieku*, II [Sketches on musical culture in the nineteenth century], Warsaw, PWN, 1973, pp. 181–231

Lissa, Zofia, 'Nicht publizierte Lemberger Chopiniana', *Annales Chopin*, V (1960), pp. 225–36

SNOC   'Du style national des oeuvres de Chopin', *Annales Chopin*, II (1958), pp. 100–78

Lissa, Zofia (ed.), *The Book of the First International Musicological Congress devoted to the Works of Frederick Chopin*, Warsaw, PWN, 1963

Liszt, Franz, *F. Chopin*, Leipzig, Breitkopf & Härtel, 1923, 6th edition

Litzmann, Berthold, *Clara Schumann. Ein Künstlerleben nach Tagebüchern und Briefen*, Leipzig, Breitkopf & Härtel, 1920, 7th edition, 3 vols

Lockspeiser, Edward, *Debussy. His Life and Mind*, Cambridge University Press, 1978, 2 vols

Long, Marguerite, *Au piano avec Claude Debussy*, Paris, Julliard, 1960

Long, Pauline, 'Charles Samuel Bovy-Lysberg (1821–1873)', *Schweizerisches Jahrbuch für Musikwissenschaft*, III (1928), pp. 140–54

Lussy, Mathis, *Traité de l'expression musicale*, Paris, Fischbacher, 1904, 8th edition

Marix-Spire, Thérèse, *Lettres inédites de George Sand et de Pauline Viardot (1839–1849)*, Paris, Nouvelles Editions Latines, 1959

Les Romantiques et la Musique. Le cas George Sand (1804–1838), Paris, Nouvelles Edition Latines, 1954

HP   Marmontel, Antoine, *Histoire du piano et de ses origines*, Paris, Heugel, 1885

PC   *Les Pianistes célèbres*, Paris, Heugel, 1878

VC   *Virtuoses contemporains*, Paris, Heugel, 1882

Mathias, Georges, Preface to Isidore Philipp, *Exercices quotidiens tirés des oeuvres de Chopin*, Paris, Hamelle, [1897]

Meister, Edith, *Stilelemente und die geschichtliche Grundlage der Klavierwerke Friedrich Chopins*, Hamburg, Holler, 1936

Mendelssohn-Bartholdy, Felix, *Briefe aus den Jahren 1830 bis 1847*, edited by Paul Mendelssohn-Bartholdy, Leipzig, Mendelssohn, 1882, 9th edition, 2 vols

Methuen-Campbell, James, *Chopin Playing from the Composer to the Present Day*, London, Gollancz, 1981

Meyerbeer, Giacomo, *Briefwechsel und Tagebücher*, edited by Heinz Becker, Berlin and New York, De Gruyter, 1960–75, 3 vols; further volumes in preparation

Michałowski, Aleksander, 'Jak grał Fryderyk Szopen?' [How did Chopin play?], *Muzyka*, IX/7–9 (1932), pp. 72–7

Michałowski, Kornel, *Bibliografia Chopinowska (1849–1969)*, Kraków, PWM, 1970

'Bibliografia Chopinowska (1970–1973)', *Rocznik Chopinowski*, IX (1975), pp. 121–76

Mickiewicz, Adam, *Correspondance*, French translation by Ladislas Mickiewicz, Paris, Les Belles-Lettres, [1924]

Miketta, Janusz, *Mazurki Chopina*, Kraków, PWM, 1949

Mikuli, Carl, *Vorwort* to *Fr. Chopin's Pianoforte-Werke*, edited by Mikuli, Leipzig, Kistner, [1880], 17 vols

Milstein, Jakow Isaakovitch, *Chopin's advice to pianists* [in Russian], Moscow, Editions Muzyka, 1967

Mirska, Maria and Hordyński, Władysław, *Chopin na obczyźnie* [Chopin Abroad], Kraków, PWM, 1965

Montabré, Maurice, 'Le dernier élève de Chopin nous parle de son Maître', *Comoedia*, No. 2261, 10 December 1913, pp. 3–4

Montal, Claude, *L'Art d'accorder soi-même son piano*, Paris, Meissonnier, 1836; Geneva, Minkoff Reprint, 1976

Morsch, Anna, 'Friedrich Chopin in seiner Lehrmethode', *Der Klavier-Lehrer*, XXII/20–1 (1899), pp. 269–71, 288–91

Moscheles, Charlotte, *Aus Moscheles' Leben. Nach Briefen und Tagebüchern*, Leipzig, Duncker & Humblot, 1872–3, 2 vols

Mozart, Leopold, *Versuch einer gründlichen Violinschule*, Augsburg, 1756; facsimile edition, Frankfurt, Grahl Musik-Verlag, 1956

Mozart, Wolfgang Amadeus, *Briefe und Aufzeichnungen*, edited by Wilhelm A. Bauer and Otto Erich Deutsch, Kassel and Basle, Bärenreiter, 1962–75, 7 vols

Murdoch, William, *Chopin. His Life*, London, Murray, 1934

Musioł, Karol, 'Frédéric Chopin im Lichte unbekannter Quellen aus der ersten Hälfte des XIX. Jahrhunderts', *Die Musikforschung*, XXV/4 (1972), pp. 430–7

'Echoes of Chopin's Wrocław Concert in Musical Criticism and in Literature', *Chopin in Silesia* (Fascicles of the archives 'Music Culture in Silesia'/Music College Library, Katowice/No. 1), Katowice, 1974, pp. 6–8

Mycielski, Zygmunt, 'Rękopis "Metody" Chopina' [The manuscript of Chopin's 'Méthode'], *Ruch muzyczny*, XII/1 (1968), pp. 3–7

Niesmieyanova, Tatiana and Siemienovski, Sergueï, 'The diary of a pupil of Chopin' [Elizavieta S. Cheriemietieff; in Russian], *Muzykalnaja Żyźńm* Moscow, 1960/4, pp. 13–14

Neuhaus, Heinrich, *The Art of Piano Playing*. Translated from Russian edition of 1958 by K. L. Leibovitch, London, Barrie & Jenkins, 1983

Niecks, Frederick, *Frederick Chopin as a Man and Musician*, London, Novello, [1902], 3rd edition, 2 vols

Friedrich Chopin als Mensch und als Musiker, translated by Wilhelm Langhans, Leipzig, Leuckart, 1890, 2 vols

Nikolaiev, Victor, 'Rosyjscy znajomi Chopina. Kilka nowych szczegółów' [Chopin's Russian acquaintances. Some new information], *Ruch muzyczny*, XXVII/12 (1983), p. 25

Šopen pedagog [Chopin as a teacher], Moscow, Editions Muzyka, 1980

ZCB   Nowik, Wojciech, 'Do związków Chopina z Bellinim. Chopinowski autograf arii Belliniego "Casta Diva"' [Connections between Chopin and Bellini: Chopin's manuscript of Bellini's 'Casta Diva'], *Pagine. Polsko-Włoskie materiały muzyczne*, IV (1980), pp. 241–71

Ostrzyńska, Ludwika, *Wspomnienia o F. Chopinie i uczniu jego F.-H. Peru* [Recollections of Chopin and his pupil F.-H. Peru], Warsaw, Reduta, 1927

Ottich, Maria, 'Chopins Klavierornamentik', *Annales Chopin*, III (1958), pp. 7–62

Paderewski, Ignace Jan and Lawton, Mary, *The Paderewski Memoirs*, London and Glasgow, Collins, 1939

Panigel, Armand and Beaufils, Marcel, *L'Oeuvre de Frédéric Chopin. Discographie générale*, Paris, Editions de la Revue Disques, 1949

Paskhalow, Viatcheslav, *Chopin a polska muzyka ludowa* [Chopin and Polish folk music], Kraków, PWM, 1951

Peru, F.-H., 'Mes souvenirs de Frédéric Chopin', *Revue de la S.I.M.*, IX/12 (1913), pp. 25–30

Philipp, Isidore, *Quelques considérations sur l'enseignement du piano*, Paris, A. Durand & fils, 1927

The Piano Quarterly (Robert J. Silverman, Editor and Publisher), Special Chopin Edition, Wilmington, 1981 XXIX/113

Piętaszewska, Zofia and Turło, Dalila Teresa, *Katalog zbiorów. Fototeka. Ikonografia Fryderyka Chopina i Jego epoki* [Catalogue of collections. Photographs. Iconography of F. Chopin and his epoch], Warsaw, TiFC, 1971

Pilipczuk, Alexander, 'Der polnische Tanz Mazurek', Unpublished Ph.D. dissertation, University of Hamburg, 1969

Piron, Constantin, *L'Art du piano*, Paris, Arthème Fayard, 1949

Planté, Francis, 'Lettres sur Chopin', *Le Courrier musical*, XIII/1 (1910), p. 36

Pozniak, Bronislaw von, *Chopin. Praktische Anweisungen für das Studium der Chopin-Werke*, Halle, Mitteldeutscher Verlag, 1949

Preisnerowa, Anna, 'Fryderyk Chopin jako pedagog w świetle pracy M.A. Szulca' [Frederick Chopin as a teacher in the light of the work of M. A. Szulc], *Materiały informacyjno-dyskusyjne* No. 36, Warsaw, Centralny ośrodek pedagogiczny szkolnictwa artystycznego, 1974, pp. 29–36

Procházka, Jaroslav, *Frédéric Chopin et la Bohême*, French translation by Yvette Joye, Prague, Artia, 1969

Prod'homme, Jacques-Gabriel, 'Gutmann, élève de Chopin', *Revue Pleyel*, [III]/29 (1926), pp. 8–9

CCR   'Un Concert de Chopin à Rouen en 1838', *Revue Pleyel*, [III]/31 (1926), pp. 8–10

C   Pugno, Raoul, *Les Leçons écrites de Raoul Pugno*. *Chopin*, Paris Librairie des Annales, 1909

V   *Les leçons écrites de Raoul Pugno*. *Chopin*. *Les Quatorze Valses*, Paris, Librairie des Annales, 1912

Pukińska-Szepietowska, Hanna, 'Życie koncertowe w Warszawie (lata 1800–1830)' [Warsaw concert life 1800–30], *Szkice o kulturze muzycznej XIX wieku*, II [Sketches on musical culture in the nineteenth century], Warsaw, PWN, 1973, pp. 35–104

Quantz, Johann Joachim, *Versuch einer Anweisung die Flöte traversiere zu spielen*, Breslaw, 1789, 3rd edition; facsimile edited by Hans-Peter Schmitz, Kassel and Basle, Bärenreiter, 1953

EV   Saint-Saëns, Camille, 'Etude des variantes', in Cortot and Ganche, *Trois manuscrits de Chopin*, Paris, Dorbon aîné, 1932, p. 19–26

QM   'Quelques mots sur l'exécution des oeuvres de Chopin', *Le Courrier musical*, XIII/10 (1910), pp. 386–7

CGS   Sand, George, *Correspondance*, edited by Georges Lubin, Paris, Garnier, 1964–, 19 vols (up to 1985)

HV   *Histoire de ma vie*, in *Oeuvres autobiographiques*, edited by Georges Lubin, Paris, Gallimard, Bibliothèque de la Pléiade, 1970–1, 2 vols

Impressions et souvenirs, Paris, Calmann and Lévy, 1896, new edition

BCOC Sandelewski, Wiarosław, 'Les éléments du "bel canto" italien dans l'oeuvre de Chopin', *in* Lissa (ed.), pp. 230–5

IROC 'Influssi rossiniani nell'opera di Chopin', *Bollettino del Centro Rossiniano degli Studi*, V/3–4 (1959), pp. 45–9, 69–72

PERP 'Sulle prime esecuzioni rossiniane in Polonia', *Rivista Italiana di Musicologia*, II/1 (1967), pp. 152–61

Schelling, Ernest, 'Chez un élève de Chopin', *La Revue musicale*, XII/121 (1931), pp. 68–70

BP   Schindler, Anton, *Beethoven in Paris*, Münster, Aschendorff, 1842

BLB   *Biographie von Ludwig van Beethoven*, edited by Eberhardt Klemm, Leipzig, Reclam, 1973

HVOB *Histoire de la vie et de l'oeuvre de Ludwig van Beethoven*, French translation [of *BLB*] by Albert Sowiński, Paris, Garnier frères, 1865

Schonberg, Harold C., *The Great Pianists*, London, Gollancz, 1965, 3rd edition

RSB   Schumann, Robert, *Robert Schumanns Briefe, Neue Folge*, edited by F. Gustav Jansen, Leipzig, Breitkopf & Härtel, 1904, 2nd edition

EFM   *Erinnerungen an Felix Mendelssohn Bartholdy*, edited by Georg Eismann, Zwickau, Predella-Verlag, 1947

GS   *Gesammelte Schriften über Musik und Musiker von Robert Schumann*, edited by F. Gustav Jansen, Leipzig, Breitkopf & Härtel, 1891, 4th edition

Siemienovski, Serguei, 'Les connaissances et les amis russes de Chopin' [in Russian], *Russko-polskije muzykalnyje swiazi*, Moscow, Izdatielstwo Akadiemii Nauk, 1963, pp. 119–37

Sietz, Reinhold, *Aus Ferdinand Hillers Briefwechsel*, Köln, Arno Volk-Verlag, 1958–70, 7 vols

Simonides, Jaroslav, 'Češti pianisté – Žáci Fryderyka Chopina' [Czech pianist pupils of Fryderyk Chopin], *Chopiniana Bohemica et Slovenica*, II (1964), pp. 73–85

Skarbowski, Jerzy, 'O przekazach dotyczących działalności pedagogicznej Chopina' [On the transmission of facts about Chopin's teaching activity], *Ruch muzyczny*, XVI/20 (1972), pp. 8–10

Sobiescy, Jadwiga and Marian, *Polska muzyka ludowa i jej problemy* [Polish folk music and its problems], Kraków, PWM, 1973

Sobieska, Jadwiga and Sobieski, Marian, 'Das Tempo rubato bei Chopin und in der polnischen Volkmusik', *in* Lissa (ed.), pp. 247–54

Sowiński, Albert, *Les Musiciens polonais et slaves anciens et modernes*, Paris, Le Clère, 1857

Stavenow, Bernhard, 'Der Lieblingsschüler Friedrich Chopin's. Biographische Skizze' [Gutmann], in *Schöne Geister*, Norden, H. Fischer Nachfolger, 1883, 4th edition

CK   Steglich, Rudolf, 'Chopins Klaviere', *Chopin-Jahrbuch* [II], Vienna, Notring-Verlag, 1963, pp. 139–60

CEdE   'Über Chopins E-dur-Etüde op. 10, Nr. 3', *Chopin-Jahrbuch* [I], Vienna, Amalthea-Verlag, 1956, pp. 132–41

Stookes, Sacha, 'Chopin the Teacher', *The Monthly Musical Record*, LXXXIV/957 (1954), pp. 119–24

Stradal, August, *Erinnerungen an Franz Liszt*, Bern and Leipzig, Haupt, 1929

Strelezki, Anton (pseudonym of Burnand, Arthur Bransby), *Personal Recollections of Chats with Liszt*, London, E. Donajowski, [1887]; New York, Musical Scope Publishers, [*c.* 1970]

Stromenger, Karol, 'How Chopin Played', *Poland of Today*, IV/10 (1949), pp. 17–18, 23

Sydow, Bronisław Edward, *Bibliografia F. F. Chopina*, Warsaw, Towarzystwo Naukowe Warszawskie, 1949; supplement: Warsaw, PWN, 1954

KF   'Karol Filtsch (1830–1845)', *Ruch muzyczny*, Kraków, 1947, No. 21, pp. 10–12

Tarnowski, Stanisław, 'Księżna Marcelina Czartoryska' [Princess Marcelina Czartoryska], *Przegląd Polski*, XXIX/116 (1895), pp. 249–94

Tartini, Giuseppe, *Traité des Agréments de la Musique*, edited by Erwin R. Jacobi, Celle, Moeck, 1961

Tasset, Aline, *La main et l'âme au piano d'après Schiffmacher*, Paris, Delagrave, [1908]

Tellefsen, Thomas, *Thomas Tellefsens Familiebreve*, Kristiania, Steenske Forlag, 1923

Thalberg, Sigismond, *L'Art du chant appliqué au piano* [op. 70], Leipzig, Breitkopf & Härtel, no date, 24 vols

Tosi, Pier Francesco, *see* Agricola

Türk, Daniel Gottlob, *Klavierschule*, Leipzig and Halle, 1789; facsimile edited by Erwin R. Jacobi, Kassel and Basle, Bärenreiter, 1962

Turło, Dalila Teresa, *Katalog zbiorów. Fototeka. Utwory Fryderyka Chopina* [Catalogue of collections. Photographs. Works of Chopin], TiFC, 1969

'Registers of Chopin Manuscripts in Polish Collections', *Studies in Chopin*, Warsaw, The Chopin Society [TiFC], 1973, pp. 90–115

'Problemy identyfikacji i chronologii pierwszych wydań Chopina' [Problems of identification and chronology of the first editions of Chopin], *Rocznik Chopinowski*, XIV (1982), pp. 33–53

Valetta, Ippolito, *Chopin. La Vita, Le Opere*, Turin, Bocca, 1910

Vancea, Zeno, 'Der Chopin-Schüler Carol Mikuli, ein Bindeglied zwischen rumänischer und polnischer Musikkultur', *in* Lissa (ed.), pp. 410–12

Vogel, Bernhard, *Raoul Koczalski. Skizze*, Leipzig, Pabst, no date

Walker, Alan (ed.), *Frédéric Chopin. Profiles of the Man and the Musician*, London, Barrie and Rockliff, 1978, revised edition

Walther, Johann Gottfried, *Musicalisches Lexicon*, Leipzig, 1732; facsimile edited by Richard Schaal, Kassel and Basle, Bärenreiter, 1953

Wangermée, Robert, 'Les techniques de la virtuosité pianistique selon Fétis', *Revue belge de Musicologie*, XXVI–XXVII (1972–3), pp. 90–105
'Tradition et innovation dans la virtuosité romantique', *Acta Musicologica*, XLII/1–2 (1970), pp. 5–32

Weill, Janine-, *see* Janine-Weill

Wierzyński, Kazimierz, *The Life and Death of Chopin*, translated by Norbert Gutermann, with a foreword by Artur Rubinstein, New York, Simon & Schuster, 1949

Wilkońska, Paulina, *Moje wspomnienia o życiu towarzyskim w Warszawie* [My recollections of social life in Warsaw], Warsaw, PIW, 1959

Windakiewicz, Helena, *Wzory ludowej muzyki polskiej w Mazurkach Fryderyka Chopina* [Polish folksong motifs in Chopin's Mazurkas], Kraków, Akademia Umiejętności, 1926

Wiora, Walter, 'Chopins Préludes und Etudes und Bachs Wohltemperiertes Klavier', *in* Lissa (ed.), pp. 73–81

Wodziński, Comte [Antoni], *Les Trois Romans de Frédéric Chopin*, Paris, Calmann and Lévy, 1886

Woźna, Małgorzatas, 'Jan Kleczyński – pisarz, pedagog, kompozytor' [Kleczyński – writer, teacher, composer], *Szkice o kulturze muzycznej XIX wieku*, III (1976), pp. 130–323

Wróblewska, Hanna, *Katalog zbiorów. Muzeum. Ikonografia, pamiątki i sztuka użytkowa* [Catalogue of collections. Museum. Iconography, souvenirs and *objets d'art*], Warsaw, TiFC, 1970
Katalog zbiorów. Muzeum. Korespondencja F. Chopin [Catalogue of collections. Museum. Letters of Chopin], Warsaw, TiFC, 1969

Wróblewska-Straus, Hanna, 'Listy Jane Wilhelminy Stirling do Ludwiki Jędrzejewiczowej' [Letters from Jane Wilhelmina Stirling to Ludwika Jędrzejewicz], *Rocznik Chopinowski*, XII (1980), pp. 55–193

Wróblewska, Hanna and Gendaszek-Lewkowicz, Maria, *Katalog zbiorów. Muzeum. Rękopisy, druki, grafika, fotografie* [Catalogue of collections. Museum. Manuscripts, editions, prints, photographs], Warsaw, TiFC, 1971

Zagiba, Franz, 'Chopin als Mozartverehrer', *Chopin-Jahrbuch* [I] Vienna, Amalthea-Verlag, 1956, pp. 177–207

Ziffer, Agnes, *Katalog des Archivs für Photogramme musikalischer Meisterhandschriften. Widmung Anthony van Hoboken*, Vienna, Prachner, 1967, Vol. 1

Index of names

Bold numbers indicate the more important references. In the case of references to notes, the page given is that of the *first* occurrence of the subject *only*.

Abraham, Gerald: 107n.62; 110n.70; 111n.75; 124n.106
Adam, Louis: 107n.61; 119n.95; 135n.36
Adelung, Sophie von: 6n.11, n.12; 9n.16; 11; 28; 167–8
Agoult, Marie d': 112n.77
Agricola, Johann Friedrich: 113n.82
Aguettant, Louis: 28; 31; 45; 47; 48; 54; 58; 129n.121; 130n.122; 162
Alard, Delphin: 164; 178; 185
Albéniz, Isaac: 20; 130n.124
Albrecht, Thomas: 185
Alkan, Charles-Valentin (Morhange): 1; 95n.15; 120n.97; 134n.129; 146n.170
André, Antoinette: *see* Couturier
André, Claire (née Le Mire): 228n.53
André, Edouard: 228n.53
André, Elisabeth: *see* Pénicaud
André, Louise (née Franchomme): 228n.53
André, René-Edouard: 228n.53; 229n.55
André, Yvonne: *see* Faure
Anonymous (author/compiler of *Conseils aux jeunes pianistes*): 29; 32; 41; 48; 57; 101n.32; 120n.97; 159n.205
Anonymous (correspondent of *Edinburgh Advertiser*): 295
Anonymous (correspondent of *Neue Leipziger Zeitschrift*): 291 and n.36
Anonymous (correspondent of *Le Pianiste*): 291–2
Anonymous (correspondent of *Wiener Theaterzeitung*): *see* Bäuerle
Anonymous Scottish lady (Chopin's pupil): 9n.16; 27; 30; 41; 44; 59; **161**; 277; 279; scores: 198n.1
Appony, Thérèse (née Nogarola): 181
Artôt, Alexandre-Joseph: 178
Ashdown, Edwin (publisher): 95n.15
Auber, D.-F.-Esprit: 279n.15; 286; 289n.34

Bach, Carl Philipp Emanuel: 110n.74; 119n.95

Bach, Johann Sebastian: 15n.25; 60–1; 93n.11; 107n.62; 111n.77; 131n.126; 135n.134; n.136; n.137; 136n.142; 144n.168; 146n.170; 165; 181; 184; 276
Bach, Wilhelm Friedemann: 131n.126
Badura-Skoda, Paul: 125n.112; 126n.114; 211; 215; 219
Balzac, Honoré de: 6n.11; **168**; 285
Barcińska, Izabela (née Chopin): 92n.8
Bardac, Emma: *see* Debussy
Bargiel, W.: 102n.32
Basso, Alberto: 110n.70
Bäuerle, Adolf (? anonymous correspondent of *Wiener Theaterzeitung*): 125n.109; 147n.172; 288–9 and n.31
Beaufils, Marcel: 97n.20
Bechstein (company): 127n.116; 128n.120
Becker, Marta: 292n.37
Beethoven, Ludwig van: 16n.29; 17; 21; 55; 59; 61; 62; 63; 109n.69, n.70; 111n.77; 115n.83; 116n.85; 119n.95; 124n.107; 125n.110, n.111; 127n.118; 128n.120; 130n.122; 135n.134, n.136, 136n.142; 137n.143; 140n.156; 165–6; 169; 178; 185; 267; 276; 277–8; 285; 288; 292n.37
Bellini, Vincenzo: 86; 110n.75; 124n.108; 144n.161
Belotti, Gastone: 95n.15; 110n.70; 113n.82; 119n.95; 121n.99; 124n.106; 129n.121; 140n.154; 147n.172; 177; 202n.9; 294n.41
Bérard, Jean-Antoine: 109n.70
Berger, Ludwig: 107n.61
Berlioz, Hector: 3n.5; 16n.29; 20; 67; 71; 104n.41; 110n.73; 118n.92; 125n.112; 135n.137; 140n.156; 143n.160; 144n.168; 153n.187; 270n.8; 272; 285
Bertha, A. de: 120n.97
Bertini, Henri (the younger): 92n.9; 107n.61
Bertini, Paolo: 174
Biegański, Krzysztof: 146n.169
Bielawski, Ludwik: 146n.169

Bischoff, Ferdinand: 27; 29; **97n.19**; 144n.161
Bizet, Georges: 130n.124
Blaze de Bury, Henri (Hans Werner): 91n.7;
   124n.108; 287n.29
Boieldieu, François-Adrien: 107n.61; 288n.32
Boissier, Mme Auguste: 16n.28; 94n.14; 97n.18
Bone, Audrey Evelyn: 161; 180
Bory, Robert: 113n.82; 240; 295n.44
Borzęcka, Emilia: *see* Hoffmann
Boschot, Adolphe: 67; 143n.160
Bourbon-Parma (family): 189
Bouvaist, Marthe: *see* Granche
Brahms, Johannes: 102n.32; 172
Brandus (publishers): 101n.32; 228n.54; 229;
   230; 234
Branson, David: 108n.64; 116n.84; 124n.106
Brée, Malwine: 104n.45
Breitkopf & Härtel (publishers): 95n.15;
   102n.32; 139n.148; 151n.183; 226n.50;
   228n.54; 229n.55; 230n.58; 268n.4; 273n.9
Broadwood (company): 26; 92n.10; 93n.11
Bronarski, Ludwik: 7n.15; 111n.75; 139n.148;
   146n.169; 220; 222
Brülow, Emilie von: *see* Gretsch
Brzowski, Józef: 139n.150
Bülow, Hans von: 2n.1; 5n.8; 73; 115n.84;
   147n.172; 168; 177
Burnand, Arthur Bransby: *see* Strelezki

Calmann–Lévy (publishers): 284n.25
Calza, Edvige: 2n.1
Canaux (publishers): 110n.75
Caraman, Juliette de: 6n.11; 13
Carreño, Teresa: 170
Carter (Mrs, pupil of Chopin): 9n.15
Caswell, Austin: 113n.82
Cavalcabo (composer): 239
Chabal, Jean-Louis (publishers): 276n.12
Chainaye, Suzanne and Denise: 7n.14; 282n.21
Champlatreux (pupil of Chopin): 9n.15
Chandet, Henriette: 186
Chateaubriand, François-René de: 13
Cheriemietieff, Anna Serguéïevna: 161; 169;
   278 and n.14
Cheriemietieff, Elizavieta Serguéïevna: 5n.8;
   6n.11; 11n.18; 27; 161–2; 169; 278 and
   n.14
Cherkassky: *see* Tcherkassky
Cherubini, Luigi: 140n.156
Chicardinsky: 168
Chmara, Barbara: 116n.84
Chodzko, Aleksander: 95n.15
Choknosowski (Prince): 168
Chopin, Frédéric: *passim*
Chopin, Izabela: *see* Barcińska
Chopin, Justyna (née Krzyżanowska, mother
   of Frédéric): 92n.8

Chopin, Ludwika: *see* Jędrzejewicz
Chopin, Nicolas: 94n.14
Chouquet, Gustave: 176
Ciechomska, Ludwika (née Jędrzejewicz):
   100n.29; 106n.52; 144n.161; 167; 184
Ciechomska, Ludwika (grand-daughter of the
   above): 220
Ciechomskie, Maria and Laura: 106n.52
Cinti-Damoreau (Laure-Cinthie Montalant):
   110n.75
Clementi, Muzio: 4; 28; 32; 59; 61; 95n.17;
   104n.41; 105n.47; 107n.61; 109n.70;
   111n.77; 135n.134, n.136; 136n.142; 162;
   189; 274; 290
Clésinger, J.-B.-Auguste: 181; 280n.17, n.18
Clésinger, Solange (née Sand-Dudevant):
   135n.135; 138n.145; 139n.151; 180; 280–1
   and n.17, n.18, n.19; 282n.21
Coeuroy, André: 158n.203
Coignet, Jules: 99n.27
Colombier (publishers): 134n.129
Cooper (Mrs, pupil of Chopin): 9n.15
Cortot, Alfred: 90n.1; 104n.45; 105n.47;
   113n.80; 144n.164; 157n.201; 179
Couperin, François: 107n.62
Courty (Mme, pupil of Chopin): 28; 31; 45;
   47; 48; 54; 58; 129n.121; 130n.122; 162
Couturier, Antoinette (née André): 228 and
   n.54; 229; 230; 231n.62
Cramer, Jean-Baptiste: 16; 32; 60; 104n.41;
   106n.54; 107n.61; 109n.69; 115n.83;
   135n.134; 146n.171
Custine, Astolphe de: 286
Czartkowski, Adam: 28; 30; 31; 32; 57;
   95n.15; 99n.28; 139n.150
Czartoryska, Marcelina (née Radziwiłł): 3; 5
   and n.8; 30; 31; 32; 57; 75; 90n.1; 94n.13;
   99n.28; 102n.32, n.34; 120n.97; 125n.112;
   131n.125; 140n.155; 154n.188; 156n.194;
   162–3; 176; 184; 280
   scores: 172; 198n.1; 240n.73
Czernicheff, Elizavieta: *see* Tschernischeff
Czerny, Carl: 4; 16 and n.28; 74; 95n.17;
   107n.61; 135n.133; 137n.142; 138n.145;
   149n.174; 163; 228n.54

Davison, James William: 127n.118; 242n.78
Debussy, Claude-Achille: 20; 21; 103n.39;
   104n.41; 128n.120, n.121; 130n.122, n.124
Debussy, Emma (née Bardac): 128n.120
Déchelette, Albert: 276
Delacroix, Eugène: 1; 4; 99n.26; 101n.31;
   131n.124; 135n.137; 137n.143; 163; 179;
   188; 231n.65; 282; 283 and n.22
Delaroche, Paul: 143n.161
Delioux, Charles: 98n.21
Denis, Ferdinand: 13n.20; 142n.157

Desternes, Suzanne: 186
Diabelli, Anton (publisher): 209n.24
Dieffenbach, Johann Friedrich: 144n.162
Diehl, A.M.: 93n.11; 163
Diémer, Louis: 98n.21; 130n.124; 212
Dietschy, Marcel: 129n.121
Dirichlet, Rebecka (née Mendelssohn): 268
   and n.2
Döhler, Theodor: 287
Donizetti, Gaetano: 86; 110n.75
Dorn, Heinrich: 164; 269
Drachman, Mrs Daniel: 111n.75
Drath, Jan Bogdan: 219 and n.40
Dreyschock, Alexander: 287
Drzewiecki, Zbigniew: 92n.7
Dubois, Camille (née O'Meara): 3; 5; 9n.16;
   27; 29; 34; 49; 60–3 passim; 83; 87;
   95n.15; 98n.21; 101n.32; 102n.34;
   105n.49; 120n.97; 124n.107; 131n.125;
   136n.139, n.142; 139n.152; 143n.154; 164;
   172; 178; 181; 212; 215; 217; 228; 232;
   280
   scores: 19n.38; 98n.23; 107n.60; 108n.66,
   n.68; 112n.79; 113n.82; 116n.85; 117n.86,
   n.88, n.90; n.91; 119n.95; 123n.105;
   125n.112; 131n.126; 133n.127, n.128;
   149n.173, n.175; 150n.179, n.180, n.183;
   152n.184, n.186; 154n.189, n.190;
   155n.191; 156n.192; 157n.197, n.201;
   158n.202; 164; 198; 200; 203n.12;
   205n.14, n.15, n.16, n.17; 206n.18;
   207n.20, n.21; 208 and n.23; 210; 212–19
   and notes; 221n.43; 224; 230n.56, n.57;
   231; 232; 233; 235n.70; 237; 238; 244
Dubois, Georges: 175
Dudevant, Casimir: 280n.17
Dufour (publishers): 228n.54; 230
Dunn, John Petrie: 110n.70; 124n.106;
   131n.126
Duperré, Laure: 98n.21
Dupin, Aurore: see Sand, George
Durand, Jacques (publisher): 103n.39;
   128n.120; 130n.122
Dussek, Jan Ladislav: 136n.142; 235
Dworzaczek, Ferdinand: 284 and n.24
Działyńska, Cecylia: 28; 30; 31; 32; 57;
   99n.24, n.28; 163

Egert, Paul: 139n.148
Eichtal (Baron d'): 140n.156; 271
Eichtal, A. (Baronne d', daughter of the
   above, pupil of Chopin): 140n.156
Eigeldinger, Jean-Jacques: 110n.70; 113n.82;
   119n.95; 124n.106; 143n.158; 155n.190;
   210; 211; 227; 231n.64; 232; 236; 238
Eismann, Georg: 269

Ekier, Jan: 101n.32; 148n.172; 151n.184; 211;
   215 and n.36; 217; 219; 221n.43, n.46;
   222; 227
Elsner, Józef: 95n.17; 119n.95; 153n.188
Erard (company): 17; 26; 91n.7; 92n.9; 93n.10;
   124n.107; 146n.171; 169
Erskine, Katherine: 180; 181
Escudier, Léon: 293–4 and n.39
Esudier, Mårie: 293n.39
Eustafiew, Elise: see Peruzzi

Falmouth (Lord): 294n.42
Faucher, Aleksandra (née Wołowska): scores:
   198n.1
Faure, Yvonne (née André): 101n.32; 228 and
   n.54; 229; 231n.62
Fauré, Gabriel: 20
Federhofer, Hellmut: 27; 29; 97n.19; 156n.193;
   172; 182
Fesca, Alexander Ernst: 239
Fétis, François-Joseph: 106n.54; 118n.93;
   127n.120; 135n.136; 147n.171; 170; 290
Field, John: 1; 16; 18; 46; 52; 61; 62; 77;
   92n.9; 104n.41; 107n.61; 108n.64;
   112n.78; 115n.83; 116n.84; 124n.106;
   136n.142; 146n.171; 152n.184; 168; 276
Filtsch, Carl: 5; 6n.12; 10; 13; 66–7; 97n.20;
   140n.157; 143n.158; 166; 169; 182; 281
Filtsch, Joseph (brother of the above):
   141n.157
Fontana, Julian: 3n.5; 80; 102n.34; 104n.44;
   123n.105; 134n.130; 139n.151; 153n.188;
   181; 209; 273n.9; 282
   edition: 101n.32; 107n.63; 108n.66; 113n.82;
   117n.91; 121n.99; 154n.188, n.189;
   156n.192; 158n.201; 178; 209; 218; 229;
   234
Forest, Adèle: 228; 229
Forest, Jules: 228
Forkel, Johann Nikolaus: 15n.25
Fortescue, Virginia: 237–8
Franchomme, Auguste: 3n.5; 4; 29; 32; 41; 48;
   57; 95n.15; 101n.32; 120n.97; 159n.205;
   163; 172; 178; 181; 184; 185; 187; 200;
   201; 202; 209; 228 and n.53; 229 and
   n.55; 231–2 and n.65; 270n.8; 293n.40
   scores: 19n.38; 107n.60; 108n.66; 117n.85,
   n.86; 132n.126; 151n.183, n.184; 200;
   205n.17; 210; 213n.30; 217; 218; 224;
   228–33 and notes; 237; 238; 244
Franchomme, Cécile: 101n.32; 217; 228; 232
Franchomme, Louise: see André
Franchomme, René: 101n.32; 179
Frère, Charles-T. ('Frère Bey'): 99n.27
Friedman, Ignacy: 118n.94
Froberville, Eugénie de: 177

Gaillard, Emile: 166; 202; 204; 205n.13; 220; 276 and n.12
Gaillard, Paul-André: 154n.188
Gailloux (Mr, pupil of Chopin): 9n.15
Gajewski, Ferdinand: 157n.196; 239n.72; 240; 241
Ganche, Edouard: 6n.11; 9n.16; 29; 61; 62; 95n.15; 99n.27; 102n.33; 122n.100; 136n.137; 164; 175; 178; 180; 181; 184; 200; 202n.8, n.9; 210n.25; 211 and n.26; 214n.31; 215; 219; 232; 240n.73 edition: 102n.33; 207–8 and n.22, n.23
Ganche, Marthe (née Bouvaist): 200
Garate, Roger de: 282n.21
Garcia, Manuel: 186
Garcia, Maria: see Malibran
Garcia, Pauline: see Viardot
Gavard, Charles: 163; 167
Gavard, Elise: 95n.15
Gaymüller (female pupil of Chopin): 9n.15
Gebethner & Wolff (publishers): 154n.188; 188
Gendaszek, Maria: 227; 243
Gérard, E. (publisher): 188; 234
Gide, André: 179
Gieseking, Walter: 16; 95n.16
Gille, Philippe: 98n.21; 144n.166
Gille, Victor: 2n.1; 98n.21 and n.23; 106n.59; 113n.80; 144n.166; 175
Gładkowska, Konstancja: 133n.127
Goddard, Arabella: 57; 127n.118
Goddard (Mrs, mother of the above): 57
Goethe, Wolfgang von: 14; 284
Goria, Alexandre-Edouard: 239
Gottschalk, Louis Moreau: 179
Goubault, Christian: 143n.158
Gounod, Charles: 163
Graf, Conrad: 91n.6; 92n.7
Gräfe, Carl Ferdinand: 144n.162
Granados, Enrique: 20
Gretsch, Emilie von (née von Timm; first married to von Brülow): 3; 5; 6 and n.11; 9n.16; 11 and n.18; 13; 26; 27; 34; 45; 57; 61; 77; 109n.70; 112n.79; 137n.143; 161; 164–6
Grewingk, Maria von: 5; 6n.11; 9n.16; 11n.18; 12; 13n.21; 26; 27; 34; 45; 57; 61; 77; 109n.70; 110n.73; 137n.143; 166
Grieg, Edvard: 20
Grisi, Giulia: 45; 110n.75
Grzymała, Wojciech: 134n.129; 139n.151; 167; 208; 282
Gunsberg, Paul: 5; 11n.18
Gutmann, Adolf: 3; 9n.16; 10; 41; 56; 61; 68; 78; 79; 80; 81; 83; 85; 95n.15; 101n.31; 123n.105; 126n.114, n.115; 127n.117; 151n.184; 157n.199; 166–7; 238

Hadden, James Cuthbert: 9n.16; 27; 30; 41; 44; 59; 74; 95n.15; 126n.112; 149n.176; 161; 277; 279
Hallé, Charles: 3n.5; 6n.11; 65; 66; 73; 82; 95n.15; 96n.17; 122n.100; 125n.112; 127n.120; 138n.143, n.146; 140n.156; 147n.172; 156n.194; 177; 271; 279n.16
Handel, Georg Friedrich: 136n.142; 143n.161
Harasowski, Adam: 180
Harder, Maria Alexandrowna von: 6n.11, n.12; 9n.16; 11; 28; 167–8
Harding, Rosamond E.M.: 92n.7, n.10; 130n.122
Härtel, Hermann: 268 and n.4
Härtel, Raimund: 268n.4
Hartmann, Caroline: 5
Haslinger, Tobias (publisher): 137n.142; 200n.4; 228n.54
Haydn, Joseph: 136n.142
Hedley, Arthur: 6n.11; 13; 93n.11; 95n.15; 107n.62; 140n.155; 142n.157; 161; 294n.41; 295
Heine, Heinrich: 71; 284 and n.25
Heller, Stephen: 1; 9; 16n.27; 95n.15, n.17; 98n.22; 101n.31; 138n.145; 139n.148, n.150; 140n.156; 156n.193; 158n.201; 168; 177; 239; 279n.16; 287
Henle, G. (edition): 129n.121; 149n.175; 150n.180; 154n.189; 156n.192; 157n.201; 215; 276n.12
Hensel, Fanny (née Mendelssohn): 268 and n.1
Hensel, Sebastian: 268
Henselt, Adolf: 1; 13; 72; 146n.170; 147n.172; 164; 165; 168; 287
Herz, Henri: 16; 92n.9; 95n.17; 104n.41, n.45; 137n.142; 176; 291
Heugel (publishers): 131n.124
Heygendorf, R. (Mme, née de Könneritz): 151n.184; 198n.1
Higgins, Thomas: 120n.98; 125n.112; 129n.121; 144n.163
Hiller, Ferdinand: 6n.11; 92n.9; 95n.15, n.17; 124n.107; 128n.120; 135n.136; 136n.142; 140n.156; 144n.168; 172; 186; 188; 267; 270 and n.8; 279n.16; 291
Hipkins, Alfred James: 3n.5; 19; 26; 30; 41; 48; 55; 57; 65; 92n.10; 93n.11; 95n.15; 106n.58; 110n.70; 117n.90; 127n.120; 140n.155; 174
Hipkins, Edith J.: 93n.11
Hirt, Franz Josef: 92n.7; 130n.122
Hławiczka, Karol: 146n.169
Hoesick, Ferdynand: 2; 9n.15; 95n.15; 153n.187
Hoffman-Tańska, Klementyna: 188; 283 and n.23

Hoffmann, Emilia (née Borzęcka): 163
Hofmeister, F.: 200n.4; 228n.54
Hogarth, George: 294–5 and n.41
Holcman, Jan: 124n.106
Holland, Jeanne: 7n.15; 215; 217; 219
Hordyński, Władysław: 6n.11; 9n.16; 11n.17;
    28; 31; 129n.121; 188; 189; 237; 238
Houstoun, Anne D.: 200; 202n.8
Hugo, Victor: 13
Hummel, Johann Nepomuk: 1; 4; 16; 18; 20;
    29; 40; 61; 63; 94n.14; 100n.29; 104n.41;
    106n.54; 107n.61, n.64; 110n.74; 111n.77;
    112n.78; 115n.83; 119n.95; 124n.106;
    131n.126; 135n.134, n.135; 136n.142;
    146n.170, n.171; 235n.69; 270n.8; 276;
    288
Hünten, Franz: 137n.142

Indy, Vincent d': 130n.124
Ingres, J.-A.-Dominique: 283n.22
Ivry (Baronne d', pupil of Chopin): 98n.21

Jaeger, Bertrand: 9n.15; 241
Janin, Jules: 163
Janine-Weill: 128n.120
Janotha, Natalia: 90n.1; 113n.80; 163
Jędrzejewicz, Ludwika (née Chopin): 11n.18;
    90n.1; 102n.33; 164; 178; 180; 181; 182;
    184; 189; 199; 209; 210; 220; 226 and
    n.50; 232
    PM fragments: 29; 34; 37; 41; 90n.1; 174
    scores: 19n.38; 107n.63; 113n.79, n.82;
    116n.85; 117n.86, n.91; 123n.105;
    126n.114; 132n.126; 150n.179; 151n.183;
    152n.184, n.186; 153n.187; 154n.189;
    155n.191; 156n.192, n.193; 157n.201; 198;
    205n.14, n.15, n.16, n.17; 206n.18, n.19;
    207n.20, n.21; 214n.32; 215; 217; 218;
    220–7 and notes; 231; 232; 233; 235n.70;
    237; 238; 241 and n.76; 244
Jędrzejewicz, Ludwika: see Ciechomska
Jełowicki, Aleksander: 96n.17
Jerger, Wilhelm: 135n.134; 164
Jeżewska, Zofia: 28; 30; 31; 32; 57; 95n.15;
    99n.28; 139n.150

Kahlert, August: 289–90 and n.34
Kalergis, Marie (née Nesselrode): 2n.1; 5n.8
Kalkbrenner, Arthur: 9; 96n.17; 178
Kalkbrenner, Frédéric: 1; 4; 7; 9; 16; 18; 27;
    40; 41; 55; 92n.9; 94n.14; 95n.17; 96n.18;
    104n.41, n.45; 106n.54; 107n.61; 108n.65,
    n.67; 112n.77; 115n.83; 127n.118;
    140n.156; 146n.171; 164; 170; 174; 177;
    178; 184; 271; 290 and n.35; 291
Kallberg, Jeffrey: 177
Kamieński, Lucjan: 110n.70; 119n.95; 121n.99

Kamieński, Maciej: 119n.95
Kann, Hans: 109n.69
Kapp, Julius: 2n.1
Karasowski, Maurycy: 2; 3n.5; 6n.11; 9; 15;
    26; 44; 45; 54; 91n.7; 92n.8; 93n.11;
    105n.49, n.51; 109n.69; 114n.82; 120n.97;
    122n.100; 180
Karłowicz, Mieczysław: 6n.11; 9n.15;
    138n.144; 141n.157; 179; 181; 182; 186
Kessler, Joseph Christoph: 92n.9; 135n.134
Kistner (publishers): 95n.15; 172; 226n.50
Kleczyński, Jan: 2; 3n.5; 5n.8; 19n.39; 30; 31;
    33; 34; 38; 39; 42; 44; 45; 51; 54; 58; 60;
    69; 79; 80; 90n.1; 92n.8; 102n.34;
    103n.40; 105n.46, n.47, n.49; 106n.51,
    n.60; 107n.62, n.63; 109n.69; 110n.71;
    113n.80, n.81; 118n.92; 120n.97, n.98;
    122n.101; 125n.112; 130n.122; 131n.125;
    134n.130; 150n.182; 151n.184; 152n.185,
    n.186; 157n.195; 163; 189
Klein, Marie: 142n.157
Kobylańska, Krystyna: 149n.175; 150n.179;
    154n.188; 156n.193; 158n.201; 199; 211;
    215; 217; 219; 220; 227; 230; 231n.64;
    236; 241
Koczalski, Raoul: 5; 27; 29; 42; 49; 52; 56; 57;
    59; 72; 74; 97n.20; 106n.54; 120n.97;
    121n.98; 123n.105; 126n.114; 132n.126;
    145n.169; 148n.173; 152n.184; 154n.189;
    157n.197; 158n.202; 172; 174; 218
Kolberg, Oskar: 147n.172
Kologrivoff, Vera de: see Rubio
Komar, Delfina: see Potocka
Könneritz, R. de: see Heygendorf
Krasiński, Zygmunt: 143n.161
Kreutz, Alfred: 110n.70; 119n.95; 121n.99
Kreutzer (Mme): 142n.157
Krudner, Marie de: 161; 162; 277n.13; 278n.14
Krzyżanowska, Justyna: see Chopin
Kurpiński, Karol: 111n.75; 119n.95
Kwiatkowski, Teofil: 95n.15; 99n.27; 179

Lablache, Luigi: 110n.75
Lacassagne, Joseph: 109n.70
Lachmund, Carl V.: 82; 83; 114n.82; 122n.100
La Fontaine, Jean de: 188
Lakatos, István: 142n.157
La Mara (pseudonym of Marie Lipsius): 5n.8;
    94n.14; 168
Landowska, Wanda: 94n.13; 103n.34
Latouche, H.-J.-A. ('Henri de'): 184
Launer (publishers): 135n.136
Laurecka, Johanna: 84
Lauth, Aurore (née Sand-Dudevant): 282n.21
Lauverjat, Adèle de: see Forest
Lawton, Mary: 164
Legouvé, Ernest: 136n.142

Lehman, Robert Owen: 90n.1; 113n.80;
    144n.163; 153n.187
Leichtentritt, Hugo: 95n.15; 107n.62
Leimer, Karl: 16; 95n.16
Le Mire, Claire: see André
Lemoine, Henry (editions): 220n.41; 228n.54;
    234; 235 and n.70; 236
Lenartowicz, Teofil: 154n.188
Lenz, Wilhelm von: 2n.1; 3; 6n.11; 9n.16; 25;
    32; 44; 50; 52; 55; 65–89 passim; 91n.7;
    92n.9; 96n.17; 107n.61; 109n.69; 111n.76;
    113n.82; 115n.83; 116n.84, n.85; 118n.93;
    120n.97; 122n.102, n.104, n.105;
    124n.107; 125n.110, n.111; 127n.117;
    134n.130; 135n.137; 137n.143; 138n.144;
    139n.150, n.153; 142n.157; 143n.158;
    146n.170; 147n.172; 150n.178, n.180,
    n.181, n.183; 151n.184; 155n.191;
    156n.193; 157n.199; 158n.201, n.203;
    159n.206; 161; 163; 166; 168–70; 207n.21;
    238; 277
    scores: 198n.1; 218
Leo, Auguste: 157n.197; 177; 279n.16
Leo(-Dellevie), Sophie Augustine: 279–80 and
    n.16
Leschetizky, Theodor: 94n.12; 104n.45; 118n.94
Leszkiewicz, Antoni: 31; 103n.37
Lévy brothers (publishers): 284n.25
Lichocherstoff, Anna de: 113n.80
Lind, Jenny: 95n.15
Lindenau, Bernhard: 142n.153
Lisowska, Agnieszka: 111n.75
Lissa, Zofia: 97n.19; 146n.169
Liszt, Franz: 1; 2n.1; 3n.5; 4; 5 and n.8; 7; 13;
    16 and n.28, n.29; 17 and n.33; 20 and
    n.41; 21; 25; 27; 51; 55; 62; 67; 70; 74; 82;
    83; 92n.9; 94n.14; 95n.15, n.17; 96n.18;
    97n.19; 98n.21; 102n.32; 112n.77;
    115n.83; 121n.99; 122n.100; 123n.106;
    124n.107; 125n.110; 129n.121; 135n.134,
    n.136, n.137; 137n.142; 138n.143, n.145;
    139n.150; 140n.156; 141n.157; 144n.168;
    146n.170; 163; 164; 167; 168; 169; 170;
    176; 182; 186; 242; 267; 268; 270 and n.8;
    272; 273–4 and n.9, n.10, n.11; 281; 285;
    287; 290; 291 and n.36; 292
Litzmann, Berthold: 170
Locard, Paul: 17n.31
Lockspeiser, Edward: 129n.121
Logier, Johann Bernhard: 96n.17
Long, Marguerite: 128n.121; 130n.122
Louis-Philippe (King of France): 71; 139n.150;
    147n.171; 163; 286n.28; 292n.37
Lubin, Georges: 281n.20; 282n.21
Ludre (Viscountess of): 9n.15
Lussy, Mathis: 103n.34; 110n.71
Łyszczyński, Adam: 95n.15

Maberly, Catherine: 180
Mainzer, Joseph: 291n.36
Makomaski (Mr, pupil of Tellefsen): 78
Malibran, Maria (née García): 45; 110n.75;
    186
Mangold, Alice: 93n.11; 163
Marcello, Benedetto: 144n.161
Marix-Spire, Thérèse: 182
Marmontel, Antoine-François: 3n.5; 9; 58;
    91n.7; 98n.21; 103n.41; 105n.49;
    128n.120, n.121; 130n.122, n.123, n.124;
    134n.126; 136n.142; 142n..157; 164; 170;
    182; 274–5
Marmontel, Antonin: 131n.124
Marpurg, Friedrich Wilhelm: 106n.54
Massé, Victor: 98n.21
Massenet, Jules: 175
Mathias, Georges: 3; 5; 12; 27; 31; 32; 41; 44;
    50; 56; 61; 79; 88; 94n.12; 95n.15; 98n.21,
    n.22; 102n.34; 105n.49; 118n.92; 120n.98;
    124n.107; 126n.114; 127n.115; 129n.121;
    131n.125; 135n.135; 137n.143; 138n.144,
    n.148; 158n.203; 164; 170–1; 277
Maurin, N.-E.: 280n.18
Mauté de Fleurville, Antoinette-Flore:
    129n.121
Mauté, Mathilde: see Verlaine
Mayer, Charles: 168
Mayer (Mme, singer): 133n.127
Mechetti (publishers): 228n.54; 231n.62
Meissonnier, Gérard (publisher): 228n.54; 234
Meissonnier, Joseph (publisher): 110n.75;
    154n.188; 228n.54; 234
Meister, Edith: 110n.70; 111n.75; 124n.106
Mendelssohn-Bartholdy, Fanny: see Hensel
Mendelssohn-Bartholdy, Felix: 1; 3n.5; 62; 65;
    95n.17; 118n.92; 135n.136; 136n.142;
    138n.146; 140n.154; 144n.164; 146n.171;
    157n.197; 267–8; 269n.7; 270n.8; 274n.11;
    279n.16
Mendelssohn-Bartholdy, Paul: 140n.154; 268
Mendelssohn-Bartholdy, Rebecka: see
    Dirichlet
Meyer (publishers): 234
Meyerbeer, Giacomo: 73; 122n.100; 140n.156;
    157n.197; 167; 279n.16
Michałowski, Aleksander: 5n.8; 26; 50; 56; 75;
    94n.13; 103n.40; 125n.112; 127n.116;
    134n.133; 158n.202; 163; 172; 174
Mickiewicz, Adam: 96n.17; 139n.148;
    154n.188; 188; 283n.22, n.23
Miketta, Janusz: 146n.169
Mikuli, Karol: 3; 5; 6 and n.11; 10–11; 17n.32;
    19n.39; 25–37 passim; 40–6 passim; 49–
    62 passim; 67; 72; 74; 77; 82; 84; 94n.13;
    97n.19, n.20; 102n.32; 103n.38, n.40;
    105n.47, n.49; 106n.54, n.58; 110n.73;

Mikuli, Karol (*cont.*)
 113n.82; 116n.84; 118n.92; 120n.97;
 122n.105; 126n.114; 127n.116; 131n.126;
 134n.129; 135n.134, n.135, n.136;
 136n.142; 142n.157; 144n.161, n.162;
 156n.194; 157n.197; 158n.202; 161; 164;
 166; 172–4; 182; 184; 185; 275–6
 edition: 107n.60, n.63; 116n.84; 148n.173;
 149n.175; 150n.178, n.179, n.183;
 151n.184; 152n.185; 154n.189, n.190;
 156n.192, n.193; 157n.197, n.200, n.201;
 158n.202; 172–4; 182; 198n.1; 213n.30;
 214n.32; 218; 230n.56, n.57; 237; 240n.73
Mittag, August: 141n.157
Moke (Mme): *see* Pleyel
Montabré, Maurice: 174
Montal, Claude: 91n.7; 93n.10
Montalant, Laure-Cinthie: *see* Cinti-Damoreau
Monteverdi, Claudio: 1
Moscheles, Charlotte: 147n.171; 157n.197; 179
Moscheles, Emily: *see* Roche
Moscheles, Ignaz: 1; 3n.5; 9; 15; 16; 28; 32;
 57; 63; 73; 94n.13; 104n.41; 106n.54;
 107n.61; 118n.92, n.93; 120n.97;
 122n.100; 126n.114; 135n.134, n.135,
 n.136; 136n.142; 139n.150; 140n.156;
 142n.157; 146n.171; 147n.172; 157n.197;
 166; 176; 177; 189; 272–3; 279n.16
Moszkowski, Maurycy: 94n.12
Mozart, Leopold: 109n.70; 110n.74; 119n.95
Mozart, Wolfgang Amadeus: 1; 15n.25; 21;
 108n.64; 110n.75; 111n.77; 119n.95;
 136n.142; 142n.157; 163; 178; 186; 188;
 276; 277; 284; 285; 288
Müller, Friederieke: *see* Streicher
Murdoch, William: 95n.15
Murray (Lady, pupil of Chopin): 99n.28
Musielak, H.: 180

Nectoux, Jean-Michel: 155n.190; 210; 211;
 235n.70
Niesmieyanova, Tatiana: 6n.11; 162
Nesselrode, Marie: *see* Kalergis
Neuhaus, Heinrich: 94n.13; 100n.30; 104n.45;
 105n.47, n.48
Neukomm, Sigismund: 201; 209 and n.24
Ney, Casimir: 185
Niecks, Frederick: 2; 5; 6n.11; 9n.16; 11n.18;
 12n.19; 14; 15; 29; 30; 32; 34; 41; 45; 46;
 49; 51; 54; 56; 57; 61; 62; 63; 68; 78; 79;
 80; 81; 83; 87; 95n.15; 99n.27; 101n.31;
 105n.49; 106n.59; 118n.92; 120n.97;
 124n.107; 127n.115; 135n.134, n.135;
 136n.137, n.142; 138n.145; 139n.148,
 n.150, n.152; 143n.160; 144n.162;
 151n.184; 157n.197; 158n.201; 159n.206;
 167; 170; 176; 179; 180; 181; 182; 183;
 238; 242n.78; 269

Niedźwiecki, Leonard: 95n.15
Nogarola, Thérèse: *see* Appony
Nourrit, Adolphe: 110n.75
Nowik, Wojciech: 102n.32; 111n.75

Obreskoff, Natalia: 162
Odéon (publishers): 240
Okińczyc, Joseph: 237
Okińczyc, Maryla Bohdana: 234
O'Meara, Camille: *see* Dubois
Onslow, Georges: 139n.150
Orda, Napoléon: 242 and n.78
 scores: 242–3
Orłowski, Antoni: 103n.37; 143n.158
Osborne, George Alexander: 95n.15;
 140n.156; 178
Ostrzyńska, Ludwika: 126n.113; 174; 175
Ottich, Maria: 110n.70; 113n.82; 124n.106
Oury, Caroline: 159n.206

Pachmann, Vladimir de: 118n.94
Paderewski, Ignacy Jan: 83; 94n.12; 118n.94;
 144n.166; 157n.197; 164
Paganini, Nicolò: 16 and n.29; 94n.14; 95n.17;
 119n.95; 123n.106; 124n.108; 267; 285
Panigel, Armand: 97n.20
Panofka, Heinrich: 291n.36
Pape, Henri: 93n.10
Pasta, Giuditta: 14; 44; 77; 85; 110n.75
Pénicaud, Elisabeth (née André): 228
Pénicaud, Georges: 228
Pénicaud, Laurent: 179; 228 and n.54; 229;
 230; 231n.62; 232
Pergolesi, Giovanni Battista: 144n.161
Peru, F.-Henry: 2n.1; 32; 55; 56; 98n.21;
 126n.113; 174–6
Peruzzi, Elise (née Eustafiew): 3; 9n.16;
 11n.18; 56; 63; 101n.31; 118n.92; 120n.97;
 143n.158; 159n.206; 176; 186
Peters (publishers): 134n.132; 135n.136;
 151n.184; 157n.201
Philipp, Isidore: 27; 98n.22; 170; 171
Piatigorsky, Gregor: 111n.75
Picquet, Charles (Mme, née Jeanne Pillot): 29;
 32; 41; 48; 57; 101n.32; 120n.97; 159n.205
Pictet, Adolphe: 20n.41
Pilipczuk, Alexander: 146n.169
Pillot, Jeanne: *see* Piquet
Piron, Constantin: 31
Pixis, Johann Peter: 137n.142
Planat (female pupil of Chopin): 9n.15
Planté, Francis: 99n.28; 120n.97; 130n.124
Plater (Countess): 159n.206
Pleyel, Camille: 92n.9; 136n.142
Pleyel, Ignace: 136n.142
Pleyel (company): 11; 17; 25; 26; 55; 58; 86;
 91n.7; 92n.9; 93n.10; 96n.17; 115n.83;
 127n.116; 128n.120; 130n.121, n.122,

n.123; 144n.167; 169; 174; 180; 286n.26;
    290; 293 and n.40
Pleyel (Mme, née Moke): 291
Poirée, Elie: 176
Pomey, Louis: 188
Potocka, Delfina (née Komar): 67; 97n.19;
    101n.32; 120n.97; **143n.161**
    scores: 172; 198n.1
Pougin, Arthur: 170
Pozniak, Bronislaw von: 82; 84; 156n.194;
    157n.201; 174
Proch, Heinrich: 239
Prod'homme, Jacques-Gabriel: 143n.158
Pugno, Raoul: 79; 88; 118n.94; 152n.186;
    158n.202, n.203; 170
Pukińska-Szepietowska, Hanna: 111n.75

Quantz, Johann Joachim: 109n.70; 110n.74;
    119n.95
Queiroz Ribeiro, Aleixo de: 239

Radziwiłł, Marcelina: see Czartoryska
Radziwiłł, Wanda: 15
Rameau, Jean-Philippe: 14n.22
Raphael (Raffaello Sanzio): 284; 285
Rappoldi-Kahrer, Laura: 2n.1
Rauch, Nicolas: 137n.142; 242
Ravel, Maurice: 21
Reber, Henri: 59; **134n.129**; 172; 179; 184
Reinecke, Carl: 94n.13; 102n.32
Rejcha, Antonin: 134n.129
Rellstab, H.F. Ludwig: 144n.162
Richards, Henry Brinley: 95n.15
Richault, Simon (publishers): 95n.15; 185;
    209n.24; 228n.54; 231n.62; 234
Richter, Jean Paul: 138n.148
Ries, Ferdinand: 136n.142; 143n.158
Rinck, J. Chr. Heinrich: 140n.156
Ritter, Théodore: 98n.22
Roche, Emily (née Moscheles): 9; 73;
    147n.171; 157n.197; **176–8**
Roche, Jean-Antoine: 175
Rocheblave, Samuel: 282n.21
Rolland, Romain: 111n.77
Rosen (?): 287
Rosengardt, Zofia: see Zaleska
Rosenhain, Jacob: 179
Rosenthal, Maurycy: 118n.94; 174
Rossini, Gioacchino: 62; 110n.75; 119n.95;
    133n.127; 285
Rothschild (Baroness): 159n.205
Roubaud de Cournand, Marie: 6n.11; 9n.16;
    61; 98n.21; 99n.27; 102n.33; 122n.100;
    175; **178**
Rousseau, Jean-Jacques: 169
Rozières, Marie de: 10; 138n.144; 188; 280
    and n.17, **n.18**
Rubini, Giovanni Battista: 12; 14; 45; 86; 111n.75

Rubinstein, Nicolas: 274.11
Rubio, Luigi: 179
Rubio, Vera (née de Kologrivoff): 3; 5; 10; 45;
    95n.15; 135n.135; 172; **178–9**; 180
    scores: 156n.193; 198n.1
Rudorff, E.: 102n.32

Saint-Saëns, Camille: 49; 54; 59; 66; 98n.22;
    118n.92, n.94; 131n.126; 188
Salabert (publishers): 105n.47; 144n.164
Samuel, Jacques: 159n.206
Sand, Aurore: see Lauth
Sand, George (née Aurore Dupin): 2; 4; 6;
    99n.26; 135n.137; 138n.144; 139n.151;
    142n.157; 150n.180; 169; 184; 186; 187;
    280n.17, n.18; 281 and n.19, n.20; 282–3
    and n.21, n.22
Sand, Maurice Dudevant: 138n.145; 186; 283
    and n.22
Sand, Solange Dudevant: see Clésinger
Sandelewski, Wiarosław: 111n.75
Santa María, Tomás de: 107n.62
Scarlatti, Domenico: 136n.142
Scheffer, Ary: 143n.161
Schelling, Ernest: 3n.5; 26; 44; **93n.12**;
    129n.121; 170
Schenker, Heinrich: 174
Scherbatoff, Marie de: **239** and **n.72**
    scores: 157n.196; **239–41** and **notes**
Schiffmacher, Joseph: 88; 159n.205; **179**
Schindler, Anton: 3n.5; 72; 74; 109n.69, n.70;
    112n.77; 115n.83; 119n.95; 149n.174;
    292–3 and **n.37**, n.38
Schlesinger, Adolf (publisher): 154n.188
Schlesinger, Maurice (publisher): 137n.139;
    142n.157; 147n.171; 154n.188; 177; 179;
    209; 220n.41; 228n.54; 229n.55; 230;
    235n.70; 237; 242 and n.79
Schmitt, Hans: 103n.34
Schneider, Hans: 137n.142
Scholtz, Herrmann: 151n.184
Schubert, Franz: 1; 17; 62; 63; 110n.75;
    124n.107; 138n.145; 143n.158; 239
Schuberth (publishers): 95n.15
Schulhoff, Julius: 179
Schumann, Clara (née Wieck): 144n.164; 170;
    269; 279n.16
Schumann, Robert: 1; 3n.5; 14n.22; 16 and
    n.29; 62; 65; 69; 70; 95n.15; 135n.136;
    136n.142; 138n.148; 140n.154; 144n.164;
    164; 268–9 and n.5; 274n.11; 289n.34;
    291n.36
Schunke, Carl: 92n.9; 291
Schwabe (Mr and Mrs; of Manchester):
    209n.24
Scott, Walter: 294n.41
Scriabin, Alexander: 20
Seligmann, Julius: 3n.5; 74; 126n.112; **149n.176**

Shakespeare, William: 153n.187
Siemienowski, Serguei: 6n.11; 27; 162
Sietz, Reinhold: 270n.8
Simonides, Jaroslav: 63; 185; 186
Sloper, Lindsay: 95n.15; 180
Słowacki, Juliusz: 188; 283n.23
Smith, Ronald: 102n.32
Smithson, Harriet: 153n.187
Sobiescy, Jadwiga and Marian: 119n.95;
    121n.99; 146n.169
Soliva, Carlo: 119n.95
Sontag, Henriette: 114n.82
Souzzo, Catherine: 162
Sowiński, Wojciech: 99n.24; 127n.119;
    143n.161; 149n.174; 163; 242n.78
Spiess (Fr.): 234
Stargardt, J.A.: 153n.187
Stavenow, Bernhard: 9n.16; 126n.114; 167
Steglich, Rudolf: 91n.6; 144n.163
Steinway (company): 127n.116
Stern (publishers): 226n.50
Stetson, John B. (junior): 239
Stirling, Jane Wilhelmina: 3; 9n.15; 11n.18;
    29; 62; 83; 101n.32; 102n.33; 125n.112;
    136n.137; 139n.149; 161; 164; 179; 179–
    81; 184; 189; 208–10; 225–6; 232
  scores: 19n.38; 102n.33; 107n.60, n.63;
    108n.66; 116n.85; 117n.86, n.91;
    123n.105; 125n.112; 126n.114; 132n.126;
    139n.149; 149n.173; 150n.179, n.183;
    151n.184; 153n.187; 154n.189, n.190;
    155n.191; 156n.192, n.193; 157n.200,
    n.201; 180; 198 and n.1; 199; 200–11 and
    notes; 214n.32, n.36; 215n.37; 217; 218
    and n.39; 221n.43, n.46, n.47; 222–6; 231
    and n.64; 232; 233; 235n.70; 237; 238;
    241; 244
Stoepel, Franz: 291n.36
Stradal, August: 138n.143
Stradella, Alessandro: 144n.161
Streicher, Friederike (née Müller): 3; 5; 6 and
    n.11; 9n.16; 12n.19; 30; 46; 49; 54; 57; 63;
    68; 95n.15; 118n.92; 124n.107; 135n.134;
    136n.137; 137n.142; 141n.157; 143n.158;
    161; 181–3; 231n.66; 287
  scores: 156n.193; 172; 182; 198n.1;
    240n.73
Streicher, Johann Baptist: 181
Strelezki, Anton (Arthur Bransby Burnand):
    274 and n.11
Stricker, Rémy: 17n.31
Sudre (Viscountess of): see Ludre
Sutherland (Duchess of): 9n.15
Sydow, Bronisław Edward: 142n.157
Szulc, Marceli Antoni: 153n.187
Szymanowska, Maria (née Wołowska):
    115n.83; 158n.202

Tamburini, Antonio: 111n.75
Tańska, Klementyna: see Hoffman
Tartini, Giuseppe: 104n.43
Tasset, Aline: 88; 159n.205; 179
Tausig, Carl: 94n.13; 155n.191; 274n.11
Tcherkassky, Alexei Borissovitch: 239n.72
Tcherkassky, Marie: see Scherbatoff
Telemann, Georg Philipp: 111n.77
Tellefsen, Thomas: 3; 5; 6n.11; 9n.16; 78; 79;
    123n.105; 134n.129; 138n.144; 163; 172;
    181; 184–5
  edition: 5; 102n.32; 151n.184; 185; 198n.1;
    210 and n.25; 234
Thalberg, Sigismond: 1; 104n.41; 112n.77;
    114n.82; 124n.107; 127n.118; 130n.122;
    137n.142; 141n.157; 166; 270; 285; 287
Thun-Hohenstein, Anna: 137n.142; 185
Thun-Hohenstein, Bedřich: 63; 185–6
Thun-Hohenstein, Josefina ('Juža'): 137n.142;
    185; 186
Tiersot, Julien: 136n.142; 212; 217
Timm, Emilie von: see Gretsch
Tosi, Pier Francesco: 113n.82; 118n.95;
    121n.99; 122n.103
Trémont, Louis-Philippe-Joseph de: 279n.15;
    286–7 and n.28, n.30
Troupenas (publishers): 228n.54
Tschernischeff, Elizavieta: 162
Tulou, Jean-Louis: 111n.75
Türk, Daniel Gottlob: 106n.54; 109n.70;
    111n.77; 119n.95
Turło, Dalila Teresa: 284n.24

Valetta, Ippolito: 95n.15
Verlaine, Mathilde (née Mauté): 129n.121
Vernet, Horace: 165
Veyret (Mme; pupil of Chopin): 98n.21
Viardot, Alice: 186
Viardot, Pauline (née Garcia): 3; 5; 49; 54; 59;
    65–6; 110n.75; 118n.92; 131n.126; 164;
    167; 182; 186–8; 293n.40
Vigneron, Pierre Roche: 242
Vogel, Bernhard: 97n.20
Voigt, Henriette: 269 and n.5, n.7

Wagner, Richard: 20; 140n.156; 172; 274n.11
Walther, Johann Gottfried: 114n.82
Weber, Carl Maria von: 1; 12; 17; 18; 50; 61;
    62; 63; 136n.142; 139n.151; 169; 276
Wedgwood (Mrs; pupil of Chopin): 9n.15
Weill, Janine: see Janine-Weill
Werner, Hans: see Blaze de Bury
Wieck, Clara: see Schumann
Wieck, Friedrich: 141n.157; 170
Wierzyński, Kazimierz: 95n.15
Wildt, J. (publisher): 158n.201; 159n.206

Wilkońska, Paulina: 284
Windakiewicz, Helena: 146n.169
Wiora, Walter: 110n.70
Witwicki, Stefan: 188; 283 and n.23
Wodzińska, Maria: 113n.82; 123n.106;
  133n.127; 240; 280n.18
Wodziński, Antoni (brother of Maria):
  280n.18
Wodziński, Antoni (nephew of Maria):
  104n.42
Wolff, Edward: 95n.15; 107n.61; 287
Wolff, Pierre-E.: 95n.14
Wołowska, Maria: see Szymanowska
Wornum, Robert: 92n.10
Wotpol (Wodpol), Michał: 28; 99n.24
Woyciechowski, Tytus: 95n.17; 104n.41
Woźna, Małgorzata: 103n.34

Wróblewska-Straus, Hanna: 11n.18; 83; 178;
  180; 181; 189; 226n.51; 227; 243
Würfel, Wilhelm: 117n.90

Zagiba, Franz: 110n.70
Zaleska, Zofia (née Rosengardt): 6n.11; 9n.16;
  11n.17; 28; 31; 60; 102n.34; 103n.40;
  105n.47; 188–9; 234–7 passim; 283n.23
  scores: 117n.86; 137n.142; 150n.179; 189;
  205n.14; 217; 221n.43; 234–8 and notes
Zaleski, Bohdan: 188; 189; 234; 283–4 and n.23
Zaleski, Dionizy: 234
Zamoyski (family): 92n.8
Zamoyski, Adam: 238
Zimmermann, Pierre-J.-G.: 98n.21; 107n.61;
  130n.124
Żywny, Wojciech: 16; 119n.95

Index of musical works

Works cited in Appendix II (pp. 198–243) have not been indexed.
Bold numbers indicate the more important references. Illustrations have not been indexed. In the case of notes, the page given is that of the *first* occurrence of the subject only.

Auber, D.-F.-Esprit
  La Muette de Portici: 289n.34
Bach, Johann Sebastian
  Chromatic Fantasy: 93n.11
  Clavier-Büchlein for Wilhelm Friedemann:
    131n.126
  Concerto for three keyboards (BWV 1063):
    135n.136; 144n.168
  Goldberg Variations (Clavier-Übung IV):
    93n.11
  Inventions and Sinfonias: 15n.25; 111n.77;
    135n.136
  Partitas (Clavier-Übung I): 135n.136
  Suites for keyboard: 60; 135n.136
  Das Wohltemperierte Klavier (the '48'): 60;
    135n.136, n.137; 181
Beethoven, Ludwig van
  Adelaïde for voice and piano op. 46:
    124n.107
  (Piano) Concertos: 62; 63
  (Piano) Concerto No. 5, op. 73 ('Emperor'):
    137n.143
  Fidelio: 142n.157
  Quartet for piano and strings [transcription
    of Quintet op. 16 for piano and wind]:
    185
  (Piano) Sonatas: 127n.118; 130n.122;
    140n.156
  Sonata op. 14/2: 116n.85; 137n.143
  Sonata op. 26: 55; 59; 61; 62; 109n.69;
    127n.110, n.111; 128n.120; 161; 169;
    277–8
  Sonata op. 27/2: 62; 115n.83
  Sonata op. 31/2: 137n.143; 165–6
  Sonata op. 31/3: 138n.143
  Sonata op. 57: 62
  Sonata op. 101: 130n.122
  Sonata op. 106: 130n.122; 138n.143
  Symphonies: 16n.29
  Symphony No. 6, op. 68 ('Pastoral'):
    124n.107

Bellini, Vincenzo
  Norma: 110n.75; 124n.108; 'Casta Diva':
    111n.75
  Il Pirata: 86; 110n.75
  I Puritani: 110n.75; 124n.108
  La Sonnambula: 110n.75
  La Straniera: 111n.75
Berlioz, Hector
  Harold in Italy: 143n.160
  Symphonie fantastique: 16n.29
Boieldieu, François-Adrien
  La Dame blanche: 288n.32
Chopin, Frédéric
  [Album leaf dedicated to E. Gaillard,
    Brown 133]: 276n.12
  Allegro de concert op. 46: 131n.126; 177;
    182
  Andante spianato op. 22: 19; 20; 58; 65;
    93n.11; 103n.35; 106n.58; 115n.82;
    117n.90; 123n.106; 124n.108; 126n.114;
    128n.120; 130n.121; 131n.125; 140n.154;
    146n.169; 177; 293n.40; 294; 295n.44
  Ballades: 139n.148; 268; 269; 294n.43;
    295n.44
  Ballade op. 23: 97n.20; 120n.98; 126n.114;
    156n.193; 177
  Ballade op. 38: 62; 65; 97n.20; 113n.81;
    114n.82; 138n.148; 140n.155; 177; 269
    and n.6
  Ballade op. 47: 62; 97n..20; 100n.30;
    128n.120; 134n.128; 177; 293n.40
  Ballade op. 52: 97n.20; 114n.82; 128n.120
  Barcarolle op. 60: 18n.36; 66; 100n.30;
    108n.66; 125n.112; 127n.120; 130n.121;
    131n.126; 133n.128
  Berceuse op. 57: 4n.6; 19; 20; 39; 51;
    97n.20; 107n.63; 108n.66; 117n.85, n.91;
    123n.106; 133n.128; 164; 176; 283; 294;
    295n.44
  Bolero op. 19: 177
  Concertos: 54; 63

Concerto op. 11: 10; 19; 63; 96n.17;
   108n.64; 139n.153; 142n.157, n.158; 176;
   177; 286n.28; *Allegro maestoso*: 66–7;
   107n.63; 111n.76; 115n.82; 123n.105,
   n.106; 126n.114; 132n.126; 133n.127,
   n.128; 139n.153; *Romance*: 53; 67;
   114n.82; 123n.106; 143n.158, n.160;
   Rondo: 126n.114; 145n.169; 289n.34
Concerto op. 21: 19; 62; 67; 142n.158; 176;
   177; 290 and n.35; *Maestoso*: 108n.66;
   113n.82; 123n.106; 131n.126; 133n.127;
   134n.128; *Larghetto*: 53; 58; 63; 67;
   108n.66; 113n.82; 117n.85; 123n.106;
   132n.126; 134n.128; 143n.160; *Allegro
   vivace*: 121n.99; 126n.114
(Grand) Duo Concertant sur des Thèmes de
   Robert le Diable (Brown 70): 101n.32;
   108n.66
Ecossaises op. 72/[3–5]: 97n.20
Etudes: 13; 100n.30; 107n.61; 147n.171; 162;
   178; 182; 268; 269; 273; 291 and n.36;
   294; 295n.44
Etudes op. 10: 16n.27; 60; 62; 96n.17;
   97n.20; 124n.107; 125n.112; 153n.187;
   177; 272; 289; No. 1: 18; 68; 91n.3;
   144n.162; 159n.205; No. 2: 19 and n.38;
   39; 40; 106n.54; 107n.62; 130n.121; No.
   3: 68; 110n.72; 113n.79; 120n.98;
   144n.163, n.165; 182; No. 4: 18;
   126n.114; 144n.165; 182; No. 5: 19; No.
   6: 130n.21; No. 7: 19; 130n.21; No. 8: 18;
   No. 9: 18; 114n.82; 153n.187; No. 10:
   100n.30; No. 11: 18; No. 12: 126n.114
Etudes op 25: 16n.27; 60; 62; 68; 97n.20;
   125n.112; 144n.164; 177; 269; 293n.40;
   No. 1: 18; 69; 100n.30; 144n.164, n.165;
   174; 293n.40; No. 2: 18; 19; 69; 70;
   118n.93; 125n.112; 144n.165; 174;
   293n.40; No. 3: 70; No. 6: 20; 40;
   106n.55; No. 7: 19; 108n.66; 116n.85;
   120n.96; 131n.126; 174; No. 8: 106n.56;
   No. 9: 174; No. 10: 19; 108n.67;
   126n.114; 130n.121; 174; No. 11: 20; 38;
   107n.60; 126n.114; No. 12: 18; 91n.3;
   126n.114; 293n.40
(3 Nouvelles) Etudes (Brown 130): 97n.20;
   118n.93; 128n.120; 147n.171; 177; No. 1:
   19; 117n.85; 118n.93; No. 3: 19; 100n.30;
   113n.81; 118n.93; 128n.120; 130n.121
Fantaisie op. 49: 62; 70; 144n.166; 162; 177
Fantasia on Polish National Airs op. 13: 52;
   177
Impromptus: 100n.30; 129n.121; 175; 189;
   295n.44
Impromptu op. 39: 19; 20; 28; 38; 51; 53;
   58; 62; 70; 97n.20; 100n.30; 107n.60;
   117n.85; 122n.101; 123n.106; 133n.127;
   134n.128; 177; 245–7

Impromptu op. 36: 18n.36; 19; 28; 62;
   97n.20; 100n.30; 12n.79; 123n..106;
   132n.126; 177
Impromptu op. 51: 62; 70; 117n.85; 293n.40
[Fantaisie-] Impromptu op. posth. 66: 19;
   97n.20; 118n.93; 178
Krakowiak. Grand Rondeau de Concert op.
   14: 145n.169; 177; 289n.33
Lento con gran espressione (Brown 49):
   100n.30; 123n.106
Mazurkas: 52; 70–4; 122n.100; 123n.105;
   128n.120; 144n.167; 145n.168, n.169;
   147n.172; 148n.173; 153n.187; 156n.193;
   157n.197; 162; 168; 268; 269; 272; 278;
   283; 293n.40; 294 and n.43; 295 and n.44
Mazurkas op. 6: 177; No. 1: 121n.99;
   148n.172; 188; No. 2: 121n.99; 148n.172;
   No. 3: 148n.172; No. 4: 146n.169;
   148n.172; 188
Mazurkas op. 7: 62; 177; No. 1: 74;
   110n.72; 121n.99; 124n.107; 125n.112;
   131n.126; 169; 188; 249–50; No. 2: 74;
   115n.82; 123n.105; 148n.173; 149n.175;
   No. 3: 115n.82; 117n.91; 120n.96;
   121n.99; 188; 247
Mazurkas op. 17: 177; No. 1: 188; No. 4:
   58; 74; 114n.82; 123n.106; 146n.169
Mazurkas op. 24: 62; 121n.99; 177; No. 1:
   115n.82; 121n.99; 123n.105; 148n.172;
   149n.173; 188; 251–2; No. 2: 121n.99;
   146n.169; 188; No. 3: 110n.72; 116n.85;
   No. 4: 74–5; 120n.98; 133n.128
Mazurkas op. 30: 177; No. 3: 75; No. 4:
   132n.126
Mazurkas op. 33: 62; 177; No. 2: 75;
   125n.112; 146n.169; 150n.178; 188; No. 3:
   73; 131n.125; 134n.128; 146n.169;
   147n.172; 188; No. 4: 75–6; 97n.20;
   110n.72; 117n.91; 150n.179, n.180
Mazurkas op. 41: 144n.167; 177; No. 1:
   150n.177, n.178; No. 2: 150n.177; No. 3:
   76
Mazurkas op. 50: No. 1: 76; 146n.169;
   150n.181; 188; No. 2: 188; No. 3:
   150n.178
Mazurkas op. 56: 180; No. 1: 146n.169;
   No. 2: 146n.169; No. 3: 146n.169;
   150n.177
Mazurkas op. 59: 62; 226n.50; No. 1:
   132n.126; 188; No. 3: 146n.169
Mazurkas op. 63: 62; No. 1: 148n.172; No.
   2: 101n.32; 116n.85
Mazurkas op. posth. 67: No. 1: 188; No. 3:
   121n.99
Mazurkas op. posth. 68: No. 1: 146n.169;
   No. 2: 97n.20; 115n.82; 132n.126;
   146n.169; 188; No. 3: 97n.20; 146n.169;
   148n.172; No. 4: 102n.32

Mazurka dedicated to E. Gaillard (Brown 140): 276n.12
Mazurka from the Szymanowska album (Brown 85): 158n.202
Nocturnes: 12; 19; 20; 45; 46; 77; 100n.30; 111n.76; 123n.105; 148n.173; 150n.182; 151n.184; 155n.191; 156n.193; 162; 268; 269; 278; 291 and n.36; 293n.40; 294; 295n.44
Nocturnes op. 9: 62; 140n.154; 177; 180; No. 1: 39; 107n.63; 114n.82; 117n.85; 126n.114; 152n.184; No. 2: 19; 28; 46; 47; 53; 77–9; 97n.20; 111n.76; 113n.79; 114n.82; 116n.84; 117n.86, n.87; 121n.99; 123n.105; 125n.112; 126n.114; 132n.126; 133n.127; 134n.128, n.130; 148n.173; 150n.183; 151n.184;152n.185; 154n.189; 155n.191; 156n.193; 189; 257–61; No. 3: 115n.82; 116n.85; 126n.114
Nocturnes op. 15: 62; 121n.99; 137n.142; 140n.154, n.156; 177; 270n.8; No. 1: 53; 58; 112n.79; 115n.82; 117n.91; 123n.106; 124n.108; 130n.121; 131n.125; 133n.127; 134n.128; No. 2: 53; 58; 79; 97n.20; 100n.30; 113n.79; 114n.82; 116n.85; 117n.91; 123n.105, n.106; 126n.113; 130n.122; 132n.126; 133n.127, n.128; 149n.173; 152n.184, n.186; No. 3: 79; 110n.72; 121n.99; 139n.148; 153n.187; 174
Nocturnes op. 27: 62; 140n.154; 177; 181; No. 1: 18; 20; 38; 39; 79; 107n.63; 114n.82; 116n.85; 124n.108; 126n.114; 133n.127; No. 2: 18; 20; 38; 58; 79–80; 97n.20; 113n.79; 114n.82; 123n.105; 126n.114; 128n.120; 133n.127, n.128; 134n.130; 152n.184; 154n.189; 261–2; 293n.40
Nocturnes op. 32: 62; 177; No. 1: 20n.40; 97n.20; 109n.68; 110n.72; 116n.85; 123n.105; 131n.126; 133n.127; 152n.184; 262–3; No. 2: 19; 51; 53; 113n.79; 115n.82; 123n.106; 131n.126; 133n.127
Nocturnes op. 37: 62; 177; No. 1: 20; 48; 53; 58; 80; 114n.82; 116n.85; 117n.89, n.91; 123n.106; 132n.126; 133n.127; 134n.128; 152n.184; 154n.190; 174; 273n.9; No. 2: 38; 117n.85; 126n.114; 128n.120; 140n.154; 273 and n.9
Nocturnes op. 48: 62; 177; No. 1: 18; 19; 48; 58; 61; 80–1; 97n.20; 108n.67; n.68; 112n.79; 117n.88; 133n.127, n.128; 155n.191; 156n.192; 170; 264–6; No. 2: 81; 123n.105; 132n.126; 134n.128; 156n.192; 293n.40
Nocturnes op. 55: 62; 101n.32; 180; No. 1: 114n.82; 132n.126; 162; No. 2: 19; 117n.85; 123n.105; 132n.126; 133n.127

Nocturnes op. 62: 151n.184; No. 1: 97n.20; 108n.66; 115n.82; 123n.106; 131n.126; 133n.127; No. 2: 108n.66; 123n.105, n.106; 131n.126; 133n.127
Nocturne op. posth. 72/1: 107n.63; 108n.66; 114n.82; 117n.91; 123n.106
Polonaises: 100n.30; 156n.194; 189; 283
Polonaise op. 22: 61; 65; 140n.154; 143n.158; 156n.194; 177
Polonaises op. 26: 62; 177; No. 1: 51; 58; 81; 114n.82; 120n.96; 126n.114; 156n.193, n.194; No. 2: 81; 120n.98; 126n.114; 156n.193, n.194; 169
Polonaises op. 40: 177; No. 1: 82; 97n.20; 126n.114; 156n.194; No. 2: 58; 112n.79; 114n.82; 126n.114; 156n.194
Polonaise op. 44: 19; 108n.67; 157n.194; 177
Polonaise op. 53: 62; 82–3. 97n.20; 131n.126; 156n.194; 157n.195, n.196; 279n.16
Polonaise-Fantaisie op. 61: 130n.121; 156n.194
Polonaise in G ♯ minor (Brown 6): 121n.99
(Introduction et) Polonaise brillante op. 3 for piano and 'cello: 177; 185
Preludes: 175; 273n.9; 274 and n.10; 295n.44
Preludes op. 28: 2n.1; 62; 92n.9; 162; 177; 182; 273; 281 and n.19; 293n.40; 294; No. 1: 113n.79; No. 2: 110n.72; 130n.121; No. 4: 110n.72; 116n.85; 281n.19; No. 6: 108n.68; 116n.85; 117n.81; 120n.96; 248–9; No. 7: 97n.20; No. 8: 274; No. 9: 97n.20; 132n.126; 281n.19; No. 10: 97n.20; No. 11: 97n.20; 113n.79; No. 12: 97n.20; No. 13: 58; 97n.20; 100n.30; 133n.128; No. 14: 97n.20; 110n.72; 125n.112; 130n.121; No. 15: 19; 116n.85; 117n.91; 123n.106; 124n.108; 129n.121; 133n.127; 134n.128; 255–6; 281n.19; 293n.40; No. 16: 100n.30; No. 17: 83; 97n.20; 100n.30; 113n.79; 157n.197; 177; No. 18: 108n.66; 110n.72; 126n.114; 132n.126; No. 19: 18; No. 20: 83; 97n.20; 281n.19; No. 21: 117n.85; 128n.120; 133n.127; No. 24: 18; 20; 112n.79; 126n.114; 132n.126
Prelude op. 45: 4n.6; 97n.20; 128n.120; 162; 177; [?283]
Rondeau op. 1: 177
Rondeau à la Mazurka op. 5: 177
Rondo op. 16: 121n.99; 177
Rondo op. posth. 73 for two pianos: 122n.103
Scherzos: 100n.30
Scherzo op. 20: 58; 83–4; 124n.108; 126n.114; 157n.198; 177; 185
Scherzo op. 31: 38; 81; 84–5; 97n.20; 100n.30; 106n.60; 111n.76; 169; 177; 294

Scherzo op. 39: 19; 85–6; 108n.67; 126n.114;
    166; 177
Scherzo op. 54: 18n.36; 118n.93
Sonata op. 4: 135n.136; n.137; 177
Sonata op. 35: 12n.19; 62; 100n.30; 101n.32;
    126n.114; 177; *Marche funèbre*: 20; 38;
    86; 97n.20; 111n.76; 116n.85; 132n.126;
    134n.129; 157n.200; 175; *Finale*: 6n.6;
    110n.72; 130n.121
Sonata op. 58: 62; 178; *Largo*: 61; 112n.79;
    Finale: 18n.36
Sonata op. 65 for piano and 'cello: 62;
    101n.32; 135n.137; 189
Songs op. posth. 74: Nos. 8, 11, 13, [19]:
    283n.23
Tarentelle op. 43: 97n.20
Trio op. 8 for piano, violin and 'cello:
    121n.99; 177
Variations sur un Air national allemand
    (Brown 14): 122n.103
Variations sur 'La ci darem la mano' op. 2
    for piano and orchestra: 114n.82;
    126n.114; 132n.126; 138n.148; 177; 274;
    288; 289n.33; 290n.35
Variations brillantes on the much-loved
    Rondo 'Je vends des scapulaires' from
    Ludovic by Hérold and Halévy op. 12:
    177
Veni creator (unpublished): 189
Waltzes: 100n.30; 158n.202; 294 and n.43;
    295 and n.44
Waltz op. 18: 20n.40; 62; 97n.20; 177;
    252–5
Waltzes op. 34: 177; No. 1: 97n.20;
    100n.30; 174; 186; No. 2: 86–7; 97n.20;
    98n.23; 108n.66; 117n.85, n.91; 120n.96;
    132n.126; 156n.193; 157n.201; 162; No. 3:
    97n.20; 131n.126; 140n.156; 158n.202;
    174
Waltz op. 42: 19; 87; 97n.20; 100n.30;
    108n.66; 118n.93; 132n.126; 158n.202
Waltzes op. 64: 62; 93n.11; No. 1: 87;
    97n.20; 106n.59; 132n.126; 158n.202,
    n.203; No. 2: 58; 88; 97n.20; 120n.98;
    159n.204, n.205; 179; No. 3: 97n.20;
    100n.30; 122n.102
Waltzes op. posth. 69: No. 1: 43–4; 97n.20;
    100n.30; 123n.106; 133n.127; 159n.206;
    176; No. 2: 158n.201; 159n.206; 162
Waltzes op. posth. 70: No. 1: 97n.20; No.
    2: 89; 158n.201; 159n.206; 162; No. 3: 89
Waltz in E minor (Brown 56): 97n.20
Clementi, Muzio:
    Gradus ad Parnassum: 60; 61
    Préludes et Exercices: 28; 59; 60; 105n.47;
    [189]
Cramer, Jean-Baptiste
    [84] *Etudes*: 60; 109n.69

Debussy, Claude-Achille
    Douze Etudes: 128n.120; No. IV 'Pour les
        sixtes': 128n.120
    Pelléas et Mélisande: 128n.120
Donizetti, Gaetano
    Don Pasquale: 110n.75
    Lucia di Lammermoor: 62; 86; 138n.147
Dussek, Jan Ladislav
    Trois Sonates op. 19: 137n.142
Field, John
    (Piano) Concertos: 62
    (Piano) Concerto No. 2 in A♭: 276
    Nocturnes: 46; 52; 62; 77; 115n.83, n.84;
        276
    Nocturne No. 1 in E♭: 116n.84; 152n.184
    Nocturne No. 9 in E♭: 152n.184
Handel, Georg Friedrich
    Ode for Saint Cecilia's day: 137n.142
    Six fugues for harpsichord or organ op. 3:
        137n.142
    Te Deum ('Dettingen'): 143n.161
Heller, Stephen
    Etudes opp. 16, 45, 46 and 47: 16n.27
    Pensées fugitives op. 30: 177
    Scherzo op. 24: 177
Henselt, Adolf
    (Piano) Concerto op. 16: 146n.170
    Douze Etudes caractéristiques op. 2: 146n.170
Herz, Henry
    Variations brillantes on the 'Dernière Valse'
        by C.M. von Weber op. 51: 137n.142
Hiller, Ferdinand
    Grand Duo for two pianos op. 135:
        128n.120; 186
Hummel, Johann Nepomuk
    *La Bella Capricciosa. Introduzione e Alla
        Polacca* op. 55: 61
    (Piano) Concertos: 63; 276
    (Piano) Concerto op. 85: 61; 108n.64;
        135n.135
    (Piano) Concerto op. 89: 61
    Grand Duo for piano duet op. 92: 63
    Fantasy [op. 18?]: 276
    Nocturne for piano duet op. 99: 137n.142
    Rondo brillant mêlé d'un Thème russe op.
        98: 61
    Septet op. 74: 29; 61; 276
    Sonata for piano duet op. 51: 137n.142
    Sonata op. 81: 61
Hünten, Franz
    Much-loved cavatina from the opera *Il
        Pirata* by Bellini for piano duet op. 36:
        137n.142
Kalkbrenner, Frédéric
    Introduction, March and Grand Polonaise
        [for six pianos] op. 92: 290n.35
Kessler, Joseph Christoph
    [24] *Etudes* op. 20: 135n.134

Liszt, Franz
'Au bord d'une source' (Années de
Pèlerinage, Vol I: Suisse, No. 4): 274n.10
Consolations, No. 6: 122n.100
Etudes d'exécution transcendante d'après
Paganini: 16n.29; 124n.107; 'Mazeppa'
(No. 4): 292
Grandes Etudes de Paganini: 16n.29
Grand galop chromatique: 124n.107, 292
Piano transcriptions: Beethoven, Adelaïde:
124n.107; Beethoven, Symphonies:
16n.29; 124n.107; Berlioz, Symphonie
fantastique: 16n.29; Donizetti, Andante
final de Lucie de Lammermoor, 2e acte:
62; 124n.107; 138n.147; Rossini,
Tarentelle (Soirées musicales, No. 9): 62,
Schubert, Ave Maria: 124n.107; Schubert,
Ständchen (Schwanengesang, No. 4):
124n.107; 138n.145
Mayer, Charles
Concerto symphonique for piano and
orchestra op. 89: 168
Mendelssohn-Bartholdy, Felix
(Piano) Concerto op. 25: 62
Songs without Words: 62; 138n.146; op. 19,
No. 1: 138n.146
Meyerbeer, Giacomo
L'Africaine: 73
Moscheles, Ignaz
[24] Etudes op. 70: 28; 60; 135n.135;
147n.171; [189]
Grande Sonate for piano duet op. 47: 63;
139n.150; 147n.171
[12] Nouvelles Grandes Etudes
caractéristiques op. 95: 60; 147n.171
Rondo brillant for piano duet op. 30:
137n.142
Mozart, Wolfgang Amadeus
Adagio K540: 119n.95
(Piano) Concertos: 119n.95
Fantasy K397: 119n.95
Fantasy K475: 119n.95
Requiem K626: 110n.75; 188
Rondo K511: 119n.95
(Piano) Sonatas: 119n.95
Onslow, Georges
Sonata for piano duet op. 22: 139n.150
Paganini, Nicolò
Cantabile spianato e Polacca brillante:
125n.108
Caprices: 16 and n.29
(Violin) Concertos: 119n.95
Pixis, Johann Peter
[Paraphrase on] Robert le Diable
(Meyerbeer) for piano duet: 137n.142
Reber, Henri

Orchestration of the Marche funèbre from
Chopin's op. 35: 134n.129
Ries, Ferdinand
Overture: 143n.158
Rossini, Gioacchino
The Barber of Seville: 111n.75
La Gazza Ladra: 133n.127
An Italian Girl in Algiers: 111n.75
Otello: 111n.75
Tarentelle (Soirées musicales, No. 9): 62
Scarlatti, Domenico
Harpsichord Sonatas: 137n.142
Schubert, Franz
Ave Maria op. 52, No. 6: 124n.107
Divertissement Hongrois for piano duet op.
54: 63
Impromptus opp. 90 and 142: 138n.145
Ländler: 62
Lieder: 110n.75
Marches for piano duet: 63
Moments musicaux op. 94: 138n.145
Polonaises for piano duet opp. 61 and 75:
63
(Piano) Sonatas: 138n.145
Ständchen (Schwanengesang, No. 4):
124n.107; 138n.145
Symphony: 143n.158
Waltzes: 62
Schumann, Robert
Carnaval op. 9: 139n.148
Etude: 269
Kreisleriana op. 16: 138n.148
Sechs Concert-Etüden nach Capricen von
Paganini op. 10: 16n.29
Sonata: 269
(Piano) Sonata op. 22: 269n.7
Studien nach Capricen von Paganini op. 3:
16n.29
Tellefsen, Thomas
Three Mazurkas: 185
Variations for piano: 185
Viardot, Pauline
Le chêne et le roseau for voice and piano
(text by La Fontaine): 188
Transcriptions of Chopin's Mazurkas for
voice and piano (texts by Louis Pomey):
188
Weber, Carl Maria von
Concertstück for piano and orchestra op.
79: 50; 138n.144; 276
(Piano) Duets opp. 3, 10 and 60: 63;
139n.151
Invitation to the Dance op. 65: 138n.144
(Piano) Sonata op. 24: 62
(Piano) Sonata op. 39: 12; 50; 61; 62; 276
(Piano) Sonata op. 70: 276